Lynne Kelly

Communicating Mental Health

LEXINGTON STUDIES IN HEALTH COMMUNICATION

Series Editors: Leandra H. Hernández and Kari Nixon

National and international governments have recognized the importance of widespread, timely, and effective health communication, as research shows that accurate, patient-centered, and culturally competent health communication can improve patient and community health care outcomes. This interdisciplinary series examines the role of health communication in society and is receptive to manuscripts and edited volumes that use a variety of theoretical, methodological, interdisciplinary, and intersectional approaches. We invite contributions on a variety of health communication topics including but not limited to health communication in a digital age; race, gender, ethnicity, class, physical abilities, and health communication; critical approaches to health communication; feminisms and health communication; LGBTQIA health; interpersonal health communication perspectives; rhetorical approaches to health communication; organizational approaches to health communication; health campaigns, media effects, and health communication; multicultural approaches to health communication; and international health communication. This series is open to contributions from scholars representing communication, women's and gender studies, public health, health education, discursive analyses of medical rhetoric, and other disciplines whose work interrogates and explores these topics. Successful proposals will be accessible to an interdisciplinary audience, advance our understanding of contemporary approaches to health communication, and enrich our conversations about the importance of health communication in today's health landscape.

Recent Titles in This Series

Communicating Mental Health: History, Contexts, and Perspectives by Lance R. Lippert, Robert D. Hall, Aimee E. Miller-Ott, and Daniel Cochece Davis

CTE, Media, and the NFL: Framing of a Public Health Crisis as a Football Epidemic by Travis R. Bell, Janelle Applequist, and Christian Dotson-Pierson

Challenging Reproductive Control and Gendered Violence in the Americas: Intersectionality, Power, and Struggles for Rights by Leandra Hinojosa Hernández and Sarah De Los Santos Upton

Politics, Propaganda, and Public Health: A Case Study in Health Communication and Public Trust by Laura Crosswell and Lance Porter

Communication and Feminist Perspectives on Ovarian Cancer by Dinah Tetteh

Communicating Mental Health

History, Contexts, and Perspectives

Edited by Lance R. Lippert,
Robert D. Hall, Aimee E. Miller-Ott and
Daniel Cochece Davis

LEXINGTON BOOKS
Lanham • Boulder • New York • London

Published by Lexington Books
An imprint of The Rowman & Littlefield Publishing Group, Inc.
4501 Forbes Blvd., Ste. 200, Lanham, MD 20706
www.rowman.com

6 Tinworth Street, London SE11 5AL, United Kingdom

British Library Cataloguing in Publication Information Available

Library of Congress Cataloging-in-Publication Data available

Library of Congress Control Number:2019950759

ISBN 978-1-4985-7801-1 (cloth : alk. paper)
ISBN 978-1-4985-7802-8 (electronic)

∞™ The paper used in this publication meets the minimum requirements of American National Standard for Information Sciences—Permanence of Paper for Printed Library Materials, ANSI/NISO Z39.48-1992.

Contents

Acknowledgments

The editors would like to thank Dr. Lindsey Thomas, Samantha Dunn, Joshua Fitzgerald, and Alex Kritselis at Illinois State University for their help in reading and finalizing each of the chapters for publication. Thank you also to the Illinois State University School of Communication, College of Arts and Sciences, and Office of Research and Graduate Studies for their support of our project.

Section 1

AN INTRODUCTION TO COMMUNICATING ABOUT MENTAL HEALTH

Chapter One

Communicating about Mental Health

What We Know, What We Need, and What We Give

Robert D. Hall
Aimee E. Miller-Ott

Our goal for this book is to provide readers with a resource in theory, research, and practice of the study of mental health in the communication discipline. While communication scholars and instructors use work by psychologists, sociologists, and practitioners to inform their own teaching and research, communication scholars are conducting a significant amount of research that plays a vital role in the study of mental health. This book can start to address the needs of people from different areas of our discipline. Researchers may use this book to locate theoretical approaches to use in their own work. Students may use this book to find ideas for their next study on communication and mental health. Instructors may use this book as a supplement in their courses for addressing how to best use a communication lens to understand mental health issues across a variety of contexts. People may read this book because they have experienced communication issues about mental health themselves or these issues have touched their family members, friends, romantic partners, and colleagues in some way. The costs and prevalence of mental health–related issues are expected to rise exponentially to 47 trillion dollars and 13 percent of all global disease burden by 2030 (Hock et al., 2016). It is imperative that research regarding communication and mental health continues as a primary research agenda item for those concerned about mental health–related issues.

Unfortunately, there is a dearth of textbooks and course readers on mental health issues in the communication discipline, even though there are scholars moving us ahead on our understanding of mental health issues in communication contexts in various chapters within communication publications (e.g., du Pré, 2014; Golden, 2011; Mattox, McSweeney, Ivory, & Sullivan, 2011; Segrin & Flora, 2017; Thompson, Parrott, & Nussbaum, 2011; Weathers &

Bell, 2013). When mentioned in other publication outlets, communication scholars often amalgamate mental health into *chronic conditions* (Barak & Grohol, 2011; Beck, Paskewitz, Anderson, Bourdeaux, & Currie-Mueller, 2017; Constonguay, Filer, & Pitts, 2016; Davis & Calitz, 2014; DeAndrea, 2015; Gammage & Foster, 2017), despite the fact that mental health conditions are categorically and medically distinguishable from physical chronic ailments (recognizing that both may be present at the same time) (National Institute for Mental Health, n.d.). This leaves communication scholars with very few resources for teaching and generating research ideas about mental health. Scholars from other disciplines address mental health in their textbooks, although they utilize a more generalized approach (for public health law, see Hodge, 2016; for counseling ethics and decision-making, see Moyer & Crews, 2017; for a sociological approach to mental health, see Scheid & Wright, 2016; for mental health in schools, see Shute & Slee, 2016).

Therefore, our text takes a five-step approach to addressing mental health in the communication field. The first step is addressing mental health generally, as it pertains to the communication field. The second step is analyzing communication about mental health in action using narrative. The third step is applying communication about mental health to various contexts. The fourth step is examining the role of family because of the salience of mental health issues and communication within families. The fifth and final step is addressing how scholars and practitioners have conceptualized mental health in the past and are offering new directions for its study in the future. Before taking the first step, we must first understand mental health and its history within the communication discipline.

COMMUNICATION AND MENTAL HEALTH

The chapters cover a range of ontological traditions in communication—postpositivism, interpretive, and critical. Despite variations in subjective experiences of mental health (Canino & Alegría, 2008), mental health reflects the universal experience of humanity. It is important to consider mental health from the three main communicative traditions because there are universal facets, subjective experiences, and power issues to consider when discussing mental health. There has been a call for further investigation into mental health utilizing Craig's (1999) seven traditions of communication (see Rudick & Dannels, 2018), indicating that communication scholars contribute significantly to our understanding of mental health. Although the three paradigms are represented in the work in this chapter, at the heart of our understanding of mental health and what we ideally wanted this book to embody is that communication about mental health is constitutive, in that the person, other, and relationship do not exist in isolation from each other.

The self, other, and relationship are interwoven together to become indistinguishable through communication (Wilmot, 1995). Citing Durkheim's fundamental research on mental health, Horwitz (2017) notes that one's mental health is constituted by their own communication, the audience with whom they are communicating, and the social institutions within which they are communicating. Thus, mental health as a constitutive topic leads us to believe that the person experiencing a mental health issue does not exist in isolation; rather, the essence of the communication regarding a mental health condition is the "interweaving of the self/other/relationship" (Wilmot, 1995, p. 51). The individual managing a mental health condition or concern cannot be seen as a separate entity from others or the nature of their relationships, but rather meanings regarding mental health are co-constructed and experienced in interaction with the other (Baxter, 2004). The self, now identified with a mental health label, does not change the relationship until the communication about the mental health occurs as with other invisible conditions (Horan et al., 2009). Thus, mental health concerns cause a fundamental shift in the self, other, and relationship.

However, up until this point, the communication discipline has not treated mental health constitutively. Rather, communication scholars utilize mental health as an outcome of communication as "communication is implicitly needed to achieve mental health" (Smith & Applegate, 2018, p. 389). In other words, scholars in the communication discipline have tended to treat mental health almost exclusively as an outcome in a biomedical manner. However, the thought that mental health is not inherently biomedical is not new information. Scheid and Wright (2016) note that the *Diagnostic and Statistical Manual* (DSM) that most psychologists use to diagnose mental illness often does not take into account contextual factors that may influence mental health and illness.

In examining the influence of communication on mental health outcomes, many communication researchers have explored mental health regarding information-seeking behaviors and campaign or media messages (e.g., DeFoster & Swalve, 2018; Francis, 2018; Ki & Jang, 2018; Pace, Silk, Nazione, Fournier, & Collins-Eaglin, 2018; Wozney, Radomski, & Newton, 2018). While there is ample evidence that aspects of communication can produce mental health outcomes (e.g., Armstrong et al., 2017; Arroyo, Segrin, & Curran, 2016; Crowley & Knowles, 2014; Curran & Arroyo, 2018; Hoffner & Cohen, 2018; Kuosmanen, Fleming, & Barry, 2018; Law, Rush, Schoon, & Parsons, 2009; Quintero Johnson, Yilmaz, & Najarian, 2017; Vangelisti, 2009), the literature generally does not expand its conceptualization to consider how these mental health outcomes influence the constituted self/ other/relationship despite the fact that individuals do communicate about their mental health with one another (Butler, 2016; Umberson & Montez, 2010; Venetis, Chernichky-Karcher, & Gettings, 2018). While it is worth noting that relational and communicative behaviors can cause mental health outcomes, the conversation should not end there as relationships live on beyond analysis of mental health outcomes of a lived experience. Thus, this text will provide multiple perspectives on communication and mental health including outcome-oriented frameworks, constitutive approaches, and other perspectives to provide a well-rounded approach to communication and mental health.

ORGANIZATION OF THIS TEXT

In this text, you will find some of the cutting-edge research in communication and mental health. We begin with this overview of the book and a chapter by Kreps that orients us toward how the communication discipline identifies mental health stigma and what scholars should begin to consider in understanding mental health stigma. The editors were the sole reviewers of these first two chapters to provide the most effective introductory structure and framing of the text.

The next four sections of chapters in this text underwent a double-anonymous peer review and an additional review by the editors. The second section provides an overview of a growing approach toward understanding health in communication research: narrative. Flood-Grady, Koenig Kellas, and Chernin provide an overview of a narrative theory with health tenets (Communicated Narrative Sense-Making Theory) and explicate how this theory applies to mental health. Goldsmith and Terui describe how those who work with at-risk individuals approach mental health literacy. Norval and Riforgiate describe a lived experience of sense making with mental illness. Finally, Willer and Koenig Kellas provide us with an intervention focused on mental health outcomes and continuing conversations to mitigate the relationships at play in these mental health outcomes.

Our third section examines mental health in various contexts: media, the college classroom, healthcare, military, and underserved communities. First, Hoffner provides an analysis of parasocial relationships in response to celebrity mental health disclosures. Next, Meluch and Starcher explore the college classroom as an arena for mental health disclosure. Piercy and Zanin investigate the role of the advocate in community-based mental healthcare. Hagmajer and Strekalova explore support of nurses experiencing burnout. Samp and Cohen describe the experiences of living with mental health concerns after military deployment. Finally, Ball and Strekalova provide an analysis of mental health in underserved black communities.

Section four explores mental health in families. Family relationships may be the longest ongoing connections that an individual may have in their lives (Floyd, Mikkelson, & Judd, 2006) and thus serves as a pivotal area of inquiry about mental health in our text. In citing both twin and adoption studies, Schwartz and Corcoran (2016) note that the environmental influence of families is a particularly strong area of inquiry for mental health research. Thus, separating families into a unique section has both communicative and mental health heuristic value. First, Craig and Moore look at how families manage ambiguous loss. Next, Curran and Scharp examine the role of mental health in conflict from the mother and father perspectives. Finally, Smith-Frigerio analyzes postpartum depression and stigma.

The final section of the text provides an understanding of where we have been and where we can go in research about communication and mental health. First, El-Shall challenges conventional ways of mental health conceptualization. Next, McLemore explores the perceptions of mental health as both portrayed by media and consumed by the public. Finally, Delaney and Basinger describe the past and future directions for social scientific research regarding communication and mental health.

After reading this text, we hope that you find yourself with a solid orientation of mental health as a communicative issue. Our hope is that this book not only serves as a comprehensive and informational toolkit for understanding mental health in communication, but also as a springboard for further inquiry into its study.

REFERENCES

Armstrong, R., Arnott, W., Copland, D. A., McMahon, K., Khan, A., Najman, J. M., & Scott, J. G. (2017). Change in receptive vocabulary from childhood to adulthood: Associated mental health, education and employment outcomes. *International Journal of Language & Communication Disorders, 52*(5), 561–572. doi:10.1111/1460-6984.12301

Arroyo, A., Segrin, C. G., & Curran, T. M. (2016). Maternal care and control as mediators in the relationship between mothers' and adult children's psychosocial problems. *Journal of Family Communication, 16*(3), 216–228. doi:10.1080/15267 431.2016.1170684

Barak, A., & Grohol, J. M. (2011). Current and future trends in Internet-supported mental health interventions. *Journal of Technology in Human Services, 29*(3), 155–196. doi:10.1080/15228835.2011.616939

Baxter, L. A. (2004). Relationships as dialogues. *Personal Relationships, 11*(1), 1–22. doi:10.1111/j.1475-6811.2004.00068.x

Beck, S. J., Paskewitz, E. A., Anderson, W. A., Bourdeaux, R., & Currie-Mueller, J. (2017). The task and relational dimensions of online social support. *Health Communication, 32*(3), 347–355. doi:10.1080/10410236.2016.1138383

Butler, H. (2016). College students' disclosure of mental health counseling utilization. *Iowa Journal of Communication, 48*(1/2), 156–170. Retrieved from https://uni .edu/ica/journal/ica_journal/48_2/48-2_156-170_mental-health.pdf

Canino, G., & Alegría, M. (2008). Psychiatric diagnosis—Is it universal or relative to culture? *The Journal of Child Psychology and Psychiatry, 49*(3), 237–250. doi:10.1111/j.1469-7610.2007.01854.x

Castonguay, J., Filer, C. R., & Pitts, M. J. (2016). Seeking help for depression: Applying the health benefit model to illness narratives. *Southern Communication Journal, 81*(5), 289–303. doi:10.1080/1041794X.2016.1165729

Craig, R. T. (1999). Communication theory as a field. *Communication Theory, 9*(2), 119–161. doi:10.1111/j.1468-2885.1999.tb00355.x

Crowley, J. P., & Knowles, J. H. (2014). Gender differences in perceived happiness and well-being of individuals who engage in contemptuous communication. *Communication Reports, 27*(1), 27–38. doi:10.1080/08934215.2013.835850

Curran, T., & Arroyo, A. (2018). Emulating parental levels of taking conflict personally: Associations with behavioral mental health outcomes in adult children. *Journal of Family Communication, 18*(3), 171–184. doi:10.1080/15267431.2018 .1450254

Davis, D. Z., & Calitz, W. (2014). Finding healthcare support in online communities: An exploration of the evolution and efficacy of virtual support groups. *Journal of Virtual Worlds Research, 7*(3), 1–16. doi:10.4101/jvwr.v7i3.7068

DeAndrea, D. C. (2015). Testing the proclaimed affordances of online support groups in a nationally representative sample of adults seeking mental health assistance. *Journal of Health Communication, 20*(2), 147–156. doi:10.1080/10810730.2014 .914606

DeFoster, R., & Swalve, N. (2018). Guns, culture or mental health? Framing mass shootings as a public health crisis. *Health Communication, 33*(10), 1211–1222. doi :10.1080/10410236.2017.1350907

du Pré, A. (2014). *Communicating about health: Current issues and perspectives* (4th ed.). New York, NY: Oxford University Press.

Floyd, K., Mikkelson, A. C., & Judd, J. (2006). Defining the family through relationships. In L. H. Turner & R. West (Eds.), *The family communication sourcebook* (pp. 21–41). Thousand Oaks, CA: Sage.

Francis, D. B. (2018). Young black men's information seeking following celebrity depression disclosure: Implications for mental health communication. *Journal of Health Communication, 23*(7), 687–694. doi:10.1080/10810730.2018.1506837

Gammage, R. J., & Foster, J. L. (2017). Leadership in community mutual support groups for mental health: A qualitative case study from the leaders' perspective. *Journal of Community & Applied Social Psychology, 27,* 463–475. doi:10.1002/ casp.2327

Golden, M. A. (2011). When love is not enough: Communication challenges and social support experienced when placing a spouse with dementia in a residential care facility. In Brann, M. (Ed.), *Contemporary case studies in health communication: Theoretical & applied approaches* (pp. 61–73). Dubuque, IA: Kendall Hunt.

Hock, R. S., Or, F., Kolappa, K., Burkey, M. D., Surkan, P. J., & Eaton, W. W. (2016). A new resolution for global mental health. *Lancet, 379*(9824), 1367–1368. doi:10.1016/S0140-6736(12)60243-8

Hodge, Jr., J. G. (2016). *Public health law in a nutshell* (2nd ed.). St. Paul, MN: West Academic Publishing.

Hoffner, C. A., & Cohen, E. L. (2018). Mental health-related outcomes of Robin Williams' death: The role of parasocial relations and media exposure in stigma, help-seeking, and outreach. *Health Communication, 33*(2), 1573–1582. doi:10.10 80/10410236.2017.1384348

Horan, S. M., Martin, M. M., Smith, N., Schoo, M., Eidsness, M., & Johnson, A. (2009). Can we talk? How learning of an invisible illness impacts forecasted relational outcomes. *Communication Studies, 60*(1), 66–81. doi:10.1080/10510970802623625

Horwitz, A. V. (2017). An overview of sociological perspectives on the definitions, causes, and responses to mental health and illness. In T. L. Scheid & E. R. Wright (Eds.), *A handbook for the study of mental health: Social contexts, theories, and systems* (3rd ed., pp. 6–19). New York, NY: Cambridge University Press.

Ki, E., & Jang, J. (2018). Social support and mental health. *Journal of Asian Pacific Communication, 28*(2), 226–250. doi:10.1075/japc.00011.ki

Kuosmanen, T., Fleming, T. M., & Barry, M. M. (2018). Using computerized mental health programs in alternative education: Understanding the requirements of students and staff. *Health Communication, 33*(6), 753–761. doi:10.1080/10410236.2 017.1309620

Law, J., Rush, R., Schoon, I., & Parsons, S. (2009). Modeling developmental language difficulties from school entry into adulthood: Literacy, mental health, and employment outcomes. *Journal of Speech, Language, & Hearing Research, 52*(6), 1401–1416. doi:10.1044/1092-4388(2009/08-0142)

Mattox, R., McSweeney, J., Ivory, J., & Sullivan, G. (2011). A qualitative analysis of Christian clergy portrayal of anxiety disturbances in televised sermons. In A. N. Miller & D. L. Rubin (Eds.), *Health communication and faith communities* (pp. 187–202). New York, NY: Hampton Press.

Moyer, M., & Crews, C. (2017). *Applied ethics and decision making in mental health.* Thousand Oaks, CA: Sage.

National Institute of Mental Health. (n.d.). *Chronic illness & mental health.* Retrieved from https://www.nimh.nih.gov/health/publications/chronic-illness-mental-health/index.shtml.

Pace, K., Silk, K., Nazione, S., Fournier, L., & Collins-Eaglin, J. (2018). Promoting mental health help-seeking behavior among first-year college students. *Health Communication, 33*(2), 102–110. doi:10.1080/10410236.2016.1250065

Quintero Johnson, J. M., Yilmaz, G., & Najarian, K. (2017). Optimizing the presentation of mental health information in social media: The effects of health testimonials and platform on source perceptions, message processing, and health outcomes. *Health Communication, 32*(9), 1121–1132. doi:10.1080/10410236.2016.1214218

Rudick, C. K., & Dannels, D. P. (2018). Yes, and . . . : Continuing the scholarly conversation about mental health stigma in higher education. *Communication Education, 67*(3), 404–408. doi:10.1080/03634523.2018.1467563

Scheid, T. L., & Wright, E. R. (Eds.) (2016). *A handbook for the study of mental health: Social contexts, theories, and systems* (3rd ed.). New York, NY: Cambridge University Press.

Schwartz, S., & Corcoran, C. (2016). Biological approaches to psychiatric disorders: A sociological approach. In T. L. Scheid & E. R. Wright (Eds.), *A handbook for the study of mental health: Social contexts, theories, and systems* (3rd ed., pp. 98–125). New York, NY: Cambridge University Press.

Segrin, C. G., & Flora, J. (2017). Family conflict is detrimental to physical and mental health. In J. A. Samp (Ed.), *Communicating interpersonal conflict in close relationships: Contexts, challenges, and opportunities* (pp. 207–224). New York, NY: Routledge.

Shute, R. H., & Slee, P. T. (2016). *Mental health & wellbeing through schools: The way forward.* London: Routledge.

Smith, R. A., & Applegate, A. (2018). Mental health stigma and communication and their intersections with education. *Communication Education, 67*(3), 382–393. doi :10.1080/03634523.2018.1465988

Thompson, T. L., Parrott, R., & Nussbaum, J. F. (Eds.) (2011). *The Routledge handbook of health communication* (2nd ed.). New York, NY: Routledge.

Umberson, D., & Montez, J. K. (2010). Social relationships and health: A flashpoint for health policy. *Journal of Health and Social Behavior, 51*(1), 54–66. doi:10.1177/0022146510383501

Vangelisti, A. L. (2009). Challenges in conceptualizing social support. *Journal of Social and Personal Relationships, 26*, 39–51. doi:10.1177/0265407509105520

Venetis, M. K., Chernichky-Karcher, S., & Gettings, P. E. (2018). Disclosing mental illness information to a friend: Exploring how the disclosure decision-making model informs strategy selection. *Health Communication, 33*(6), 653–663. doi:10.1080/10410236.2017.1294231

Weathers, M. R., & Bell, G. C. (2013). Assessing health disparities through communication competence, social support, and coping among Hispanic lay caregivers for loved ones with Alzheimer's Disease. In M. J. Dutta & G. L. Kreps (Eds.), *Reducing health disparities: Communication interventions* (pp. 59–74). New York, NY: Peter Lang.

Wilmot, W. W. (1995). *Relational communication.* New York, NY: McGraw-Hill.

Wozney, L., Radomski, A. D., & Newton, A. S. (2018). The gobbledygook in online parent-focused information about child and adolescent mental health. *Health Communication, 33*(6), 710–715. doi:10.1080/10410236.2017.1306475

Chapter Two

The Chilling Influences of Social Stigma on Mental Health Communication

Implications for Promoting Health Equity

Gary L. Kreps

INTRODUCTION

The increasing incidence and negative outcomes of mental health problems have become a serious and widespread health challenge in modern society (National Academy of Sciences, Engineering, and Medicine [NASEM], 2016; Smith & Applegate, 2018; World Health Organization [WHO], 2014). It is estimated that one in four Americans will suffer from serious mental health issues (NASEM, 2016). Many of the people confronting mental health problems go undiagnosed, and many more do not follow or even receive needed professional care treatments for their mental health problems (Stolzenburg et al., 2018; Turner, Mota, Bolton, & Sareen, 2018). The lack of clear diagnoses and effective treatment for mental health challenges has served to exacerbate these mental health problems, as well as increase suffering from a range of related co-morbid health conditions (Scott et al., 2016; WHO, 2014). This chapter examines the influences of social stigma and communication on mental health problems, especially for members of at-risk and vulnerable populations.

MENTAL HEALTH, HEALTH EQUITY, AND COMMUNICATION

Mental health problems are especially challenging health concerns for members of many marginalized populations, including minority group members, many members of immigrant groups, the poor, the homeless, people with serious disabilities (both physical and mental disabilities), and the ill-elderly, who already suffer from a range of serious physical health inequities (Bor, 2015; Dutta & Kreps, 2013; Kreps, 2006, 2017). For example, many members of ethnic and racial minority groups in the United States encounter worse health outcomes from a number of serious physical health problems such as cancers, heart disease, diabetes, and HIV/AIDS than majority group members in the United States; these minority group members also suffer significant inequities in outcomes from challenging mental health conditions such as manic-depression, psychotic disorders, and suicidal tendencies (Allen, Balfour, Bell, & Marmot, 2014; Bostwick et al., 2014; Jimenez, Cook, Bartels, & Alegría, 2013; Cook et al., 2014; Williams & Williams-Morris, 2000). It is important to note that epidemiological data suggest that the actual incidence rates of mental health problems are not significantly higher for many racial and ethnic groups in the United States; a large body of research shows that members of these minority groups, especially African Americans and Latino Americans, often do not receive adequate professional care for their mental health problems, resulting in many unmet needs for mental health care and significantly poorer mental health outcomes (Alegría et al., 2008; Cook et al., 2014; Fiscella, Franks, Doescher, & Saver, 2002; Jimenez et al., 2013; Lo, Cheng, & Howell, 2014; Neighbors et al., 2007; Obasi & Leong, 2009). It is my contention that stigma and communication barriers are major factors leading to these mental health outcome disparities.

An array of serious communication issues can often discourage members of at-risk and minority populations from sharing information with others about their mental health challenges and deter them from actively seeking professional treatment for their mental health concerns (Aggarwal et al., 2016). These communication problems often include intercultural interaction barriers between mental health sufferers and health care providers, issues with English language fluency, low levels of health literacy, and limited knowledge (and often misinformation) about the causes and treatments for mental health problems (Kreps, 2017). These serious communication barriers become impediments to accessing needed support and care for mental health sufferers, and lead to mental health outcome disparities for many members of minority communities in the United States.

In addition to general reluctance to disclose mental health problems, evidence suggests that minority group members who do take the risk to disclose their mental health struggles often encounter inappropriate responses from family members, friends, and even by health care professionals (Clement et al., 2015; Robinson, 2013; Rogers & Pilgrim, 2014; Wood & Watson, 2016). These inappropriate communication responses to mental health problem disclosures include expressions of verbal and nonverbal avoidance, fear, blaming, hostility, and rejection. These inappropriate reactions to mental health disclosures are directly related to a widespread and detrimental social stigma concerning mental illness in society. This stigma is often magnified in many minority communities, which can significantly discourage mental health sufferers from disclosing concerns about mental health problems and from seeking mental health care (Clement et al., 2015; Corrigan, Druss, & Perlick, 2014; Robinson, 2012, 2013; Schomerus et al., 2018).

The serious health communication barriers that make discussing mental health concerns problematic have been closely related to growing disparities in mental health outcomes (Corrigan et al., 2014; Neely, 2015). Evidence shows that minority group members are less likely than other segments of society in the United States to disclose mental health diagnoses, receive adequate support from significant others about such diagnoses, seek care for mental health problems, and receive and continue mental health care treatments (Anglin, Alberti, Link, & Phelan, 2008; Corrigan et al., 2010; Robinson, 2012; Whaley, 2001; Williams, 2009). Cook, Doksum, Chen, Carle, and Alegría (2013) indicate that the number of mental health care providers within minority communities is often limited, making access to high-quality mental health care difficult for residents of these communities. There are numerous serious social determinants of care, such as limited financial resources, lack of health insurance coverage, low education levels, and limited levels of health literacy that are serious problems confronting members of minority communities in the United States that are likely to reduce access to mental health care services and treatments, so that mental health problems for members of these communities are exacerbated (Clement et al., 2015; Corrigan et al., 2014; Robinson, 2012, 2013; Rüsch, Brohan, Gabbidon, Thornicroft, & Clement, 2014; WHO, 2014).

Research has shown that access to relevant and accurate information about mental health issues is often limited among the members of minority communities (Grohol, Slimowicz, & Granda, 2014; Obasi & Leong, 2009; Snowden, 2012). Relevant and accurate health information is the most important resource consumers can have for making important health decisions about seeking care and adopting health behaviors (Kreps, 1988). The lack of relevant information about available mental health services has been found to reduce the understanding of mental health problems that is needed to diagnose them accurately, seek the best treatments, and reduce the burden of mental health problems in minority communities (Grohol et al., 2014; Obasi & Leong, 2009; Snowden, 2012). Even when the symptoms of mental health problems are detected by the individuals experiencing them, such people tend to self-treat their mental health disorders in ways that often make them worse (Lipsky, Kernic, Qiu, & Hasin, 2016; Lo, Tenorio, & Cheng, 2012; Turner, 2016). In many cases, members of minority groups choose self-treatment for mental health problems, typically with overuse of alcohol and illicit drugs (Lo et al., 2012; Turner, 2016; Turner et al., 2018). Although a self-medication approach may appear to these individuals to be an easier route than seeking professional treatments for coping with mental health problems, masking symptoms with substance abuse rarely solves their underlying mental health problems; instead, this common and dangerous strategy often leads to additional problems, such as addiction (Clement et al., 2015; Corrigan et al., 2014; Hatzenbuehler, Phelan, & Link, 2013; U.S. Department of Health and Human Services, 2001).

MENTAL HEALTH COMMUNICATION AND STIGMA

Social stigma is a problem that reduces the perceived status of the people who are stigmatized, including those confronting mental health problems (Goffman, 1963). Stigma concerning mental health problems involves widespread pervasive beliefs portraying those who experience mental health problems as dangerous, evil, weak, or purposely uncooperative, beliefs that often lead to the avoidance and disparagement of the mentally ill in the United States (Robinson, 2012, 2013; Thoits, 2011). The stigma surrounding mental health promotes dangerous stereotypes that portray people with mental health struggles as being violent, dangerous, and hostile. This discourages others from providing needed support and assistance to those with mental health problems.

Social stigma is a primary factor inhibiting discussion about mental health concerns and leads directly to reluctance to seek mental health treatment in many minority communities. This stigma discourages individuals from disclosing their concerns about mental health problems, assisting others facing mental health challenges, and seeking mental health treatment for themselves or others (Hatzenbuehler et al., 2013; Parcesepe & Cabassa, 2013; Pescosolido, Boyer, & Medina, 2013; Pescosolido, Medina, Martin, & Long, 2013; Robinson, 2012, 2013). However, because of the importance of communication in the prevention, diagnosis, and treatment of serious health problems, it is critical to address these complex communication barriers that derive from the social stigma related to mental health problems to help increase the use of effective communication for reducing mental health risk and incidence, and to improve outcomes from mental health care, especially within minority communities (Neumann et al., 2010; Turner, 2016). Access to relevant health information can enable individuals to make good decisions about mental health, identify their best strategies for improving mental health outcomes, and reduce uncertainty about helping others with mental health problems (Grohol et al., 2014; Kreps, 1988; Schomerus et al., 2016).

Unfortunately, popular media, such as movies and television programs, have often promoted the stigma of mental health problems with the widespread dissemination of messages that help to establish and reinforce prejudice against those with mental health problems, portraying these sufferers as violent, dangerous, and out of control (Klin & Lemish, 2008; Neely, 2015; Parcesepe & Cabassa, 2013; Sirey, Franklin, McKenzie, Ghosh, & Raue, 2014; Stout, Villegas, & Jennings, 2004). Mental health stigma is rooted in feelings of shame, fear, embarrassment, discomfort, guilt, uncertainty, and lack of control (Corrigan et al., 2014; Klin & Lemish, 2008; Neely, 2015). The stigma-related discomfort associated with communicating about mental health issues makes it difficult for those who have such issues to acknowledge their problems and seek help in confronting them, even from members of their own families (Robinson, 2012, 2013). The groundbreaking research of Robinson (2012) on African Americans living with mental health problems suggests that their family members are often unreceptive to hearing about mental health problems and do not provide needed social support to those who have them. It is important to raise consciousness and awareness within minority communities that mental health issues are legitimate health concerns and that as significant health problems they require professional attention and treatment to be remedied.

Discomfort concerning communication about mental health issues is closely related to the stigmatization of those within minority communities who experience them; they are often categorized as crazy, dangerous, violent, hostile, and out of control (*loco*). In Latino communities, it is not uncommon for people with mental health problems to be perceived as possessed by the devil and in need of exorcism (Moodley & Palmer, 2014; Sperry, 2015). People confronting mental health problems are often perceived as weak, undisciplined, and untrustworthy. Therefore, it is common for individuals with mental health problems to try to hide them, treat themselves for their mental health disorders, and refrain from seeking professional assistance. Lack of therapeutic communication about mental health issues inevitably leads to an increase in mental health problems and poor health outcomes for many members of minority communities.

SUICIDE PREVENTION AND COMMUNICATION

The many stressors associated with living as a member of a racial or ethnic minority in the United States can intensify mental health problems (Cokley, McClain, Enciso, & Martinez, 2013; Sirin, Ryce, Gupta, & Rogers-Sirin, 2013). Prejudicial public stereotypes about competence, intelligence, responsibility, and intentions often lead to negative views and expectations of members of minority groups (Sirey et al., 2014; Sirin et al., 2013). Similarly, public assumptions about antisocial behaviors, including violence, substance abuse, and criminality, can increase the sensitivity of minority group members to public scrutiny and suspicion, leading to feelings of limited self-worth and a poor public image (Turner, 2016; Whaley, 2001; Williams & Williams-Morris, 2000; Williams, 2009). Living with the stress of prejudice and marginalization can promote depressive symptoms among members of minority groups that can increase the risk for suicide (Bostwick et al., 2014). Suicide has become a major mental health–related problem in the United States that is closely related to a lack of access to sensitive, caring, and supportive communication (Kleiman & Liu, 2013; Lai, Maniam, Chan, & Ravindran, 2014; Silk, Perrault, Nazione, Pace, & Collins-Eaglin, 2017).

The communication problems encountered in addressing stress disorders and depression are especially problematic in efforts to reduce the risk for suicide in minority communities, where individuals can experience high levels of stress due to social bias and prejudice (Cokley et al., 2013; Sirin et al., 2013). It is difficult for members of minority communities to let others know about the stresses that are confronting them, and it is very difficult to diagnose and treat serious stress disorders. Suicidal tendencies can grow from unaddressed feelings of stress. Communication programs need to be developed to help recognize stress-related problems in minority communities; provide needed health services, such as counseling, therapy, and medications, to individuals confronting stress; and reduce the progression from stress disorders to depression and suicidal attempts (Kleiman & Liu, 2013; Lai et al., 2014; Silk et al., 2017).

COMMUNICATION STRATEGIES FOR ADDRESSING MENTAL HEALTH DISPARITIES

Mental health problems are complex, often difficult to diagnose, and challenging to manage (Pescosolido et al., 2013). Serious mental health problems often require long-term treatments with a variety of therapies (Nathan & Gorman, 2015). Those who have mental health problems may not recognize their need for help, and others may interpret their symptoms as bad or antisocial behavior. The stigma surrounding mental health problems often leads to stereotyping and limited knowledge about the best ways to interact with and help persons with mental health problems. Inappropriate responses to those with mental health problems can often make the problems worse by frustrating, frightening, or provoking those who are experiencing them (Rogers

& Pilgrim, 2014; Wood & Watson, 2016). It can sometimes be difficult to reason with people who have mental health problems. Training and educational programs can help increase understanding about the best strategies for recognizing, responding to, and providing assistance for those with mental health problems.

New communication strategies, programs, and policies must be proposed to help address the stigma of mental health problems in minority communities and to encourage open discussion about mental health issues, promoting the provision of needed interventions for effectively addressing these serious health problems. Strategic communication interventions have the potential to help address many of the inequities in the management of mental health problems that are prevalent in minority communities in the United States. For example, training for mental health care providers in communicating in culturally sensitive ways with members of minority groups who have mental health issues has been found to improve health outcomes (Copeland, 2006; Pearson et al., 2015). Similarly, culturally sensitive multimedia health education campaigns have been designed to help reduce the significant discomfort that members of many minority communities feel when discussing mental health issues (Corrigan et al., 2014; Silk et al., 2017; Thornicroft et al., 2016). Schomerus et al. (2016) found that an online internet-based educational intervention that provided information about viewing mental illness as a normal part of a continuum of mental health helped to combat the stigma of mental illness by influencing attitudes toward people with mental illness.

Ngo et al. (2016) found that community engagement programs can promote improvements in key mental health functional outcomes, reduce barriers to care, and increase participation in mental health care services. Ali, Farrer, Gulliver, & Griffiths (2015) found that the use of online peer-to-peer social support showed promise as a communication intervention for addressing mental health problems. African American churches have been found to hold great potential for providing needed social support and treatment referrals for members experiencing mental health problems (Blank, Mahmood, Fox, & Guterbock, 2002; Bryant et al., 2014; Hankerson & Weissman, 2012). Bridges et al. (2014) found preliminary evidence indicating that the use of integrated mental health services, which seek to reduce stigma and barriers to service utilization by embedding mental health professionals into primary care teams, can help reduce mental health disparities for Latinos. In addition, programs that promote the expression of social support have been found to reduce risks for suicide by encouraging resilience, combatting loneliness, and promoting feelings of self-worth (Farrell, Bolland, & Cockerham, 2015; Silk et al., 2017).

Communication research can help identify the best strategies for reducing the stigmatization of mental health problems in minority communities.

Basic research studies are needed to examine how key communication processes, such as relational coordination, information sharing, social influence, social support, and intercultural communication sensitivity, are related to providing help to individuals confronting mental health problems. We also need surveillance research programs to track how societal communication practices that stigmatize mental health issues can be reduced to promote a greater understanding of mental health issues and support for those living with mental health challenges. Most of all, we need to continue to develop and test evidence-based communication intervention programs for educating key audiences about mental health, as well as for training professional and lay caregivers to interact effectively with people seeking care for mental health concerns. There is great promise for improving mental health outcomes among members of minority communities if we can develop key communication strategies to reduce mental health stigma, increase access to relevant mental health information, and introduce communication programs that make high-quality mental health care easily available to all people who need such care. Increasing access, understanding, and the exchange of relevant mental health information can help to reduce disparities in mental health outcomes.

There is a dire need to reexamine the ways that mental health is conceptualized in modern society. Mental health must be recognized as a legitimate health issue and not a personal weakness or deficiency. We need to stop blaming people for experiencing mental health challenges, and to find ways to help them address these health issues. At the population level, education programs that portray mental health as a common health issue that can be treated effectively can be used to combat mental health stigma and the dangerous stereotypes that derive from stigma. Entertainment-based media education programs, such as movies and television shows, can be powerful communication channels for portraying mental health in realistic and optimistic ways, providing guidance for responding effectively to mental health issues, both for those confronting these issues themselves and for those who can help mental health sufferers (Singhal & Rogers, 2002).

On a personal level, interpersonal communication is an essential social process for helping people who are suffering from mental health challenges. Through observant interpersonal communication we can help identify when people we know are engaging in behaviors and demonstrating symptoms that may suggest they are confronting mental health challenges. Those confronting mental health problems may not recognize changes in their behaviors or physical conditions that may be obvious to others and can indicate mental health issues. We can also endeavor to exhibit sensitive and caring interpersonal communication behaviors with those confronting mental health problems to provide them with needed support and encouragement to help them address their problems, to encourage them to disclose their problems and seek professional care, as well as to help them follow recommended treatment regimens. It is very difficult for those who are confronting mental health problems to overcome the stigma and communication barriers concerning mental health issues all by themselves. They need interpersonal support and encouragement. This is especially important for helping those who may be experiencing suicidal thoughts. They may not be inclined to seek help themselves, may not feel worthy of help or support, or may think the world would be better off without them around. Interpersonal support and encouragement can go a long way to help mitigate these feelings and help them access needed care to save their lives. Effective communication can make a major contribution to addressing serious mental health challenges on an individual and at a societal level, helping to improve mental health outcomes for all members of society.

REFERENCES

Aggarwal, N. K., Pieh, M. C., Dixon, L., Guarnaccia, P., Alegría, M., & Lewis-Fernández, R. (2016). Clinician descriptions of communication strategies to improve treatment engagement by racial/ethnic minorities in mental health services: A systematic review. *Patient Education and Counseling, 99*(2), 198–209. doi:10.1016/j.pec.2015.09.002

Alegría, M., Chatterji, P., Wells, K., Cao, Z., Chen, C. N., Takeuchi, D., . . . Meng, X. L. (2008). Disparity in depression treatment among racial and ethnic minority populations in the United States. *Psychiatric Services, 59*(11), 1264–1272. doi:10.1176/ps.2008.59.11.1264

Ali, K., Farrer, L., Gulliver, A., & Griffiths, K. M. (2015). Online peer-to-peer support for young people with mental health problems: A systematic review. *JMIR Mental Health, 2*(2), e19. doi:10.2196/mental.4418

Allen, J., Balfour, R., Bell, R., & Marmot, M. (2014). Social determinants of mental health. *International Review of Psychiatry, 26*(4), 392–407. doi:10.3109/09540261.2014.928270

Anglin, D. M., Alberti, P. M., Link, B. G., & Phelan, J. C. (2008). Racial differences in beliefs about the effectiveness and necessity of mental health treatment. *American Journal of Community Psychology, 42*(1–2), 17–24. doi:10.1007/s10464-008-9189-5

Blank, M. B., Mahmood, M., Fox, J. C., & Guterbock, T. (2002). Alternative mental health services: The role of the Black church in the South. *American Journal of Public Health, 92*(10), 1668–1672. doi:10.2105/ajph.92.10.1668

Bor, J. A. (2015). Among the elderly, many mental illnesses go undiagnosed. *Health Affairs, 34*(5), 727–731. doi:10.1377/hlthaff.2015.0314

Bostwick, W. B., Meyer, I., Aranda, F., Russell, S., Hughes, T., Birkett, M., & Mustanski, B. (2014). Mental health and suicidality among racially/ethnically diverse sexual minority youths. *American Journal of Public Health, 104*(6), 1129–1136. doi:10.2105/AJPH.2013.301749

Bridges, A. J., Andrews A. R. III, Villalobos, B. T., Pastrana, F. A., Cavell, T. A., & Gomez, D. (2014). Does integrated behavioral health care reduce mental health disparities for Latinos? Initial findings. *Journal of Latina/o Psychology, 2*(1), 37–53. doi:10.1037/lat0000009

Bryant, K., Haynes, T., Yeary, K., Hye-cheon, K., Greer-Williams, N., & Hartwig, M. (2014). A rural African American faith community's solutions to depression disparities. *Public Health Nursing, 31*(3), 262–271. doi:10.1111/phn.12079

Clement, S., Schauman, O., Graham, T., Maggioni, F., Evans-Lacko, S., Bezborodovs, N., . . . Thornicroft, G. (2015). What is the impact of mental health–related stigma on help-seeking? A systematic review of quantitative and qualitative studies. *Psychological Medicine, 45*(1), 11–27. doi:10.1017/s0033291714000129

Cokley, K., McClain, S., Enciso, A., & Martinez, M. (2013). An examination of the impact of minority status stress and impostor feelings on the mental health of diverse ethnic minority college students. *Journal of Multicultural Counseling and Development, 41*(2), 82–95. doi:10.1002/j.2161-1912.2013.00029.x

Cook, B. L., Doksum, T., Chen, C. N., Carle, A., & Alegría, M. (2013). The role of provider supply and organization in reducing racial/ethnic disparities in mental health care in the U.S. *Social Science & Medicine, 84*, 102–109. doi:10.1016/j.socscimed.2013.02.006

Cook, B. L., Zuvekas, S. H., Carson, N., Wayne, G. F., Vesper, A., & McGuire, T. G. (2014). Assessing racial/ethnic disparities in treatment across episodes of mental health care. *Health Services Research, 49*(1), 206–229. doi:10.1111/1475-6773.12095

Copeland, V. (2006). Disparities in mental health service utilization among low-income African American adolescents: Closing the gap by enhancing practitioner's competence. *Child and Adolescent Social Work Journal, 23*(4), 407–431. doi:10.1007/s10560-006-0061

Corrigan, P. W., Druss, B. G., & Perlick, D. A. (2014). The impact of mental illness stigma on seeking and participating in mental health care. *Psychological Science in the Public Interest, 15*(2), 37–70. doi:10.1177/1529100614531398

Corrigan, P. W., Morris, S., Larson, J., Rafacz, J., Wassel, A., Michaels, P., . . . Rüsch, N. (2010). Self-stigma and coming out about one's mental illness. *Journal of Community Psychology, 38*(3), 259–275. doi:10.1002/jcop.20363

Dutta, M., & Kreps, G. L. (2013). Reducing health disparities: Communication interventions. In M. J. Dutta & G. L. Kreps, (Eds.), *Reducing health disparities: Communication interventions* (pp. 1–14). New York: Peter Lang Publishers.

Farrell, C. T., Bolland, J. M., & Cockerham, W. C. (2015). The role of social support and social context on the incidence of attempted suicide among adolescents living in extremely impoverished communities. *Journal of Adolescent Health, 56*(1), 59–65. doi:10.1016/j.jadohealth.2014.08.015

Fiscella, K., Franks, P., Doescher, M. P., & Saver, B. G. (2002). Disparities in health care by race, ethnicity, and language among the insured: Findings from a national sample. *Medical Care, 40*(1), 52–59. doi:10.1097/00005650-200201000-00007

Goffman, E. (1963). *Stigma: Notes on management of a spoiled identity.* Engelwood Cliffs, NJ: Prentice Hall.

Grohol, J. M., Slimowicz, J., & Granda, R. (2014). The quality of mental health information commonly searched for on the Internet. *Cyberpsychology, Behavior, and Social Networking, 17*(4), 216–221. doi:10.1089/cyber.2013.0258

Hankerson, S. H., & Weissman, M. M. (2012). Church-based health programs for mental disorders among African Americans: A review. *Psychiatric Services, 63*(3), 243–249. doi:10.1176/appi.ps.2011000216

Hatzenbuehler, M. L., Phelan, J. C., & Link, B. G. (2013). Stigma as a fundamental cause of population health inequalities. *American Journal of Public Health, 103*(5), 813–821. doi:10.2105/ajph.2012.301069

Jimenez, D. E., Cook, B., Bartels, S. J., & Alegría, M. (2013). Disparities in mental health service use of racial and ethnic minority elderly adults. *Journal of the American Geriatrics Society, 61*(1), 18–25. doi:10.111/jgs.12063

Kleiman, E. M., & Liu, R. T. (2013). Social support as a protective factor in suicide: Findings from two nationally representative samples. *Journal of Affective Disorders, 150*(2), 540–545. doi:10.1016/j.jad.2013.01.033

Klin, A., & Lemish, D. (2008). Mental disorders stigma in the media: Review of studies on production, content, and influences. *Journal of Health Communication, 13*(5), 434–444. doi:10.1080/10810730802198813

Kreps, G. L. (2017). Stigma and the reluctance to address mental health issues in minority communities. *Journal of Family Strengths, 17*(1), 1–11. Retrieved from https://digitalcommons.library.tmc.edu/jfs/vol17/iss1/3

Kreps, G. L. (2006). Communication and racial inequities in health care. *American Behavioral Scientist, 49*(6), 760–774. doi:10.1177/0002764205283800

Kreps, G. L. (1988). The pervasive role of information in health and health care: Implications for health communication policy. *Annals of the International Communication Association, 11*(1), 2318–276. doi:10.1080/23808985.1988.11678988690

Lai, M. H., Maniam, T., Chan, L. F., & Ravindran, A. V. (2014). Caught in the web: A review of web-based suicide prevention. *Journal of Medical Internet Research, 16*(1), e30. doi:10.2196/jmir.2973

Lipsky, S., Kernic, M. A., Qiu, Q., & Hasin, D. S. (2016). Posttraumatic stress disorder and alcohol misuse among women: Effects of ethnic minority stressors. *Social Psychiatry and Psychiatric Epidemiology, 51*(3), 407–419. doi:10.1007/s00127-015-1109-z

Lo, C., Cheng, T., & Howell, R. (2014). Access to and utilization of health services as pathway to racial disparities in serious mental illness. *Community Mental Health Journal, 50*(3), 251–257. doi:10.1007/s10597-013-9593-7

Lo, C., Tenorio, K., & Cheng, T. (2012). Racial differences in co-occurring substance use and serious psychological distress: The roles of marriage and religiosity. *Substance Use & Misuse, 47*(6), 734–744. doi:10.3109/108226084.2012.666312

Moodley, R., & Palmer, S. (2014). *Race, culture and psychotherapy: Critical perspectives in multicultural practice.* Abingdon, UK: Routledge.

Nathan, P. E., & Gorman, J. M. (Eds.). (2015). *A guide to treatments that work.* New York, NY: Oxford University Press.

National Academy of Sciences, Engineering, and Medicine. (2016). *Ending discrimination against people with mental and substance use disorders: The evidence for stigma change.* Washington, DC: The National Academies Press. doi:10.17226/23442

Neely, S. Y. (2015). *Mental illness knowledge, stigma, help seeking behaviors, and perceptions of media portrayals of Black culture: The role of spirituality and the African American church* (Doctoral dissertation). University of Cincinnati, Cincinnati, Ohio.

Neighbors, H. W., Caldwell, C., Williams, D. R., Nesse, R., Taylor, R. J., Bullard, K. M., . . . Jackson, J. S. (2007). Race, ethnicity, and the use of services for mental disorders: Results from the National Survey of American Life. *Archives of General Psychiatry, 64*(4), 485. doi:10.1001/archpsyc.64.4.485

Neumann, M., Edelhäuser, F., Kreps, G. L., Scheffer, C., Lutz, G., Tauschel, D., & Visser, A. (2010). Can patient-provider interaction increase the effectiveness of medical treatments or even substitute them? A methodological reflection of the specific effect of the provider. *Patient Education and Counseling, 80*, 307–314. doi:10.1016/j-pec.2010.07.020

Ngo, V. K., Sherbourne, C., Chung, B., Tang, L., Wright, A. L., Whittington, Y., . . . Miranda, J. (2016). Community engagement compared with technical assistance to disseminate depression care among low-income, minority women: A randomized controlled effectiveness study. *American Journal of Public Health, 106*(10), 1833–1841. doi:10.2105/ajph.2016.303304

Obasi, E. M., & Leong, F. T. L. (2009). Psychological distress, acculturation, and mental health-seeking attitudes among people of African descent in the United States: A preliminary investigation. *Journal of Counseling Psychology, 56*(2), 227–238. doi:10.1037/a0014865

Parcesepe, A. M., & Cabassa, L. J. (2013). Public stigma of mental illness in the United States: A systematic literature review. *Administration and Policy in Mental Health and Mental Health Services Research, 40*(5), 384–399. doi:10.1007/s10488-012-0430-z

Pearson, G. S., Hines-Martin, V. P., Evans, L. K., York, J. A., Kane, C. F., & Yearwood, E. L. (2015). Addressing gaps in mental health needs of diverse, at-risk, underserved, and disenfranchised populations: A call for nursing action. *Archives of Psychiatric Nursing, 29*(1), 14–18. doi:10.1016/j.apnu.2014.09.004

Pescosolido, B. A., Boyer, C. A., & Medina, T. R. (2013). The social dynamics of responding to mental health problems. In C. Aneshensel, J. C. Phelan, & A. Bierman (Eds.), *Handbook of the sociology of mental health* (pp. 505–524). Dordrecht, the Netherlands: Springer.

Pescosolido, B. A., Medina, T. R., Martin, J. K., & Long, J. S. (2013). The "backbone" of stigma: Identifying the global core of public prejudice associated with mental illness. *American Journal of Public Health, 103*(5), 853–860. doi:10.2105/ ajph.2012.301147

Robinson, N. (2013). Addressing the stigma of mental illness: Promoting greater receptivity of mental health disclosures in co-cultural group members. In G. L. Kreps & S. Kodish (Eds.), *DC Health Communication (DCHC) Conference proceedings* (p. 92). Fairfax, VA: Center for Health and Risk Communication.

Robinson, N. (2012). *To tell or not to tell: Factors in self-disclosing mental illness in our everyday relationships* (Doctoral dissertation). Fairfax, VA: George Mason University.

Rogers, A., & Pilgrim, D. (2014). *A sociology of mental health and illness.* London, UK: McGraw-Hill Education UK.

Rüsch, N., Brohan, E., Gabbidon, J., Thornicroft, G., & Clement, S. (2014). Stigma and disclosing one's mental illness to family and friends. *Social Psychiatry and Psychiatric Epidemiology, 49*(7), 1157–1160. doi:10.1007/s00127-014-0871-7

Schomerus, G., Angermeyer, M. C., Baumeister, S. E., Stolzenburg, S., Link, B. G., & Phelan, J. C. (2016). An online intervention using information on the mental health–mental illness continuum to reduce stigma. *European Psychiatry, 32,* 21–27. doi:10.1016/j.eurpsy.2015.11.006

Schomerus, G., Stolzenburg, S., Freitag, S., Speerforck, S., Janowitz, D., Evans-Lacko, S., . . . Schmidt, S. (2018). Stigma as a barrier to recognizing personal mental illness and seeking help: A prospective study among untreated persons with mental illness. *European Archives of Psychiatry and Clinical Neuroscience,* 1–11. doi:10.1007/s00406-018-0896-0

Scott, K. M., Lim, C., Al-Hamzawi, A., Alonso, J., Bruffaerts, R., Caldas-de-Almeida, J. M., . . . Kessler, R. C. (2016). Association of mental disorders with subsequent chronic physical conditions: World mental health surveys from 17 countries. *JAMA Psychiatry, 73*(2), 150–158. doi:10.1001/jamapsychiatry.2015.2688

Silk, K. J., Perrault, E. K., Nazione, S. A., Pace, K., & Collins-Eaglin, J. (2017). Evaluation of a social norms approach to a suicide prevention campaign. *Journal of Health Communication, 22*(2), 1–8. doi:10.1080/10810730.2016.1258742

Singhal, A., & Rogers, E. M. (2002). A theoretical agenda for entertainment-education. *Communication Theory, 12*(2), 117–135. doi:10.1111/j.1468-2885.2002.tb00262.x

Sirey, J. A., Franklin, A. J., McKenzie, S., Ghosh, S., & Raue, P. (2014). Race, stigma and mental health recommendations among depressed older persons in aging services. *Psychiatric Services, 65*(4), 537. doi:10.1176/appi.ps.201200530

Sirin, S. R., Ryce, P., Gupta, T., & Rogers-Sirin, L. (2013). The role of acculturative stress on mental health symptoms for immigrant adolescents: A longitudinal investigation. *Developmental Psychology, 49*(4), 736–748. doi:10.1037/a0028398

Smith, R. A., & Applegate, A. (2018). Mental health stigma and communication and their intersections with education. *Communication Education, 67*(3), 382–393. doi :10.1080/03634523.2018.1465988

Snowden, L. R. (2012). Health and mental health policies' role in better understanding and closing African American–White American disparities in treatment access and quality of care. *American Psychologist, 67*(7), 524–531. doi:10.1037/a0030054

Sperry, L. (2015). Effective spiritually oriented psychotherapy practice is clinically, ethically, and culturally sensitive practice. *Spirituality in Clinical Practice, 2*(2), 103–105. doi:10.1037/scp0000073

Stolzenburg, S., Freitag, S., Evans-Lacko, S., Speerforck, S., Schmidt, S., & Schomerus, G. (2018). Individuals with currently untreated mental illness: Causal beliefs and readiness to seek help. *Epidemiology and Psychiatric Sciences*, 1–12. doi:10.1017/S2045796017000828

Stout, P. A., Villegas, J., & Jennings, N. A. (2004). Images of mental illness in the media: Identifying gaps in the research. *Schizophrenia Bulletin, 30*(3), 543–561. doi:10.1093/oxfordjournals.schbul.a007099

Thoits, P. A. (2011). Resisting the stigma of mental illness. *Social Psychology Quarterly, 74*(1), 6–28. doi:10.1177/0190272511398019

Thornicroft, G., Mehta, N., Clement, S., Evans-Lacko, S., Doherty, M., Rose, D., . . . Henderson, C. (2016). Evidence for effective interventions to reduce mental-health–related stigma and discrimination. *The Lancet, 387*(10023), 1123–1132. doi:10.1016/s0140-6736(15)00298-6

Turner, S., Mota, N., Bolton, J., & Sareen, J. (2018). Self-medication with alcohol or drugs for mood and anxiety disorders: A narrative review of the epidemiological literature. *Depression and Anxiety, 35*(9), 851–860. doi:10.1002/da.22771

Turner, T. (2016). *Substance abuse and mental disorders among African Americans.* (Doctoral dissertation). Fort Lauderdale, FL: Kaplan University.

U.S. Department of Health and Human Services. (2001). *Mental health: Culture, race, and ethnicity—A supplement to mental health: A report of the Surgeon General.* 2001. Rockville, MD: U.S. Department of Health and Human Services, Substance Abuse and Mental Health Services Administration, Center for Mental Health Services. Retrieved from https://www.ncbi.nlm.nih.gov/books/NBK44243/

Whaley, A. L. (2001). Cultural mistrust and mental health services for African Americans: A review and meta-analysis. *The Counseling Psychologist, 29*(4), 513–531. doi:10.1177/0011000001294003

Williams, D. R., & Williams-Morris, R. (2000). Racism and mental health: The African American experience. *Ethnicity and Health, 5*(3/4), 243–268. doi:10.1080/713667453

Williams, T. M. (2009). *Black pain: It just looks like we're not hurting.* New York, NY: Simon & Schuster.

Wood, J. D., & Watson, A. C. (2016). Improving police interventions during mental health–related encounters: Past, present and future. *Policing and Society*, 1–11. doi:10.1080/10439463.2016.1219734

World Health Organization. (2014). *Social determinants of mental health.* Geneva: World Health Organization. Retrieved from https://www.who.int/mental_health/publications/gulbenkian_paper_social_determinants_of_mental_health/en/

Section 2

MENTAL HEALTH IN ACTION: NARRATIVE APPROACH

Chapter Three

Communicated Sense-Making

A Theoretical Compass for Exploring Family Communication and Sense-Making about Mental Health and Illness

Elizabeth Flood-Grady
Jody Koenig Kellas
Kelly A. Chernin

My dad was only in the hospital for about two weeks and then he came home for Christmas Eve . . . [My dad] was on medication and [my sisters and I] were understanding of that . . . Like [my mom and dad] explained to us, both my parents were like, "Okay, so [your] dad is going to be taking medication right now. He's trying to figure out his depression. You know he has [depression]. [As a family], we're just going to see what happens." [My dad] was very weird on Christmas, he was super off, like he wasn't very (pauses), present. [My dad] just seemed like a little over medicated, if that makes sense. Then [my dad], I think (pauses) yeah, in mid-January, all the sudden he wasn't taking the medication anymore, but he seemed a lot better, like really randomly seemed a whole lot better. I remember the three days before he died, we had a snow day. We had a three-day snow day, so everyone [my mom, my dad, my two sisters, and me] was home, and everyone was snowed into the house . . . it was the best thing in my whole life, [my family] had three days of [our] family. And my dad was getting dressed. He wasn't in his pajamas. He was awesome. He was great. (pauses) and then he committed suicide on the fourth. (Female, Age 21)

This account was shared by a young woman during an interview for a study on mental health and illness communication within the family. Her story is heart-wrenching; the devastating loss of her father and the complexities associated with this experience will likely take years—if not a lifetime—of which to make sense. In this brief narrative, the participant uses attributions to explain her dad's behavior on Christmas Eve (e.g., "[my dad] was super off, like he wasn't very (pauses), present. [My dad] just seemed like a little over medicated") and the events preceding his suicide. The harrowing experience she shared illustrates the salience of family in understanding mental health and illness, and, in our opinion, underscores the critical need for communication and sense-making in this context. In this chapter, we explore the communicated sense-making (CSM) processes individuals and families use to communicate about mental health and illness.

Our goal in this chapter is to illuminate the utility of the CSM theoretical model (Koenig Kellas & Kranstuber Horstman, 2015) to investigate individual and family communication in sense-making about mental health and illness. We begin by contextualizing mental health and illness as a process embedded in family communication and in need of sense-making. Second, we provide an overview of the CSM theoretical model and review research using sense-making devices to explicate the content, process, and effects of individual and family communication about mental health and illness. Third, we offer recommendations for extending the CSM theoretical model and using CSM devices to inform the development of mental health and illness interventions.

FAMILY COMMUNICATION AND SENSE-MAKING ABOUT MENTAL HEALTH AND ILLNESS

Despite the significance of family communication to mental health and illness (see Segrin, 2013), and the ubiquity of mental health conditions across the globe (Kessler, Aguilar-Gaxiola, Alonso, & Chatterji, 2009), there is limited research on individual and family communication in sense-making about mental health and illness. Expanding this line of research is important for several reasons.

First, the constructs of mental health and illness are confusing, and individuals have generally low levels of mental health literacy (e.g., Lauber, Ajdacic-Gross, Fritschi, Stulz, & Rössler, 2005). For instance, mental health is not merely the absence of mental illness, but also reflects the ways in which mental and psychological well-being are promoted and maintained (World Health Organization [WHO], 2018). On the other hand, the American Psychiatric Association [APA] (2018) describes mental illnesses as "health conditions involving changes in emotion, thinking, and behavior, and are associated with distress and/or impaired social, work, or family functioning" (para. 1). Adding to the complexity, several illnesses are characterized by common symptoms, including trouble sleeping and eating (e.g., depression and mood disorders, eating disorders), bouts of intense anxiety (e.g., mood disorders, anxiety disorders), and consuming alcohol at a rate that hinders one's ability to hold a job or maintain personal relationships (e.g., substance abuse disorders, mood disorders) (Aneshensel, Phelan, & Bierman, 2013). Because families are central to sense-making (Pecchioni & Keeley, 2011), individuals likely rely on family communication to understand and make sense of mental health and illness in the face of its complexities.

Second, mental health concerns are social illnesses anchored in family communication. For instance, certain communication patterns within the family of origin, including criticism, excessive emotional involvement among parents, and high levels of family conflict, serve as risk factors for developing mental health concerns (see Segrin, 2013, for review). Communication about mental illness from parents and older family members teach younger members important lessons (e.g., Aleman & Helfrich, 2010; Flood-Grady & Koenig Kellas, 2018) and influence their perceptions of help-seeking and personal relationships (Greenwell, 2018). Thus, family communication both contributes to and helps family members understand mental health and illness.

In the U.S. and many developing countries (e.g., India according to Patel et al., 2011), family and community members also play a significant role in loved ones' mental illnesses through caretaking (e.g., Aleman & Helfrich, 2010; Rose, Mallinson, & Walton-Moss, 2002; Saxena, Thornicroft, Knapp, & Whiteford, 2007). Taking responsibility and caring for the loved one with a mental illness, such as schizophrenia or depression, can be a significant burden. Many family caregivers struggle to balance family, work, and caretaking and can experience poor physical and emotional health and burnout (Chan, 2011). Given the links between family communication and increased risk of mental illness, socialization, treatment-seeking, and care provision for family members afflicted, more research on family communication about mental health and illness is needed.

Third, families are exposed to and affected by mental illness stigma (e.g., Corrigan & Miller, 2004), and reinforce stigma through family communication or its absence (e.g., avoidance). Stigmas reflect "attributes that are deeply discrediting and serve to dehumanize, making those with stigmas easier to discriminate against" (Goffman, 1963, p. 3). The stigma surrounding mental illness results from negative reactions of individuals without a mental illness in their attempts to separate themselves from the stigmatizing label and associated stereotypes (see modified labeling theory, Link, 1987; Link & Phelan, 2013, for reviews). Due to their association with afflicted family members, family members of those diagnosed with mental illness are affected by stigma and make sense of the member's diagnosis by experiencing elevated feelings of shame (Corrigan & Miller, 2004). For example, individuals in Mexican American families sometimes use the word nervios, rather than schizophrenia, to protect afflicted members against psychiatric stigma (Carpenter-Song et al., 2010; Jenkins, 1988). Although mental illness stigma has changed in recent years, such that there is "less" stigma associated with psychiatric treatment (Mojtabai, 2007), mental illness stigma persists across several areas, such as dangerousness (see Schnittaker, 2013 for review) and culture (see Fischer & Sartorius, 1999), and is shaped, in part, through communication about mental illness within the family (e.g., Flood-Grady & Koenig Kellas, 2018).

Finally, it is also possible that some individuals and families do not talk about mental health and illness. For instance, family members may choose to avoid conversations about mental illness in order to protect younger members or to spare them the confusion and pain that may accompany knowledge of certain familial mental health information (e.g., parents may not tell children about a family member with schizophrenia who went off their medication and then committed suicide). Uncertainty about how to initiate conversations about mental health and illness, or fears about what to say during conversations, could also preclude communication about this topic.

Refraining from mental health and illness communication could also be guided by privacy rules and cultural norms (e.g., mental illness may be viewed as inappropriate to discuss outside the family). In African American families, for example, serious mental illness is considered "family business" and is expected to remain private (Carpenter-Song et al., 2010). Family members may avoid talking to aging parents about Alzheimer's dementia in order to avoid worry or insult. Thus, the decision to avoid communicating about mental illness could also be intentional and done strategically to benefit certain family individuals. Regardless of their motivations, avoidance influences mental health and illness sense-making by increasing perceptions of mental illness stigma (Link & Phelan, 2013).

The complexities surrounding mental health and illness and stigma increase the need for individual and family communicated sense-making. Sense-making is the process of organizing and interpreting one's thoughts and turning them into action (i.e., behavior, according to Weick, Sutcliffe, & Obstfeld, 2005). Communicated sense-making refers to the way in which people communicate to make sense of their relationships and lives, particularly during times of difficulty (Koenig Kellas & Kranstuber Horstman, 2015), since stress, trauma, illness, and the unexpected require cognitive and communicated work to incorporate into a person's or a family's sense of understanding and (co-created) reality. The CSM theoretical model was introduced by Koenig Kellas and Kranstuber Horstman (2015) to synthesize research on the common processes by which people communicate to make sense. In the current chapter, we introduce the CSM theoretical model as a particularly useful lens for understanding family communication about mental health and illness.

DEFINING COMMUNICATED SENSE-MAKING
AND SENSE-MAKING DEVICES

Koenig Kellas and Kranstuber Horstman (2015) introduced communicated sense-making as a theoretical model for synthesizing research constructs relevant to the ways in which individuals and families make sense of their relationships, difficulty, and lives. They contend that,

> Research in CSM is guided by theorizing related to psychological processing (e.g., Bruner, 1990; Heider, 1958), identity construction (e.g., McAdams, 1993), self-presentation and face (e.g., Brown & Levinson, 1987), and the process of communicating explanations (e.g., Scott & Lyman, 1968), and helps illuminate the ways in which humans come to make sense of their lives through communication. (Koenig Kellas & Kranstuber Horstman, 2015, p. 80)

The authors position sense-making devices, including memorable messages, accounts, communicated narrative sense-making (CNSM), attributions, communicated perspective-taking, and, in more recent work, metaphors (see Horstman & Holman, 2018) as primary ways individuals and families communicate to make sense of their lives and experiences (see Figure 3.1).

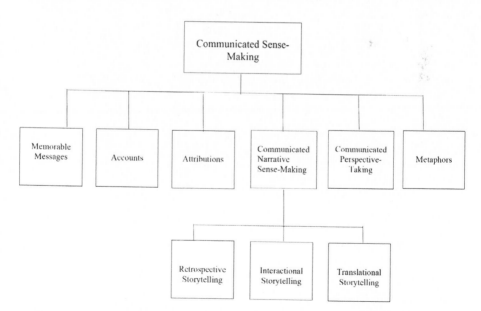

Figure 3.1. Communicated sense-making model. Adapted from Koenig Kellas & Kranstuber Horstman (2015).
Image provided courtesy of the author.

Unlike other cognitive approaches to sense-making, Koenig Kellas and Kranstuber Horstman (2015) argue that communication (i.e., content and process) is at the heart of sense-making. The theoretical model synthesizes previously siloed bodies of research into a parsimonious approach to understanding sense-making in interaction. In other words, the CSM theoretical model synthesizes concepts to explicate the everyday ways individuals and families make sense of their experiences and communicate that sense-making to others (Koenig Kellas & Kranstuber Horstman, 2015). CSM devices are particularly relevant to understanding the individual and family communication surrounding difficult, confusing, or complex situations and experiences, such as mental health and illness. In the sections that follow, we explain each of the sense-making devices included in the CSM theoretical model, highlight examples of CSM from existing research to study mental health and illness communication and sense-making, and offer several avenues for future research.

MEMORABLE MESSAGES

Individuals and families communicatively make sense of difficult, complex experiences, such as mental health and illness through memorable messages. Memorable messages are the verbal messages people recall hearing over long periods of time and can have a significant impact on one's life (Knapp, Stohl, & Rierdon, 1981). The content of memorable messages provide individuals with social knowledge and information to guide their future actions (Stohl, 1986). Memorable messages can be positive or negative (Knapp et al., 1981) and offer a way for individuals to make sense of their everyday experiences (e.g., gendered messages about work-life balance, see Medved, Brogan, McClanahan, Morris, & Shepherd, 2006).

Memorable messages are powerful socializing devices, particularly when delivered by family members (e.g., Lucas & Buzzanell, 2012), and are used to communicate about health topics and stigmatized illnesses (see Cooke-Jackson & Rubinsky, 2018 for review). Greenwell (2018), for example, examined the content of memorable messages about mental health that young adults recalled receiving from their family members. Participant's reports of memorable messages were gathered via survey, and analysis of the open-ended questions revealed three themes about mental health: strategizing, normalizing, and minimizing messages. Strategizing messages reflected the need to engage in proactive mental health self-care; normalizing messages validated mental health and mental health care as acceptable and in non-stigmatized ways; finally, minimizing messages diminished the reality of mental health and the need for care. The content (i.e., type, theme) of memorable messages from family members in Greenwell's (2018) study has a socializing influence on young adults' attitudes toward clinical help-seeking and relational closeness with the message source, such that minimizing messages were negatively associated with help-seeking intentions and closeness with the message sender.

Finally, Flood-Grady, Starcher, and Bergquist (2018) examined the memorable messages that young adults who were diagnosed with clinical depression reported receiving from their parents about depression and the impact of those messages on young adults' reported satisfaction with the message source. Findings revealed seven themes of memorable messages, including It's not real; Depression is a temporary experience (and things will get better); We will be there; Depression is serious; Depression is no big deal; Get over it and try to be happy; It's normal. Moreover, message theme predicted young adult children's reported satisfaction with the parental message sender such that those who recalled hearing messages that reflected the first theme— It's not real—reported significantly lower levels of relational satisfaction compared to those who received parental memorable messages from parents communicating any of the other themes.

Though limited, evidence from these studies suggest that the content of memorable messages about mental health and illness influence recipient's attitudes, values, and relationships. Memorable messages about mental health and illness delivered from family members (e.g., parents, grandparents, aunts and uncles) influence how young adult family members make sense of clinical help-seeking for mental illness and their relationship (satisfaction, closeness) with the message source. The importance of this cannot be overstated. Parents (often the senders of memorable messages in families) play a crucial role in managing their children's mental illness, particularly when children are diagnosed in adolescence. In addition to building a treatment team, ensuring adherence to therapeutic and possible pharmaceutical interventions, parents (and other influential adults such as therapists, teachers, guidance counselors, and extended family members) may send messages that stick with adolescents and young adults that either reinforce stigma and shame (e.g., Greenwell, 2018) or encourage self-acceptance and provide hopeful or encouraging wisdom or advice that guides future behavior. Future research should examine the development of these memorable messages longitudinally and their impact over time on decision-making (e.g., decision to seek treatment if needed), self-concept (e.g., self-esteem), and family relationships (e.g., closeness). Memorable message studies should also investigate the extent to which recipients of stigmatizing mental illness messages are likely to share those messages with future generations (see Koenig Kellas, 2005).

ACCOUNTS

In order to explain their own and others' negative experiences and behaviors, people provide accounts. Accounts are verbal offerings used to explain unanticipated and untoward behavior (Scott & Lyman, 1968), including excuses, justifications, concessions, and refusals (see Schönbach, 1980). They are often used to protect one's face and maintain social expectations (Cupach & Metts, 1994). Because mental illness is often stigmatized (and therefore may be seen as negative and untoward), accounts are likely used for communicating to make sense of one's own and others' mental illnesses. For example, even prior to a receiving a mental illness diagnosis, family members make sense of their loved one's confusing behaviors by explaining them as symptoms of the illness (Rose et al., 2002) (e.g., he is crying because he is depressed).

Individuals also communicate and justify mental illness decision-making through accounts. Patients provide accounts to explain the reasons why they stopped taking medication to manage their mental illness, which can include limited insight into the illness, missed appointments (to get prescriptions for refills), and the complexity of treatment (see Osterberg & Blaschke, 2005 for review). Interestingly, the presence of a psychological disorder (e.g., depression) is also cited by patients to justify non-adherence to medication (Osterberg & Blaschke, 2005). In the mental health context, individuals diagnosed with schizophrenia, a chronic psychotic disorder, report forgetfulness, carelessness, and medication side effects to justify their non-adherence to treatment recommendations (DiBonaventura, Gabriel, Dupclay, Gupta, & Kim, 2012).

Psychiatrists also use accounts to communicate with patients about treatment. After analyzing thirty-six patient-provider interactions, Angell and Bolden (2015) found that psychiatrists justify their treatment recommendations to patients using patient-centered accounts (i.e., accounts addressing patient concerns and needs) and authority-based accounts (i.e., by invoking their own expertise) that are typically deployed in response to patient resistance (e.g., questions, silence) or refusals (e.g., request for a new medication) with regard to treatment. For instance, if a patient is unhappy with their current medication and requests an alternative treatment (e.g., a different drug or medication), a physician could respond by saying, "I've prescribed that medication to patients with similar symptoms and it was ineffective at changing their mood" to justify their refusal to change a patient's treatment. Although this example does not reflect family communicated sense-making, it highlights the interactional nature of mental illness communication and underscores the need for sense-making among individuals living with a mental illness and others affected by (i.e., involved in decision-making) by the disorders.

Collectively, these studies demonstrate the ability of accounts to illuminate mental health and illness sense-making. These studies also highlight the utility of the CSM devices to investigate mental health and illness communication using qualitative (e.g., Easter, 2012) and quantitative methods (DiBonaventura et al., 2012). Future studies should investigate how families account for their loved one's mental illnesses and how accounts (e.g., type, content) influence the relationship between the family member providing the account and the family member with the mental illness. For example, a young adult who hears his parent denying his depression (a type of refusal account) to extended family members may feel disconfirmed, rejected, and may take steps to distance himself from the parent. Research is also needed to understand how familial mental illness accounts influence the identity (e.g., sick role, development, changes) of the family member with the mental illness.

ATTRIBUTIONS

Whereas accounts are verbal offerings to explain untoward behavior, attributions are people's assessments of the cause of or degree of responsibility associated with an action or behavior (Manusov & Spitzberg, 2008). Although typically considered cognitive judgements, Manusov (2006) argues that attributions are communicated in at least three ways. First, they can be seen as the explanation—or the verbal reasons people give for a behavior (e.g., "discontinuing therapy made her relapse"). Second, they can serve as ways to categorize explanations (e.g., positive, negative; "mental illness is horrible" vs. "some mental illnesses get easier to manage"). Third, they can emerge as the actual meaning we cognitively assign or verbally communicate to describe a behavior (e.g., "this [depression] sucks").

Attributions are widely used to explain the cause and controllability of mental health concerns (e.g., Corrigan et al., 2000; Corrigan et al., 2001). Cause is located (i.e., causal loci) in internal or external factors. Attributions about the cause and controllability of mental illness are often based on beliefs about mental illness. For example, beliefs about the causes of mental illness include both nurture (e.g., social, environmental) and nature (e.g., genetic, biomedical) explanations (Schnittker, 2013). In the United States, some people believe mental illness results from chemical imbalances, explained through genetic composition (Pescosolido et al., 2010). Although severe mental illnesses (e.g., schizophrenia) are often attributed to genetic factors, certain mental illnesses, such as major depression, are attributed to a combination of biomedical and social influences (e.g., life's "ups" and "downs," family) (Pescosolido et al., 2010). For example, someone might attribute another person's depression as an internal character trait (or flaw) or external causes, such as situational trauma or grief.

Individuals with a mental illness make attributions (i.e., perceive, consider) about their own and other members' mental health concerns (e.g., Rose et al., 2002). For example, females in treatment and recovery from Anorexia Nervosa (AN) and Bulemia Nervosa (BN) attribute the cause to social (e.g., abuse in childhood, problematic parental interactions) and biomedical (i.e., genetic) factors (Easter, 2012). Participants, however, cautioned exclusive use of genetic attributions to explain these illnesses, citing their potential to increase stigma, serve as "a crutch" to prevent recovery, or minimize the role of aversive factors (e.g., childhood abuse) in contributing to the development of these illnesses (Easter, 2012).

Family members also make attributions about loved ones with mental illnesses (e.g., Hinrichsen & Lieberman, 1999; Lauber & Rössler, 2007). In Thailand, family caregivers attribute their loved one's mental illness to karma and past wrong doings (Sethabouppha & Kane, 2005), whereas individuals in China attribute mental illness to ancestral misconduct, cosmological forces, and even food (Lin & Lin, 1981). Karp and Tanarugsachock (2000) conducted in-depth interviews with family members (e.g., child, spouse) whose loved ones (e.g., parent, spouse, sibling) were suffering from depression, manic-depression, or schizophrenia to understand family caregiver strategies for managing and making sense of a loved one's mental illness. In the early stages of a mental illness, some family members attributed their own actions as the cause of their loved one's illness. Although attributions were often made pre-diagnosis and to minimize confusion, this example highlights the relevance of families and their need for sense-making in this context. The collection of studies reviewed here focus, primarily, on the cognitive attributions (e.g., beliefs) made about mental health and illness. Thus, future studies should explore the ways in which individuals and families verbally communicate mental health attributions over the course of an illness (e.g., recover, relapse, outside of etiology and diagnosis) and with what consequences for individual and relational health (Koenig Kellas & Kranstuber Horstman, 2015).

COMMUNICATED PERSPECTIVE-TAKING

Although accounts and attributions serve to explain behavior or causality, communicated perspective-taking is a type of communicated sense-making that focuses on understanding. Communicated perspective-taking (CPT) refers to the process through which individuals acknowledge, attend to, confirm, and create space for the views and perspectives of others (Koenig

Kellas & Trees, 2006). Behavioral indicators of CPT include communicating similarity, making relevant contributions, giving the other person space to tell her or his version of the story, coordination, attentiveness, and positive tone (Koenig Kellas, Willer, & Trees, 2013). Individuals' use of CPT during interactions is positively associated with relational functioning (e.g., satisfaction) (Koenig Kellas, 2005) and negatively associated with family stress (Trees & Koenig Kellas, 2009). In addition, CPT benefits both the person whose perspective is being confirmed and perspective-takers (i.e., person who is validating the experience). For example, Koenig Kellas, Trees, Schrodt, LeClair-Underberg, and Willer (2010) found that wives' use of CPT during jointly told stories about difficulty led to a decrease in mental health symptoms and perceived stress among husbands. Horstman et al. (2015) found that daughters' own perspective-taking during mother-daughter conversations about a daughter's difficult experiences helped daughters reframe these experiences more positively over time. In the context of mental illness communication, young adults with bipolar disorder reported their preference for receiving supportive communication that confirms and validates their illness experiences (Doherty & MacGeorge, 2013). These investigations reveal that CPT during conversations about difficulty (i.e., mental health) benefits conversational partners. CPT positively influences the mental health of those whose perspectives are being validated during conversations about difficult experiences, and CPT facilitates sense-making among individuals with bipolar disorder. More research is needed, however, on how to facilitate CPT about mental health among families. As noted earlier, talking about mental health can be difficult or even considered taboo. Thus, creating interventions, instructional materials, or training that can enhance CPT in families should improve understanding, compassion, and communicated sense-making (see also Koenig Kellas, 2018).

Research is also needed on the ways in which engaging in CPT during conversations about mental health may differ across cultures. Specifically, cultures that subscribe to a traditional Asian familial model, wherein maintaining harmony takes precedence over the expression of one's own opinions or feelings (Pearson, 1993), may perceive CPT as irrelevant or violating filial hierarchies. Filial piety is the Confucian belief that one respects their elders and must adhere to familial and ancestral beliefs (Confucius, 2003). As a show of respect, individuals may refrain from contributing their ideas during conversations, be overly attentive, and coordinate their behaviors to match their elders at the expense of one's own opinions or feelings. Thus, more research is needed to understand cultural perceptions of CPT among individuals and families from diverse cultural backgrounds and to what extent they engage in perspective-taking behaviors and with what effects.

NARRATIVES AND STORYTELLING

Finally, narratives and storytelling are a primary means of making sense of difficulty. Koenig Kellas and Kranstuber Horstman (2015) refer to storytelling as communicated narrative sense-making (CNSM) in order to emphasize the communicated nature of narrative as central to making sense of difficulty despite decades of research on narratives as psychological constructs (e.g., McAdams, 1993). CNSM elucidates the communicated nature of narratives by examining the content, process, and outcomes of retrospective, interactional, and translational storytelling within the family (Koenig Kellas, 2018). Family stories exert influence over individuals and family members and function to create individual and family identity, facilitate coping, and socialize members under a set of common values, expectations, and behaviors (e.g., Koenig Kellas & Trees, 2013).

Family illness narratives teach younger family members about their family's orientation toward difficulty (e.g., suicide) and illness (Stone, 2004). Through the process of narrative inheritance (Goodall, 2005), younger members learn of their families' experiences with health issues and illness, and family illness stories "reveal and influence their health practices" (Koenig Kellas & Trees, 2013, p. 398). In the following section, we discuss how the three heuristics presented as part of CNSM[1]—retrospective, interactional, and translational storytelling (see Figure 3.1 and Koenig Kellas & Kranstuber Horstman, 2015; Koenig Kellas, 2018)—have illuminated the ways in which family stories and storytelling communication in the context of mental health and illness influence sense-making.

Retrospective storytelling. The first heuristic, retrospective storytelling, refers to the stories individuals hear and tell that can have a potentially long-lasting effect on their values, beliefs, health, and behaviors (Koenig Kellas, 2018). Retrospective storytelling illuminates the content (i.e., theme, tone) of narratives and storytelling. Investigations of the content of retrospective stories told within families reveal that individuals and families tell stories about multiple health contexts, such as adolescents' reports of parental stories about love and mistakes in the context of sex (see Holman & Koenig Kellas, 2018), and young adults' reports of stories about mental illness (Flood-Grady & Koenig Kellas, 2018). In addition, Aleman and Helfrich (2010) investigated the stories mothers and daughters constructed about family members' experiences with Alzheimer's Dementia (AD) and found that families pass on other members' experiences with AD to younger generations though stories. By inheriting narratives of AD, younger generations learned of family members' illness experiences and what it is like to be a caretaker for a family member with this mental illness (Aleman & Helfrich, 2010). Flood-Grady and Koenig

Kellas (2018) used CNSM theory's (Koenig Kellas, 2018) retrospective storytelling heuristic to examine young adults' reports of the content and lasting influence of family stories about mental illness. Young adults reported hearing stories, primarily from parents, about family members' experiences with mental illness. Although mental illness narratives were characterized by themes of caution and struggle, young adult children reported learning important lessons including a greater awareness (e.g., of mental illness signs and symptoms, their own risk), as well as the importance of understanding the experiences of others diagnosed with mental illnesses.

Sharing mental illness narratives among individuals and families is not unique to Western culture (e.g., Tang & Bie, 2016), but research on the cultural differences in storytelling lags. In an exception to this, Tang and Bie (2016) studied college students from China and identified five prominent narratives through their analysis of stories about mental illnesses. Participants told stories about individuals with mental illnesses whom they knew personally or learned about through media. Story themes included the tragic genius, psychotic criminal, fragile victim, antisocial recluse, and homosexual. Although family was not discussed in relation to these narratives, they found that narratives were based on and reinforced highly cultural-specific stereotypes and biases about mental illness in China. Those stereotypes are likely passed down, at least in part, in the family. In another study, Ueno and Kamibeppu (2008) found that Japanese mothers who are diagnosed with depression make sense of their illnesses by telling stories about their illness experiences and the effects of their depression on their parenting and the lives of their children. Their findings revealed several themes, including conflicting responsibilities (for mothers with mental illnesses), the need to balance self- and child-care, and understanding (i.e., mothers' feelings that children understood their mental health and distress). Maternal narratives illuminate the mix of emotions (e.g., sadness, gratitude) mothers experienced at their own struggles and children's ability to make sense of and respond to their depression and needs (e.g., my child gave me a gift to make me happy). These findings illustrate how narrative content facilitates meaning making about one's own and others' mental illnesses across different cultural contexts.

Interactional storytelling. The second heuristic, interactional storytelling, illuminates the patterned ways in which individuals and families jointly or collaboratively construct narratives (Koenig Kellas & Kranstuber Horstman, 2015). Interactional storytelling underscores the verbal and nonverbal communicative process associated with telling stories and how storytelling links to health and well-being (Koenig Kellas, 2018). For example, researchers found that joint storytelling characterized by engagement, turn-taking, perspective-taking, and collaboratively constructed coherence report higher levels of family satisfaction and functioning (see Koenig Kellas, 2005; Trees & Koenig Kellas, 2009). Koenig Kellas and colleagues refer to these processes as interactional sense-making (ISM) behaviors, and CNSM theory proposes that storytelling characterized by ISM behaviors should result in greater mental and relational health (see Koenig Kellas, 2018). For example, Koenig Kellas et al. (2010) investigated married couples' joint storytelling about stressful marital events and found that when couples' storytelling interactions were characterized by higher levels of ISM, husbands experienced fewer mental health symptoms and perceived stress. Koenig Kellas and Trees (2006) further specified that families who told stories about difficulty tended to make family-level meanings when they engaged in ISM behaviors, in contrast with families who make individual to little or no discernable sense-making. Future research situated in the interactional storytelling heuristic should examine the nuanced ways in which families from diverse cultural backgrounds engage in storytelling about mental health and with what health effects.

Translational storytelling. The third heuristic in CNSM, translational storytelling, positions narratives (e.g., methods, theorizing) as the basis for developing interventions and contends that narrative interventions predict health and well-being among intervention recipients (Koenig Kellas, 2018). Narratives and storytelling have served as the basis for several evidence-based mental health intervention programs (see Miller-Day & Hecht, 2013 for review). Hecht and Miller-Day (2007, 2009, 2010), for example, used narratives to build anti–substance use programs for adolescents. They grounded their intervention approach in narrative by collecting adolescent narratives to understand the active strategies young people use to avoid substance use. Moreover, most translational storytelling interventions are aimed at improving mental health symptoms and participant well-being. Thus, mental health is at the heart of translational storytelling and could readily be developed for contexts involving narratives and storytelling about mental health and illness in the family. Willer and Koenig Kellas (Ch. 6, this volume) present a translational storytelling intervention designed to ameliorate negative mental health consequences of social aggression among middle school girls that illustrates the type of translational storytelling efforts that might be translated to families.

In sum, family stories and storytelling about mental health and illness provide members of younger generations with information about mental health and illness and provide a framework for coping and making sense of complex illness experiences. In addition to storytelling—or CNSM—the CSM theoretical model positions accounts, attributions, memorable messages, and communicated perspective-taking as key devices that people use to make sense of life's difficulties such as mental illness in the family. The studies reviewed in this chapter provide initial evidence in support of CSM's ability to synthesize siloed bodies of narrative research to illuminate how individuals and families communicate to make sense of mental health and illness. In the following section, we provide recommendations to researchers interested in using the CSM theoretical model to study mental health and illness communication and sense-making within the family.

DIRECTIONS FOR FUTURE RESEARCH USING THE CSM THEORETICAL MODEL

The preceding research highlights the utility of the CSM theoretical model to study individual and family communication and sense-making about mental health and illness. Future research opportunities for family and interpersonal scholars to investigate mental health and illness communication and sense-making are plentiful. In what follows, we offer suggestions for extending the CSM theoretical model to study mental health and illness communication and using the CSM theoretical framework to develop individual and family communication interventions in the context of mental health and illness.

Extending the CSM Theoretical Model

As noted earlier in this chapter, the CSM theoretical model integrates previously siloed bodies of work on communicated sense-making, including accounts, attributions, memorable messages, communicated perspective-taking, and CNSM, and highlights the ways in which individuals and families communicate to make sense of their lives, difficulties, and experiences surrounding mental health and illness. Despite our thorough review of sense-making devices, additional devices, such as metaphors and metaphorical language, are also commonly used by individuals and families to communicate about and make sense of difficult and complex health experiences (e.g., Arroliga, Newman, Longworth, & Stoller, 2002). Metaphors help individuals structure and make sense of their thoughts and actions and simply "explain one thing in terms of another" (Lakoff & Johnson, 1980, p. 3). Thus, along with Horstman and Holman (2018), we argue for the inclusion of metaphors as a sense-making device into subsequent iterations of the CSM theoretical model as our next direction for future inquiry (see Figure 3.1).

Individuals in the biomedical community (e.g., physicians, hospital systems) use metaphors to discuss diagnoses with patients (e.g., Arroliga et al., 2002) and explain complex information about clinical trials (e.g., randomization) in interpersonal (e.g., Krieger, Neil, Strekalova, & Sarge, 2017) and mediated contexts (i.e., online) (e.g., Flood-Grady et al., 2017). Individuals and families experiencing difficult or complex health challenges also use a range of metaphors to explain, understand, and make sense of their experiences, including the use of metaphors to describe infertility (e.g., Palmer-Wackerly & Krieger, 2015), asthma (e.g., Peterson & Sterling, 2009), cancer (e.g., Gibbs & Franks, 2002), and mental illness (e.g., Levitt, Korman, & Angus, 2000). For example, Fullagar and O'Brien (2012) examined the metaphors females who were recovering or recovered from an experience of depression used to make sense of their experiences and to create meaning about their experiences with depression. In qualitative interviews, females described depression as being trapped (e.g., in a "hole," "hell," "dark room") and recovery from depression as "a battle" (p. 20). Metaphors also emerge in mental illness recovery narratives (e.g., Ridgeway, 2001) and are used experimentally to track and evaluate client changes in psychotherapy (Levitt et al., 2000). As evidenced from these studies, and true to the CSM theoretical model, metaphors can illuminate communication and sense-making about health and illness across paradigms.

Although incorporating metaphors into the CSM theoretical model makes sense, we caution scholars interested in using these devices to illuminate mental health communication and sense-making to inform interventions. Indeed, metaphors of mental illness could serve to unite mental health clinicians, families, and patients by providing an opportunity to engage similar language to communicate about mental health and illness, and thus it warrants investigation. However, without careful consideration and attention to the power embedded in the construction and interpretation of metaphors, using metaphors and metaphorical language to explain mental illness could lead to misunderstandings about what mental illness is and is not, and potentially increase stigma. Thus, research and feedback on the use of metaphors is needed from those directly affected by mental illness (i.e., individuals with a mental illness, caregivers, therapists) to understand how metaphors may or may not be stigmatizing.

MENTAL HEALTH INTERVENTION DEVELOPMENT USING THE CSM THEORETICAL MODEL

In light of existing recommendations to incorporate narratives (e.g., Kreuter et al., 2007) and CSM devices into family health interventions (see Koenig Kellas & Kranstuber Horstman, 2015), as well as the abundance of scholarly interventions aimed at decreasing mental illness stigma (see Corrigan, Morris, Michaels, Rafacz, & Rüsch, 2012), we limit our suggestions to incorporating specific CSM devices (processes) to develop mental health and illness interventions. With this in mind, we offer the following suggestions.

We recommend interviewing family caregivers, patients, and practitioners about stories of mental illness and suicide to inform the development of mental health interventions aimed at identifying the signs that precede mental illness–related suicides. For instance, gathering personal narratives, like the one presented at the beginning of this chapter, from mental illness and suicide survivors might illuminate factors that exacerbate mental illness and/or precede suicide ideation or attempts. CNSM theory suggests that retrospective storytelling reveals individual, relational, and intergenerational attitudes, values, and beliefs (see Proposition 1, Koenig Kellas, 2018). Asking survivors, bereaved family members, and/or trained, clinical professionals to narrate stories of mental illness–related suicide might reveal patterns of behavior, risk, and successful prevention that could be used to develop future translational storytelling interventions. Incorporating personal narratives from individuals affected by mental illness along with information from experts (e.g., medical information about mental illness from a psychiatrist) are effective practices in designing mental health interventions (Janoušková et al., 2017).

Although the act of storytelling can benefit tellers and listeners (Horstman et al., 2015), participating in storytelling interventions, or attending mental illness support group meetings wherein attendees verbally share their experiences, may be difficult for individuals with mental illnesses, suicide survivors, and/or family caretakers. Because writing the story of a traumatic or stressful event positively predicts mental health, physical health, and psychological functioning among those writing (see Frattaroli, 2006), storytelling interventions anchored in the expressive writing paradigm may be particularly helpful for individuals with mental illnesses, suicide survivors, and family caregivers. Storytelling interventions wherein individuals with mental illnesses, suicide survivors, and family caregivers write the story of their illness, suicide, or caretaking will help them to make sense of these complex, life-changing experiences, without compromising their privacy.

Next, mental health interventions anchored in CPT could also benefit individuals communicating interpersonally and within the family about mental health and illness. We believe CPT interventions aimed at teaching individuals the behavioral components associated with communicating their mental illness perspective-taking to others will be particularly useful during mental illness disclosures, conversations about relapses, as well as conversations about medication and side effects between patients, physicians, and family members. For instance, teaching family members about the importance of listening and giving loved one's space to talk about their illness (see Koenig Kellas et al., 2013) would benefit individual members who may be fearful about disclosing their mental illness to family members. In addition, teaching physicians and family members how to communicate their understanding of patient concerns—verbally and nonverbally—regarding the side effects that can accompany certain mental health medications would benefit patients and their families. CPT is needed because mental illness is poorly understood and extensively stigmatized. Moreover, CPT should build understanding, be identity-affirming, and help to ameliorate the stress associated with mental illness stigma and poor self-esteem (e.g., self-blame) that can accompany mental illness.

Finally, communication experts are not mental health practitioners. Thus, they are limited in their ability to implement and evaluate the efficacy of certain mental health interventions (e.g., clinical trials involving treatment). However, communication scholars can contribute substantially to mental health interventions through theoretical (e.g., narrative methods) and context expertise (e.g., the importance of family and interpersonal communication to mental health), both of which are necessary to developing effective individual and family-based mental health interventions. Thus, our final recommendation is to identify and forge interdisciplinary partnerships with scholars and practitioners outside of the communication field (e.g., medicine, bioinformatics, epidemiology, sociology). Individuals in these fields are actively working to improve mental health and mental illness communication (e.g., treatment, decision-making) around the world (e.g., Patel et al., 2011), and would benefit substantially from the scholarly contributions of communication experts.

CONCLUSION

Our goal with this chapter was to demonstrate the significance of family communication to mental health and illness communication and sense-making. In the current chapter, we contextualize mental health and illness as a family communication context in need of sense-making and introduce the CSM theoretical model, as well as argue for its utility to illuminate individual and family communication and sense-making about mental health and illness and stigma. We offer recommendations for extending the model and using CSM processes to inform the development of mental health and illness interventions. The CSM theoretical model is uniquely positioned to advance the study of mental health and illness by illuminating the content, process, and effects of mental health and illness communication and sense-making. It is our hope that scholars will embrace this theoretical model as they endeavor to advance scientific inquiry in this important communication context by responding to the sense-making needs of individuals and families affected by mental health, illness, stigma, and suicide.

NOTE

1. First introduced as a sub-part of the CSM theoretical model, CNSM has now been developed into its own theory (Koenig Kellas, 2018). Guided by the assumptions and heuristics presented by Koenig Kellas & Kranstuber Horstman (2015) in the CSM theoretical model, CNSM theory proposes seven propositions exploring the links between storytelling and psychosocial, relational, and physiological health.

REFERENCES

Aleman, M. W., & Helfrich, K. W. (2010). Inheriting the narratives of dementia: A collaborative tale of a mother and daughter. *Journal of Family Communication, 10*(1), 7–23. doi:10.1080/15267430903385784

American Psychiatric Association. (2018). What is mental illness? Retrieved from https://www.psychiatry.org/patients-families/what-is-mental-illness

Aneshensel, C. S., Phelan, J. C., & Bierman, A. (2013). The sociology of mental health: Surveying the field. In C. S. Aneshensel, J. Phelan, & A. Bierman (Eds.), *Handbook of sociology of mental health* (2nd ed., pp. 1–19). New York, NY: Springer.

Angell, B., & Bolden, G. B. (2015). Justifying medication decisions in mental health care: Psychiatrists' accounts for treatment recommendations. *Social Science & Medicine, 138*, 44–56. doi:10.1016/j.socscimed.2015.04.029

Arroliga, A., Newman, S., Longworth, D., & Stoller, J. K. (2002). Metaphorical medicine: Using metaphors to enhance communication with patients who have pulmonary disease. *Annals of Internal Medicine, 137*(5, Part 1), 376–379. doi:10.7326/0003-4819-137-5_part_1-200209030-00037

Brown, P., & Levinson, S. C. (1987). *Politeness: Some universals in language usage.* Cambridge, UK: University Press.

Bruner, J. (1990). *Acts of meaning.* Cambridge, MA: Harvard University Press.

Carpenter-Song, E., Chu, E., Drake, R. E., Ritsema, M., Smith, B., & Alverson, H. (2010). Ethno-cultural variations in the experience and meaning of mental illness and treatment: Implications for access and utilization. *Transcultural Psychiatry, 47*(2), 224–251. doi:10.1177/1363461510368906

Chan, S. W. C. (2011). Global perspective of burden of family caregivers for persons with schizophrenia. *Archives of Psychiatric Nursing, 25*(5), 339–349. doi:10.1016/j.apnu.2011.03.008

Confucius. (2003). *Analects: With sections from traditional commentaries* (E. Slingerland, Trans.). Cambridge: Hackett Publishing Company.

Cooke-Jackson, A., & Rubinsky, V. (2018). Deeply rooted in memories: Toward a comprehensive overview of 30 years of memorable message literature. *Health Communication, 33*(4), 409–422. doi:10.1080/10410236.2016.1278491

Corrigan, P. W., & Miller, F. E. (2004). Shame, blame, and contamination: A review of the impact of mental illness stigma on family members. *Journal of Mental Health, 13*(6), 537–548. doi:10.1080/09638230400017004

Corrigan, P. W., Morris, S. B., Michaels, P. J., Rafacz, J. D., & Rüsch, N. (2012). Challenging the public stigma of mental illness: A meta-analysis of outcome studies. *Psychiatric Services, 63*(10), 963–973. doi:10.1176/appi.ps.201100529

Corrigan, P. W., River, L. P., Lundin, R. K., Penn, D. L., Wasowski, K. U., Campion, J., . . . Kubiak, M. A. (2001). Three strategies for changing attributions about severe mental illness. *Schizophrenia Bulletin, 27*(2), 187–195. doi:10.1093/oxfordjournals.schbul.a006865

Corrigan, P. W., River, L. P., Lundin, R. K., Wasowski, K. U., Campion, J., Mathisen, J., . . . Kubiak, M. A. (2000). Stigmatizing attributions about mental illness. *Journal of Community Psychology, 28*(1), 91–102. doi:10.1002/(SICI)1520-6629(200001)28:1<91::AID-JCOP9>3.0.CO;2-M

Cupach, W. R., & Metts, S. (1994). *Facework*. Thousand Oaks, CA: Sage.

DiBonaventura, M., Gabriel, S., Dupclay, L., Gupta, S., & Kim, E. (2012). A patient perspective of the impact of medication side effects on adherence: Results of a cross-sectional nationwide survey of patients with schizophrenia. *BMC Psychiatry, 12*(20), 1–7. doi:10.1186/1471-244X-12-20

Doherty, E. F., & MacGeorge, E. L. (2013). Perceptions of supportive behavior by young adults with bipolar disorder. *Qualitative Health Research, 23*(3), 361–374. doi:10.1177/1049732312468508

Easter, M. M. (2012). "Not all my fault": Genetics, stigma, and personal responsibility for women with eating disorders. *Social Science & Medicine, 75*(8), 1408–1416. doi:10.1016/j.socscimed.2012.05.042

Fischer, W., & Sartorius N. (1999). *The image of madness: The public facing mental illness and psychiatric treatment*. Basel, Switzerland: Karger.

Flood-Grady, E., & Koenig Kellas, J. (2018). Sense-making, socialization, and stigma: Exploring narratives told in families about mental illness. *Health Communication*, 1–11. doi:10.1080/10410236.2018.1431016

Flood-Grady, E., Paige, S. R., Karimipour, N., Harris, P. A., Cottler, L. B., & Krieger, J. L. (2017). A content analysis of Clinical and Translational Science Award (CTSA) strategies for communicating about clinical research participation online. *Journal of Clinical and Translational Science, 1*(6), 340–351. doi:10.1017/cts.2018.2

Flood-Grady, E., Starcher, S., & Bergquist, G. (2018, November). Exploring the content and influence of parental memorable messages about depression on young adult children diagnosed with clinical depression. Paper presented at the annual meeting of the National Communication Association, Salt Lake City, UT.

Frattaroli, J. (2006). Experimental disclosure and its moderators: A meta-analysis. *Psychological Bulletin, 132*(6), 823–865. doi:10.1037/0033-2909.132.6.823

Fullagar, S., & O'Brien, W. (2012). Immobility, battles, and the journey of feeling alive: Women's metaphors of self-transformation through depression and recovery. *Qualitative Health Research, 22*(8), 1063–1072. doi:10.1177/1049732312443738

Gibbs, R. W., & Franks, H. (2002). Embodied metaphor in women's narratives about their experiences with cancer. *Health Communication, 14*(2), 139–165. doi:10.1207/s15327027hc1402_1

Goffman, E. (1963). *Stigma: Notes on the management of spoiled identity.* Englewood Cliffs, NJ: Prentice-Hall.

Goodall, H. L. (2005). Narrative inheritance: A nuclear family with toxic secrets. *Qualitative Inquiry, 11*(4), 492–513. doi:10.1177/1077800405276769

Greenwell, M. R. (2018). Memorable messages from family members about mental health: Young adult perceptions of relational closeness, message satisfaction, and clinical help-seeking attitudes. *Health Communication,* 1–9. doi:10.1080/1041023 6.2018.1431021

Hecht, M. L., & Miller-Day, M. (2007). The Drug Resistance Strategies Project as translational research. *Journal of Applied Communication Research, 35*(4), 343–349. doi:10.1080/00909880701611086

Hecht, M. L., & Miller-Day, M. A. (2009). The Drug Resistance Strategies Project: Using narrative theory to enhance adolescents' communication competence. In L. Frey & K. Cissna (Eds.), *The Routledge handbook of applied communication* (pp. 535–557). New York, NY: Routledge.

Hecht, M. L., & Miller-Day, M. A. (2010). "Applied" aspects of the Drug Resistance Strategies Project. *Journal of Applied Communication Research, 38*(3), 215–229. doi:10.1080/00909882.2010.490848

Heider, F. (1958). *The psychology of interpersonal relations.* New York: Wiley.

Hinrichsen, G. A., & Lieberman, J. A. (1999). Family attributions and coping in the prediction of emotional adjustment in family members of patients with first–episode schizophrenia. *Acta Psychiatrica Scandinavica, 100*(5), 359–366. doi:10.1111/j.1600-0447.1999.tb10879.x

Holman, A., & Koenig Kellas, J. (2018). "Say something instead of nothing": Adolescents' perceptions of memorable conversations about sex-related topics with their parents. *Communication Monographs, 85*(3), 357–379. doi:10.1080/036377 51.2018.1426870

Horstman, H. K., & Holman, A. (2018, November). Expanding the communicated sense-making model: Men's use of metaphors to make sense of their spouse's miscarriage. Paper presented at the annual meeting of the National Communication Association, Salt Lake City, UT.

Horstman, H. K., Maliski, R., Hays, A., Cox, J., Enderle, A., & Nelson, L. R. (2015). Unfolding narrative meaning over time: The contributions of mother-daughter conversations of difficulty on daughter narrative sense-making and well-being. *Communication Monographs, 83*(3), 326–348. doi:10.1080/03637751.2015.1068945

Janoušková, M., Tušková, E., Weissová, A., Trančík, P., Pasz, J., Evans-Lacko, S., & Winkler, P. (2017). Can video interventions be used to effectively destigmatize mental illness among young people? A systematic review. *European Psychiatry, 41*, 1–9. doi:10.1016/j.eurpsy.2016.09.008

Jenkins, J. H. (1988). Ethnopsychiatric interpretations of schizophrenic illness: The problem of nervios within Mexican-American families. *Culture, Medicine and Psychiatry, 12*(3), 301–329. doi:10.1007/bf00051972

Karp, D. A., & Tanarugsachock, V. (2000). Mental illness, caregiving, and emotion management. *Qualitative Health Research, 10*(1), 6–25. doi:10.1177/104973200129118219

Kessler, R. C., Aguilar-Gaxiola, S., Alonso, J., & Chatterji, S. (2009). The global burden of mental disorders: An update from the WHO (WMH) surveys. *Epidemiology and Psychiatric Sciences, 15*(1), 23–33. doi:10.1017/S1121189X00001421

Knapp, M. L., Stohl, C., & Reardon, K. K. (1981). "Memorable" messages. *Journal of Communication, 31*(4), 27–41. doi:10.1111/j.1460-2466.1981.tb00448.x

Koenig Kellas, J. (2005). Family ties: Communicating identity through jointly told stories. *Communication Monographs, 72*(4), 365–389. doi:10.1080/03637750500322453

Koenig Kellas, J. (2018). Communicated narrative sense-making theory: Linking storytelling and health. In D. O. Braithwaite, E. Suter, & K. Floyd (Eds.), *Engaging theories in family communication* (2nd ed., pp. 62–74). New York, NY: Routledge.

Koenig Kellas, J., & Kranstuber Horstman, H. (2015). Communicated narrative sensemaking: Understanding family narratives, storytelling, and the construction of meaning through a communicative lens. In L. M. Turner & R. West (Eds.), *Handbook of family communication* (2nd ed., pp. 76–90). Thousand Oaks, CA: Sage.

Koenig Kellas, J., & Trees, A. (2006). Finding meaning in difficult family experiences: Sense-making and interaction processes during joint family storytelling. *Journal of Family Communication, 6*(1), 49–76. doi:10.1207/s15327698jfc0601_4

Koenig Kellas, J., & Trees, A. R. (2013). Family stories and storytelling: Windows into the family soul. In A. L. Vangelisti (Ed.), *The Routledge handbook of family communication* (2nd ed., pp. 391–406). New York, NY: Routledge.

Koenig Kellas, J., Trees, A. R., Schrodt, P., LeClair-Underberg, C., & Willer, E. K. (2010). Exploring links between well-being and interactional sense-making in married couples' jointly told stories of stress. *Journal of Family Communication, 10*(3), 174–193. doi:10.1080/15267431.2010.489217

Koenig Kellas, J., Willer, E. K., & Trees, A. R. (2013). Communicated perspective-taking during stories of marital stress: Spouses' perceptions of one another's perspective-taking behaviors. *Southern Communication Journal, 78*(4), 326–351. doi:10.1080/1041794X.2013.815264

Kreuter, M. W., Green, M. C., Cappella, J. N., Slater, M. D., Wise, M. E., Storey, D., . . . Woolley, S. (2007). Narrative communication in cancer prevention and control: A framework to guide research and application. *Annals of Behavioral Medicine, 33*(3), 221–235. doi:10.1007/bf02879904

Krieger, J. L., Neil, J. M., Strekalova, Y. A., & Sarge, M. A. (2017). Linguistic strategies for improving informed consent in clinical trials among low health literacy patients. *Journal of the National Cancer Institute, 109*(3), djw233. doi:10.1093/jnci/djw233

Lakoff, G., & Johnson, M. (1980). Metaphors we live by. Chicago, IL: University of Chicago Press.

Lauber, C., Ajdacic-Gross, V., Fritschi, N., Stulz, N., & Rössler, W. (2005). Mental health literacy in an educational elite—an online survey among university students. *BMC Public Health, 5*(1), 1–9. doi:10.1186/1471-2458-5-44

Lauber, C., & Rössler, W. (2007). Stigma towards people with mental illness in developing countries in Asia. *International Review of Psychiatry, 19*(2), 157–178. doi:10.1080/09540260701278903

Levitt, H., Korman, Y., & Angus, L. (2000). A metaphor analysis in treatments of depression: Metaphor as a marker of change. *Counselling Psychology Quarterly, 13*(1), 23–35. doi:10.1080/09515070050011042

Lin, T. Y., & Lin, M. C. (1981). Love, denial and rejection: Responses of Chinese families to mental illness. In A. Kleinman & T. Y. Lin (Eds.), *Normal and abnormal behavior in Chinese culture vol. 2: Culture, illness, and healing* (pp. 387–407). Dordrecht: Springer. doi:10.1007/978-94-017-4986-2_20

Link, B. G. (1987). Understanding labeling effects in the area of mental disorders: An assessment of the effects of expectations of rejection. *American Sociological Review, 52*(1), 96–112. doi:10.2307/2095395

Link, B. G., & Phelan, J. C. (2013). Labeling and stigma. In C. S. Aneshensel, J. Phelan, & A. Bierman (Eds.), *Handbook of sociology of mental health* (2nd ed., pp. 525–541). New York: Springer.

Lucas, K., & Buzzanell, P. M. (2012). Memorable messages of hard times: Constructing short- and long-term resiliencies through family communication. *Journal of Family Communication, 12*(3), 189–208. doi:10.4135/9781483346427.n332

Manusov, V. (2006). Attribution theories: Assessing interpretation processes in families. In D. O. Braithwaite & L. A. Baxter (Eds.), *Family communication theories.* Mahwah, NJ: Lawrence Erlbaum Associates.

Manusov, V., & Spitzberg, B. (2008). Attribution theory: Finding good cause in the search for theory. In L. A. Baxter & D. O. Braithwaite (Eds.), *Engaging theories in interpersonal communication: Multiple perspectives* (pp. 37–49). Thousand Oaks, CA: Sage Publications.

McAdams, D. P. (1993). *The stories we live by: Personal myths and the making of the self.* New York: Guilford Press.

Medved, C. E., Brogan, S. M., McClanahan, M. A., Morris, J. F., & Shepherd, G. J. (2006). Family and work socializing communication: Messages, gender and ideological implications. *Journal of Family Communication, 6*(3), 161–180. doi:10.1207/s15327698jfc0603_1

Miller-Day, M., & Hecht, M. L. (2013). Narrative means to preventative ends: A narrative engagement framework for designing prevention interventions. *Health Communication, 28*(7), 657–670. doi:10.1080/10410236.2012.762861

Mojtabai, R. (2007). Americans' attitudes toward mental health treatment seeking: 1990–2003. *Psychiatric Services, 58*(5), 642–651. doi:10.1176/ps.2007.58.5.642

Osterberg, L., & Blaschke, T. (2005). Adherence to medication. *New England Journal of Medicine, 353*(5), 487–497. doi:10.1056/nejmra050100

Palmer-Wackerly, A. L., & Krieger, J. L. (2015). Dancing around infertility: The use of metaphors in a complex medical situation. *Health Communication, 30*(6), 612–623. doi:10.1080/10410236.2014.888386

Patel, V., Weiss, H. A., Chowdhary, N., Naik, S., Pednekar, S., Chatterjee, S., . . . Kirkwood, B. R. (2011). Lay health worker led intervention for depressive and anxiety disorders in India: Impact on clinical and disability outcomes over 12

months. *The British Journal of Psychiatry, 199*(6), 459–466. doi:10.1192/bjp
.bp.111.092155

Pearson, V. (1993). Families in China: An undervalued resource for mental health? *Journal of Family Therapy, 15*(2), 163–185. doi:10.1111/j.1467-6427.1993.00752.x

Pecchioni, L., & Keeley, M. (2011). Insights about health from family communication theories. In T. L. Thompson, R. Parrott, & J. F. Nussbaum (Eds.), *The Routledge handbook of health communication* (pp. 363–376). New York, NY: Routledge.

Pescosolido, B. A., Martin, J. K., Long, J. S., Medina, T. R., Phelan, J. C., & Link, B. G. (2010). "A disease like any other"? A decade of change in public reactions to schizophrenia, depression, and alcohol dependence. *American Journal of Psychiatry, 167*(11), 1321–1330. doi:10.1176/appi.ajp.2010.09121743

Peterson, J. W., & Sterling, Y. M. (2009). Children's perceptions of asthma: African American children use metaphors to make sense of asthma. *Journal of Pediatric Health Care, 23*(2), 93–100. doi:10.1016/j.pedhc.2007.10.002

Ridgeway, P. (2001). Restorying psychiatric disability: Learning from first person recovery narratives. *Psychiatric Rehabilitation Journal, 24*(4), 335–343. doi:10.1037/h0095071

Rose, L., Mallinson, R. K., & Walton-Moss, B. (2002). A grounded theory of families responding to mental illness. *Western Journal of Nursing Research, 24*(5), 516–536. doi:10.1177/019394502400446397

Saxena, S., Thornicroft, G., Knapp, M., & Whiteford, H. (2007). Resources for mental health: Scarcity, inequity, and inefficiency. *The Lancet, 370*(9590), 878–889. doi:10.1016/s0140-6736(07)61239-2

Schnittker, J. (2013). Public beliefs about mental illness. In C. Aneshensel, J. Phelan, & A. Bierman (Eds.), *Handbook of sociology of mental health* (2nd ed., pp. 75–93). New York, NY: Springer.

Schönbach, P. (1980). A category system for account phases. *European Journal of Social Psychology, 10*(2), 195–200. doi:10.1002/ejsp.2420100206

Scott, M. B., & Lyman, S. M. (1968). Accounts. *American Sociological Review, 33*(1), 46–62. doi:10.2307/2092239

Segrin, C. (2013). Mental health. In A. Vangelisti (Ed.), *The Routledge handbook of family communication* (2nd ed., pp. 512–527). New York, NY: Routledge.

Sethabouppha, H., & Kane, C. (2005). Caring for the seriously mentally ill in Thailand: Buddhist family caregiving. *Archives of Psychiatric Nursing, 19*(2), 44–57. doi:10.1016/j.apnu.2005.02.004

Stohl, C. (1986). The role of memorable messages in the process of organizational socialization. *Communication Quarterly, 34*(3), 231–249. doi:10.1080/01463378609369638

Stone, E. (2004). *Black sheep and kissing cousins: How our family stories shape us.* London, England: Transaction Publishers.

Tang, L., & Bie, B. (2016). Narratives about mental illness in China: The voices of Generation Y. *Health Communication, 31*(2), 171–181. doi:10.1080/10410236.2014.940673

Trees, A. R., & Koenig Kellas, J. (2009). Telling tales: Enacting family relationships in joint storytelling about difficult family experiences. *Western Journal of Communication, 73*(1), 91–111. doi:10.1080/10570310802635021

Ueno, R., & Kamibeppu, K. (2008). Narratives by Japanese mothers with chronic mental illness in the Tokyo metropolitan area: Their feelings toward their children and perceptions of their children's feelings. *Journal of Nervous and Mental Disease, 196*(7), 522–530. doi:10.1097/nmd.0b013e31817cf721

Weick, K. E., Sutcliffe, K. M., & Obstfeld, D. (2005). Organizing and the process of sensemaking. *Organization Science, 16*(4), 409–421. doi:10.1287/orsc.1050.0133

World Health Organization. (2018, May 30). Mental health: Strengthening our response. Retrieved September 13, 2019, from https://www.who.int/news-room/fact-sheets/detail/mental-health-strengthening-our-response

Chapter Four

Mental Health Literacy at the House of Grace

Advancing Relational Health Literacy as a Conceptual Model

Joy V. Goldsmith

Sachiko Terui

> You know substance abuse usually is . . . what everybody sees and they won't see the underlying diagnosis of unmediated mental illness. (Participant HS006)

While working on a health literacy project, we were led to a little-trafficked area in rural Alabama. The pursuant and stalwart research-seeking behaviors eventually opened the doors to a recovery house. There, we collected interview data to support a larger project that explores a new model for health literacy. Without knowing it, we landed in the living room of one of the most hard-to-reach populations. Those in the house fit the definitions of "disadvantaged," "underserved," and "extremely impoverished," and were struggling in every way to put one foot in front of the other. We had arrived at the House of Grace.[1]

Disadvantaged populations, which include those with mental health problems, are difficult for researchers to access and study. Additionally, groups with lower socioeconomic status have been underresearched (Bonevski et al., 2014). Individuals in the United States with mental health problems have complex and often unmet support needs. Housing, provision of day-to-day health care, transportation, and social support quickly slip through the holes in many societies (Pope, Malla, & Iyer, 2018). Individuals struggling with depression, schizophrenia, and bipolar disorder are at increased risk for contracted illnesses, chronic diseases, comorbidities, injury, and death (Bahorik, Satre, Kline-Simon, Weisner, & Campbell, 2017). Those with mental health challenges and illness are disproportionately represented among those who cannot afford to meet basic food, housing, and health needs (Harper, 2018). Among those living with mental health issues and using a free clinic, a higher level of health literacy (e.g., locating, understanding, enacting, and communicating about health care) was associated with better physical health functioning, and better mental health functioning is associated with higher social support (friends, family, organizations) (Kamimura, Christensen, Tabler, Ashby, & Olson, 2013). Each disadvantaged factor figures prominently in the lives of those we were privileged to interview and improves our understanding of the construction of health literacy.

HEALTH LITERACY AND MENTAL HEALTH

Health literacy is predominantly placed in the hands of individuals and their skills in obtaining, reading, understanding, and using health information—all of which collide with communication behaviors (Laidsaar-Powell, Butow, Boyle, & Juraskova, 2018). In this collision, we question the common definition of health literacy, which places the onus on the individual and proposes a new way of thinking about health literacy.

Dominating definitions of health literacy lopsidedly distribute responsibilities of health literacy on patients and caregivers (Ad Hoc Committee on Health Literacy for the Council on Scientific Affairs, 1999; Cutilli & Bennett, 2009), particularly those with low socioeconomic status and low educational achievements (Denning & DiNenno, 2017). Another challenge with current health literacy work is that researchers and clinicians typically study individuals who are already accessing healthcare systems (Batterham, Hawkins, Collins, Buchbinder, & Osborne, 2016).

New voices in health literacy and health communication argue that health literacy involves not only patients' cognitive and functional skills, but also the collaborative efforts among patients, caregivers, healthcare organizations, healthcare providers, and communities (Batterham et al., 2016; Chou, Gaysynsky, & Persoskie, 2015). This collaborative view of health literacy identifies the impactful role that each stakeholder plays in reducing health literacy barriers and inequities/disparities across all groups. The deficiencies of existing health literacy models warrant the development of a comprehensive model that is representative of the transactional nature of interactions among patients, caregivers, providers, systems, and communities (Batterham et al., 2016; Goldsmith & Terui, 2018; Young, Stephens, & Goldsmith, 2017).

The concept of mental health literacy (MHL) emerges from developed work in health literacy. Health literacy began as an assessment strategy to improve health outcomes for the individual, but has since expanded to explore entire populations and stakeholder factors in co-creating health literacy (Kutcher, Wei, & Coniglio, 2016). These elements of health literacy continue to guide and inform the evolving science of MHL. MHL includes knowledge that benefits the mental health of a person or others, including knowledge of how to prevent a mental disorder, recognition of disorders when developing, knowledge of effective self-help strategies, and skills to help others (Jorm, 2012). MHL, self-stigma, and help-seeking behaviors are key variables that are now linked to one another (Cheng, Wang, McDermott, Kridel, & Rislin, 2018). Individuals with low MHL frequently do not recognize the need for treatment and, thus, take longer to attain it (Thompson, Hunt, & Issakidis, 2004). The first onset of mental disorders is often in adolescence and early adulthood; developing recognitions of mental disorders in family units can improve attitudes toward mental health treatment and, in turn, increase help-seeking efficacy (Kessler, 2012; Wright et al., 2005). The complexities of mental health are often not studied or examined with health literacy models or measures.

ENVISIONING A NEW WAY

Proposing a new health literacy model for development is the result of a long program of research. The COMFORT Model, an alternative to current provider communication training, teaches healthcare providers how to deliver life-altering news, assess patient/family health literacy needs, practice mindful communication, integrate family caregivers into care, and support patient/family goals of care (Wittenberg, Ferrell, Goldsmith, Ragan, & Buller, 2018; Wittenberg-Lyles, Goldsmith, Ferrell, & Ragan, 2012). The concepts are grounded in communication theory and include evidence-based communication practices and materials rooted in narrative medicine that situate the patient's story at the center of quality care (Charon, 2004, 2008). We will also address narrative and the patient later in this chapter as we remember the work of Walter Fisher (1989) and the narrative paradigm.

Across the last decade of growth for COMFORT, health literacy became an increasingly prominent aspect of the model. A shift in COMFORT toward the development of patient and caregiver materials and training has progressed steadily (Goldsmith, Young, Dale, & Powell, 2017; Wittenberg-Lyles et al., 2012). COMFORT is predicated on the transactional nature of communication: that all communication is co-created. It therefore stands that the health literacy concept developed here emerges from the work on COMFORT.

OVERVIEW OF RELATIONAL HEALTH LITERACY

The mainstream conceptual model of health literacy limits one's understanding by placing the responsibilities of knowing, acquiring, communicating, and decision-making about health predominantly on patients and/or their family caregivers (Young et al., 2017). As an alternative, the model of Relational Health Literacy (RHL) emphasizes the collaborative efforts among stakeholders for fortifying or dissolving MHL barriers. RHL is predicated on the communication co-created among patients, family caregivers, providers, communities, and healthcare systems (Chou et al., 2015; Goldsmith & Terui, 2018).

Patients

A variety of factors shape patients' health literacy and health outcomes, including their linguistic, numeracy, and cognitive skills and their beliefs and/or expectations regarding health treatment and relationships with their healthcare providers (Berkman, Sheridan, Donahue, Halpern, & Crotty, 2011; Fernandez et al., 2004; Leung, Bo, Hsiao, Wang, & Chi, 2014; Sentell & Braun, 2012). Patients with high health literacy tend to experience better health outcomes (Berkman et al., 2011). However, unsettling emotions during the treatment and/or distrust toward healthcare providers, regardless of the direct associations with the health concerns in question, function as barriers in reaching better health outcomes even when patients' health literacy is high (Schinckus, Dangoisse, Van den Broucke, Mikolajczak, 2018; Schulz & Nakamoto, 2013). Such barriers can be alleviated by enhancing "therapeutic alliances" (Street, Makoul, Arora, & Epstein, 2009, p. 297) across stakeholders (caregiver, provider, community, and system), which includes interaction, goal sharing, and creating information together. Patients' active communication about their perspectives and struggles can help medical providers promote patient-centered care (Arnold, Coran, & Hagen, 2012).

Caregivers

Untrained and unpaid caregivers (e.g., family members or friends of the patient) are a significantly important aspect of healthcare delivery. They play a vital role in making decisions with and/or for patients, planning care, and managing treatment to assist their loved ones in navigating the health journey. As a part of caregiving tasks, caregivers often study the names, functions, and side effects of medications so they can coordinate with healthcare providers across different care settings (Schumacher et al., 2014). Caregivers decide to what extent, when, and how they share information with the patients and provide treatments at home (Ewing et al., 2016). Some tasks (e.g., cleaning a ventricular assist device) require a high level of accuracy to maintain a loved one's life, thus compounding caregiver burden and emotional distress (Dilger, 2013). Communicating with other stakeholders can help caregivers cope with stress (Fletcher, Miaskowski, Given, & Schumacher, 2012) and increase their skills in assisting patients with safe and effective treatment at home (Roter et al., 2018), which leads to decreased rate of hospital re-admission (Rodakowski et al., 2017).

Providers

People may believe that healthcare providers have high health literacy; that is, they have the skills and knowledge necessary for making diagnoses and providing information and guidance to patients and their caregivers. However, RHL questions such an assumption, and instead proposes that all stakeholders are responsible for creating health literacy barriers. One barrier example is the use of complex medical language, which contributes to low heath literacy among other stakeholders (Parnell, 2015). Moreover, in the different types of interactions with patients and their family, providers do not always possess or seek information specific to the patients' and caregivers' needs in terms of healthcare treatment and resources or support (Robotin et al., 2017). Productive communication skills among healthcare providers can a) promote patients' and caregivers' participation in decision making processes, b) increase shared understandings of treatment procedures, and c) pursue the recommended regimens (D'Agostino et al., 2017; Huntington & Kuhn, 2003).

Communities

Each stakeholder is surrounded by various communities, which can both prohibit and promote patients' health and health management. In our present mental health study, local, illness, and cultural/religious communities are most prominent. Communicating with others in the local community may help patients and caregivers learn about local resources (Rikard, Thompson, McKinney, & Beauchamp, 2016). When fatalistic views are prevalent in a community, patients are less likely to actively seek and receive treatments despite a high level of health literacy (Lee & Vang, 2010). Contrarily, by following the actions of others in the community, patients with low health literacy may possess good health practices without understanding why or how (Fang, Machtinger, Wang, & Schillinger, 2006; Molina et al., 2014). The power of community is recognized and utilized in community-based intervention for HIV prevention and other chronic illnesses (Center for Disease Control and Prevention, 2018). Through the community network, health literacy can be expanded through communication, and individuals who distribute health literacy are more likely to have higher levels of health literacy (Edwards, Wood, Davies, & Edwards, 2015).

Systems

In light of the negative effects of low health literacy, governmental regulations and policies, such as the Plain Writing Act of 2010 and Culturally and Linguistically Appropriate Services (CLAS) (Federal Drug Administration, 2018), require that all written and spoken communication must be understandable in all U.S. healthcare systems (Nouri & Rudd, 2015). Along with these guidelines, Kaphingst et al. (2012) developed a plain language index that proposes the following practices for written material: a) 6th grade reading level, b) active voice, c) address patients directly, d) reduce medical words, e) fifteen words or less per utterance, and f) simple phrasing. Developing wayfinding and signage both in electronic and on-site forms that are compliant with plain language recommendations significantly contributes to improved health literacy. Despite governmental efforts to promote linguistically and culturally appropriate care, the regulations are not fully followed by medical providers and healthcare organizations because many parts of the regulations rely on providers' and organizations' interpretations (Youdelman, 2008). More effective communication among all stakeholders is necessary to reduce this gap.

THEORETICAL LENS

Mental illnesses, like narratives, simultaneously unfold with and redefine place and time. Both influence how people communicate, which can in turn reshape relationships in a person's life. This project is guided by the narrative paradigm (Fisher, 1989), which informed the narrative research movement and its role in the study of health communication. RHL is heavily informed by the meanings created by community stories, family stories, and the ways in which stories are communicated. One of Fisher's primary aims was to account for and better understand how people come to believe and adopt stories that guide their behavior. This is a particularly salient point of interest for this chapter.

The narrative paradigm assumes that all forms of human communication can be seen fundamentally as stories, as interpretations or aspects of the world occurring in time and shaped by history, culture, and character (Fisher, 1989). A woman's experience of navigating mental illness, like narrative, occurs within her life at the same time that it reshapes her life. These health experience stories can order and disorder the navigation of health care systems, seeking help, accessing information, and finding resources. Personal narratives serve as building blocks for public knowledge about the ways in which mental health challenges can be engaged, treated, and talked about. The stories of individuals cannot be built and understood separately from public narrative. Stories are biased, incomplete, conflicting, fragmentary, and contradictory; even so, they become a vehicle for sense- and meaning-making.

Earlier efforts to forge a path into health communication studies using the tools of narrative have left their mark. Charon (2004, 2008) and COMFORT (Wittenberg-Lyles et al., 2012) both feature work that privileges the patient's voice and experience in an effort to improve patient outcomes and quality of care. Narratives in culturally concordant and discordant clinical interactions are now an area of study and understanding in health communication (Terui, 2017). Social support, sharing of health experiences on digital platforms (Rains & Keating, 2015), and pediatric coping (Manning, Hemingway, & Redsell, 2017) also include examinations of mental health care and the role of narrative. The influence of this class of research can be seen in the work of nursing clinicians (Hall & Powell, 2011) and interprofessional teams (Goldsmith, Wittenberg-Lyles, Rodriguez, & Sanchez-Reilly, 2010).

Turning to the storied experiences of underserved mental health patients, one can see challenging and beneficial communication events described by the women in the House of Grace. Fisher (1989) helps us discern where MHL arises in a population that is out-of-network, out-of-system, out-of-good-graces, and out-of-help. The matter of narrative coherence and fidelity is central to Fisher's (1989) approach because "good reasons are elements in human discourse or performance that we take as warrants for belief or action" (p. 194). If a motive for an action is a) consistent with what one knows and values, b) appropriate to the decision at hand, c) promising in its benefits for one's communities and ourselves, and d) consonant with what one thinks about basic action, the reason for the action can be deemed "good." This presents a potential problem in the context of the setting and sample we engaged with for this project and may point to the heart of the credibility and trust challenges that the women in the House of Grace face. When one considers mental illness, poverty, and lack of social support, the credibility of the storyteller is called into question.

For participants in this study, narrative can be called into question as a cost of their diagnosis and their past legal and behavioral challenges. However, the story can be all that is left to represent the self when removing other resources (e.g., independence, time, money, abilities, freedom). Especially for this group of participants, narrative is agency. In this project, we investigated the following research questions:

RQ1: How can the MHL needs of patients be informed by the conceptual model of RHL?

RQ2: How do patients perceive that family intersects with their MHL needs?

METHODS

We used directed qualitative content analysis (Hsieh & Shannon, 2005) informed by the narrative paradigm approach to examine the research questions identified above and develop a deeper understanding of the various components of mental health and RHL. The narrative features of content-ordering (e.g., making sense of events, meanings, activities, and identities) (Fisher, 1989) determined the units of meaning in our analysis.

SETTING

A larger research effort was designed for execution near the site of the Tuskegee Syphilis Study. Using the components of the RHL model, we collected interviews addressing health literacy from individuals living in extreme poverty. Individuals living on less than $2 a day before government support met our criteria. The rural community that served as the setting for this project earns an average household income of less than $29,000 per year with a poverty rate above 30 percent (United States Census Bureau, n.d.). Health indicators based on the prevalence of mental illness and access to mental health treatment in Alabama are low compared with the national average (Mental Health America, n.d.). In cultivating multiple sites for the parent study, one of the authors gained a research invitation into a halfway house. Women residing there were in recovery from a variety of difficulties including drug addition, suicide attempts, homelessness, prostitution, and incarceration. The issues of mental health and mental illness figured prominently in the lives of all participants.

PARTICIPANTS AND RECRUITMENT

Researchers recruited a subset of eleven participants who were living in or had lived in the House of Grace. Residents, past and current, had been directed to this housing facility as part of sentencing enforced by the judicial system. This residential environment is closely associated with a local church, and a religious orientation to recovery is strongly emphasized in its day-to-day operations. Participants' length of residency in the House of Grace varied, as the program has no required end point.

Research Design and Ethics Review

We developed interview prompts to improve our understanding of RHL and elicit stories about health literacy from this hard-to-reach population. Data gathering followed an open-ended protocol (see Table 4.1).

Table 4.1. Interview Prompts About Health Literacy

Have you had any experiences in your life that would identify you as a patient? Or a caregiver to a family member or friend? A health care provider?
- Could you describe a positive communication experience as a patient/caregiver/provider that you feel okay sharing?
  - What made it positive?
- Could you describe a negative communication experience as a patient/caregiver/provider that you feel okay sharing?
  - What made it negative?
  - What could be different if you could do it again?

In your experience as a patient/caregiver/provider, can you describe a time when you had a <u>challenge</u> in trying to figure out what to do in terms of care?
- Was communication a part of this challenge?
- Was communication a part of accessing care? Not accessing care?

In your experience as a patient/caregiver/provider, can you describe a time when you found a <u>pathway</u> to clarify what to do in terms of care?
- How do you/those you care for learn about available resources?
- How do you communicate about available resources?
- Have you ever brought the information (ideas, literature, pictures, etc.) to a health care appointment?/Have you ever had patients and family caregivers bring information to a health care appointment?
  - If yes: What kind of information did you/they bring? How did that go?
  - If no: Can you share why you did not share the info?/Why do you think they do not bring information?

How do nurses, doctors, and other health care workers you see play a part in helping you figure out what to do in terms of care?/ How do patients and caregivers you see play a part in helping you figure out what to do in terms of care?

How does the community you are a part of (religious, neighborhood, illness, shared experience) play a part in helping you figure out what to do in terms of care?

How does the health care system (hospital, clinic, emergency room) you use/belong play a part in helping you figure out what to do in terms of care?

Interviews were conducted and recorded by the authors and three research team members, yielding a total of 126 transcribed pages. All procedures were reviewed and approved by the Institutional Review Board at our institution. Participant confidentiality was protected by our coding labels and the consent process. Location, provider, institution, and other identifiers have been changed.

PROCEDURE

At the beginning of each interview session, we obtained both verbal and written informed consent. First, we collected a demographic profile. Some participants preferred that the interviewer read items out loud, and others completed demographic items with pen and paper. Second, the interviewer presented a series of open-ended questions about health literacy. The interview protocol prompted participants to share mental health needs, mental health information-seeking patterns, shared decision-making experiences, and barriers and pathways to mental health care. If the participant needed further explanation or clarification for a prompt, it was provided through a semi-structured interview format. The interviews lasted between fifteen and ninety minutes and were conducted face to face in private rooms at both the House of Grace and the church that sponsors the House of Grace. All house members participated and were given a $10 gift card upon completion of the interview.

DIRECTED QUALITATIVE CONTENT ANALYSIS

Hsieh and Shannon (2005) note that researchers examining a phenomenon that would "benefit from further description" and completeness may select a directed approach to content analysis. This directed approach has a more structured procedure than is typically used in conventional content analysis (Hickey & Kipping, 1996). The directed approach allowed us to identify the five key elements in the RHL model and treat them as coding categories (See Table 4.2).

Table 4.2.   Exemplar Units of Analysis Per Relational Health Literacy (RHL) Element

RHL Element	Narrative Unit of Analysis
Patient	"I lost about four months of my memory because I had a mild stroke. So I'm starting over. I don't remember going to the hospital. I had shot myself in the stomach. So from then on, I don't even remember the paramedics, ambulance, any of that. I have no memory. That's why part of my memory is gone" (Participant HS003).
Caregiver	"My ex's grandfather uh actually threw an oxygen tank in the fire. And he blew himself up. And he had nylon pants on. Yeah, so it burned to his skin. And they had to scrub it all off and I had to doctor him quite a few times. And he had a hernia in his stomach and they put mesh over it. So we had to. It was just an open hole for a long time we had to pack stuff in there" (Participant HS002).

Provider	"I was kind of unconscious for a while. Not unconscious, but the pain medicine made me 'out.' And when I came to, they were just loving and caring. They even came, I did some at-home physical therapy and all, and she was awesome" (Participant HS006).
Community	"The community of the illness, the other diabetics. People know you're diabetic, when they get the diagnosis, they come to you. Several times I've talked to people and told them what to do, and told them about diabetic school. Do go to diabetic school. Because if you don't know, you're making mistakes. I mean, you could hurt yourself or you could do damage" (Participant CH007).
System	"Because you're going to bill my insurance company, or you're gonna send me a bill in the thousands or ten thousands, and you know you're gonna charge $45 for a Band-Aid" (Participant SH005).

Element Combinations

Patient/ Provider	"And he was like 'Oh my God. They left that in you.' I was like 'yeah, I told that lady that you said that it is supposed to be pulled out but she said they would dissolve it and cut both of them off.' And he said 'OK well I'm gonna pull on this. If it don't come out we're going to have to cut you back open.' And you know I went to my six-week check up just by myself you know I got an infant right here on the floor. And he starts tugging on it and it, he tugs the first time and it, it didn't come. And he takes his scissors and he puts it straight down in my incision and opens it like that" (Participant HS002).
Patient/ Caregiver	"I had to stay there for a while till I found somewhere to go when I got out. They won't let you just go. But my sister-in-law, my brother, which is her husband, and my older son, they were all there for me" (Participant HS009).
Patient/ Community	"They didn't get infected. I would never think to do that. He said it burned really bad. When he first put it in there. I assume so. I mean, I thought that was pretty cool. I would never do it. But you know if you had to. So that's definitely something interesting when you're I guess just around certain people and they do certain things and that like helps you think about health in new ways and stuff. And ways to care for wounds and stuff. But really what is like uh the liquid stitches? What is that really? Is it just super glue? So if you don't say have the money for it all the kind of stuff and they go to the hospital you might try to use that" (Participant HS002).
Provider/ System	"I came here for about a week and then I left and actually relapsed, and I had to go to a mental hospital. I had a psychiatrist there, a social worker. And I told her my problem with my mental health meds is I can't afford it right now. And she told me going in that that wasn't going to be a problem, because that was one of my worries and one of the reasons I didn't go to the hospital ever. Because I would take the medicine there, get on the medicine, and then when I would leave there, I would be stuck without it. So she basically lied to me and said that I would be able to get it for four dollars, or this or that. I was not able to" (Participant HS006).

Next, we determined the nature of an element in RHL and its potential properties (Potter & Levine-Donnerstein, 1999). In doing this, the five elements operated as an initial framework for us to identify co-created health literacy features in the interview data, underscoring MHL barriers and pathways. We identified subcategories depending on the type and breadth of a category. This method allowed us to provide examples of coding categories from the interview data. It also helped us generate descriptive evidence to support the theoretical model.

In designing the study with the directed content analysis approach, we built open-ended questions along with targeted questions (Hsieh & Shannon, 2005) about the predetermined five categories specifically to learn about mental health challenges surrounding patient, caregiver, provider, community, and system. Reported are rank-order comparison of code frequency and newly identified subcategories and supported and non-supported categories for each participant and the total sample (Curtis et al., 2001). The RHL model guided the discussion of findings. This method extended RHL by directly recognizing that the research underway is not employing a naïve perspective, which is often viewed as the only and best approach in naturalistic research design (Hsieh & Shannon, 2005).

We were familiar with participants and their interviews prior to the directed content analysis coding process. Initially, both authors reviewed the data independently to identify narrative content-ordering units. Disagreements about unit identification were resolved during one extended meeting. We compiled units into a new document, and 20 percent of the total units for analysis were coded independently for the five RHL elements (e.g., patient, caregiver, provider, community, and system). We compared coding and achieved 80 percent agreement. We divided the remaining units in half between us for coding completion as well as identification of new subcategories.

RESULTS

A total of eleven individuals were part of this study. Interviews were conducted on two separate occasions four months apart. All available house residents (n = 9) or former residents (n = 2) took part in each of the two collection visits.

Participants had a wide range of mental health challenges. We did not include this variable in the demographic collection; however, all participants readily shared mental health information during the interviews. We identified these referents in the data and included them in the overview of participant characteristics (Table 4.3).

Table 4.3. Overview of Participant Characteristics

Characteristics	n (%)
Self-Identified Mental Health Challenge	
Drug use	9 (81.8%)
Schizophrenia	2 (18.1%)
Bipolar	4 (36.3%)
Trauma/abuse	4 (36.3%)
Depression	6 (54.5%)
Gender	
Female	10 (90.9%)
Male	1(9.1%)
Ethnicity	
Caucasian	9 (81.8%)
African American	2(18.2%)
Age	
21–30 years	1 (9.1%)
31–40 years	3 (27.2%)
41–50 years	2 (18.2%)
51–60 years	4 (36.4%)
61–70 years	1 (9.1%)
Years of Education	
Less than high school	1 (9.1%)
Completed high school and some higher education	10 (90.9%)
Income	
Less than 10,000 a year	5 (45.4%)
10,000–20,000 a year	2 (18.2%)
Selected not to answer	4 (36.4%)
Marital Status	
Single	1 (9.1%)
Married	3 (27.2%)
Divorced or separated	5 (45.5%)
Widowed	2 (18.2%)
Employment Status	
Unemployed	7 (63.6%)
Disabled	3 (27.3%)
Retired	1 (9.1%)
Has a Primary Doctor	
Yes	4 (36.4%)
No	7 (63.6%)
Has a Living Will	
Yes	1 (9.1 %)
No	10 (90.9%)

Most participants in our sample noted drug addiction challenges (81.8%), but other mental health issues included schizophrenia, bipolar disorder, trauma, and depression. The sample was predominantly Caucasian (81.8%) and ranged in age from twenty-eight to sixty-two (M = 47.36). All but one participant was female. The sole male participant was a resident in the past, but currently works with the church that sponsors the House of Grace. The majority of participants completed high school and some higher education (90.9%). All who chose to disclose income information fell below the poverty rate (63.6%), with most living in extreme poverty (less than $10,000 a year) (45.4%). The majority of the sample was divorced, separated, or widowed (63.7%), and none were employed. Most participants did not have a primary doctor (63.6%), and only one had a living will.

RHL Element Frequencies

We reported content analysis frequencies by individual and by sample, and two-element frequencies for the sample are reported here (Table 4.4).

We identified units of meaning as content-ordered narratives (Fisher, 1989). Here, we include one example of an identified content ordered narrative:

> Fentanyl patches, I had enough Fentanyl in my body to kill an elephant, because my kidneys weren't flushing it out. I died and they gave me Narcan three times in four hours. I still was dead for four and a half weeks, in intensive care on life support. (Participant CH008)

We identify this as a narrative passage that is content-ordered because of the recall of events and time. We coded for one of five RHL elements: patient, caregiver, provider, community, or system. For this passage of talk, we coded the narrative for patient, as the participant is describing the events of her own health.

Across fifty single-spaced pages of narratives identified for coding, there were a total of 101 narrative units of meaning. Within those units, we coded for 181 instances of RHL elements. Code frequencies include fify-seven patient elements, forty-one provider elements, thirty-three caregiver elements, twenty-seven system elements, and twenty-three community elements (Table 4.5).

We also collected frequency counts for two and three or more elements appearing in one unit of analysis. The most common two-element combination was patient/provider (n = 12), followed by patient/caregiver (n = 11), patient/community (n = 6), system/provider (n = 6), patient/system (n = 3), caregiver/community (n = 3), caregiver/provider (n = 2), caregiver/

Table 4.3. Relational Health Literacy Code Frequencies and Combination Frequencies

Participant/ RHL Element Code Frequencies	Patient	Caregiver	Provider	Community	System	Frequency of One Element in Narrative	Frequency of Two Elements in Narrative	Frequency of More Than Two Elements in Narrative
CH007	8	2	8	7	2	9	7	1
CH008	5	—	4	1	3	—	2	3
HS001	1	—	—	—	—	1	—	—
HS002	8	3	4	2	—	—	6	1
HS003	2	2	—	1	—	2	—	1
HS004	10	10	7	3	4	5	5	6
HS005	3	2	6	—	1	2	2	2
HS006	5	—	3	3	4	2	4	1
HS007	8	2	1	1	2	4	6	—
HS008	4	9	8	4	11	13	10	1
HS009	3	3	—	1	—	4	1	—
Sample Frequencies	57	33	41	23	27	44	43	16

Table 4.4. Two-Element Combination Frequencies

Patient +	Provider	Caregiver	Community	System
	12	11	6	3

Caregiver +	Provider	Patient	Community	System
	2	11	3	1

System +	Provider	Patient	Community	Patient
	6	-	1	-

*Unit of Analysis Narratives Totaled 181

community (n = 3), caregiver/system (n = 1), and finally, system/community (n = 1).

We also coded three or more elements per unit of analysis, which resulted in sixteen instances of three or more RHL codes. Four of those sixteen included more than three elements.

Communication Frequencies

Because the health literacy model proffered here is driven by communication theory and predicated on the transacted nature of health, we also observed references to communication within units of analysis. This is supported by Fisher's (1989) theory that people are storytelling animals that use stories to communicate and provide reason for action. Noting this phenomenon within the MHL narratives is important to understanding the RHL model and the role that communication plays in establishing its unique explanatory value. No current theoretical construct of health literacy employs communication as a central epistemological component.

Of the 101 units of analysis, forty-one included communication as a central topic. In the first instance, a participant describes the interaction between himself and another man who has the same challenges, exemplifying communication and the community element of RHL.

> The value of communicating back and forth, I didn't have to make the mistakes that I would have made, because John helped me. He instructed me what to do. When certain things happened, I could immediately go to him. (Participant CH007)

A second instance of communication figures prominently as this participant describes how she is unsure of how to tell her love interest about her past experiences with cocaine addiction.

> I talk to my housemother about it all the time. How would I tell him, you know, about the situation? And she said, some things you don't tell. I try to be honest and I'm trying to live honest. But my mind is made up today so I don't have to think about tomorrow, about that again (Participant HS007).

Over 40 percent of the narratives we analyzed predicated on communication as the key subject. Most commonly, participants relived the role that communication played in creating a circumstance, good or bad. However, some participants were reflective about the potential role of communication in repairing situations in the future or navigating health and mental health challenges ahead.

MENTAL HEALTH AND NARRATIVE

Many of our interviews included clarifying and insightful narratives from people facing a significant range of mental health challenges. Our data also improved our understanding of the impact of mental health challenges on that act of content-ordering (e.g., making time, place, events clear to others). The following narratives are indicative of the array of difficulties faced by our participants.

> Interviewer: Okay. How does the community that you're a part of play a part in how you look at care? So let's say your community is this household and the people that live in it. How do they support you in terms of what to do about your care? Or maybe it's your church?

> Participant: I would say that, um they're, well, I definitely would say that I haven't, given that, given that people say I am overly sweet or I'm overly a challenging person or things of that nature, I definitely would say that I have been still given time, I have still been given time. And although, although my path, I am, the job, the things that I am hoping for, I don't, I really don't know how the things that they're going to ask of me or from me. (Participant HS001)

Demonstrated throughout HS001's interview, she struggles to orient to the interview questions. However, her cadence, phrasing, conversational timing, turn-taking, and nonverbal interaction demonstrated competence (Thomason & Hopper, 1992). Not until the examination of the transcripts did it become clear that this participant never responded with coherent content. We learned from others in the house that this participant remained untreated for schizophrenia and had suffered sexual abuse for an untold number of years.

The descriptions of health behaviors and diagnoses were confusing and difficult to understand in some interviews.

> Four years ago I was schizophrenic and seventy-nine pounds. And I don't even take nothing anymore for all that. So I know what it took for me to get over that. I know what it took. I mean, I've been in rehabs probably sixteen times in the past twenty years. So I know what it takes as far as like clinically. I've prayed, I was like God, I don't know who to call so I can be a testimony to the medical community. So me just sitting here and be able to share these things with you is such an answer to prayer. (Participant CH008)

Our setting leaves us with many questions. The operating philosophy is derived from the leader of the supporting church, as well as from the house parents—a couple who has been overseeing the house for two years. The House of Grace is populated via the court system, but also through word-of-mouth channels. The house cannot be an official placement site for the court system due to its church-related status; instead, judges make casual recommendations to people facing criminal charges. We were not able to learn about the house's operating budget or how its operational costs may be tied to those of the church. All of these observations affect the mental health care of the residents. The house parents are not mental health workers, and the house does not appear to have a mental health/physical health budget or standardized set of care procedures for its residents. Instead, group sessions and religious study are used to structure residents' time and assist in their recovery.

> You know I came here to get help a year and a half ago myself. I was addicted to Lortabs, pain medication. Anyway, I was in Birmingham. Somehow this happened. I was in a smoking area. And this other person had been talking. We was just talking every day for a couple of days. Anyway, a long story short, I ended up, something had been put in a drink. I know it had to have been. Because I cannot remember leaving that place that I was at. And I woke up in a motel with three men, being raped. (Participant HS008)

> The girl that came in on the meth. I mean, she had sores all over her body. And I've never been around anything like that. That was something new for me. We didn't have any gloves. We didn't have anything that could help. So we had to get some gloves. And those things are not cheap. But I had to call a healthcare provider . . . She's doing this, doing that. Because I really didn't know. Do I need to get her somewhere? Is she going to die here? This girl was pitiful. She was burning up with a fever. And I mean, she was just bleeding. Actually, she was picking at her face real bad. (Participant HS008)

Both narratives from this participant demonstrate the need for mental and physical health care. Only one participant out of eleven did not mention physical health needs. All other participants spoke about chronic illnesses (e.g., hepatitis C, H. pylori, diabetes, heart disease, cirrhosis of the liver, high blood pressure, irritable bowel syndrome, chronic obstructive pulmonary disease) as well as acute health events (e.g., surgeries, childbirth, shotgun injury). This community of recovering participants not only endured a complete lack of regular mental health care, but an absence of physical health care as well. Without these two types of care working in tandem, residents are unlikely to achieve the desired outcomes for recovery.

DISCUSSION

We were given access to residents in a recovery house in rural Alabama during 2017 and 2018 as part of larger study to develop the relational health literacy (RHL) model. We asked participants to share their experiences regarding finding care; the collaborative roles of patient, caregiver, provider, community and system in achieving care; and barriers and pathways to obtaining health care. The subset of data is limited to participants with treated and untreated mental health challenges. This project sought to understand further how the RHL model might be inclusive of mental health concepts and issues, how the mental health needs of patients might be better understood with the use of the model, and finally, how family caregivers intersect with the mental health literacy (MHL) needs of patients.

Of the 181 narratives in our data, we found that the highest frequency of narratives shared were inclusive of the patient (57) as the primary element, followed closely by the provider (41), the caregiver (33), the system (27), and the community (23). The spread of RHL elements across narrative units supports the elements as substantive factors in the pursuit and achievement of care.

Of the 101 units of analysis studied in this data set, 64 included two or more RHL elements. In other words, more than half of the time, participants described health care events in a way that included more than one stakeholder group. This lends support to the concept that health literacy is co-created among and between stakeholder groups. Additionally, we emphasize the finding that nearly half of all units of analysis feature communication as the

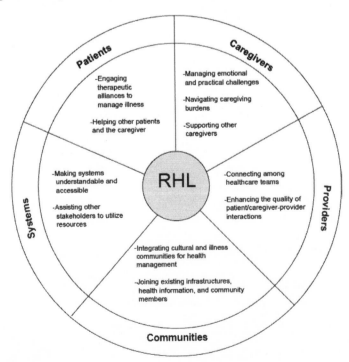

Figure 4.1.   Relational health literacy conceptual model.
Image provided courtesy of the author.

primary subject matter. This finding highlights the communication-driven orientation of this RHL conceptual model (see Figure 4.1).

These discoveries are important to the advancement of RHL, and the potential for this model to introduce health communication more saliently into the discourse and research on health literacy and MHL. Importantly, the mental health needs of patients can be more specifically engaged and understood utilizing the elements of RHL and integrating communication as a driving force for improving interventions and access of care for all stakeholders. This data underscores the complexity of mental health and its challenges, and the impact of each stakeholder group on finding and achieving effective care.

> For depression, I would say, I've had the worst time trying to find what to do. Because my primary nurse practitioner that I see wanted me to go to mental health. But mental health was so far away, and it was hard to get in with them as far as them making appointments, and timely appointments. And then my appointments would come and go, and I didn't have a ride there. So it was hard to get to the appointments. And even when I did go, you'd have to wait four or five hours. And then you were back there with the doctor maybe two and half minutes. And he never connected with you physically. Like he just came in for two and a half minutes, typed in his computer on his keyboard, and walked back out. Never even looked at you. So it was hard for mental health to figure out what to do for myself to get over the hump. (Participant CH008)

This exemplar's richness is also grounded in the communication recalled by the participant. The patient, the system, and the provider are at all play for this participant.

One of the five elements of the model is the caregiver. We did not expect that the caregiver would appear in narratives in the way that it did. Though often included in descriptions (n = 33), the absence or disappointment in the caregiver was a pattern.

> My whole family, I look at where I was at, not one of them, not one of them, have came to see what my life is about. Not my grown kids. Not my mother, for sure. I've got three sisters. (Participant HS008)

> I think its four girls here, they don't have nobody. Not one soul. Not one person in their life. Sad. One girl on frigs so bad, but actually, she lost her mom. Her mom died while she was in jail. Her dad is on meth. He's out there so bad. The other girl, her grandmamma raised her and she just died. It's sad. They don't have anybody. That's sad. (Participant HS008)

> So I'm kind of, I been dealing with it, the marijuana and cocaine since I was 20 years old. And I'm 33 now. And I have been a couple places. I was married.

I lost my husband. No, he didn't pass away. He just divorced me. (Participant HS007)

I go to good RX for my prescriptions. And I look for coupons. Um they give me a pretty decent discount. Um and that I found through my daughter. The pharmacist assistant. My other daughter lived here for a few years. (Participant HS004)

From the coding and narrative analysis of this data, the intersection of the family caregiver with the patient is low and not a supportive part of the picture for this group of patients. Less than five of thirty-three narratives described benefits and help in health literacy proffered by family caregivers. With that element so absent or problematic, this group of patients is further challenged in accessing and enacting mental and physical health care.

This project contributes to three areas of knowledge in health communication. First, we make a connection here between health literacy and health communication in a way that has not received evidence-based explanation before in the advancement of the RHL model. Second, mental health and mental illness receive unique attention as a result of the rare access to the sample population in this study. And finally, narrative and health communication are engaged together in ways that may extend their dual use into the area of mental health communication study.

IMPLICATIONS AND CONCLUSIONS

A final consideration here is that the directed content analysis approach can present challenges to the naturalistic paradigm as we approached the data with an informed bias. The model informed both the creation of the interview protocol and the coding process. However, this is a developmental project meant to further understand the presence or absence of these RHL elements in a certain context of health. Findings were supportive and also extend the RHL model. The role of narrative and the connection between physical and mental health needs is strongly suggested for future model analysis and intervention development. The context in which this work was collected clarified our awareness and perspective about RHL, rather than overemphasizing the model.

Next steps for the development will feature the identification and demonstration of communication as part of the model structure, and the role of communication in achieving health literacy. The work presented here supports the growth of MHL knowledge, further develops the RHL model, and contributes to perspectives on mental and physical health outcomes for a woefully underserved segment of the disadvantaged population.

NOTE

1. House of Grace is a pseudonym to protect the identities of those involved in the project.

REFERENCES

Ad Hoc Committee on Health Literacy for the Council on Scientific Affairs, American Medical Association. (1999). Health literacy: Report of the Council on Scientific Affairs. *Journal of the American Medical Association, 281*(6), 552–557. doi:10.1001/jama.281.6.552

Arnold, C. L., Coran, J. J., & Hagen, M. G. (2012). Revisiting patient communication training: An updated needs assessment and the AGENDA model. *Patient Education and Counseling, 88*(3), 399–405. doi:10.1016/j.pec.2012.06.026

Bahorik, A., Satre, D., Kline-Simon, A., Weisner, C., & Campbell, C. (2017). Serious mental illness and medical comorbidities: Findings from an integrated health care system. *Journal of Psychosomatic Research, 100*, 35–45. doi:10.1016/j.jpsychores.2017.07.004

Batterham, R. W., Hawkins, M., Collins, P. A., Buchbinder, R., & Osborne, R. H. (2016). Health literacy: Applying current concepts to improve health services and reduce health inequalities. *Public Health, 132*, 3–12. doi:10.1016/j.puhe.2016.01.001

Berkman, N. D., Sheridan, S. L., Donahue, K. E., Halpern, D. J., & Crotty, K. (2011). Low health literacy and health outcomes: An updated systematic review. *Annals of Internal Medicine, 155*(2), 97–107. doi:10.7326/0003-4819-155-2-201107190-00005

Bonevski, B., Randell, M., Paul, C., Chapman, K., Twyman, L., Brant, J., . . . Hughes, C. (2014). Reaching the hard-to-reach: A systematic review of strategies for improving health and medical research with socially disadvantaged groups. *BMC Medical Research Methodology, 14*(42), 42–71. doi:10.1186/1471-2288-14-42

Center for Disease Control and Prevention. (2018). Social network strategy for HIV testing recruitment. Retrieved from https://effectiveinterventions.cdc.gov/en/2018-design/care-medication-adherence/group-4/social-network-strategy-for-hiv-testing-recruitment

Charon, R. (2004). Narrative and medicine. *New England Journal of Medicine, 350*(9), 862–864. doi:10.1056/NEJMp038249

Charon, R. (2008). *Narrative medicine: Honoring the stories of illness.* New York, NY: Oxford University Press.

Cheng, H. L., Wang, C., McDermott, R., Kridel, M., & Rislin, J. (2018). Self-stigma, mental health literacy, and attitudes toward seeking psychological help. *Journal of Counseling and Development, 96*(1), 64–74. doi:10.1002/jcad.12178

Chou, W. S., Gaysynsky, A., & Persoskie, A. (2015). Health literacy and communication in palliative care. In E. Wittenberg, B. R. Ferrell, J. Goldsmith, T. Smith, S. L.

Ragan, M. Glajchen, & G. Handzo (Eds.), *Textbook of palliative care communication* (pp. 90–101). New York, NY: Oxford University Press.

Curtis, J. R., Wenrich, M. D., Carline, J. D., Shannon, S., Ambrozy, D. M., & Ramsey, P. G. (2001). Understanding physicians' skills at providing end-of-life care: Perspectives of patients, families and health care workers. *Journal of General Internal Medicine, 16*(1), 41–49. doi:10.1046/j.1525-1497.2001.00333.x

Cutilli, C. C., & Bennett, I. M. (2009). Understanding the health literacy of America: Results of the National Assessment of Adult Literacy. *Orthopaedic Nurses, 28*(1), 27–34. doi:10.1097/01.NOR.0000345852.22122.d6

D'Agostino, T. A., Atkinson, T. M., Latella, L. E., Rogers, M., Morrissey, D., DeRosa, A. P., & Parker, P. A. (2017). Promoting patient participation in healthcare interactions through communication skills training: A systematic review. *Patient Education and Counseling, 100*(7), 1247–1257. doi:10.1016/j.pec.2017.02.016

Denning, P., & DiNenno, E. (2017). Communities in crisis: Is there a generalized HIV epidemic in impoverished urban areas of the United States? Retrieved from https://www.cdc.gov/hiv/group/poverty.html

Dilger, D. (2013). The emotional health literacy block. Retrieved from https://www.kevinmd.com/blog/2013/11/emotional-health-literacy-block.html

Edwards, M., Wood, F., Davies, M., & Edwards, A. (2015). 'Distributed health literacy': Longitudinal qualitative analysis of the roles of health literacy mediators and social networks of people living with a long-term health condition. *Health Expectations, 18*(5), 1180–1193. doi:10.1111/hex.12093

Ewing, G., Ngwenya, N., Benson, J., Gilligan, D., Bailey, S., Seymour, J., & Farquhar, M. (2016). Sharing news of a lung cancer diagnosis with adult family members and friends: A qualitative study to inform a supportive intervention. *Patient Education and Counseling, 99*(3), 378–385. doi:10.1016/j.pec.2015.09.013

Fang, M. C., Machtinger, E. L., Wang, F., & Schillinger, D. (2006). Health literacy and anticoagulation-related outcomes among patients taking Warfarin. *Journal of General Internal Medicine, 21*(8), 841–846. doi:10.1111/j.1525-1497.2006.00537.x

Federal Drug Administration. (2018). *Federal plain language guidelines* [Data file]. Retrieved from https://www.fda.gov/downloads/AboutFDA/PlainLanguage/UCM346279.pdf

Fernandez, A., Schillinger, D., Grumbach, K., Rosenthal, A., Stewart, A., Wang, F., & Pérez-Stable, E. (2004). Physician language ability and cultural competence. *Journal of General Internal Medicine, 19*(2), 167–174. doi:10.1111/j.1525-1497.2004.30266.x

Fisher, W. (1989). *Human communication as narration: Toward a philosophy of reason, value, and action.* Columbia, SC: University of South Carolina Press.

Fletcher, B. S., Miaskowski, C., Given, B., & Schumacher, K. (2012). The cancer family caregiving experience: An updated and expanded conceptual model. *European Journal of Oncology Nursing, 16*(4), 387–398. doi:10.1016/j.ejon.2011.09.001

Goldsmith, J., & Terui, S. (2018). Family oncology caregivers and relational health literacy. *Challenges, 9*(35), 1–10. doi:10.3390/challe9020035

Goldsmith, J., Wittenberg-Lyles, E., Rodriguez, D., & Sanchez-Reilly, S. (2010). Interdisciplinary geriatric and palliative care team narratives: Collaboration practices and barriers. *Qualitative Health Research, 20*(1), 93–104. doi:10.1177/1049732309355287

Goldsmith, J., Young, A. J., Dale, L., & Powell, M. P. (2017). Plain language and health literacy for the oncology family caregiver: Examining a bilingual mHealth resource. *Seminars in Oncology Nursing, 33*(5), 498–506. doi:10.1016/j/soncn.2017.09.008

Hall, J., & Powell, J. (2011). Understanding the person through narrative. *Nursing Research and Practice, 2011*, 1–10. doi:10.1155/2011/293837

Harper, A. (2018). Relegated to chronic poverty: Financial difficulties faced by people with mental illness in the United States. *Enterprise Development and Microfinance, 29*(1), 64–79. doi:10.3362/1755-1986.17-00015

Hickey, G., & Kipping, C. (1996). A multi-stage approach to the coding of data from open-ended questions. *Nurse Researcher, 4*(1), 81–91. doi:10.7748/nr.4.1.81.s9

Hsieh, H. F., & Shannon, S. (2005). Three approaches to qualitative content analysis. *Qualitative Health Research, 15*(9), 1277–1288. doi:10.1177/1049732305276687

Huntington, B., & Kuhn, N. (2003). Communication gaffes: A root cause of malpractice claims. *Baylor University Medical Center Proceedings, 16(*2), 157–161. doi:1 0.1080/08998280.2003.11927898

Jorm, A. (2012). Mental health literacy: Empowering the community to take action for better mental health. *American Psychology, 67*(3), 231–243. doi:10.1037/a0025957

Kamimura, A., Christensen, N., Tabler, J., Ashby, J., & Olson, L. (2013). Patients utilizing a free clinic: Physical and mental health, health literacy, and social support. *Journal of Community Health, 38*(4), 716–723. doi:10.1007/s10900-013-9669-x

Kaphingst, K. A., Kreuter, M. W., Casey, C., Leme, L., Thompson, T., Cheng, M. R., . . . Filler, C. (2012). Health literacy INDEX: Development, reliability, and validity of a new tool for evaluating the health literacy demands of health information materials. *Journal of Health Communication, 17*(sup3), 203–221. doi:10.1080/10 810730.2012.712612

Kessler, R. (2012). Mental health care treatment initiation when mental health serivces are incorporated into primary care practice. *Journal of the American Board of Family Medicine, 25*(2), 255–259. doi:10.3122/jabfm.2012.100125

Kutcher, S., Wei, Y., & Coniglio, C. (2016). Mental health literacy: Past, present, and future. *Canadian Journal of Psychiatry, 61*(3), 154-158. doi:10.1177/0706743715616609

Laidsaar-Powell, R., Butow, P., Boyle, F., & Juraskova, I. (2018). Managing challenging interactions with family caregivers in the cancer setting: Guidelines for clinicians (TRIO Guidelines-2). *Patient Education and Counseling, 101*(6), 983–994. doi:10.1016/j.pec.2018.01.020

Lee, H. Y., & Vang, S. (2010). Barriers to cancer screening in Hmong Americans: The influence of health care accessibility, culture, and cancer literacy. *Journal of Community Health, 35*(3), 302–314. doi:10.1007/s10900-010-9228-7

Leung, A. Y. M., Bo, A., Hsiao, H. Y., Wang, S. S., & Chi, I. (2014). Health literacy issues in the care of Chinese American immigrants with diabetes: A qualitative study. *BMJ Open, 4*(11), 1–12. doi:10.1136/bmjopen-2014-005294

Manning, J., Hemingway, P., & Redsell, S. (2017). Stories of survival: Children's narratives of psychosocial well-being following pediatric critical illness or injury. *Journal of Child Health Care, 21*(3), 236–252. doi:10.1177/1367493517717078

Mental Health America. (n.d.). *The state of mental health in America: Ranking the states.* Retrirved from http://www.mentalhealthamerica.net/issues/ranking-states

Molina, Y., Hohl, S. D., Ko, L. K., Rodriguez, E. A., Thompson, B., & Beresford, S. A. (2014). Understanding the patient-provider communication needs and experiences of Latina and non-Latina White women following an abnormal mammogram. *Journal of Cancer Education, 29*(4), 781–789. doi:10.1007/s13187-014-0654-6

Nouri, S. S., & Rudd, R. E. (2015). Health literacy in the "oral exchange": An important element of patient-provider communication. *Patient Education and Counseling, 98*(5), 565–571. doi:10.1016/j.pec.2014.12.002

Parnell, T. A. (2015). *Health literacy in nursing: Providing person-centered care.* New York, NY: Springer Publishing Company.

Pope, M., Malla, A., & Iyer, S. (2018). Who should be responsible for supporting individuals with mental health problems? A critical literature review. *International Journal of Social Psychiatry, 64*(3), 193–302. doi:10.1177/0020764017752019

Potter, W. J., & Levine-Donnerstein, D. (1999). Rethinking validity and reliability in content analysis. *Journal of Applied Communication, 27*(3), 258–284. doi:10.1080/00909889909365539

Rains, S., & Keating, D. (2015). Health blogging: An examination of the outcomes associated with making public, written disclosures about health. *Communication Research, 42*(1), 107–133. doi:10.1177/0093650212458952

Rikard, R. V., Thompson, M. S., McKinney, J., & Beauchamp, A. (2016). Examining health literacy disparities in the United States: A third look at the National Assessment of Adult Literacy (NAAL). *BMC Public Health, 16*(1), 1–11. doi:10.1186/s12889-016-3621-9

Robotin, M. C., Porwal, M., Hopwood, M., Nguyen, D., Sze, M., Treloar, C., & George, J. (2017). Listening to the consumer voice: Developing multilingual cancer information resources for people affected by liver cancer. *Health Expectations, 20*(1), 171–182. doi:10.1111/hex.12449

Rodakowski, J., Rocco, P. B., Ortiz, M., Folb, B., Schulz, R., Morton, S. C., . . . James, A. E. (2017). Caregiver integration during discharge planning for older adults to reduce resource use: A metaanalysis. *Journal of the American Geriatrics Society, 65*(8), 1748–1755. doi:10.1111/jgs.14873

Roter, D. L., Narayanan, S., Smith, K., Bullman, R., Rausch, P., Wolff, J. L., & Alexander, G. C. (2018). Family caregivers' facilitation of daily adult prescription medication use. *Patient Education and Counseling, 101*(5), 908–916. doi:10.1016/j.pec.2017.12.018

Schinckus, L., Dangoisse, F., Van den Broucke, S., & Mikolajczak, M. (2018). When knowing is not enough: Emotional distress and depression reduce the positive effects of health literacy on diabetes self-management. *Patient Education and Counseling, 101*(2), 324–330. doi:10.1016/j.pec.2017.08.006

Schulz, P. J., & Nakamoto, K. (2013). Health literacy and patient empowerment in health communication: The importance of separating conjoined twins. *Patient Education and Counseling, 90*(1), 4–11. doi:10.1016/j.pec.2012.09.006

Schumacher, K. L., Plano Clark, V. L., West, C. M., Dodd, M. J., Rabow, M. W., & Miaskowski, C. (2014). Pain medication management processes used by oncology outpatients and family caregivers part II: Home and lifestyle contexts. *Journal of Pain and Symptom Management, 48*(5), 784–796. doi:10.1016/j.jpain symman.2013.12.247

Sentell, T., & Braun, K. L. (2012). Low health literacy, limited English proficiency, and health status in Asians, Latinos, and other racial/ethnic groups in California. *Journal of Health Communication, 17*(sup3), 82–99. doi:10.1080/10810730.2012 .712621

Street, R. L., Jr., Makoul, G., Arora, N. K., & Epstein, R. M. (2009). How does communication heal? Pathways linking clinician–patient communication to health outcomes. *Patient Education and Counseling, 74*(3), 295–301. doi:10.1016/j.pec .2008.11.015

Terui, S. (2017). Conceptualizing the pathways and processes between language barriers and health disparities: Review, synthesis, and extension. *Journal of Immigrant and Minority Health, 19*(1), 215–224. doi:10.1007/s10903-015-0322-x

Thomason, W. R., & Hopper, R. (1992). Pauses, transition relevance, and speaker change. *Human Communication Research, 18*(3), 429–444. doi:10.1111/j.1468 -2958.1992.tb00559.x

Thompson, A., Hunt, C., & Issakidis, C. (2004). Why wait? Reasons for delay and prompts to seek help for mental health problems in an Australian clinic sample. *Social Psychiatry and Psychiatric Epidemiology, 39*(10), 810–817. doi:10.1007/ s00127-004-0816-7

United States Census Bureau. (n.d.). *U.S. Census Bureau QuickFacts: United States.* Retrieved from https://www.census.gov/quickfacts/fact/table

Wittenberg, E., Ferrell, B., Goldsmith, J., Ragan, S., & Buller, H. (2018). COMFORT SM communication for oncology nurses: Program overeiw and preliminary evaluation of a nationwide train-the-trainer course. *Patient Education and Counseling, 101*(3), 467–474. doi:10.1016/j.pec.2017.09.012

Wittenberg-Lyles, E., Goldsmith, J., Ferrell, B., & Ragan, S. L. (2012). *Communication in palliative nursing.* New York, NY: Oxford University Press.

Wright, A., Harris, M., Wiggers, J., Jorm, A., Cotton, S., Harrigan, S., . . . McGorry, P. (2005). Recognition of depression and psychosis by young Australians and their beliefs about treatment. *Medical Journal of Australia, 183*(1), 18–23. doi:10.5694/ j.1326-5377.2005.tb06881.x

Youdelman, M. K. (2008). The medical tongue: U.S. laws and policies on language access. *Health Affairs, 27*(2), 424–433. doi:10.1377/hlthaff.27.2.424

Young, A. J., Stephens, E., & Goldsmith, J. (2017). Family caregiver communication in the ICU: Toward a relational view of health literacy. *Journal of Family Communication, 17*(2), 137–152. doi:10.1080/15267431.2016.1247845

Chapter Five

"They Saved My Life!"

Exploring Alternative Communication Narratives to Create Mental Health Agency

Sara "Sarie" Norval
Sarah E. Riforgiate

Lori[1] peers over the rim of her wine glass, "Girlfriend, you know I can't draw." Yet several portraits lay on the table, in a swirling cloud of disembodied faces, all with names written on them. Lori glances at the collage of sketches and drains her wine glass. She presents a small stack of papers, bits and pieces of evidence of which she has no memory. The next picture, scrawled in the handwriting of a small child, appears to be a person lying on a bed, a group of figures standing at a door to a room, a dog, and a broom. "That's me, I can tell you that because there's blood coming out of that little girl—I mean, that's me. That's my blood." Lori points to another part of the drawing, "my alters and my mom are there in the doorway, but my alters are inside the room trying to help me. My mom is outside the door," she pauses. "She knew, but. . ." she trails off and stares at the picture in silence. Lori embraces her empty wine glass with both hands and pauses. "Why I can even sit here and talk about it—because (as she points to the little girl on the bed) that's me, but it didn't happen to me."

Lori loves wine and Jesus. She is a mother of five children, three of them grown and out of the house, and is newly a grandmother. Lori watches *The Bachelor* like most people watch a football game: yelling, strong emotional outbursts, and angry Facebook status play by plays. Lori also runs a thriving business as one of the most talented hairstylists in the midwestern city she calls home.

If you ask her, Lori will tell you that she is Lori; on disorganized days, Sam; when she is nervous, Kari; when she is truly comfortable, Sarah; on really good days, Jane; on really bad days, Rosebud. Today she is Lori: mother, businesswoman, Christian, survivor of violent incest and sexual abuse, and diagnosed with dissociative identity disorder.

This chapter considers communication and mental health implications that are derived from reflections on an existing research study and ethnodrama that was based on ten qualitative interviews (lasting one to three hours each) with Lori and her alters. Reflecting on the interviews, research process, and live ethnodrama reading with Lori present, this chapter explores the power of communication narrative to: a) provide perspectives and humanize mental health, b) create opportunities for advocacy, and c) provide a potential avenue for healing. The chapter begins by explaining dissociative identity disorder, the associated stigma, and how the spiral of silence theory shapes communication pertaining to this mental health condition. A brief discussion of the research and analysis process is provided, followed by an explanation of the three communication implications of narratives.

DISSOCIATIVE IDENTITY DISORDER

Dissociative identity disorder (DID), previously labeled multiple personality disorder, refers to a psychiatric condition caused by the experience of significant trauma, categorized by an individual having at least two separate and unique personalities and experiencing memory loss (American Psychiatric Association [APA], 2018). The alternative personalities are often referred to as "others" or "alters." These alters take control of the individual's behavior, and each alter identity has individualistic and recurring patterns of understanding, thinking, interacting, and being (Jacome, 2001). In Lori's case, all of her alters are different ages, have different birthdates, some are right handed while others are left handed, and several have special skills that others do not possess (e.g., the ability to cut hair, draw, organize).

When alternative personalities present themselves, individuals experience memory loss and discontinuity that can be disruptive and confusing (Plokar, Bisaillon & Terradas, 2018). It is estimated that the prevalence of DID is between 0.5 percent to 5 percent in the general population (Parry, Lloyd & Simpson, 2018), with dissociative disorders occurring in 20 percent of clinical adult populations worldwide (Chiu et al., 2017). DID is strongly linked with child sexual abuse, with over 85 percent of DID individuals having experienced child sexual abuse (Hirakata, 2007).

The causal theories for DID are divided into two dominant perspectives: iatrogenic and traumagenic (Bailey & Brand, 2017). Those holding the *iatrogenic* position assert that DID is a direct result of exposure to and mimicry of DID-type characters on television and in movies (Traub, 2009). Iatrogenic proponents generally believe that DID (and a number of memories, including the idea that one has been sexually abused and repressed it) can be projected upon patients by therapists, also known as false memory syndrome (Piper & Merskey, 2004). In some cultures, concurrent with the iatrogenic position, DID may be explained by the presence of demon or "spirit" possession (Stickley & Nickeas, 2006).

Those of the *traumagenic* position, which is supported by the APA (2018), contend that DID is a direct result of childhood trauma, especially of an abusive nature. Proponents of the traumagenic school posit that during traumatic episodes, the other personalities (or alters) experience the pain of the episode, which allows the child abuse survivor to return to her/his body after the trauma without memory of experiencing the abuse (Brand et al., 2017). DID often manifests in childhood as a response that is defensive to a traumatizing event, such as childhood sexual abuse (much like post-traumatic stress disorder in adults) (Parry et al., 2018). Goffinet and Beine (2018) found that multiple experiences of traumatic events, including sexual, physical, and emotional abuse, are indicative of dissociative disorders. From a communication standpoint, the split in theories of origination for DID is important as one group advocates for the suppression of communication while the other does not.

As traumatic experiences accumulate, the dissociated compartments formalize, creating alters (Traub, 2009). The National Alliance on Mental Illness (2018) estimates DID individuals present with anywhere from two to one hundred alters, with an average of ten alters. Different alters often develop to handle various situations through a process of dissociation (Stickley & Nickeas, 2006). A controlling dominant personality, sometimes the usual self and sometimes a host personality, is typically present.

Distinct personality states mark DID, but the other defining symptom is amnesia: "For many with this disorder, it's as if they lived two or more different lives and only have knowledge of one—the safe one that does not involve past abuse or anything or anyone associated with it" ("Dissociative Identity Disorder," 2018). Dissociation and amnesia function as a means to survive severe trauma, but as alters persist as a part of the survivor's life, the dissociation and amnesia are diagnosed as a disorder (International Society for the Study of Trauma and Dissociation [ISSTD], 2011).

Mental health professionals often choose a goal of integration, or unity of the multiple states of self, as treatment (ISSTD, 2011). Becoming an integrated person is the process of developing awareness of the continuity of one's "coherent existence across person, place, and time while being cognizant of the multiple and various aspects of self" (Rothschild, 2009, p. 187). DID individuals consistently cannot explain time lapses, recall parts of their life, or understand or have control over their behaviors, many of which are out of the individual's character before the onset of the disorder. Clinicians who treat DID from a traumatological perspective agree that the goal is to achieve a stable sense of unity (Bromberg, 2006). Through integration, the individual begins to understand how all the pieces fit together and that all the experiences they witnessed as happening to someone else were actually happening to them. They garner the ability to learn who they are and observe the entirety of their life (van der Hart, Nijenhuis & Steele, 2006). With increasing frequency, the therapeutic goal of integration is to allow DID individuals to become aware of their alters and help them gain access to alters when appropriate (Rothschild, 2009). Finding ways to allow DID individuals to learn their full stories provides a unique communicative possibility that can assist with this goal.

DISSOCIATIVE IDENTITY DISORDER STIGMA

As most of society are non-DID individuals, one often relies on stereotypes to understand DID. There is uncertainty and unpredictability in encountering someone with several distinct alters presenting different characteristics. Stereotypical views often reduce DID individuals to entertainment value. DID is represented in media as anything from an unusual token character to a dangerous killer in television dramas (e.g., *The United States of Tara*, 2009) and motion pictures (e.g., *Frankie & Alice*, 2010; *Split*, 2016; *The Ward*, 2010), as well as a culpability defense in criminal court (ABC News, 2018; Go, 2017). Messages spread by media may not be accurate or even intentional, but they are the crux of information most people receive about DID. In reality, most DID individuals remain low profile and avoid drawing attention to their diagnosis for fear of the associated stigma of the disorder which could cause them to lose their job or status with loved ones or society (Fox, Bell, Jacobson, & Hundley, 2013). They edit their communication to downplay their mental health condition or hide the condition completely.

The idea that all DID individuals are interested in sensationalism or fame appears in the mental health community among professionals who hold an iatrogenic position (Stickley & Nickeas, 2006). When media spotlight DID, the reported cases of DID increase and lessen the credibility of DID individuals (Traub, 2009). For example, with the introduction of the 1976 American television mini-series *Sybil*, there was not only an increase in the number of reported cases of DID, but an increase in the "the average number of alternate personalities from a typical two or three to an approximate 15 alters" (Traub, 2009, p. 351). However, rather than fabricating a DID condition, this increase in reporting could equally be due to a growing awareness of this mental health condition. Brand et al. (2017) discuss that even when a DID diagnosis could help individuals, many DID individuals downplay their shameful experiences of sexual trauma and are sometimes unaware of their DID, causing them to be misdiagnosed. Thus, DID individuals do not generally seek recognition.

Considering the negative media and medical attention, DID individuals often silence their alters. This silence is compounded by some treating physicians who believe the best course of treatment is to ignore presenting alters to avoid reinforcement of pathological behavior (Gleaves, 1996). This advice ceases communication and halts understanding; silence erases individuals (Scheufele & Moy, 2000). Part of the reality for many DID individuals who are also child sexual abuse survivors is that they were first pushed into silence about the abuse, then encouraged to keep silent about their DID for fear of stigmatization.

SPIRAL OF SILENCE THEORY

Spiral of silence theory (Noelle-Neumann, 1974) explains that people are constantly aware of the opinions of the people around them and adjust their behaviors accordingly by either censoring their minority stance or editing their communication to match majority opinion (Gearhart & Zhang, 2018). Most people base the decision to communicate vocally about issues on the *perception* of opinion distributions rather than the *actual* opinion, ultimately shaping public expression (Scheufele & Moy, 2000). Those perceiving their viewpoint in the majority are more likely to communicate opinions, while those holding minority positions tend to keep silent or conform to perceived majority viewpoints (Liu & Fahmy, 2011).

Fear of isolation is a particularly important component of spiral of silence theory. Social collectives threaten individuals who deviate from majority viewpoints with isolation, increasing individual fears that their expression of unpopular views or behavior will isolate them further (Matthes et al., 2012). Spiral of silence theory predicts that those who identify in the minority are less willing to express opinions in public and appear more diminutive and weak over time (Malaspina, 2013). Ultimately, reluctance of minority members to express opinions establishes the majority opinion as the predominant view, or even as a social norm, thus triggering the creation of a spiral in which individuals fall increasingly silent (Scheufele, 2008). Importantly, silence removes individuals' voices and possibilities to create change, influencing those who have a fear of social isolation the most (Matthes et al., 2012).

Spiral of silence theory has largely been applied to the ways that individuals silence opinions regarding social issues (e.g., abortion, gay marriage, immigration) (Gearhart & Zhang, 2018). However, this chapter extends spiral of silence theory by demonstrating how individuals who are stigmatized are also silenced. Minority group individuals, particularly those who are stigmatized, stifle communication, thus reducing the potential for greater understanding, compassion, and healing. This silencing, as predicted by the theory, causes a downward spiral of silence that could be applied to stigmatized groups such as those who experience sexual abuse and mental health issues. However, as will be further explained, using creative communication methods, such as creating ethnodramas, can break spirals and facilitate important discussions.

COMMUNICATION NARRATIVE AND DISSOCIATIVE IDENTITY DISORDER

Communication scholars and medical practitioners alike have turned to narrative, to the telling of stories, to enhance the richness and expand the scope of the data they collect (Charon, 2009; Harter & Bochner, 2009). Further, Goffinet and Beine (2018) call for longitudinal qualitative research to better understand the complexities of dissociative mental health experiences. The narrative research shift impacts the study of DID individuals by including survivor accounts to explore the subjective experience of DID individuals through interviews (Parry et al., 2018). Through sharing their stories, DID individuals can maintain positive relationships, reframe and normalize their symptoms as challenges, organize and deal with DID experiences, reduce explanation of idiosyncrasies in personal relationships, and empower others to find resolutions to their difficulties (Fox et al., 2013).

Clinical case studies dominate DID literature, most frequently ascribing statistics and lists of symptoms to the diagnosis (Sar & Ross, 2006). Understanding could be enhanced by incorporating qualitative methods that humanize communication research regarding identity, agency, and lived truth for DID individuals (Parry et al., 2018). Additionally, using story and narrative methods provides a potential vehicle to diagnose DID in children to help these individuals receive help at a younger age (Plokar et al., 2018). Thus, narrative qualitative methodologies can extend communication research and enhance understanding of DID and child sexual abuse.

NARRATIVE METHODS TO SHARE LORI'S STORY IN HER OWN VOICE

This research project began with an invitation to the first author to interview Lori (a DID individual who is also a child sexual abuse survivor), talk with

Lori's alters, and observe Lori at work. Precautions were taken due to the sensitive nature of interviewing someone diagnosed with DID. First, the first author met with Lori and her therapist to create a code of ethics to ensure the safety of Lori, her friends, and family. The code of ethics included such protections as: participants involved in this study will sign a release of information, direct interviews will occur with a third party of the focus participant's choosing on call, if an alter discloses abuse, the researcher will disclose the information to the participant's therapist to decide the method of disclosure to the participant, and no direct interview will last longer than two to three hours in any twenty-four-hour period.

Both researchers engaged in extensive discussions with the university Institutional Review Board (IRB) to determine the most appropriate ways to protect Lori and those involved with the study. IRB approved the study to record an oral history of Lori's life. Further, Lori signed an informed consent form acknowledging that she would be recorded, she could stop the recording at any time, and the information would be used for research purposes with the intent to publish her story. Explicit discussions about confidentiality were an important part of the agreement; Lori specifically requested to use her own name, but no names of friends or family.

The first author met with Lori ten times over the course of a year for one to three hours per session and audio recorded informal discussion sessions, resulting in over one hundred pages of double-spaced transcription. These sessions allowed for the exploration of open-ended and follow-up questions to better understand Lori's experiences. During the interactions, the first author paid particular attention to relational ethics, or "an ethics of care" (Ellis, 2007, p. 4). Relational ethics include being true to one's character, being responsible for one's own actions and their consequences on others, and acknowledgment of one's interpersonal relationships while maintaining mutual respect and dignity (Slattery & Rapp, 2003). Working within the "ethic of friendship, a stance of hope, caring justice, even love . . . a level of investment in participants' lives . . . puts fieldwork relationships on par with the project" (Tillmann-Healy, 2003, p. 735). The first author remains in contact with Lori who, after pushing down and swallowing her story for many years, now wants to share her story with as broad of an audience as possible.

The original project involved creating an ethnodrama using quotations directly from Lori's interview transcripts to tell Lori's story in her own words (see Norval, 2015). Ethnodrama presents an opportunity to depart from more scientific practices to allow participants greater voice: "The point is not for some expert to show how much more he or she knows, but to allow people . . . to say what they have learned at such an enormous cost" (Gray & Sinding, 2002, p. viii). Existing narrative work with DID individuals emphasizes the importance of listening to first-person stories and the way the narratives reflect meaning-making to better understand DID experiences (Parry et al., 2018). Lori's therapist reviewed the full ethnodrama in detail and supported Lori attending a draft reading of the ethnodrama.

This chapter is a result of reflection on the research process, the ethnodrama reading, and others' reactions to the work to determine implications. The implications presented emerged from an iterative process beginning with open conversations between the authors regarding the data and research experience, and free journaling about our engagement with the project. From there, we used memo-writing to organize predominant themes, which involved identifying prominent ideas and refining the ideas by adding support (Charmaz, 2014). Specifically, we articulated each theme and then added quotations from Lori's interview transcripts, the original research study and ethnodrama (203 double-spaced pages), and verbal and email notations from others' reactions to the ethnodrama. Then, we engaged in multiple memo-drafts to fine tune where each element of information best fit to develop the three themes discussed in this chapter. Finally, we engaged in discussion with communication experts and sought additional research to further interpret and support our findings (Tracy, 2013).

The research process and ethnodrama reading point to important implications for communication research and mental health. As will be discussed below, communicating Lori's narrative: a) provides perspectives and humanizes mental health; b) creates opportunities for advocacy through stories; and c) provides a potential avenue for healing.

PROVIDING PERSPECTIVES AND CHALLENGING UNCERTAINTIES ABOUT MENTAL HEALTH

As previously explained, DID is classified as a mental health condition: a disorder. However, from Lori's perspective, DID is the *only* reason she was able to survive traumatic and repeated child sexual abuse. Lori explains:

> LORI: I was abused as a child, sexually abused, severely. And um—because of that, as a child, I developed something that was called DID, which is dissociative identity disorder. When I would be abused, my mind would drift off, and it would create another personality, and so, that's how I survived it. I mean, people look at me and they think, "That happened to *you*?" Well, they don't see—well, I'm functioning, I'm behind a [beauty salon] chair, and I'm doing my job. You know, I'm a church-going person—I'm—but they have no clue, for the last twenty-six years, they've had somebody with DID cutting their hair. That's because that's how I survived extreme, severe sexual abuse. You, Sarie, you are writing a play on how I survived all of that, and what this means, and how our

society doesn't understand what sexual abuse can do to a child, and yet, how I am so functional, how I've managed to raise a family, how I've managed—I say lightly—being married (*Both laugh.*), but my DID literally ended up costing me my marriage.

I: And saved your life.

LORI: Yeah. (*Tearing up*)

Later, Lori continues:

I was lucky. I've got multiple personalities. What about the kids that don't? What about them? Those are the ones that are underneath the viaduct. Those are the ones that are shootin' up. Those are the ones that are hookers. Those are the ones that are selling their bodies. Those are the ones that have no lives whatsoever.

These comments offer a very different perspective on mental health—that a mental health condition is beneficial.

However, Lori faced many difficulties in communicating this perspective to medical providers and was silenced through heavy medications by one doctor who took an iatrogenic approach to her mental health. She recalls:

When I was at General West, after the suicide attempt, there was a doctor by the name of Dr. Kyle, who did not believe in DID at all. And it felt like I was on display. Dr. Kyle was very mean, and um—very mean. *Very* mean. He just wants to medicate everybody. And he would ask me trick questions. Um—I was excited about . . . *The Bachelor*, or somethin' like that. And he goes, "I think you are overreacting, I think you need Seraquil." And I was like, "What?!" Because I was happy! We were just talking about the show, you know, *The Bachelor*. And I thought to myself, "Do you give your wife Seraquil every time she has an orgasm?" Because that's how—he just *(in a robotic tone)* pumps the meds, pumps the meds, pumps the meds, instead of talking to the person? He's a quack, and if I woulda had the energy, and the knowledge to have his job, I would of. Dr. Kyle didn't believe in DID. I've seen him medicate people to where they are complete zombies. And you know, here's the thing. I got close enough to some of the therapists there—*they* even feel that way about him, but they're intimidated enough, they'd never say it. He's a quack. He never once asked me how I felt about anything, about what happened to me as a child. Instantly thought the worst, instead of looking at me as a whole person.

Reading about Lori's experiences not only provides a different perspective, but her account also humanizes her and allows readers to understand the obstacles she faced interacting with a medical professional who was supposed to be "helping" her. Because her DID was stigmatized and she was the patient, her perspective was not only silenced, but other medical professionals were also silenced in speaking out against medicating patients. Charon (2009) advocates for the importance of listening to patients and the beneficial outcomes hearing patients' stories has for their treatment. Yet in Lori's case, she was medicated by Dr. Kyle and encouraged by other medical professionals to stay quiet and wait for her release. Silencing made healing more difficult for Lori and removed any agency she may have had in her own healing process. While doctors have important medical training that positions them as experts, patients also have information that could allow for the most beneficial treatment plans.

Lori was also aware and discussed how her condition was stigmatized and misrepresented by media. She explained, "I've never seen the movie *Sybil*, but I know I've had enough people that know I have DID that ask, 'Is that like the movie *Sybil*?'" Lori expressed that media portrayals served as a point of reference for others to understand her condition; she was concerned about the stigma and implications which caused her to limit her disclosures to others.

While Lori offers one person's story, researchers have begun to advocate for more qualitative accounts of DID experiences (e.g., Parry et al., 2018). Acknowledging that research often perpetuates authoritative, hierarchical and distanced observations, which displace the voice of survivors, and frequently casts them as "the other," a spectacle (Fine, 1994), we designed the ethnodrama project to allow Lori to talk about her experiences as a human being so others could better understand her perspective. Lori and her alters' direct quotations were compiled into an ethnodrama manuscript to share with others (see Norval, 2015). Because mental health is both stigmatized and therefore silenced, narratives created a methodological opportunity to better comprehend the "worlds of experience that are unknown to us, show us the concrete daily details of people whose lives have been underrepresented . . . reduce their marginalization . . . [and] show us how partial and situated our understanding of the world is" (Ellis & Bochner, 2000, p. 748). Communicating these untold stories encourages perspective-taking while allowing audiences to question current practices. In other words, ethnodrama breaks the spiral of silence for marginalized groups by bringing to light lived experiences (Gray & Sinding, 2002) and reaching larger audiences than traditional academic outlets (Richardson, 2000).

Ethnodrama removes layers of interpretation by using dramatic format to create a live performance of research participants' lived experiences from qualitative data (Saldana, 2005). A playwright of ethnodrama is not a storyteller, s/he is a "story *re*-teller" who combines interviews into one three-dimensional character (Saldana, 2005, p. 17). Importantly, an ethnodrama must be true to the qualitative data and not include fictional material (Mienczakowski & Morgan, 2001). As such, ethnodrama "exposes oppression and challenges the existing social order through an artistic rendering or moral and political discourse" (Saldana, 2005, p. 3). This research can live and breathe to do the most justice and the least violence (Ellis, Adams & Bochner, 2010).

Lori's narrative humanizes and gives voice to her experiences to provide a realistic account of DID and mental health. She wants others to respect her and understand her perspective. At one point she explained:

> I kinda want your professor to meet me, so you know, when she reads that paper, she has spent a little time with me, and she doesn't think I'm a nutcase, because God gave me—I would have died, girlfriend. I'd a-died. . . . I wanna have a chance to meet her or spend a little time with her before she reads the paper because it's so important to me that she understands fully.

Instead of seeing alters as something to be medicated into submission or sensationalized by media and as something to be feared, Lori views her alter identities as protectors who "saved her life" and "sacrificed themselves" by repeatedly bearing child sexual abuse occurrences so that she did not have to remember these events.

Through Lori's stories in ethnodrama readings, audiences can come to understand her preferred identity of a survivor: someone delivered from harm through the protective capacity of her own mind. Lori's words are powerful. Her story is unbelievably horrific, but also quite real. Importantly, Lori uses her own words to narrate her story. She is a *real* person with a sense of humor about DID, explaining, "If what you write helps people understand child sexual abuse, I don't care [what name you use]. I'm not protecting who I am anymore because, good or bad, I am who I am. And I mean—if I gotta pick a name, ya know, I have 17 to choose from."

Her alters also have a voice through ethnodrama. They share the pain they experienced on her behalf, but they also talk like any other human being would, comparing zodiac signs and gossiping about each other. For example, Kari (one alter) comments that Nichole (another alter) is left handed and "odd as hell!" They also talk about Lori's family members.

> KARI (Lori's alter): My memaw told me I'd never be rich unless I reused my foil [to save money], so I resorted to reusing cream cheese and sour cream containers to compromise.
> I: Memaw is your grandma?
> KARI: Yes, my grandma, and Mother Theresa reincarnated. Just Mother Theresa hasn't stepped aside yet (laughs).

Through Lori and her remaining five alters, Sam, Sarah, Kari, Jane, and Rosebud, the reader/viewer realizes the alters each have their own opinions, personalities, and individual roles in Lori's life. Humanizing DID as a mental health condition and presenting Lori's life in her own words counteracts sensationalized accounts and helps others understand DID. The ethnodrama serves as a powerful communication device to break spirals of silence and prompt others to talk about mental health, sexual abuse, and medical practices.

CREATING OPPORTUNITIES FOR ADVOCACY THROUGH STORIES

"I am not sure I could explain what I heard or fully understood what happened! That was a wild experience, but I know that that is exactly the type of thing communication scholars should be engaging in." (Observer at the ethnodrama reading)

This quote is in response to a reading of Lori's ethnodrama and indicates how narratives can make deep impressions and provoke profound understandings that other communication cannot; stories can call people to action. During the interviews and in the ethnodrama, Lori and her alters break the spiral of silence to share accounts of childhood sexual abuse. She does this because she is hopeful her experiences can help others by preventing child sexual abuse occurrences and help foster resilience in children who are unfortunately affected. As a child, one of Lori's neighborhood friends was abused alongside Lori and was diagnosed with schizophrenia. Sam, one of Lori's alters, discloses: "I ended up messed up, too. But we have a blessing, whether it be her schizophrenia, or my DID, or whatever it is, we're ok . . . I hope that when you write this book, it can reach her." Lori tirelessly and passionately expressed her interest in increasing awareness of child sexual abuse, feeling that if she could finally share her story, she could help others. She exemplifies:

Girl. I just want sexual abuse to STOP! I DON'T NEED GLORY OR KUDOS . . . I just want the ABUSE to STOP! THAT'S ALL! This is not about me or for me . . . it is to GLORIFY THE CREATOR OF HEAVEN AND EARTH! ROMANS 8:28 [for all things come together for the glory of God]. I LIVE FOR IT EVERY DAY.

Indeed, children do need adults' help. The reality is that one in ten children will be sexually abused before the age of eighteen (Darkness to Light, 2018). Child sexual abuse is the number one health issue facing children. This epidemic thrives in a culture of silence, feeding off power dynamics in families, hegemony in society, embarrassment, shame, fear, stigma, threats, and manipulation (Hornor, 2010). Research suggests that more than two-fifths of females and more than one-third of males who have been sexually abused in the United States have never disclosed the experience to anyone (Stop the

Silence, 2018). Even when evidence of sexual abuse exists and children are interviewed, significant numbers of children deny victimization (McGuire & London, 2017). Most child survivors silence themselves, waiting long periods of time and sometimes never disclosing the abuse (Alaggia, Collin-Vézina, & Lateef, 2019). Child sexual abuse happens in secret, and there is rarely physical evidence. Often the responsibility to end the abuse through disclosure rests on the child and their willingness to speak out.

A child's self-disclosure of sexual abuse is a critical component in initiating intervention to halt the abuse, address its immediate effects, and decrease the likelihood of negative long-term outcomes. Because of the silence and hidden nature of child sexual abuse, children often must make the decision whether to disclose without the advice, support, or encouragement of others (McElvaney, 2013). The lack of voice for survivors reduces the platform for these issues and hinders dissemination of information for prevention, perpetuating a culture of silence and shame. Narrative provides an important way to heighten awareness and build understanding.

There are organizations currently collecting child abuse survivor stories for investigation and prosecution utilization. Many centers have in-house therapy, and ethnodrama and other forms of drama therapy can provide a space for child sexual abuse victims to speak out and heal. Using their own words and experiences to process and share their most painful and personal experiences through drama therapy can allow survivors to reshape their experiences, communicate their truth, and support each other in a dynamic and tangible way. Further, narrative can also be used to diagnose sexual abuse trauma and mental health conditions (Plokar et al., 2018). Finally, sharing the stories through ethnodrama readings breaks spirals of silence by heightening awareness of child sexual abuse and mental health, encouraging victims to come forward and seek care, and creating better prevention and healthcare programs.

NARRATIVE PROVIDING A POTENTIAL AVENUE FOR HEALING

In addition to providing important findings, the qualitative research process can be beneficial for participants (Manning, 2010; Rossetto, 2014). While the intent of the original study was to give voice to Lori's story through demystifying DID and advocating for children, engaging in the interviews and narratives from the project through ethnodrama provided important opportunities for Lori and her alters to heal.

Part of the writing process of an ethnodrama is to have a reading to hear the manuscript flow and make editing decisions. Acknowledging that the researchers involved in this project do not have clinical training or experience, precautions were taken before the reading to confirm that Lori could be present. Specifically, Lori's therapist was asked to read and approve the full ethnodrama script that came directly from Lori's interview transcripts, and he granted Lori permission to attend the reading.

Students working on their masters' degree in drama therapy agreed to read the ethnodrama, were provided the script in advance, and signed consent forms that their reading could be recorded. The researchers sat on both sides of Lori as she grasped their hands and took a deep breath. During the reading, several alters presented to hear the stories and process the experiences. Breaks were taken when Lori or her alters needed to breathe and process, but Lori insisted that she hear the full ethnodrama. The reading allowed the alters to exist as they exist for Lori: as separate entities that have function and emotions and goals and stories. Using different people to play each alter gave honor to the alters as independent beings, the way Lori understands them.

The ethnodrama reading touched people differently than clinical language could and showed Lori that others were listening, absorbing, and understanding her story. After being silenced for so many years, she felt heard. Others cared without sensationalizing her and wanted to hear her story without judgment and without thinking she was "a freak," as she often worries. The narratives highlighted her experiences through the perspective that Lori and her alters shared.

Importantly, the reading allowed Lori to encounter her alters for the first time. This unexpected outcome was incredibly rewarding. Lori has amnesia-type DID: she only knows of her transitions because of loss of time or headaches. Lori also only knows of her remaining alters' personalities from testimony of others close to her and her therapist. Lori was able to attend the live reading and, for the first time, hear her alters speaking in their own words. Lori was fully aware that the reading was by drama therapy students and acknowledged this in discussions, but still felt connected to her alters. Lori was most moved by meeting the actor that read Rosebud's lines. Lori was able to share with the actor emotions and gratitude she had always wanted to share with Rosebud, but never had the chance. Weeks after the reading, Lori recounted,

She [Rosebud] needed to know that I loved her. I know it really wasn't my alter. It was the closest I ever felt to being able to tell her that she had to know how much she saved me and the others. I felt complete when I saw her and held her. She [actor reading Rosebud] will never know what she did for me that day. She was as much of a gift to me as Rosebud herself.

Lori reached a new level of connectedness and developed greater understanding with her alters. Those on the outside of Lori may have had the opportunity to talk to and hear from her alters, but Lori had not, and without this experience, she may have never had the chance. While the reading was intense and emotionally draining, Lori's therapist acknowledged the importance of this event in Lori's healing process. Allowing people to deeply reflect and to re-narrate their stories provides a method that can be profoundly healing for those suffering from mental health issues (Tuval-Mashiach, Patton & Drebing, 2018). For example, after the ethnodrama experience Lori shared:

My life is in a different place now, but I have always had this passion to tell people about child sexual abuse and how DID can help survivors. Doctors need to know, they aren't just treating one person, they are treating all the individual people within the person. You are treating all the alters—not just the person that was abused. You know, I was just looking at that picture of us from that day . . . when I heard the play and met the alters. I'll never forget when I met Rosebud . . . I'll never forget it. Now my life is so different. I have been [re-]married a year, it was small—28 people which was 27 too many, and of course I am busy with my precious grandson. I am completely integrated now. They're gone. I'd pay good money to have them back—get some cleaning done! I truly think I was integrated completely when my therapist moved out of town, which was after the play. We were both whooped. But I'll never, ever forget meeting Rosebud. I'd fly out to you to do some more interviews if it would help raise awareness. Anything you can do to help anyone, use it.

Recognizing that Lori's narrative is one case and that further clinical research is needed to explore implications of narrative for mental health patients responsibly, this study provides areas to explore in terms of how narrative offers a potential way to enhance self-understanding and healing.

Ethnodrama and narrative accounts promote fuller understanding of others and offer benefits to those experiencing mental health conditions. Patients can feel heard for the first time and understand aspects of themselves that they may not previously know. Nurses and physicians can gain important information to help them address their patients' needs. Family members can gain perspective, compassion, and understanding mental health conditions from the perspective of their loved one. Further, those who share in the ethnodrama experience can see a *real* non-sensationalized representation of the mental health condition, which can diminish uncertainty and lead to more accurate understandings of the condition. Some viewers may even see themselves in the story, letting them know they are not alone and providing them with the impetus to seek help. In health communication, narrative has increasingly been identified as a useful tool because narrative and medicine are both deeply involved with human suffering and expectations gone awry, as are most good stories (Charon, 2009).

THE CLOSING SCENE

Throughout this chapter, we shared the importance of narrative for mental health issues and DID in particular. We discussed how spiral of silence theory can be extended beyond controversial issues to also understand how stigmatized individuals with mental health conditions are silenced by providing examples of how medical professionals and media contribute to this silencing. Stories provide a powerful vehicle to better understand patient perspectives and humanize mental health conditions and advocate to change negative experiences that contribute to mental health issues and create possibilities for healing. Ethnodrama possesses emancipatory potential for motivating social change within participants and audiences, especially when a non-minority audience can experience the perspective of a minority voice (Mienczakowski & Morgan, 2001; Saldana, 2005). The drama allows others to establish a connection through empathy. Through ethnodrama, Lori was able to utilize a space to present her perspective of DID and sexual abuse; she wasn't silenced.

NOTE

1. "Lori" gave the authors permission to use her real name. This was also validated by the authors' Institutional Review Board.

REFERENCES

ABC News. (2018). *Using multiple personality disorder as a legal defense*. Retrieved from https://abcnews.go.com/Primetime/story?id=132119&page=1

Alaggia, R., Collin-Vézina, D., & Lateef, R. (2019). Facilitators and barriers to child sexual abuse (CSA) disclosures: A research update (2000–2016). *Trauma, Violence, & Abuse, 20*(2), 260–283. doi:10.1177/1524838017697312

American Psychiatric Association. (2018). *Dissociative disorders*. Retrieved from https://www.psychiatry.org/patients-families/dissociative-disorders/what-are -dissociative-disorders

Bailey, T., & Brand, B. (2017). Traumatic dissociation: Theory, research, and treatment. *Clinical Psychology: Science and Practice, 24*(2), 170–185. doi:10.1111/cpsp.12195

Berry, H., Cirrincione, V., DeKaric, S., & Zaidi, H. (Producers), & Sax, G. (Director). (2010). *Frankie & Alice* [Motion Picture]. Canada: CodeBlack Films.

Brand, B. L., Sar, V., Stavropoulos, P., Krüger, C., Korzekwa, M., Martinez-Taoas, A., & Middleton, W. (2017). Separating fact from fiction: An empirical examination of six myths about dissociative identity disorder. *Harvard Review of Psychology, 24*(4), 257–270. doi:10.1097/HRP.0000000000000100

Bromberg, P. M. (2006). *Awakening the dreamer: Clinical journeys.* Mahwah, NJ: Analytic Press.

Capice, P., & Dunne, P. (Producers). (1976). *Sybil.* United States: Lorimar Productions.

Charmaz, K. (2014). *Constructing grounded theory* (2nd ed.). Los Angeles, CA: Sage.

Charon, R. (2009). Narrative medicine as witness for the self-telling body. *Journal of Applied Communication Research, 37*(2), 118–131. doi:10.1080/00909880902792248

Chiu, C., Meng Tseng, M. C., Chien, Y. L., Liaos, S. C., Li, C. M., Yeh, Y., . . . Ross, C. (2017). Dissociative disorders in acute psychiatric inpatients in Taiwan. *Psychiatry Research, 250*, 285–290. doi:10.1016/j.psychres.2017.01.082

Darkness to Light. (2018). Retrieved from https://www.d2l.org/the-issue/

Dissociative Identity Disorder. (2018). Retrieved from: https://www.dissociative-identity-disorder.org

Ellis, C. S. (2007). Telling secrets, revealing lives: Relational ethics in research with intimate others. *Qualitative Inquiry, 13*(1), 3–29. doi:10.1177/1077800406294947

Ellis, C., Adams, T. E., & Bochner, A. P. (2010). Autoethnography: An overview. *Forum Qualitative Sozialforschung/Forum: Qualitative Social Research, 12*(1) Art. 10. Retrieved from http://www.qualitative-research.net/index.php/fqs/article/view/1589/3095

Ellis, C., & Bochner, A. (2000). Autoethnography, personal narrative, reflexivity. In N. K. Denzin & Y. S. Lincoln (Eds.), *Handbook of qualitative research* (pp. 733–768), Thousand Oaks, CA: Sage Publications.

Fine, M. (1994). Working the hyphens: Reinventing self and other in qualitative research. In N. K. Denzin & Y. S. Lincoln (Eds.), *Handbook of qualitative research* (2nd ed., pp. 70–82). Thousand Oaks, CA: Sage Publications.

Fox, J., Bell, H., Jacobson, L., & Hundley, G. (2013). Recovering identity: A qualitative investigation of a survivor of dissociative identity disorder. *Journal of Mental Health Counseling, 35*(4), 324–341. doi:10.17744/mehc.35.4.g715qt65qm281117

Gearhart, S., & Zhang, W. (2018). Same spiral, different day? Testing the spiral of silence across issue types. *Communication Research, 45*(1), 34–54. doi:10.1177/0093650215616465

Gleaves, D. H. (1996). The sociocognitive model of dissociative identity disorder: A reexamination of the evidence. *Psychological Bulletin, 120*(1), 42–59. doi:10.1037/0033-2909.120.1.42

Go, G. (2017). Amnesia and criminal responsibility. *Journal of Law and the Biosciences, 4*(1), 194–204. doi:10.1093/Jlb/lsx003

Goffinet, S. J. L., & Beine, A. (2018). Prevalence of dissociative symptoms in adolescent psychiatric inpatients. *European Journal of Trauma & Dissociation, 2*(1), 39–45. doi:10.1016/j.ejtd.2017.10.008

Gray, R. E., & Sinding, C. (2002). *Standing ovation: Performing social science research about cancer.* Walnut Creek, CA: AltaMira Press.

Harter, L., & Bochner, A. (2009). Healing through stories: A special issue on narrative medicine. *Journal of Applied Communication Research, 37*(2), 113–117. doi:10.1080/00909880902792271

Hirakata, P. E. (2007). *Narratives of dissociation: Insights into the experience and treatment of dissociation in individuals who have been sexually abused in childhood* (Doctoral dissertation). Retrieved from: https://open.library.ubc.ca/cIRcle/collections/ubctheses/831/items/1.0053642

Hornor, G. (2010). Child sexual abuse: Consequences and implications. *Journal of Pediatric Health Care, 24*(6), 358–364. doi:10.1016/j.pedhc.2009.07.003

International Society for the Study of Trauma and Dissociation. (2011). Guidelines for treating Dissociative Identity Disorder in adults (Third Revision). *Journal of Trauma & Dissociation, 12*(2), 115–187. doi:10.1080/15299732.2011.537247

Jacome, D. E. (2001). Transitional interpersonality thunderclap headache. *Headache, 41*(3), 317–320. doi:10.1046/j.1526-4610.2001.111006317.x

Liu, X., & Fahmy, S. (2011). Exploring the spiral of silence in the virtual world: Individuals' willingness to express personal opinions in online versus offline settings. *Journal of Media and Communication Studies, 3*(2), 45–57. Retrieved from http://www.academicjournals.org/jmcs

Malaspina, C. (2013). *The spiral of silence and social media: Analysing Noelle-Neumann's phenomenon application on the web during the Italian political elections of 2013* (Unpublished doctoral dissertation). London School of Economics and Political Science, London, England.

Mankoff, D., Block, P., Marcus, M., & Spaulding, A. (Producers), & Carpenter, J. (Director). (2010). *The ward.* United States: Echo Lake Entertainment.

Manning, J. (2010). There is no agony like bearing an untold story inside you: Communication research as interventive practice. *Communication Monographs, 77*(4), 437–439. doi:10.1080/03637751.2010.520019

Matthes, J., Hayes, A. F., Rohas, H., Shen, F., Seong-Jae, M., & Dylko, I. B. (2012). Exemplifying a dispositional approach to cross-cultural spiral of silence research: Fear of social isolation and the inclination to self-censor. *International Journal of Public Opinion Research, 24*(3), 287–305. doi:10.1093/ijpor/eds015

McGuire, K., & London, K. (2017). Common beliefs about child sexual abuse and disclosure: A college sample. *Journal of Child Sexual Abuse, 26*(2), 175–194. doi: 10.1080/10538712.2017.1281368

McElvaney, R. (2013). Disclosure of child sexual abuse: Delays, non-disclosure and partial disclosure: What the research tells us and implications for practice. *Child Abuse Review, 24*(3), 159–169. doi:10.1002/car.2280

Mienczakowski, J., & Morgan, S. (2001). Ethnodrama: Constructing participatory experiential and compelling action research through performance. In P. Reason &

H. Bradbury (Eds.), *Handbook of action research: Participative inquiry and practice* (pp. 219–227). London, England: Sage.

National Alliance on Mental Illness. (2018). NAMI: National Alliance on Mental Illness. Retrieved from http://NAMI.org

Noelle-Neumann, E. (1974). The spiral of silence: A theory of public opinion. *Journal of Communication, 24*(2), 43–51. doi:10.111/j.1460-2466.1974.tb00367.x

Norval, S. M. (2015). *Altering perceptions of individuals with dissociative identity disorder* (Master's thesis). Retrieved from: https://krex.k-state.edu/dspace/bitstream/handle/2097/19235/SaraNorval2015.pdf?sequence=1&isAllowed=y

Parry, S., Lloyd, M., & Simpson, J. (2018). "It's not like you have PSTD with a touch of dissociation": Understanding dissociative identity disorder through first person accounts. *European Journal of Trauma & Dissociation, 2*(1), 31–38. doi:10.1016/j.ejtd.2017.08.002

Piper, A., & Merskey, H. (2004). The persistence of folly: Critical examination of dissociative identity disorder. Part II. The defense and decline of multiple personality or dissociative identity disorder. *Canadian Journal of Psychiatry, 49*(10), 678–683. doi:10.1177/070674370404901005

Plokar, A., Bisaillon, C., & Terradas, M. M. (2018). Development of the child dissociation assessment system using a narrative story stem task: A preliminary study. *European Journal of Trauma & Dissociation, 2*(1), 21–29. doi:10.1016/j.ejtd.2017.07.004

Richardson, L. (2000). Evaluating ethnography. *Qualitative Inquiry, 6*(2), 255–257. doi:10.1177/107780040000600207

Rossetto, K. R. (2014). Qualitative research interviews: Assessing the therapeutic value and challenges. *Journal of Social and Personal Relationships, 31*(4), 482–489. doi:10.1177/0265407514522892

Rothschild, D. (2009). On becoming one-self: Reflections on the concept of integration as seen through a case of Dissociative Identity Disorder. *Psychoanalytic Dialogues, 19*(2), 175–187. doi:10.1080/10481880902779786

Saldana, J. (Ed.). (2005). *Ethnodrama: An anthology of reality theatre.* Lanham, MD: AltaMira Press.

Sar, V., & Ross, C. (2006). Dissociative disorders as a confounding factor in psychiatric research. *Psychiatric Clinics of North America, 29*(1), 129–144. doi:10.1016/j.psc.2005.10.008

Scheufele, D. A. (2008). Spiral of silence theory. In W. Donsbach & M. W. Traugott (Eds.), *The SAGE handbook of public opinion research* (pp. 175–183). Thousand Oaks, CA: Sage.

Scheufele, D. A., & Moy, P. (2000). Twenty-five years of the spiral of silence: A conceptual review and empirical outlook. *International Journal for Quality in Health Care, 12*(1), 3–28. doi:10.1093/ijpor/12.1.3

Shyamalan, M. N., Blum, J., Bienstock, M. (Producers), & Shyamalan, M. N. (Director). (2016). *Split* [Motion Picture]. United States: Universal Pictures.

Slattery, P., & Rapp, D. (2003). *Ethics and the foundations of education: Teaching convictions in a postmodern world.* Boston, MA: Allyn & Bacon.

Spielberg, S. Cody, D., Junge, A., Frank, D., Falvey, J. & Zisk, C. (Executive Producers). (2009–2011). *The United States of Tara* [Television Series]. United States: DreamWorks Television Showtime Networks.

Stickley, T., & Nickeas, R. (2006). Becoming one person: Living with dissociative identity disorder. *Journal of Psychiatric and Mental Health Nursing, 13*(2), 180–187. doi:10.1111/j.1365-2850.2006.00939.x

Stop the Silence. (2018). Retrieved from https://stopthesilence.org/

Tillmann-Healy, L. M. (2003). Friendship as method. *Qualitative Inquiry, 9*(5), 729–749. doi:10.1177/1077800403254894

Tracy, S. J. (2013). *Qualitative research methods: Collecting evidence, crafting analysis, communicating impact*. Malden, MA: Wiley-Blackwell.

Traub, C. M. (2009). Defending a diagnostic pariah: Validating the categorization of dissociative identity disorder. *South African Journal of Psychology, 39*(3), 347–356. doi:10.1177/008124630903900309

Tuval-Mashiach, R., Patton, B. W., & Drebing, C. (2018). "When you make a movie, and you see your story there, you can hold it": Qualitative exploration of collaborative filmmaking as a theraputic tool for veterans. *Frontiers in Psychology, 9*, 19–54. doi:10.3389/fpsyg.2018.01954

van der Hart, O., Nijenhuis, E., & Steele, K. (2006). *The haunted self: Structural dissociation and the treatment of chronic traumatization*. New York, NY: W.W. Norton & Company.

Chapter Six

Testing a Social Aggression and Translational Storytelling Intervention

The Impact of Communicated Narrative Sense-Making on Adolescent Girls' Mental Health

Erin K. Willer

Jody Koenig Kellas

INTRODUCTION

The experience of social aggression, including behaviors such as malicious gossip, rumor spreading, and exclusion, can be distressing, particularly for girls (e.g., Paquette & Underwood, 1999). Young females face challenges making sense of their experiences with relational aggression (Miller-Ott & Kelly, 2013) and report related mental and physical health challenges. For example, Crick and Bigbee (1998) determined that aggression victims were significantly more maladjusted than their non-victim peers in that victims were less accepted, more rejected, lonelier, and suffered more emotional distress than non-victims. Further, Crick and Grotpeter (1995) found that being a target of aggression was significantly related to social-psychological distress, including depression, social anxiety, social avoidance, and loneliness. Social aggression also has been shown to be related to affective and emotional outcomes including sadness, hurt, embarrassment, anger, guilt, shame, and jealousy (e.g., Owens, Shute, & Slee, 2000; Willer & Cupach, 2008; Willer & Soliz, 2010).

Despite these mental health and affective correlates, parents and teachers interested in supporting girl victims of social aggression face challenges. Existing lay advice is not always theoretically grounded or empirically tested and, therefore, may be ineffective or more harmful for girls than it is helpful (Geiger, Zimmer-Gembeck, & Crick, 2004; Willer & Cupach, 2011).

Studies that are grounded in theory and research are often designed to reduce aggressive behaviors through prosocial competency education (e.g., Boyle & Hassett-Walker, 2008; Cappella & Weinstein, 2006; Leff, Goldstein, Angelucci, Cardaciotto, & Grossman, 2007; Dellasega & Adamshick, 2005; Ostrov et al., 2009; Van Schoiack-Edstrom, Frey, & Beland, 2002). Although these types of programs indeed are promising (see Leff, Waasdorp, & Crick, 2010 for a review), extant research has not addressed the mental health symptoms associated with targets' experiences of social aggression (Safran & Safran, 2008; Willer & Cupach, 2011).

In order to address these limitations, the current study tested a communication-based intervention method designed to be accessible to parents and teachers. The intervention is grounded in Communicated Narrative Sense-Making Theory (CNSM) (Koenig Kellas, 2018; Koenig Kellas & Kranstuber Horstman, 2015), and aimed to reduce adolescent girls' negative affective and mental health symptoms associated with experiences of social aggression. Research and practice indicate that telling and retelling narratives about difficult or traumatic experiences facilitate communicative coping in ways that help people shape new and hopeful storylines (e.g., Pennebaker, 1997a; Sunwolf, Frey, & Keränen, 2005; White, 2007). Therefore, the following section provides an overview highlighting why a narrative intervention was a viable option for reducing social aggression's associated negative mental health and affective consequences.

NARRATIVE SENSE-MAKING AS A MEANS OF COPING

As Fisher (1989) argues, unlike other forms of rationality that are restricted to experts, narrative is accessible to all humans. Thus, narrative theories and methods are particularly well suited to interventions that might be applied beyond clinical contexts. A central assumption of narrative theorizing is because life is complicated, individuals find ways to explain it in more coherent terms. Such explanation occurs as people interpret their experiences in the form of stories that help them make sense of the diverse events that constitute their lives (e.g., Bruner, 1991; Fisher, 1984, 1985). CNSM Theory (Koenig Kellas, 2018; Koenig Kellas & Kranstuber Horstman, 2015) asserts that storytelling is one of the primary ways one makes sense of difficulty and identity and examines the links between storytelling content, process, and psychosocial well-being. CNSM is organized around three heurisitcs. The first, retrospective storytelling, focuses primarily on storytelling content and the ways in which the stories one hears and tell have a lasting impact in ways that affect and reflect individual and relational health. The second, interactional storytelling, centers research on the verbal and nonverbal communication processes that animate narrative sense-making. The third heuristic, translational storytelling, orients research toward the ways in which narrative theories, methods, and empirical results can be used to design and/ or inform interventions geared toward improving the health and well-being of certain populations.

The current study is situated within the translational storytelling heuristic of CNSM. According to Koenig Kellas (2018), "CNSM provides an orientation to storytelling research that can—and most often does—include the utilization of other theoretical orientations" because CNSM research and other theories

> provide evidence for the benefits of storytelling content and process across a variety of contexts [and] translational storytelling research marshals this evidence to create and test narratively-based interventions designed to improve the quality of communication and quality of lives of individuals and families coping with difficulty, trauma, illness, and stress (pp. 68–69).

In line with the theory, we draw from research on narrative health communication (see Harter, Japp, & Beck, 2005b for a review), narrative psychology (see McAdams, 1993; Pennebaker, 1997a for reviews) and narrative therapy (see White, 2007 for a review) to design and test an intervention to examine how individuals experiencing stress, such as social aggression, may use stories or narratives to decrease negative health outcomes. Specifically, we synthesized research and practice from the expressive writing paradigm (see Frattaroli, 2006), narrative (e.g., White, 2007), art-based therapies (e.g., Malchiodi, 2003), and research on narrative tone (e.g., McAdams, Reynolds, Lewis, & Bowman, 2001) to design an intervention appropriate for adolescent girls' sense-making of social aggression.

EXPRESSIVE WRITING PARADIGM

Research grounded in Pennebaker's Expressive Writing Paradigm (Pennebaker, 1997a) indicates that emotional disclosure about traumatic experiences allows individuals to experience catharsis (Frattaroli, 2006; Pennebaker, 1993), whereas rumination contributes to ongoing negative thoughts and feelings (Pennebaker & Seagal, 1999). In other words, inhibition is psychologically and physiologically taxing on health, but writing about a traumatic experience may reduce the inhibition required to keep traumatic episodes secret (Pennebaker, 1997b; Pennebaker, Colder, & Sharp, 1990). Emotional disclosure also allows people to make sense of, organize, and integrate the experience into their self-schema and allows them to engage in self-regulation as they observe themselves expressing, controlling, and mastering their stress (Frattaroli, 2006).

Numerous studies provide support that writing about stressful experiences predicts positive mental and physical health outcomes over time, particularly for adult samples (e.g., Lyubomirsky, Sousa, & Dickerhoof, 2006; Murray & Segal, 1994; Pennebaker et al., 1990; Pennebaker, Kiecolt-Glaser, & Glaser, 1988). Results are mixed, however, in relation to the beneficial impact of this method on children and adolescents (e.g., Reynolds, Brewin, & Saxton, 2000; Soliday, Garofalo, & Rogers, 2004; Warner et al., 2006). Given the overall benefits, the expressive writing method presented a theoretically and empirically useful approach to facilitating coping in the current study. Yet given the inconsistency in reported benefits for younger populations, the narrative writing approach warranted revision. First, the expressive writing technique was modified based on narrative health communication practices that focus on the interpersonal process of storysharing (Sunwolf et al., 2005). Second, the benefits of the narrative writing method was enhanced for adolescent girls by supplementing it with the narrative therapy principle of externalization (White & Epston, 1990) and with the personal myth concept of the redemption sequence (McAdams, Diamond, de St. Aubin, & Mansfield, 1997).

STORYSHARING

Although most expressive writing studies tested the effects of writing about traumatic experiences, a few studies determined that writing and talking into a tape recorder have similar effects (Lyubomirsky et al., 2006; Murray & Segal, 1994). In an interpersonal communication extension of the expressive writing paradigm, Koenig Kellas, Kranstuber Horstman, Willer, and Carr (2015) found that friends who told stories of stress experienced significantly lower levels of negative affect over time in comparison with control group participants. Moreover, Fivush, Marin, and Crawford (2007) suggested that co-constructing narratives with an adult who can provide specific directions for how to engage in sense-making might prove to be more beneficial for younger samples who may lack the analytic skills necessary to engage in productive written sense-making. Indeed, Pennebaker and Graybeal (2001) suggested that the goal of a narrative approach is not simply to reduce negative outcomes via writing, but to aid interpersonal communication. Storysharing, additionally, can be functional for those telling stories of difficulty, as the process serves to connect the teller and listener, as well as serving as a way for the teller to explain, create a reality, remember, and forecast their future (Sunwolf et al., 2005).

Based on principles from the expressive writing paradigm and research on narrative health communication, the intervention tested in the present study was based on the notion that, for adolescent girls, the process of interpersonal storysharing likely facilitates health benefits. Although previous efforts indicate that storysharing is beneficial, more research is needed on how telling stories will lead to mental health benefits. CNSM Theory (Koenig Kellas, 2018) proposes that stories that are framed positively should lead to greater levels of well-being than those framed negatively (Proposition 2). This theorizing is based in research and practices growing out of narrative therapy and narrative psychology. Therefore, the present study modified the expressive writing paradigm by using these narrative principles.

Narrative Therapy and Externalization

For children experiencing trauma, constructing life stories and using words to describe how they feel can be difficult (e.g., Harter, 2009; McAdams, 1993). In addition, girls who seek therapy often emphasize negative self-stories. Therapists, therefore, help clients construct alternative stories that run counter to the ones that are self-recriminating. Narrative therapists do so through a process called externalization, which is a way of allowing clients to make sense out of emotionally complicated relational phenomena by re-casting problems as external to the self (e.g., White, 2007). Therapists use externalization to help clients view the problem as the problem rather than the person as the problem (White, 2007; White & Epston, 1990).

Drawing externalizing metaphors is an externalization technique from the narrative therapist's multifaceted process that may be particularly useful for parents and teachers in facilitating coping in an adolescent population. Lakoff and Johnson (1980) contend that metaphors compare unlike things in order to better understand or know entities, and metaphors allow individuals to communicate about themselves and their experiences when they may not be able to do so analytically or literally (Marshak, 1996). In addition to verbalizing metaphors, Riley and Malchiodi (2003) suggest that drawing metaphors, especially for children who do not have the capacity to communicate details, is a natural way of separating the problem from the person, because doing so allows the problem to become visible. Because of this, narrative therapists use art therapies to aid in sense-making and storytelling (Malchiodi, 2003).

Researchers and narrative therapists have used art and metaphor to aid children in communicating about difficult life events. For example, children in Willer et al.'s (2018) study drew pictures capturing their experiences with the death of a baby in their families. Traumatically bereaved young people who were impacted by September 11 constructed metaphors such as "the surprise," "the burnt marshmallow," and "the cheeseburger" (i.e., "it was messy") in order to make sense of the attacks on the Twin Towers (Haen, 2005). Creative methods allow young people to make sense of emotional and anomalous events in a manner that is relevant to their everyday lives. Thus, the intervention tested in the present study was grounded in the idea that a narrative drawing approach would be useful in helping girls make sense of social aggression. In addition to including storysharing and externalizing metaphors, the present study was based on the possibility that adolescent girls also may benefit from the principle of narrative reframing.

Redemptive Framing

Life-story research (McAdams, 1993) is grounded in the idea that individuals seek to construct integrative personal myths of the self as a means of providing semblance and purpose to their lives. McAdams and his colleagues collected and coded participants' stories for themes and the manner in which they framed their story details. Some individuals framed their experiences in terms of redemption sequences, wherein "decidedly bad events are subsequently redeemed or made better, resulting in good outcomes" (McAdams et al., 1997, p. 684, e.g., a painful delivery led to the birth of a beautiful baby).

Such narrative framing consistently has been linked with individual and relational well-being (e.g., Koenig Kellas, 2005; Vangelisti, Crumley, & Baker, 1999). Research suggests that redemption sequences are positively correlated with life satisfaction, life coherence, and self-esteem, and negatively correlated with depression (McAdams et al., 2001). King and Miner (2000) similarly found that individuals who wrote about the perceived benefits of traumatic events experienced the same increased health benefits as those who wrote about trauma, including fewer visits to the health center, in comparison with participants in a control group. Thus, the intervention tested in the present study was designed based on the reasoning that telling a story of social aggression and drawing a redemption metaphor would facilitate productive meaning-making about social aggression, and therefore would help to increase girls' mental well-being.

To summarize, social aggression often impacts adolescent girls' mental health. CNSM Theory (Koenig Kellas, 2018) suggests that storytelling, externalizing, and reframing difficulty, such as social aggression, should ameliorate its negative effects. Thus, the current study, grounded itself in CNSM Theory's translational storytelling heuristic to test its Proposition 6 (Interventions that promote narrative reflection and sense-making benefit participants in the context of difficulty, trauma, illness, and/or stress) and its Proposition 7 (Interventions that incorporate (a) positive narrative (re)framing techniques . . . will result in benefits for individuals and families in the context of difficulty, trauma, illness, and/or stress) through a multi-step intervention designed to facilitate mental well-being related to adolescent girls' experiences with social aggression. Specifically, we hypothesized:

> H: Girls who participate in a communicated narrative sense-making intervention will demonstrate decreases in negative mental health symptoms and negative affect over a nine-week period.

METHOD

Sampling and Recruitment

The intervention targeted sixth-, seventh-, and eighth-grade girls given that research suggests that the greatest prevalence of social aggression occurs during the middle school years with a decline occurring during high school (Espelage & Swearer, 2003). After receiving Institutional Review Board approval, eleven middle school principals were recruited and six agreed to allow their students to be solicited for participation in the present study.

Before beginning participant recruitment, and in order to determine the number of participants necessary to detect statistical significance, a power analysis was conducted based on Frattaroli's (2006) meta-analysis of 146 studies on expressive writing. The power analysis was run using G*Power (Erdfelder, Faul, & Buchner, 1996) and revealed that thirty-nine participants were needed to obtain a moderate η^2-effect size of .06 (Cohen, 1988) when conducting a repeated measures multivariate analysis of variance (MANOVA). Thus, the recruitment goal of the present study was to obtain at least thirty-nine volunteers in order to guarantee an adequate amount of power to conduct the analysis.

Participant recruitment at each of the six schools included several strategies, such as having teachers read the details of the study to students during daily announcements, posting the study details for parents to read on the school's website, sending consent and assent forms home with report cards, setting up an informational table during an afterschool talent show, and announcing the study to groups of female students. Based on an IRB recommendation, in order to protect potential participants from the risk of identifying as victims of social aggression, recruitment was directed toward all girls in the sixth, seventh, and eighth grades of the schools.

Participants

Participants were girls from six middle schools in a medium-sized Midwestern city and included forty sixth- (n = 24, 60.00%), seventh- (n = 5, 12.50%), and eighth- (n = 11, 27.5%) graders who ranged in age from eleven to fifteen years (M = 12.18, SD = .98). Participant ethnicities included African American (n = 6, 15.00%), Asian American/Pacific Islander (n = 2, 5.00%), Caucasian American (n = 25, 62.50%), Latino/Hispanic (n = 2, 5.00%), Native American (n = 2, 5.00%), and Other (n = 3, 7.50%).

Procedures

Drawing from the expressive writing paradigm (Pennebaker & Seagal, 1999), the intervention took place over the course of nine weeks, including four meetings with the first author. As one of the goals of the present study was to test a method that would be accessible to parents and teachers, the first author did not have clinical therapeutic training.

Time 1

Building on expressive writing methods (Pennebaker, 1997a), the purpose of the first session was to engage each participant in communicated sense-making about an experience with social aggression, including telling the story of a socially aggressive episode and having it heard. At the beginning of the session, each participant completed a questionnaire comprised of demographic information, including race/ethnicity, age, and grade. Each participant also completed a pre-test measure of mental health (Dornbusch, Mont-Reynaud, Ritter, Chen, & Steinberg, 1991), which was administered at the beginning of the session to avoid treatment effects.

Next, the participant answered a few interview questions designed to get her thinking about communication among adolescent girls and social aggression in particular. In line with Willer and Cupach (2008), when referring to the socially aggressive episode, the terms *mean* and *hurtful* were used, given the terms are more colloquial and accessible to adolescents than the concept termed *social aggression*. The participant then was asked to think of a time during middle school when another girl did something that was a) mean or hurtful to her and/or her relationship with others, b) that was still bothersome to her at the present time, and c) that she would not mind exploring during the four study sessions. In order to avoid treatment effects, once the participant identified an instance of meanness and prior to telling her story, she completed a measure of negative affect (Watson, Clark, & Tellegen, 1988; Willer & Cupach, 2008) pertaining to the socially aggressive experience. Finally, the primary investigator asked her to tell the story of the episode of social aggression, including who was involved, where they were, why it happened, and how she felt as a result. The story was audio recorded. Each of the first sessions lasted approximately thirty minutes.

Time 2

The purpose of the second session not only was to allow the participant to continue to engage in communicated sense-making about her identified experience with social aggression, but also to harness the principles of narrative therapy (White, 2007) and allow her to externalize her feelings by drawing a metaphor. The primary investigator first reminded the participant of the story described during the first session and then read an explanation of the drawing activity, as well as a definition and example of a metaphor. Specifically, the participant was told that "a metaphor compares two things that are both similar and different," such as in the example, "Love is like a warm blanket." The participant then was told that she should draw a picture to illustrate what her own experience with meanness felt like to her. Examples were provided, but to avoid influencing the participant's own drawing and causing a threat to internal validity, these were examples of what niceness, as opposed to meanness, might look and feel like (e.g., "a cat licking her kitten").

In order to be consistent with the process of narrative externalization, the participant was told that "your metaphor should be something outside you and outside of the girl(s) who did the mean thing . . . and you should avoid drawing real life representations of where you were and what happened." The participant also was instructed that her metaphor should represent "what meanness feels like" (e.g., "niceness might look and feel like a fuzzy cotton ball"). Finally, the participant was encouraged to use colors to exemplify her feelings (Malchiodi, 1998; Freeman, Ebston, & Lobovits, 1997). After asking if the participant had any questions about what she was being instructed to do, the first author gave her a piece of paper and drawing tools, as well as time and the personal and physical space necessary to draw her metaphor. The metaphors ranged in theme and included those representing rejection (e.g., a girl sitting alone in a corner of a room), negative forces of nature (e.g., clouds and lightning), physical attacks (e.g., a piece of meat with a knife stabbing it), and physical/emotional responses (e.g., tears) (see Willer, 2011; Willer, 2012).

Once the participant indicated that she had completed her drawing, she was asked to explain her metaphor, including why she chose the images and the colors she did, and why it represented her experience with meanness and how it felt to her. Post-treatment, the participant again completed measures of mental health symptoms and negative affect. These sessions lasted approximately thirty to forty minutes.

Time 3

The purpose of the third session, which occurred one week after Time 2, was to have the participant engage in communicated and productive sensemaking by reframing the socially aggressive episode through the drawing of and communication about a redemption metaphor (McAdams et al., 1997). The meeting began with a reminder of the socially aggressive episode that she previously explored during the first two sessions. In order to facilitate the participant's reframing of the socially aggressive episode as one of redemption (McAdams et al., 2001), the primary investigator explained the following:

> When bad things happen to us, we usually focus on the negative, such as how sad we are or how angry we are. We tend to forget that even though we feel those bad emotions, there also might be some positive things that come out of the negative situation. So that is what you are going to try to do today; you are going to draw a metaphor of something positive that came out of your negative experience with meanness. But, that doesn't mean that we are going to forget about the negative things because feeling sad and angry, especially when girls are mean, is a healthy and natural way to feel. So for today we are not going to throw those things in the garbage, we are just going to set them aside for a while.

The participant then was offered examples of how something that typically is perceived negatively could be viewed positively (e.g., gaining strength from having to go through the death of the family dog). To illustrate how someone might draw this strength, the participant was told that someone could draw a girl flexing her arm muscle. Before the participant began drawing, she again was encouraged to use colors to represent her feelings. Next, the participant asked any questions about what she was expected to do and then had time and space necessary to complete her drawing. In a separate investigation relating to the use of redemption narratives, Willer (2012) determined that the participants' redemption metaphors represented four themes, including personal growth (e.g., a caution sign), relational growth (e.g., two people holding hands), termination of the relationship with the perpetrator (e.g., two girls going in different directions), and getting revenge against the perpetrator (e.g., devil and angel) (see Willer, 2011, 2012).

Once the participant was finished, she explained her metaphor drawing to the primary investigator and detailed why it represented the way she felt about her experience with meanness, as well as the good things that came out of the event. After the participant was finished with her explanation, she completed the post-test measures of mental health and negative affect. This third meeting lasted approximately thirty minutes for each participant and concluded the treatment process.

Time 4

The purpose of the fourth and final session was to test the impact of the three treatment sessions over time on negative mental health symptoms and negative affect. Given that narrative writing research suggests that outcome scores immediately following treatment tend to reveal increases in negative outcomes, but that scores on negative outcomes tend to decrease over time (Pennebaker & Seagal, 1999), the fourth session was scheduled six weeks after Time 3 (i.e., during week nine) (see Frattaroli, 2006 for a review of similar methods). During this final session the participant completed the post-test measures of negative health symptoms and negative affect, was debriefed, and asked to provide the first author with feedback on the study. The fourth meeting lasted approximately twenty minutes.

Measures

The pre- and post-test measures described above included the Negative Mental Health Symptoms Inventory (Dornbusch et al., 1991) and a modified version of the Negative Affect Schedule (Watson et al., 1988; Willer & Cupach, 2008). The negative mental health symptoms instrument is comprised of nine items that ask participants to report the extent to which they have experienced a number of different symptoms, including anxiety and depression. Instructions were modified such that each time participants filled out the measure, they were asked how often they experienced the feelings during the last week (as opposed to the last month). The nine items include statements such as "felt nervous or worried," "felt 'low' or depressed," and "felt apart and alone" and were measured on a scale from never (0), once (1), twice (2), to three or more times (3), such that higher scores indicated more negative mental health symptoms. The reliability of the scale had been established in previous studies with adolescents (e.g., Buchanan, Maccoby, & Dornbusch, 1991, α = .83).

Participants also completed a measure of negative affect in relation to the socially aggressive event. The scale used in the present study was a 13-item measure based on Watson et al.'s (1988) Negative Affect Schedule, which was employed in Willer and Cupach's (2008) study on social aggression among girls. The measure asks participants to rate on a five-point Likert-type scale how they currently felt about the socially aggressive experience (1 = very slightly to not at all, 5 = extremely). Samples of Watson et al.'s original ten items include "distressed," "upset," and "guilty." Willer and Cupach (2008) added three items including, "angry," "hurt," and "embarrassed." In the present study, higher scores indicated a greater degree of negative affect. This measure has produced reliable results with adolescent girls reporting on their experiences with social aggression (i.e., Willer & Cupach, α = .85).

Alpha reliabilities, means, standard deviations, and intercorrelations are presented in Table 6.1.

Table 6.1.   Means, Standard Deviations, Alpha Reliabilities, and Intercorrelations for Outcome Variables

Variables		Time 1	Time 2	Time 3	Time 4
Negative Mental Health Symptoms	M (SD)	1.11 (.70)	1.02 (.65)	.88 (.71)	.96 (.68)
	a	.83	.80	.86	.84
	Intercorrelation with Negative Affect	.51**	.60**	.65**	.57**
Negative Affect	M (SD)	2.21 (.73)	1.87 (.62)	1.78 (.66)	1.78 (.66)
	a	.84	.80	.84	.89

Note. Negative Mental Health Symptoms were measured on a scale of 0 to 3 and Negative Affect was measured on a scale of 1 to 5. ** $p < .01$.

RESULTS

The hypothesis guiding the present study predicted that participants would report decreases in negative mental health symptoms and negative affect over time as a result of the study treatments. A within-subjects repeated-measures MANOVA was conducted with time as the independent variable, and negative mental health symptoms and negative affect as the dependent variables. The analysis showed a significant multivariate within-subjects treatment effect, Wilks's $\Lambda = .07$, $F(5, 35) = 3.67$, $p < .01$, $\eta^2 = .34$.

Follow-up analyses of variances (ANOVAs) were run for mental health and negative affect, respectively, in order to assess the nature of differences identified by the MANOVA main effect. Using the Bonferoni method, each ANOVA was tested at the .05 divided by two, or .025 level (Green & Salkind, 2004). The first ANOVA revealed a trend for the reduction in negative mental health symptoms, Huynh-Feldt $F(2.23, 88.38) = 2.97$, $p = .05$, $\eta^2 = .07$. Follow-up pairwise comparisons were run on all possible combinations (i.e., Time 1–Time 2, Time 1–Time 3, Time 1–Time 4, Time 2–Time 3, Time 2–Time 4, Time 3–Time 4). Across the six comparisons and consistent with the Bonferroni method, each was tested at the .025 divided by 6 or .004 level (Green & Salkind, 2004). One of the pairwise comparisons was significant; participants reported significantly more negative mental health symptoms at Time 1 ($M = 1.11$, $SD = .70$) than at Time 3 ($M = .88$, $SD = .71$), $t(39) = 3.09$, $p = .004$, $\eta^2 = .20$.

The ANOVA on negative affect was significant, Huynh-Feldt $F(1.98, 77.39) = 10.48$, $p < .001$, $\eta^2 = 21$. Given the significant omnibus effect, post hoc independent samples t-tests were conducted for all possible pairwise comparisons. Three of the six pairwise comparisons were significant at the .004 level. Specifically, negative affect at Time 1 (M = 2.21, SD = .73) was significantly higher than negative affect at all three other times—Time 2 (M = 1.86, SD = .62), $t(39) = 3.32$, $p = .002$, $\eta^2 = .22$, Time 3 (M = 1.78, SD = .66), $t(39) = 4.07$, $p < .001$, $\eta^2 = .30$, and Time 4 (M = 1.78, SD = .66), $t(39) = 4.07$, $p < .001$, $\eta^2 = .30$. The hypothesis received partial support.

DISCUSSION

Grounded in the translational storytelling heuristic of CNSM Theory (Koenig Kellas, 2018), the current study set out to empirically test an interpersonal communication intervention with adolescent girls designed to be accessible to parents and teachers and to reduce the negative mental health correlates of social aggression. The hypothesis guiding the present study suggested that over a nine-week period, middle school girls would report decreases in negative mental health symptoms and negative affect. The results of the present study provided partial support for this prediction and, therefore, Propositions 6 and 7 of CNSM Theory. Girls experienced significant reductions in negative mental health symptoms at Time 3 after completing all three treatments in comparison with pre-treatment baseline scores at Time 1. In comparison to scores at Time 1, negative affect also decreased significantly after drawing and explaining the externalizing metaphor during Time 2, after drawing and explaining the redemption metaphor at Time 3, and six weeks post-intervention at Time 4. In light of these findings, we present theoretical and practical implications, as well as limitations that provide avenues for future research.

Practical and Theoretical Implications

Based on previous narrative research, CNSM Theory (Koenig Kellas, 2018) proposes that interventions that promote narrative reflection and sense-making benefit participants in the context of difficulty, trauma, illness, and/or stress (proposition 6) and that interventions promoting positive narrative (re) framing should be especially robust in producing these benefits (proposition 7). The current study facilitated an intervention that both promoted narrative reflection, communicated sense-making, and narrative reframing. Therefore, we expected support for the study's hypotheses. Yet this was the first study we know of to test these principles and techniques in combination.

Specifically, the current study employed the principles of storysharing (Sunwolf et al., 2005) and communicated narrative sense-making (i.e., the importance of storytelling, Koenig Kellas & Kranstuber Horstman, 2015) to supplement the methods employed within the expressive writing paradigm (e.g., Pennebaker, 1997a). We also employed art-based techniques (Malchiodi, 2003), including drawing metaphors (Riley & Malchiodi, 2003), in order to facilitate externalizing practices from narrative therapy (i.e., making the problem the problem instead of the person, White, 2007). Finally, we asked girls to reframe their metaphors about meanness based on research in narrative psychology (e.g., McAdams et al., 2001) and communication (e.g., Kranstuber Horstman et al., 2016), that shows links between narrative tone and individual well-being and communicated sense-making.

Combining these approaches resulted in health benefits for the girls in our study. Through storysharing and externalizing, girls may be able to narratively make sense of and purge their ruminative thoughts about their experiences with social aggression and feel as if they have control over what occurred. Through the process of drawing an externalizing metaphor, and therefore, establishing distance from social aggression, girls may (re)frame meanness and gain a sense of personal agency (Freeman et al., 1997). In addition, fashioning redemption metaphors by focusing on the positive that comes out of negative experiences with social aggression (McAdams et al., 1997) may allow participants to "interpret past difficulties and challenges in such a way as to conclude that good things can come from very bad events in one's life" (McAdams et al., 2001, p. 483). During sense-making about social aggression, when "bad scenes . . . precede and eventually give birth to good" (McAdams et al., 1997, p. 687), girls may be reminded that there are indeed benefits to adversity.

Previous research within the realm of narrative identity and the literature on post-traumatic growth supports the proposition that redemptive storytelling enables resilience, including improvements in health and well-being. For example, Martino and Freda (2016) found more redemption sequences in narratives of cancer patients who demonstrated higher levels of post-traumatic growth (i.e., a positive self, relationship, and life transformation following trauma). Jirek (2017) found that "trauma-related therapy, writing, informal conversations, and self-reflection played important roles in the narrative reconstruction process" (p. 166) and that coherent stories about trauma were also related to higher levels of post-traumatic growth. Thus, offering girls multiple and multi-faceted opportunities to interpersonally tell and positively reframe their stories following difficulty is an important step in helping them cope with social aggression.

Whereas externalization and redemptive framing likely impacted girls' perceptions of their well-being in the present study, the manner in which they communicated—both by drawing and storysharing with the first author—may have predicted decreases in mental health symptoms and negative affect as well. In other words, the current study adds to existing literature by including art-based methods known to promote well-being (Willer, 2011) and interpersonal storytelling or communicated narrative sense-making (Koenig Kellas & Kranstuber Horstman, 2015) as important additions to the methods employed in psychological research. Drawing metaphors as a means of representing their feelings may allow girls not only to make sense of the complexities inherent in their experience of social aggression, but also to process the myriad emotions that they feel as a result of being victimized. For children, using words to describe how they feel can be difficult (Haen, 2005; Malchiodi, 2003), and those who are traumatized can lose language altogether (Haen, 2005). Through drawing and metaphor girls can communicate their feelings about social aggression (Malchiodi, 2003) and their drawings, therefore, may serve as a conduit through which their oral sense-making can emerge.

In addition, participants in the present study may have reported increases in well-being over time as a result of interpersonally communicating about their experience with social aggression with an adult rather than engaging in emotional disclosure on their own in writing (e.g., Fivush et al., 2007). This lends further support to Koenig Kellas et al.'s (2015) findings that interpersonally telling stories (i.e., communicated narrative sense-making) and talking about stress leads to mental health benefits for tellers over time. Given the difficulty young people may experience processing their emotions, parents and teachers can employ the easily accessible methods used in the current study with their children and students. This process may support Freeman et al.'s (1997) assertion that, "Children take strands of adult input and weave them into . . . storytelling. Adult[s] . . . provide a trellis on which children's imaginations and narratives flourish like vines" (p. 7).

In sum, the process of expressing—through storysharing and drawing, externalizing, and narratively reframing—social aggression seemed to have impacted girls in significant ways, thereby providing initial support for the possible efficacy of implementing these narrative coping tools in the current context. It also supports the synthesis of narrative theories, methods, and empirical findings into interventions as advocated by the translational storytelling heuristic of CNSM Theory. Additional research is needed on the combination of such practices on individual and relational health, but the current study evidences the benefits of their implementation for adolescent girls coping with social aggression.

Limitations and Directions for Future Research

Given that the goal of emotional disclosure studies such as the one tested in the present investigation is to determine the impact of ecologically valid sense-making over time, a quasi-experimental design was an appropriate first step. However, there are a number of factors that make determining treatment effects difficult. For example, there was not a control group in the present study. Control groups could include participants who simply talk about their experiences with social aggression or those who talk about daily activities, for example (e.g., Pennebaker et al., 1988).

In the present study, we chose to supplement the expressive writing paradigm with multiple narrative means in an effort to design an intervention that not only would help girls cope with social aggression, but also would address a number of limitations in previous research and methods. Such theoretical complexity is a strength of the current design, but also limits the extent to which determining treatment effects is viable. Comparison groups should verify the effects of storysharing, metaphor, externalization, and reframing alone and in combination to see if certain aspects of treatment are more beneficial than others and/or if the effect is cumulative.

An inability to tightly control participation criteria also posed threats to the interpretation of current findings. The study was open to all female students as opposed to those who frequently were victimized and suffered considerably as a result of their experience with social aggression. Although this precaution was in line with previous research and was necessary in order to prevent the risk of social stigma and/or revictimization, all participants were not equal in relation to the degree to which they were victims or the degree to which they were experiencing distress. Some participants described instances of social aggression that were clearly ongoing and repeated (i.e., bullying), whereas others described events that were singular and only mildly bothersome to them. In one expressive writing study, adolescents who suffered the most also benefited the most from emotional disclosure (Warner et al., 2006). Thus, future studies that can control for these factors, while at the same time keeping participants safe from harm (e.g., in therapeutic settings or outside school), should be conducted to determine who benefits the most from the sense-making methods tested in the present study.

We chose to use the Dornbusch et al. (1991) general measure of mental health symptoms because it previously had been established as reliable with adolescents (Buchanan et al., 1991). Additionally, the measure's brevity was desirable given participants completed several measures, including those detailed in the present study and others. Nonetheless, given that mental health symptoms such as anxiety and depression may present differently, future studies should measure such constructs separately.

One of the ultimate goals of the study was to test an intervention that adults, such as teachers and parents, easily could use. Because the first author is not a licensed counselor or therapist, it is likely that with minimal training others can facilitate the intervention in a manner that elicits the benefits derived in the present study. Future research should be conducted in order to support this prediction. A control group could include participants' parents or teachers as facilitators of the intervention methods. Moreover, it will be important for future studies to examine the impact of listening behaviors on emotional disclosure given that not all people listen in a manner that is likely to benefit those disclosing distressful information (e.g., Koenig Kellas, Baker, Minniear, Cardwell, & Horstman, 2018). In other words, it may not be who facilitates the intervention but how they do so that helps girls cope most effectively with social aggression.

Additional populations also should be considered in future research. Although the present study focused on girls in particular, boys, too, experience social aggression and, therefore, are in need of effective strategies to help them cope with its effects. Two meta-analyses on the treatment effects of expressive writing indicated conflicting results on benefits by gender (see Frattaroli, 2006; Smyth, 1998). Thus, future research should test for these potential differences to assess whether or not individualized interventions are needed for girls and boys.

Race, ethnicity, and group membership (e.g., cliques) also can play a role in social aggression. One participant in the present study indicated that she experienced social aggression as a result of her racial identity. Previous expressive writing research has indicated that participants who write about being members of stigmatized groups experienced increases in identity specific collective self-esteem and improved self-reported health (Sexton & Pennebaker, 1997). Thus, future samples should include girls who experience social aggression as a result of their stigmatized identity, such as race, in an effort to address well-being, as well as outcomes such as collective self-esteem.

In sum, girls who are targets of social aggression often experience emotional and mental health bruises. These tend to be the result of girls' ruminative and unproductive cognitive framing about themselves, perpetrators, and their experiences with social aggression. Unfortunately, both targets and the adults in their lives seldom have the necessary tools to help girls productively communicate about, and therefore, cope with the emotional distress that often accompanies victimization. The intervention tested in the present study, however, provides support for CNSM Theory and hope for improving adolescent girls' mental health in the context of social aggression.

REFERENCES

Boyle, D., & Hassett-Walker, C. (2008). Reducing overt and relational aggression among young children: The results from a two-year outcome evaluation. *Journal of School Violence, 7*(1), 27–42. doi: 10.1300/J202v07n01_03

Bruner, J. S. (1991). The narrative construction of reality. *Critical Inquiry, 18*(1), 1–21. doi: 10.1086/448619

Buchanan, C. M., Maccoby, E. E., & Dornbusch, S. M. (1991). Caught between parents: Adolescents' experience in divorced homes. *Child Development, 62*(3), 1008–1029. doi: 10.1111/j.1467-8624.1991.tb01586.x

Cappella, E., & Weinstein, R. (2006). The prevention of social aggression among girls. *Social Development, 15*(3), 434–462. doi: 10.1111/j.1467-9507.2006.00350.x

Cohen, J. (1988). *Statistical power analysis for the behavioral sciences* (2nd ed.). Hillsdale, NJ: Lawrence Earlbaum.

Crick, N. R., & Bigbee, M. A. (1998). Relational and overt forms of peer victimization: A multi-informant approach. *Journal of Consulting and Clinical Psychology, 66*(2), 337–347. doi: 10.1037/0022-006X.66.2.337

Crick, N. R., & Grotpeter, J. K. (1995). Relational aggression, gender, and social-psychological adjustment. *Child Development, 66*(3), 710–722. doi: 10.1111/j.1467-8624.1995.tb00900.x

Dellasega, C., & Adamshick, P. (2005). Evaluation of a program designed to reduce relational aggression in middle school girls. *Journal of School Violence, 4*(3), 63–76. doi: 10.1300/J202v04n03_06

Dornbusch, S. M., Mont-Reynaud, R., Ritter, P. L., Chen, Z., & Steinberg, L. (1991). Stressful events and their correlates among adolescents of diverse backgrounds. In M. E. Colten & S. Gore (Eds.), *Adolescent stress: Causes and consequences* (pp. 111–130). New York, NY: Erlbaum.

Erdfelder, E., Faul, F., & Buchner, A. (1996). GPOWER: A general power analysis program. *Behavior Research Methods, Instruments, & Computers, 28*(1), 1–11. Retrieved from http://www.psychonomic.org/index.html

Espelage, D. L., & Swearer, S. M. (2003). Research on school bullying and victimization: What have we learned and where do we go from here? *School Psychology Review, 32*(3), 365–383. Retrieved from http://www.nasponline.org/publications/spr/sprmain.aspx

Fisher, W. (1984). Narration as a human communication paradigm: The case of public moral argument. *Communication Monographs, 51*(1), 1–22. doi: 10.1080/03637758409390180

Fisher, W. (1985). The narrative paradigm: An elaboration. *Communication Monographs, 52*(4), 347–367. doi: 10.1080/03637758509376117

Fisher, W. R. (1989). *Human communication and narration: Toward a philosophy of reason, value, and action.* Columbia, SC: University of South Carolina Press.

Fivush, R., Marin, K., & Crawford, M. (2007). Children's narratives and well-being. *Cognition and Emotion, 21*, 1414–1434. doi: 10.1080/02699930601109531

Frattaroli, J. (2006). Experimental disclosure and its moderators: A meta-analysis. *Psychological Bulletin, 132*(7), 823–865. doi: 10.1037/0033-2909.132.6.823

Freeman, J. C., Epston, D., & Lobovits, D. (1997). *Playful approaches to serious problems: Narrative therapy with children and their families.* New York, NY: W.W. Norton & Company.

Geiger, T. C., Zimmer-Gembeck, M. J., & Crick, N. R. (2004). The science of relational aggression: Can we guide intervention? In M. M. Moretti, C. L. Odgers, & M. A. Jackson (Eds.), *Girls and aggression: Contributing factors and intervention principles* (pp. 27–40). New York, NY: Kluwer Academic/Plenum Publishers.

Green, S. B., & Salkind, N. J. (2004). *Using SPSS for Windows and Macintosh: Analyzing and understanding data* (4th ed.). Upper Saddle River, NJ: Prentice Hall.

Haen, C. (2005). Rebuilding security: Group therapy with children affected by September 11th. *International Journal of Group Psychotherapy, 55*(3), 391–413. Retrieved from http://www.guilford.com/cgi-bin/cartscript.cgi?page=pr/jngr .htm&dir=periodicals/per_psych&cart_id=

Harter, L. M. (2009). Narratives as dialogic, contested, and aesthetic performances. *Journal of Applied Communication Research, 37*(2), 140–150. doi: 10.1080/00909880902792255

Harter, L. M., Japp, P. M., & Beck, C. S. (2005a). Vital problematics of narrative theorizing about health and healing. In L. M. Harter, P. M. Japp, & C. S. Beck (Eds.), *Narratives, health, and healing: Communication theory, research, and practice* (pp. 7–29). New York, NY: Routledge.

Harter, L. M., Japp, P. M., & Beck, C. S. (2005b). *Narratives, health, and healing: Communication theory, research, and practice.* New York, NY: Routledge.

Jirek, S. L. (2017). Narrative reconstruction and post-traumatic growth among trauma survivors: The importance of narrative in social work research and practice. *Qualitative Social Work, 16*(2), 166–188. doi: 10.1177/1473325016656046

King, L. A., & Miner, K. N. (2000). Writing about the perceived benefits of traumatic events: Implications for physical health. *Personality and Social Psychology Bulletin, 26*(2), 220–230. doi: 10.1177/0146167200264008

Koenig Kellas, J. (2005). Family ties: Communicating identity through jointly told family stories. *Communication Monographs, 72*(4), 365–389. doi: 10.1080/03637750500322453

Koenig Kellas, J. (2018). Communicated narrative sense-making theory: Linking storytelling and well-being. In D. O. Braithwaite, E. A. Suter, & K. Floyd (Eds.), *Engaging theories in family communication: Multiple perspectives* (2nd ed., pp. 62–74). New York, NY: Routledge.

Koenig Kellas, J., Baker, J., Minniear, M., Cardwell, M., & Horstman, H. (2018, November). *Communicated Perspective-Taking (CPT) and storylistening: Testing the impact of CPT in the context of friends telling stories of difficulty.* Presented at the National Communication Association Annual Convention, Salt Lake City, UT.

Koenig Kellas, J., & Kranstuber Horstman, H. (2015). Communicated narrative sense-making: Understanding family narratives, storytelling, and the construction of meaning through a communicative lens. In L. Turner & R. West (Eds.), *Sage handbook of family communication* (pp. 76–90). Thousand Oaks, CA: Sage.

Koenig Kellas, J., Kranstuber Horstman, H., Willer, E. K., & Carr, K. (2015). The benefits and risks of telling and listening to stories of difficulty over time:

Experimentally testing the expressive writing paradigm in the context of interpersonal communication between friends. *Health Communication, 30*(9), 843–858. doi: 10.1080/10410236.2013.850017

Kranstuber Horstman, H., Maliski, R., Hays, A., Cox, J., Enderle, A., & Nelson, L. R. (2016). Unfolding narrative meaning over time: The contributions of mother-daughter conversations of difficulty on daughter narrative sense-making and well-being. *Communication Monographs*, 83, 326–348. doi: 10.1080/03637751.2015.1068945

Lakoff, G., & Johnson, M. (1980). *Metaphors we live by*. Chicago, IL: University of Chicago.

Leff, S. S., Goldstein, A. B., Angelucci, J., Cardaciotto, L., & Grossman, M. (2007). Using a participatory action research model to create a school-based intervention program for relationally aggressive girls: The friend to friend program. In J. E. Zins, M. J. Elias, & C. A. Maher (Eds.), *Bullying, victimization, and peer harassment: A handbook of prevention and intervention* (pp. 199–218). New York, NY: Haworth Press.

Leff, S. S., Waasdorp, T. E., & Crick, N. R. (2010). A review of existing relational aggression programs: Strengths, limitations, and future directions. *School Psychology Review, 39*(4), 508–535

Lyubomirsky, S., Sousa, L., & Dickerhoof, R. (2006). The costs and benefits of writing, talking, and thinking about life's triumphs and defeats. *Journal of Personality and Social Psychology, 90*(4), 692–708. doi: 10.1037/0022-3514.90.4.692

Malchiodi, C. A. (1998). *The art therapy sourcebook*. New York, NY: McGraw Hill.

Malchiodi, C. A. (2003). *Handbook of art therapy*. New York, NY: The Guilford Press.

Marshak, R. J. (1996). Metaphors, metaphoric fields and organizational change. In D. Grant & C. Oswick (Eds.), *Metaphor and organizations* (pp. 147–165). London, England: Sage.

Martino, M. L., & Freda, M. F. (2016). Post-traumatic growth in cancer survivors: Narrative markers and functions of the experience's transformation. *The Qualitative Report*, 21, 765–780.

McAdams, D. P. (1993). *The stories we live by: Personal myths and the making of the self*. New York, NY: The Guilford Press.

McAdams, D. P., Diamond, A., de St. Aubin, E., & Mansfield, E. (1997). Stories of commitment: The psychological construction of generative lives. *Journal of Personality and Social Psychology, 72*(3), 678–694.

McAdams, D. P., Reynolds, J., Lewis, M., & Bowman, P. J. (2001). When bad things turn good and good things turn bad: Sequences of redemption and contamination in life narrative and their relation to psychological adaption in midlife adults and in students. *Personality and Social Psychology Bulletin, 27*(4), 474–485. doi: 10.1177/0146167201274008

Miller-Ott, A. E., & Kelly, L. (2013). Mean girls in college: An analysis of how college women communicatively construct and account for relational aggression. *Women's Studies in Communication, 36*(3), 330–347. doi: 10.1080/07491409.2013.829792

Murray, E. J., & Segal, D. L. (1994). Emotional processing in vocal and written expression of feelings about traumatic experiences. *Journal of Traumatic Stress, 7*(3), 391-405. doi: 10.1002/jts.2490070305

Ostrov, J. M., Massetti, G. M., Stauffacher, K., Godleski, S. A., Hart, K. C., Karch, K. M., Mullins, A. D. & Ries, E. E., (2009). An intervention for relational and physical aggression in early childhood: A preliminary study. *Early Childhood Research Quarterly, 24*(1), 15–28. doi: 10.1016/j.ecresq.2008.08.002

Owens, L., Shute, R., & Slee, P. (2000). Guess what I just heard!: Indirect aggression among teenage girls in Australia. *Aggressive Behavior, 26*(1), 67–83. doi: 10.1002/ (SICI)1098-2337(2000)26:1<67::AID-AB6>3.0.CO;2-C

Paquette, J. A., & Underwood, M. K. (1999). Gender differences in young adolescents' experiences of peer victimization: Social and physical aggression. *Merrill-Palmer Quarterly, 45*(2), 242–266. Retrieved from http://www.merrillpalmer quarterly.com/

Pennebaker, J. W. (1993). Putting stress into words: Health, linguistic, and therapeutic implications. *Behavior Research and Therapy, 31*(6), 539–548. doi: 10.1016/ 0005-7967(93)90105-4

Pennebaker, J. W. (1997a). *Opening up: The healing power of expressing emotions* (rev. ed.). New York, NY: Guilford.

Pennebaker, J. W. (1997b). Writing about emotional experiences as a therapeutic process. *Psychological Science, 8*(3), 162–166. doi: 10.1111/j.1467-9280.1997 .tb00403.x

Pennebaker, J. W., Colder, M., & Sharp, L. K. (1990). Accelerating the coping process. *Journal of Personality and Social Psychology, 58*(3), 528–537. doi: 10.1037/ 0022-3514.58.3.528

Pennebaker, J. W., & Graybeal, A. (2001). Patterns of natural language use: Disclosure, personality, and social integration. *Current Directions in Psychological Science, 10*(3), 90–93. doi: 10.1111/1467-8721.00123

Pennebaker, J. W., Kiecolt-Glaser, J. K., & Glaser, R. (1988). Disclosure of traumas and immune function: Health implications for psychotherapy. *Journal of Consulting and Clinical Psychology, 56*(2), 239–245. doi: 10.1037/0022-006X.56.2.239

Pennebaker, J. W., & Seagal, J. D. (1999). Forming a story: The health benefits of narrative. *Journal of Clinical Psychology, 55*(10), 1243–1254. doi: 10.1002/ (SICI)1097-4679(199910)55:10<1243::AID-JCLP6>3.0.CO;2-N

Reynolds, M., Brewin, C. R., & Saxton, M. (2000). Emotional disclosure in school children. *The Journal of Child Psychology and Psychiatry and Allied Disciplines, 41*(2), 151–159. doi: 10.1017/S0021963099005223

Riley, S., & Malchiodi, C. A. (2003). Solution-focused and narrative approaches. In C. A. Malchiodi (Ed.), *Handbook of art therapy* (pp. 82–92). New York, NY: The Guilford Press.

Safran, D. S., & Safran, E. R. (2008). Creative approaches to minimize the traumatic impact of bullying behavior. In C. A. Malchiodi (Ed.), *Creative interventions with traumatized children* (pp. 132–166). New York, NY: The Guilford Press.

Seagal J. D., & Pennebaker, J. D. (1997) Expressive writing and social stigma: Benefits from writing about being a group member. Unpublished Manuscript, The University of Texas, Austin.

Sharf, B. F. (2009). Observation from the outside in: Narratives of illness, healing, and mortality in everyday life. *Journal of Applied Communication Research, 37*(2), 132–139. doi: 10.1080/00909880902792297

Smyth, J. M. (1998). Written emotional expression: Effect sizes, outcome types, and moderating variables. *Journal of Consulting and Clinical Psychology, 66*(1), 174–184. doi: 10.1037/0022-006X.66.1.174

Soliday, E., Garofalo, J. P., & Rogers, D. (2004). Expressive writing intervention for adolescents' somatic symptoms and mood. *Journal of Clinical Child and Adolescent Psychology, 33*(4), 792–801. doi: 10.1207/s15374424jccp3304_14

Sunwolf, Frey, L. R., & Keränen, L. (2005). R$_x$ story prescriptions: Healing effects of storytelling and storylistening in the practice of medicine. In L. M. Harter, P. M. Japp, & C. S. Beck (Eds.), *Narratives, health, and healing: Communication theory, research, and practice* (pp. 237–257). New York, NY: Routledge.

Van Schoiack-Edstrom, L., Frey, K. S., & Beland, K. (2002). Changing adolescents' attitudes about relational and physical aggression: An early evaluation of a school-based intervention. *School Psychology Review, 31*(2), 201–216.

Vangelisti, A. L., Crumley, L. P., & Baker, J. L. (1999). Family portraits: Stories as standards for family relationships. *Journal of Social and Personal Relationships, 16*(3), 335–368. doi: 10.1177/0265407599163004

Warner, L. J., Lumley, M. A., Casey, R. J., Pierantoni, W., Salazar, R., Zoratti, E., Enberg, R., & Simon, M. R. (2006). Health effects of written emotional disclosure in adolescents with asthma: A randomized control trial. *Journal of Pediatric Psychology, 31*(6), 557–568. doi: 10.1093/jpepsy/jsj048

Watson, D., Clark, L. A., & Tellegen, A. (1988). Development and validation of brief measures of positive and negative affect: The PANAS scales. *Journal of Personality and Social Psychology, 54*(6), 1063–1070. doi: 10.1037/0022-3514.54.6.1063

White, M. (2007). *Maps of narrative practice.* New York, NY: W.W. Norton.

White, M., & Epston, D. (1990). *Narrative means to therapeutic ends.* Adelaide, South Australia: Dulwich Centre.

Willer, E. K. (2011). "My stomach was upset, like when I eat vegetables": Coping with social aggression via a narrative metaphor intervention. In R. H. Shute, P. T. Slee, R. Murray-Harvey, & K. L. Dix (Eds.), *Mental health and wellbeing: Educational perspectives* (pp. 331–334). Adelaide, Australia: Shannon Research Press.

Willer, E. K. (2012). Drawing light(ning) from the clouds of social aggression: A visual narrative analysis of girls' metaphors. *Qualitative Communication Research, 1*(3), 347–383. doi: 10.1525/qcr.2012.1.3.347

Willer, E. K., & Cupach, W. R. (2008). When "sugar and spice" turn to "fire and ice": Factors affecting the adverse consequences of relational aggression among girls. *Communication Studies, 59*(4), 415–429. doi: 10.1080/10510970802473674

Willer, E. K., & Cupach, W. R. (2011). The meaning of girls' social aggression: Nasty or mastery? In W. R. Cupach & B. H. Spitzberg (Eds.), *The dark side of close relationships—II* (pp. 297–326). New York: Routledge.

Willer, E. K., Droser, V. A., Hoyt, K. D., Hunniecutt, J., Krebs, E., Johnson, J. A., & Castaneda, N. (2018). A visual narrative analysis of children's baby loss remembrance drawings. *Journal of Family Communication, 18*(2), 153–169. doi: 10.1080/15267431.2018.1428608

Willer, E. K., & Soliz, J. (2010). Face needs, intragroup status, and women's reactions to socially aggressive face threats. *Personal Relationships, 17*(4), 557–571. doi: 10.1111/j.1475-6811.2010.01297.x

Section 3

CONTEXTS IN MENTAL HEALTH: CONSIDERING VARIOUS PERSPECTIVES

Chapter Seven

Responses to Celebrity Mental Health Disclosures

Parasocial Relations, Evaluations, and Perceived Media Influence

Cynthia A. Hoffner

In every media context, we encounter celebrities—on television, online, in magazines, on social media. People who are widely known for their accomplishments in fields such as acting, music, athletics, and politics also exert public influence on social issues, including those related to health. The media widely covers celebrity health diagnoses and experiences with illness, and many individuals discuss such topics on social networking sites. These health-related communications can affect people's beliefs, attitudes, and personal health behaviors (Myrick, 2017; Noar, Willoughby, Myrick, & Brown, 2014). Recent data indicate that nearly one in five adults in the United States have a mental health condition (Mental Health America, 2018). Thus, it is no surprise that celebrity mental health issues are often the topic of media coverage. Media focus on celebrities' mental health experiences may have unique power because mental illness is often concealed and avoided in interpersonal communication due to public stigma (Corrigan & Kosyluk, 2014).

This chapter reports a survey that assessed respondents' exposure and responses to celebrities who publicly disclosed bipolar disorder or depression. The research examines how responses to these celebrities are related to several mental health–related variables, including mental illness stereotypes, social distance, and willingness to seek mental health treatment if needed. Theoretically, the chapter draws on work related to stigma (Goffman, 1963), parasocial relationships (Horton & Wohl, 1956; Schiappa, Gregg, & Hewes, 2005), and the influence of presumed media influence model (Gunther & Storey, 2003; Tal-Or, Tsfati, & Gunther, 2009).

MENTAL HEALTH PORTRAYALS IN THE MEDIA

The media often portrays people with mental health conditions in negative and inaccurate ways by suggesting that they are violent, unpredictable, or incompetent (McGinty, Kennedy-Hendricks, Choksy, & Barry, 2016; Parrott & Parrott, 2015; Pirkis, Blood, Francis, & McCallum, 2006). Associating these types of characteristics with mental illness contributes to public stigma, reinforcing fear, perceived danger, and other stereotypes (Klin & Lemish, 2008). However, more realistic media portrayals, showing people with mental illness living meaningful lives, can challenge stereotypes and lower stigmatization (e.g., Evans-Lacko, Corker, Williams, Henderson, & Thornicroft, 2014). Media portrayals of mental health treatment can also impact people's willingness to seek or continue treatment (e.g., Maier, Gentile, Vogel, & Kaplan, 2014; Vogel, Gentile, & Kaplan, 2008).

Reducing or eliminating stigma associated with mental illness is an important public health priority. Goffman (1963) defined stigma as an "attribute that is deeply discrediting," that reduces an individual from a whole person to "a tainted, discounted one" (p. 3). Stigma can manifest in many ways, but two key components include stereotyping and social distance (Link, Yang, Phelan, & Collins, 2004). Stereotypes refer to negative or undesirable characteristics that are linked to people seen as members of particular groups or categories, leading to status loss and discrimination. Social distance refers to avoidance or unwillingness to interact with people in a variety of different contexts. Self-stigma involves personal internalization of public stigma and leads to lowered self-esteem and self-efficacy. Research found that both self-stigma and perceptions of public stigma related to mental illness can be obstacles to seeking mental health treatment (Corrigan & Kosyluk, 2014; Link & Phelan, 2013).

Contact—both direct and mediated—with members of stigmatized groups is one of the most effective ways to reduce stigma (Couture & Penn, 2003; Pettigrew, Tropp, Wagner, & Christ, 2011). The role of media portrayals in reducing stigma related to mental health conditions is especially important because many people conceal mental illness in daily life, thus reducing the potential for personal encounters that might challenge stereotypes (Corrigan & Kosyluk, 2014). Building on the work on intergroup contact theory and parasocial interaction (Allport, 1954; Horton & Wohl, 1956), Schiappa et al. (2005) proposed the "parasocial contact hypothesis," which contends that positive mediated contact with identifiable social group members can reduce prejudicial attitudes and avoidance of interaction. These beneficial effects most likely occur through sustained parasocial contact with likable, attractive media figures, especially when a parasocial relationship (PSR) develops. A PSR reflects the sense of a real, deeply felt emotional bond with a media figure (Brown, 2015; Cohen, 2009). Research on the TV series *Monk* (Hoffner & Cohen, 2012, 2015) found that a parasocial bond with the character was associated with lower stereotypes and less social distance from people with mental illness.

Celebrity Mental Health Disclosures

Celebrities can become associated with health conditions that they themselves experience, and, through media coverage, they become a source of health information for the public (Hoffman & Tan, 2013; Myrick, 2017; Noar et al., 2014). Coverage of celebrity health issues can motivate people to search for health information and communicate about related topics (Brown, 2010; Casey et al., 2003; Myrick, Noar, Willoughby, & Brown, 2014). Celebrity disclosure of stigmatized health conditions, such as HIV, lung cancer, or mental illness, also may lower stigma depending on the media coverage and audience response (e.g., Brown & Basil, 1995; Myrick, 2017; Wong, Lookadoo, & Nisbett, 2017).

Recently, many celebrities—such as Lady Gaga, Mariah Carey, and Dwayne "The Rock" Johnson—revealed experience with mental health conditions and encouraged others to seek help (Carucci, 2018). Mediated encounters with admired celebrities who reveal mental health problems could lead to more favorable group attitudes and a reduction in public stigma. These outcomes are more likely when people have a stronger parasocial bond with the celebrity (Hoffner & Cohen, 2018; Wong et al., 2017). Revelation of a stigmatized identity from someone with whom a close personal or parasocial bond already exists has greater potential to reduce stigma than an encounter with someone new who reveals the same stigmatized identity (Herek, 1996; Schiappa et al., 2005).

Typically, parasocial involvement reflects underlying positive affect, but PSR is conceptually different from liking a character or character evaluations. For example, people may have favorable evaluations of a celebrity with whom they do not feel a close emotional bond. Moreover, although many celebrities are likable and admired, some are regarded unfavorably by segments of the audience for a variety of reasons (Edwards & La Ferle, 2009; Fenimore, 2012; Gies, 2011; Miller & Laczniak, 2011; Zhou & Whitla, 2013). Research shows that responses to negative (or positive) exemplars can transfer to the social group to which the exemplar is seen as belonging (Holman & McKeever, 2017). Journalism coverage of celebrities' personal difficulties and legal problems often frames them as socially deviant, which can lead to negative evaluations and damage to their public reputation (Fenimore, 2012; Gies, 2011; Zhou & Whitla, 2013). When negative exemplars are connected to mental health issues—whether disclosed personally or labeled by others—this may increase stereotypes of mental illness and public stigma (Fenimore, 2012; McGinty et al., 2016; Quintero Johnson, & Riles, 2018).

Based on the parasocial contact hypothesis (Schiappa et al., 2005), effects of celebrity mental health disclosures on stigma should depend, in part, on whether contact with the individual is positive or negative. Thus, evaluations and perceived reputation of celebrities should play a role in the outcome of parasocial contact. Awareness that successful, admired individuals are dealing with mental health issues may normalize mental illness and lead to lower stigma. However, if knowledge of a celebrity's mental illness is connected to negative information about that person, especially if linked to pervasive stereotypes of mental illness, stigma may be increased. Examining how responses to celebrities (PSR, evaluations, perceived reputation) who disclose mental health issues relate to stigma and willingness to seek treatment can provide insight into the most socially beneficial ways to frame such disclosures. This information would be useful for celebrities hoping to make a positive difference, for journalists looking for guidance on covering mental health issues, and for designing public health campaigns.

Perceived Influence of Media Coverage of Celebrity Mental Health Disclosures

An additional way in which celebrity mental health disclosures may impact audiences is through expectations about their influence on self and others. In their presumed media influence model, Gunther and Storey (2003) contended that beliefs about other people's responses to media messages can have a wide range of attitudinal and behavioral effects (Ho & Yee, 2017; Tal-Or et al., 2009). Of the three types of outcomes included in the model (i.e., protection, coordination, normative influence), the one most relevant to understanding responses to celebrity mental health disclosures is normative influence. Believing that media favorably impacted social norms or public opinions related to mental illness may increase people's comfort in discussing mental health issues. However, based on prior research, beliefs about influence on others may not translate into greater willingness to seek mental health treatment (Hoffner & Cohen, 2015). Thus, perceived influence of celebrity disclosures on oneself also may be important (cf. Price, Tewksbury, & Huang, 1998). Self-stigma (internalization of public stigma) discourages people from seeking mental health treatment due in part to fear of associating oneself with a stigmatized group. If celebrity disclosures are perceived as lowering respondents' own stigma, this may be associated with greater willingness to seek treatment (Corrigan, Watson, & Barr, 2006).

THE CURRENT STUDY

Drawing on the work reviewed above, this research examined responses to male and female celebrities who publicly disclosed either bipolar disorder or depression. Specifically, the study explored the role of three celebrity responses—PSR, evaluations, and perceived reputation—in mental illness stigma and willingness to seek mental health treatment. Much research has addressed media depictions of mental illness (e.g., Klin & Lemish, 2008; Pirkis et al., 2006), but few studies focused specifically on depression or bipolar disorder. Celebrity gender was considered because research shows differences in stigma based on gender and mental disorder. Depression is more common among women and is perceived as more female-typical; bipolar disorder tends to occur equally among men and women (Boysen & Logan, 2017; Wirth & Bodenhausen, 2009; World Health Organization, 2018). In general, stigma associated with mental illness tends to be lower for women than for men and for mental health disorders that are more typical of women. However, people with disorders that are atypical for their gender, such as men with depression, are less stigmatized, possibly due to lower perceived responsibility for their illness (Farina, 1981; Wirth & Bodenhasen, 2009).

First, the study examined awareness of celebrities' mental health disclosures and how responses to celebrities (PSR, evaluations, reputation) differ based on the celebrity's mental health diagnosis and gender. Thus, the researchers asked two research questions:

RQ1: To what extent are respondents aware of celebrity mental health disclosures?

RQ2: How do responses to celebrities (PSR, evaluations, perceived reputation) vary based on celebrity mental health condition (bipolar disorder, depression) and gender?

Based on the parasocial contact hypothesis (Schiappa et al., 2005), a parasocial bond or sense of pseudo-friendship with a celebrity who disclosed a mental health disorder should be associated with lower mental illness stigma (stereotyping, social distance) (Hoffner & Cohen, 2012, 2015). Similarly, more positive evaluations and perceived reputation for the celebrity should translate into lower stigma (Corrigan & Kosyluk, 2014). Although evaluations and perceived reputation should be connected, certain celebrity behaviors (e.g., moral violations) may affect perceived reputation more than they impact trait evaluations (Zhou & Whitla, 2013). Therefore, both measures were included. The researchers predicted that:

H1: Stronger PSR with the celebrity will be associated with lower mental illness stigma (stereotyping, social distance).
H2: More positive evaluations and perceived reputation of the celebrity will be associated with lower mental illness stigma (stereotyping, social distance).

Stronger PSR with a celebrity dealing with mental health issues should lead to greater willingness to seek mental health treatment due to lower stigma and increased awareness of mental health issues, bolstered by the emotional bond (Hoffner & Cohen, 2018). More positive evaluations and perceived reputation of the celebrity also may facilitate willingness to seek treatment, but may not be enough without the emotional connection of PSR. Thus, the researchers proposed:

H3: Stronger PSR with the celebrity will be associated with greater willingness to seek mental health treatment.

Because little is known about the perceived reputation of the celebrity in regards to mental health disclosure and stigma, the researchers asked:

RQ3: How will evaluations and perceived reputation of the celebrity be related to willingness to seek mental health treatment?

Grounded in the presumed influence model (Gunther & Storey, 2003), additional questions addressed the perceived influence of media coverage of the celebrity's mental health issues, which necessarily measured only respondents who reported awareness of the celebrity's diagnosis. Perceived positive impact on self, but perhaps not others, should be related to lower stigma (stereotypes, social distance), and lower self-stigma should translate into greater willingness to seek treatment (Hoffner & Cohen, 2012, 2015). But given the exploratory nature of this inquiry, the researchers proposed:

RQ4: How is perceived influence of media coverage of the celebrity's mental health on self and others associated with mental illness stigma (stereotyping, social distance) and willingness to seek mental health treatment?

METHOD

Participants and Procedure

Two-hundred thirteen respondents between the ages of eighteen to sixty-five years (M = 42.02, SD = 13.58) completed a questionnaire. Slightly more females (56.3 %) than males (41.8%) participated; one respondent reported being nonbinary and three did not respond regarding gender. Most respondents (76.1%) identified as White/Caucasian, 7.5 percent as Black/African-American, 4.2 percent as Asian/Pacific Islander, 5.6 percent Hispanic/Latino(a), and 4.7 percent multiethnic, and 0.5 percent Native American; three participants did not report their ethnicity. The highest reported level of education for participants was: 0.5 percent some high school; 16.0 percent, high school diploma or GED; 32.4 percent, some college or vocational training; 32.9 percent, college degree; 17.4 percent, graduate degree; two people did not respond. On average, respondents reported a moderate political orientation (M = 4.02 on a scale of 1 to 7). All respondents resided in the United States, including thirty-eight states and the District of Columbia. Just under one third of the sample (30.5%; n = 65) reported that they had been diagnosed or treated for a mental health problem.

The researchers recruited participants in February 2017 by Survey Sampling International (SSI) from an online panel of people who agreed to participate in surveys for compensation. SSI shared an invitation and link to the survey (on surveymonkey.com) with members of the panel. Each participant was paid the equivalent of $2 for participating. At the end of the survey, a message was provided about ways media can reinforce as well as reduce stigma related to mental illness. Respondents also received a list of mental health resources. The study was approved by the university's Institutional Review Board.

Study Design

The study employed a 2 × 2 between-subjects design, with celebrity gender (male, female) and mental health condition (bipolar disorder, depression) as independent variables.[1] There were two celebrity exemplars in each of the four cells, so a total of eight celebrities were included. A review of news coverage confirmed the celebrities' personal disclosure of bipolar disorder or depression in at least two reputable news outlets. Celebrities who had heavy press coverage for serious criminal behaviors (e.g., spousal abuse) were excluded from the study.

Respondents were randomly assigned to one of eight surveys. An initial screening question asked respondents to rate their familiarity with the celebrity they were assigned. If they had not heard of that person, they rated their familiarity with the other celebrity in the same cell of the design (same gender/mental health condition). A between-subjects design was employed due to the potential for carry-over effects if respondents rated a series of celebrities.

Participants completed the survey measures in the order in which they are listed below. Ratings of the focal celebrity were completed first. PSR, evaluations, and perceived reputation of the celebrity were rated prior to the question about the celebrity's health issues. Next, the participants completed the mental health–related measures, followed by a checklist assessing familiarity with health issues of a list of celebrities, and background characteristics. The survey did not identify the mental health disclosure of any celebrity.

Measures Related to Focal Celebrity

Familiarity with celebrity. The familiarity scale ranged from 1 (I have never heard of him/her) to 5 (I am extremely familiar with him/her). Only celebrities with a familiarity rating of 2 or higher were rated on other measures.

Parasocial relationship. Respondents' PSR with the celebrity was measured with twelve items adapted from Bocarnea and Brown's (2007) Celebrity-Persona Parasocial Interaction Scale. Example items include: "[Celebrity name] makes me feel as if I was with someone I knew well"; "Sometimes I feel like contacting [Celebrity name] personally." "I find myself thinking about him/her on a regular basis." Items were rated on 5-point Likert scales (1 = disagree strongly, 5 = agree strongly) and averaged after reverse coding ($\alpha = .93$).

Evaluation and perceived reputation of the celebrity. Evaluations were made on seven items describing personal characteristics adapted from measures of mental illness stereotypes (Corrigan et al., 2006). Respondents reported the extent to which they agreed that each characteristic described the celebrity on 5-point Likert scales. The negative items were reverse coded so higher scores indicate a more positive evaluation. The characteristics were: intelligent, unpredictable, dangerous, aggressive, successful, makes important contributions to society, and trustworthy. After reverse coding of unpredictable, dangerous, and aggressive, these items were averaged ($\alpha = .71$).

A single item addressed the celebrity's perceived reputation: "[Celebrity name] has a negative reputation." This item was reverse coded so that higher scores indicate a more positive perceived reputation.

Awareness of the celebrity's health issues. Respondents were presented with a list of twelve personal circumstances and health conditions (including four mental health conditions) and asked to mark if any were true of the focal celebrity. Respondents who reported awareness that the celebrity had any mental health issues were asked to report how they had learned this information as an open-ended response.

Perceived influence of media coverage of the celebrity's mental health issues. If respondents were aware of the celebrity's mental health issues, they rated the perceived influence of related media coverage. Specifically, they rated the extent to which they thought media coverage of the celebrity's mental health problems made them personally more or less inclined to believe several statements about mental health/mental illness; they also rated the perceived media influence on others for the same statements. Ratings were made on 5-point scales (1, much less inclined to believe; 5, much more inclined to believe). The items included: "Mental health is an important social issue"; "Mental health conditions can be effectively treated"; "Mental illness can happen to anyone"; and "People with mental health problems can make important contributions to society." Items for each target were averaged (self, $\alpha = .86$; others, $\alpha = .87$).

Measures Not Related to the Focal Celebrity

Stereotypes. Stereotypes were assessed for either bipolar disorder or depression, depending on assigned condition. Respondents reported the percent of people with bipolar disorder/depression whom they believed had several characteristics (adapted from Corrigan et al., 2006): intelligent (reversed), are not able to take care of themselves, are unpredictable, are dangerous, are able to maintain a regular job (reversed), make important contributions to society (reversed), will not recover or get better, are to blame for their problems, and trustworthy (reversed). One item ("live a good, fulfilling life") was dropped because it had a near-zero item-to-total correlation. The scale ranged from 1 to 11, with points labeled in 10 percent increments (0%, 1%–10%, 11%–20%, up to 91% or more). After reverse coding, the items were averaged, so higher scores reflect greater stereotypes ($\alpha = .76$).

Social distance. Social distance was measured with three items from Martin, Pescosolido, & Tuch (2000). Respondents imagined they met someone whom they learned had bipolar disorder or depression (depending on condition) and rated how willing they would be to: spend an evening socializing with the person, make friends with the person, and have that person start working closely with you on the job. Ratings were made on a scale ranging from 1, not at all willing, to 5, very willing but were rescored so that high scores reflect greater social distance (less willingness to interact). The items were averaged ($\alpha = .91$).

Willingness to seek treatment for mental health problems. Two items assessed willingness to seek treatment if they experienced symptoms of a mental health problem in the next year regardless of past experience. Respondents rated the likelihood that they would seek help from a psychologist or therapist and a medical doctor (Sheffield, Fiorenza, & Sofronoff, 2004). Ratings were made on a scale from 1 (not likely at all) to 5 (very likely), and the items were averaged ($\alpha = .78$).

Awareness of eight celebrities' mental health diagnoses. All respondents saw a list of celebrities, including the eight who were the focus of this study, only one of whom the respondents had previously reported on. Four additional celebrities who had not disclosed any mental health conditions were included on the list to help camouflage the focus on mental health. Respondents checked which health issues, if any, they believed each celebrity had dealt with. The four health issues were: bipolar disorder, depression, cancer, and multiple sclerosis. Respondents also could indicate if they had not heard of the celebrity.

Personal experience with mental health issues. Respondents indicated whether they had been diagnosed or treated for any mental health condition (using a checklist). Personal experience with mental health issues (0, no; 1, yes) was used in some analyses.

RESULTS

Familiarity with the Celebrities

Table 7.1 provides descriptive information about the eight celebrities. Respondents were most familiar with Demi Lovato, Jean-Claude Van Damme, Winona Ryder, and Bruce Springsteen, and they were least familiar with Scott Stapp and Jenifer Lewis.

Table 7.1.   Information About Celebrities Included in the Study

Celebrity	Occupation	Initial Familiarity Mean	Initial Familiarity SD	# Who Rated Celebrity
Disclosed Bipolar Disorder				
Demi Lovato	Singer/songwriter/actor	3.31	1.14	37
Jenifer Lewis	Actor/singer	2.08	1.35	14
Jean-Claude Van Damme	Actor/martial artist	3.32	1.28	43
Scott Stapp	Singer/songwriter	1.87	1.31	12
Disclosed Depression				
Kristen Bell	Actor/singer	2.88	1.28	23
Winona Ryder	Actor	3.38	1.14	27
Wayne Brady	Actor/singer/comedian	2.65	1.15	18
Bruce Springsteen	Singer/songwriter	3.14	0.95	34

Note. N = 213 for familiarity ratings. Familiarity could range from 1 to 5. Five respondents ultimately did not rate any celebrity because they were unfamiliar with both celebrities in their assigned condition/gender.

Although approximately an equal number of people were initially assigned to each of the celebrities, the table shows that the number of celebrities rated was unequal. Respondents were not asked to rate a celebrity of whom they had not heard. If they indicated a lack of familiarity with the first assigned celebrity (rated 1 on a familiarity scale of 1 to 5), they were asked to rate the other celebrity in the same cell. All but five respondents rated one of the two celebrities in their assigned cell.

RQ1 asked about respondents' familiarity with the celebrities' mental health disclosures. Results from the checklist of health conditions for the eight celebrities show that, overall, respondents had relatively low awareness of these celebrities' specific mental health disclosures, ranging from a low of 12.2 percent to a high of 42.3 percent. About two-fifths of the respondents were aware of the mental health conditions disclosed by Demi Lovato (42.3%) and Winona Ryder (40.4%). However, less than one-fifth of the respondents reported awareness for the other six celebrities (Jenifer Lewis, 12.2%; Jean-Claude Van Damme, 13.6%; Scott Stapp, 14.1%; Kristen Bell, 17.8%; Wayne Brady, 13.3%; and Bruce Springsteen, 14.1%).

Rated Variables as a Function of Celebrity Mental Health Condition and Gender

Table 7.2 reports means and standard deviations of key measures for the four cells of the design, collapsing the two celebrities in each cell. Each rated variable was analyzed in a 2 × 2 analysis of variance (ANOVA), with celebrity mental health condition (bipolar disorder, depression) and celebrity gender (female, male) as factors.

A post hoc power analysis revealed that power to detect a medium effect size (d = .50) in this design was .997. None of the analyses revealed a main effect of celebrity gender. The main effect of mental health condition and the interaction are reported for each variable in Table 7.2.

RQ2 asked how responses to the celebrities would vary based on the celebrity's gender and mental health condition. Familiarity with the rated celebrities did not differ across the four cells. The lowest possible familiarity score was 2 on a scale of 1 to 5, since participants did not rate celebrities they did not recognize. Respondents' PSR with the celebrity they rated also did not vary based on mental health condition or gender. On average, PSR was moderate to low (between 2 and 3 on a scale of 1 to 5). Overall, respondents had less positive evaluations of the male celebrities who had bipolar disorder and perceived them to have less positive reputations than the other celebrities. Further analysis revealed that the two men in that cell did not differ significantly from each other on either measure.

The three mental health–related variables addressed either depression or bipolar disorder (depending on the condition), but did not refer to any celebrity. Significant main effects of mental health condition for both stigma measures revealed that stereotypes and desired social distance were higher for

Table 7.2. Means and Standard Deviations, and ANOVA Results for Key Variables as a Function of Rated Celebrities' Mental Health Condition and Gender

Rated Variable	Bipolar Disorder		Depression		Condition Main Effect F value	Interaction F value
	Female Celebrity	Male Celebrity	Female Celebrity	Male Celebrity		
Familiarity with celebrity	3.20 (1.14)	3.53 (1.03)	3.38 (1.05)	3.15 (0.92)	0.44	3.80
Parasocial relationship	2.73 (1.02)	2.52 (0.88)	2.64 (0.87)	2.65 (0.91)	0.18	1.21
Celebrity evaluation	3.60$_b$ (0.53)	3.33$_a$ (0.50)	3.55$_{ab}$ (0.53)	3.78$_b$ (0.57)	8.16**	12.71***
Celebrity's perceived reputation	3.50$_{ab}$ (1.04)	3.27$_a$ (1.13)	3.60$_{ab}$ (1.08)	4.19$_b$ (0.89)	12.53***	8.01**
Stereotypes	5.01$_b$ (1.47)	4.77$_b$ (1.30)	4.21$_a$ (1.41)	4.24$_a$ (1.44)	11.85***	0.47
Social Distance	2.31$_b$ (1.04)	2.42$_b$ (0.89)	2.05$_a$ (0.93)	2.03$_a$ (0.91)	6.24*	0.22
Willingness to seek mental health treatment	3.66$_{ab}$ (1.59)	3.45$_{ab}$ (1.20)	3.22$_a$ (1.31)	3.73$_b$ (1.23)	0.25	4.57*
N	51	55	50	52		

* $p < .05$. ** $p < .01$. *** $p < .001$.

Note. Stereotypes could range from 1 to 11. All other variables were rated 1 to 5, but familiarity could range from 2 to 5. For evaluation and reputation, higher scores are more positive. There were no main effects of celebrity gender. Means in the same row with no subscripts in common differ at $p < .05$ by the Tukey procedure.

people with bipolar disorder than for those with depression. For willingness to seek mental health treatment, there was no main effect of mental health condition, but, unexpectedly, there was a significant interaction. For respondents who rated a male celebrity, but not a female celebrity, willingness to seek treatment was higher if the celebrity had depression than if they had bipolar disorder.

Relationships among Celebrity Responses and Mental Health–Related Variables

Despite relatively low reported awareness of the celebrity's specific mental health disclosure, it seemed possible that respondents who were familiar with the celebrity had encountered some media coverage of the celebrity's mental health. As is common, some of the celebrities also reportedly dealt with issues such as addiction, anxiety, or an eating disorder. Thus, to address H1,

H2, H3, and RQ3, partial correlations examined the relationships between the celebrity ratings and mental health–related variables for the full sample. Partial correlations controlled for background variables (gender, age, education, political orientation, and personal mental health experience) and celebrity familiarity. Political orientation was included as a control because this variable is related to mental illness stigma (Parcesepe & Cabassa, 2013).

Preliminary analyses showed that PSR was higher for celebrities whom respondents evaluated more positively, pr = .34, p < .001, but was unrelated to the celebrity's perceived reputation, pr = -.01, p > .87. Celebrity evaluation and perceived reputation were positively correlated, pr = .54, p < .001.

Table 7.3 reports partial correlations between celebrity ratings and mental health variables. H1 and H2 predicted that more positive celebrity responses would be associated with lower mental illness stigma (stereotyping and social distance).

Table 7.3.   Ratings of Celebrity

Mental Health Variables	Parasocial Relationship	Celebrity evaluation	Celebrity perceived reputation
Stereotypes	.17*	−.25***	−.26***
Social distance	−.11	−.41***	−.26***
Willingness to seek mental health treatment	.15*	.25***	.19**

Partial correlations between ratings of celebrity and mental health variables.
* p < .05.   ** p < .01.   *** p < .001
Note. N for the correlations ranged from 200 to 205. For evaluation and reputation, higher scores are more positive. Partial correlations control for gender, age, education, political orientation, personal experience with mental health issues, and celebrity familiarity.

Contrary to H1, PSR was unrelated to social distance, and, surprisingly, was associated with *greater* mental illness stereotypes. To explore this finding, partial correlations between these two variables were calculated separately based on the celebrity's gender and mental health condition. The findings revealed that this relationship was observed only for respondents who rated female celebrities with depression, *pr* = .36, p < .03. The correlations were smaller and nonsignificant in the other three groups: depression/male, *pr* = .22, p > .14; bipolar disorder/female, *pr* = .15, p > .32; bipolar disorder/male, *pr* = .03, p > .83. In support of H2, the more positive respondents' evaluation and perceived reputation of the celebrity, the lower their stereotypes and desire for social distance from people with mental health conditions. Thus, support was obtained for H2 but not H1.

H3 predicted that the stronger respondents' PSR with the celebrity, the more willing they would be to seek mental health treatment. As Table 7.3 shows, this hypothesis was supported. Regarding RQ3, positive evaluations and perceived reputation also were associated with greater willingness to seek treatment.

Perceived Media Influence

The final set of analyses focused on the seventy-three respondents who indicated that they believed the celebrity they were rating had bipolar disorder/depression. In an open-ended question, two-thirds of these respondents (67.1%) reported being able to recall how they had first learned about the celebrity's mental health issues. Sources mentioned were: print/online, 26.0 percent, television, 17.8 percent, social media, 11.0 percent, and media (not specified), 12.3 percent. Of the seventy-three respondents, 17.8 percent mentioned a positive response in their answer (e.g., support, compassion, admiration). For example, respondents stated: "I read an article . . . in which she was coming forward with her struggle with bipolar disorder. I thought it was very admirable of her to do so." "Sympathy and appreciation for being open about it." "I like him even more than I did before I knew this." Two respondents (2.7%) included negative comments related to anti-social behavior.

Perceived influence of media coverage of the celebrity's mental health issues on the respondents' own and others' attitudes toward mental illness were examined. A 2 (celebrity mental health condition) x 2 (celebrity gender) x target (self, other) ANCOVA was conducted, with background variables (gender, age, education, political orientation, and personal mental health experience) and celebrity familiarity as covariates. Only the condition by gender interaction was significant, $F(1,62) = 4.28$, p < .05. For female celebrities, the perceived influence of media coverage tended to be more positive for bipolar disorder ($M = 4.21$) than for depression ($M = 3.83$), whereas the opposite was the case for male celebrities (bipolar disorder, $M = 3.90$; depression, $M = 4.21$).

RQ4 asked whether perceived influence of the media coverage on self and others would be related to stigma (stereotypes and social distance) and willingness to seek mental health treatment. Partial correlations between these two sets of variables were calculated with the same control variables. More positive perceived influence on self was associated with lower social distance ($pr = -.32$, p < .001) and greater willingness to seek mental health treatment ($pr = .35$, p < .01), but was unrelated to stereotypes. Perceived influence on others was not related to any of the mental health variables.

DISCUSSION

Overall, respondents had relatively low awareness of the celebrities' mental health disclosures. Over 40 percent of respondents were aware of the mental health issues experienced by two female celebrities (one with bipolar disorder, one with depression), but less than 20 percent reported awareness for the other six celebrities. However, this was a relatively high bar in that the questions required that participants be aware that the celebrity had either bipolar disorder or depression. Many reported perceiving that the celebrity they rated had problems with substance abuse or other mental health issues. Indeed, most of the celebrities included in this study had publicly disclosed other mental health problems such as anxiety, addiction, or eating disorders.

Overall, PSR was low to moderate, reflecting the fact that respondents were assigned a specific celebrity. This design had advantages of controlling key characteristics of the rated celebrities, but allowing respondents to name a person with whom they felt a closer bond may have yielded different results. For example, Carrie Fisher, who openly discussed her experience with bipolar disorder and was a passionate mental health advocate, was regarded as a role model by many people who identified with her mental health challenges (Burleson & Parker-Pope, 2016; Hoffner & Park, in press). PSR was unrelated to celebrity's gender or mental health condition. However, evaluations and perceived reputation were more negative for celebrities who had disclosed bipolar disorder than depression. Consistent with this pattern, stereotypes and social distance unrelated to a specific celebrity also were higher for bipolar disorder than for depression. When the celebrity's gender was considered, the ratings were least positive for males with bipolar disorder and most positive for males with depression. This may partially reflect the specific choices of celebrities for the cells of this design. The more favorable judgments of males with depression is consistent with evidence that people are less inclined to stigmatize people with disorders that are atypical for their gender (Wirth & Bodenhasen, 2009).

Respondents who had a stronger PSR with the celebrity also evaluated him/her more favorably, but PSR was unrelated to the celebrity's perceived reputation. In other words, respondents' bond with the celebrity appeared to be based on their own evaluations and not on how they felt others viewed the person. However, evaluations and perceived reputation were strongly positively correlated and findings for the two variables were very similar.

Correlational findings offer some clues regarding how people's responses to celebrity mental health issues relate to their beliefs and behaviors. As expected, the more positive respondents' evaluation and perceived reputation of the celebrity, the lower their stereotypes and desire for social distance from people with mental health conditions. Unexpectedly, PSR was associated with *greater* mental illness stereotypes, but follow-up analyses revealed this was limited to celebrities with depression, especially females. This could be an artifact of the specific celebrities selected. Also, since stereotypes were measured after the ratings of the celebrity, having been primed with a specific celebrity may have affected stereotype ratings. It is also possible that the traits that are considered "stereotypes," such as being unpredictable or untrustworthy, may seem intriguing in celebrities and may make them more appealing to some people (Sanders, 2010). This possibility could complicate our understanding of how celebrity mental health disclosures, coupled with their public activities and social interactions, may influence public stigma, as well as the role that PSR with the celebrity may play in this process.

All three responses to the celebrity—PSR, evaluations, and perceived reputation—were associated with greater willingness to seek mental health treatment if needed. This finding is consistent with evidence that celebrity health disclosures have the potential to influence health-related behaviors (Brown & Basil, 1995; Myrick, 2017; Noar et al., 2014). These are correlational findings, and no evidence was obtained in this study regarding respondents' awareness of the celebrity's treatment or therapy. However, the selected celebrities had all voluntarily disclosed their mental health issues publicly and had indicated that they had sought treatment. These findings suggest that positively regarded celebrities who disclose mental health issues have the potential to encourage favorable views of mental health treatment (Francis, 2018; Lee, 2018; Maier et al., 2014).

A small subsample of seventy-three respondents rated the perceived influence of media coverage of the celebrity's mental health issues. More positive perceived influence on self, but not others, was associated with lower social distance and greater willingness to seek mental health treatment if needed. The link with willingness to seek treatment is consistent with the view that self-stigma can be a barrier to seeking treatment (Corrigan & Kosyluk, 2014). The lack of associations with perceived influence on others indicates that the perception of lower public stigma from celebrity mental health disclosures did not translate into greater willingness to seek mental health treatment. This finding replicates results reported by Hoffner and Cohen (2012, 2015), in their research on the perceived influence of the TV series *Monk*. Although public stigma has been implicated in reluctance to seek or continue mental health treatment (Corrigan, Druss, & Perlick, 2014), the factors involved are complicated and unlikely to be impacted by the perceived influence of a single disclosure on others' attitudes.

Limitations and Future Research

This survey was an exploratory study, designed to gather information on responses to celebrity mental health disclosures with the goal of developing future work on the influence of media framing of celebrity mental health disclosures. Some limitations of this study should be noted. The use of a convenience sample means that the descriptive findings cannot be generalized. In addition, causal conclusions cannot be based on the correlational findings of this study. Participants were assigned to rate specific celebrities, which reduced the variations across gender and type of mental health condition and allowed a focus on clearly identified mental illnesses (bipolar disorder, depression). Some differences across conditions may reflect unique characteristics of the celebrities in each cell. Moreover, as noted above, the choice to randomly assign respondents to report on a specific celebrity (if familiar) limited the study's ability to examine responses to media figures with whom respondents had a deep parasocial bond. Some respondents may have been more familiar with other celebrities who had disclosed mental health conditions, and who may have had a stronger personal influence on them. Responses to specific celebrity disclosures should be explored in more depth in future research; the timing of the disclosure in the trajectory of the PSR also should be considered.

This study obtained no information about the content of the media coverage respondents had seen (if any) about the celebrity's mental health disclosure. Thus, it cannot be determined how message framing or content cues may have impacted people's responses (Noar et al., 2014; Smith, 2007). In addition, seeing reactions of other people to mental health disclosures in media reports or social media could be a factor in how the disclosures influence attitudes and behavioral intentions (Peter, Rossmann, & Keyling, 2014; Waddell & Bailey, 2017). Examination of responses to actual media reports of celebrities dealing with mental health challenges could add to understanding of how public figures impact stigma and mental health–related behaviors (Gekoski & Broome, 2014). One factor that may affect responses to media coverage is the source of information about a celebrity's mental health diagnosis. Does it matter whether a celebrity personally discloses or if a diagnosis is revealed by another source (e.g., journalists)? Given that cues suggesting a health issue can be openly discussed tend to lower stigma (Goffman, 1963; Myrick, 2017), personal disclosure by a celebrity may have more beneficial influence, although the circumstances surrounding the disclosure would also play a role (e.g., for public benefit vs. an excuse for bad behavior).

Due to the relatively small sample size, this study did not explore the role of personal mental health experience in responses to the celebrities. Just under one-third of this sample reported personally dealing with a mental health condition. Certainly, people who share the diagnosis of a celebrity may be more likely to identify with them and experience self-relevant effects such as self-esteem and ways of coping (Hoffner & Cohen, 2012, 2018). Indeed, recent studies demonstrated that media coverage of celebrities' mental health diagnoses motivated people to seek information and obtain mental health treatment for the same condition (Francis, 2018; Lee, 2018). The influence of celebrity disclosures on people who have or suspect they may have specific mental health conditions should be a continued focus of research.

CONCLUSION

This study is consistent with prior evidence that celebrity involvement in health issues can increase attention and amplify the impact of media coverage (Myrick, 2017; Noar et al., 2014). When celebrities make a choice to disclose mental health challenges and continue discussing their experiences in interviews and public appearances, this has the potential to reduce stigma and contribute to beneficial public health outcomes. The extent to which this occurs undoubtedly depends on the nature of the media coverage, responses to the celebrity, and interpersonal communication, among other factors (Noar et al., 2014). Future research needs to examine the causal processes that underlie associations between exposure to media coverage of celebrity mental health disclosures and mental health outcomes, as well as factors that facilitate stigma reduction.

NOTE

1. The research reported in this chapter was funded by the Waterhouse Family Institute for the Study of Communication and Society.

REFERENCES

Allport, G. W. (1954). *The nature of prejudice.* Cambridge, MA: Perseus Books.
Bocarnea, M. C., & Brown, W. J. (2007). Celebrity-Persona Parasocial Interaction Scale. In R. A. Reynolds, R. Woods, & J. D. Baker (Eds.), *Handbook of research on electronic surveys and measurements* (pp. 309–312). Hershey, PA: Idea Group Reference.
Boysen, G. A., & Logan, M. (2017). Gender and mental illness stigma: The relative impact of stereotypical masculinity and gender atypicality. *Stigma and Health,* 2(2), 83–97. doi: 10.1037/sah0000044

Brown, W. J. (2010). Steve Irwin's influence on wildlife conservation. *Journal of Communication, 60*, 73–93. doi: 10.1111/j.1460-2466.2009.01458.x

Brown, W. J. (2015). Examining four processes of audience involvement with media personae: Transportation, parasocial interaction, identification, and worship. *Communication Theory, 25*, 259–283. doi: 10.1111/comt.12053

Brown, W., & Basil, M. D. (1995). Media celebrities and public health: Responses to "Magic" Johnson's HIV disclosure and its impact on AIDS risk and high-risk behaviors. *Health Communication, 7*, 345–370. doi: 10.1207/s15327027hc0704_4

Burleson, R., & Parker-Pope, T. (2016, December 27). Fans Tweet about mental illness to honor Carrie Fisher. *The New York Times*. Retrieved from: https://www.nytimes.com/2016/12/27/arts/carrie-fisher-bipolar-disorder.html?_r=0

Carucci, J. (2018, May 17) Celebrities highlight mental health issues. *US News & World Report*. Retrieved from: https://www.usnews.com/news/healthiest-communities/articles/2018-05-17/celebrities-bring-awareness-to-mental-health-issues

Casey, M. K., Allen, M., Emmers-Sommer, T., Sahlstein, E., Degooyer, D., Winters, A. M., Wagner, A. E., & Dun, T. (2003). When a celebrity contracts a disease: The example of Earvin "Magic" Johnson's announcement that he was HIV positive. *Journal of Health Communication, 8*, 249–265. doi: 10.1080/10810730305682

Cohen, J. (2009). Mediated relationships and media effects: Parasocial interaction and identification. In R. L. Nabi & M. B. Oliver (Eds.), *The Sage handbook of media processes and effects* (pp. 223–236). Thousand Oaks, CA: Sage.

Corrigan, P. W. Druss, B. G., & Perlick, D. A. (2014). The impact of mental illness stigma on seeking and participating in mental health care. *Psychological Science in the Public Interest, 15*, 37–70. doi: 10.1177/1529100614531398.

Corrigan, P. W. & Kosyluk, K. A. (2014). Mental illness stigma: Types, constructs, and vehicles for change. In P. W. Corrigan (Ed.), *The stigma of disease and disability: Understanding causes and overcoming injustices* (pp. 35–56). Washington, DC: American Psychological Association.

Corrigan, P. W., Watson, A. C., & Barr, L. (2006). The self-stigma of mental illness: Implications for self-esteem and self-efficacy. *Journal of Social and Clinical Psychology, 25*, 875–884. doi: 10.1521/jscp.2006.25.8.875.

Couture, S., & Penn, D. (2003). Interpersonal contact and the stigma of mental illness: A review of the literature. *Journal of Mental Health, 12*, 291–305. doi: 10.1080/09638231000118276

Edwards, S. M., & La Ferle, C. (2009). Does gender impact the perception of negative information related to celebrity endorsers? *Journal of Promotion Management, 15*(1/2), 22–35. doi: 10.1080/10496490902837940

Evans-Lacko, S., Corker, E., Williams, P., Henderson, C., & Thornicroft, G. (2014). Effect of the Time to Change anti-stigma campaign on trends in mental-illness-related public stigma among the English population in 2003–13: An analysis of survey data. *Lancet Psychiatry, 1*, 121–128. doi: 10.1016/s2215-0366(14)70243-3

Farina, A. (1981). Are women nicer people than men? Sex and the stigma of mental disorders. *Clinical Psychology Review, 1*, 223–243. doi: 10.1016/0272-7358(81)90005-2

Fenimore, W. L. (2012). Bad girls: From Eve to Britney. In L. C. Rubin (Ed.), *Mental illness in popular media: Essays on the representation of disorders* (pp. 146–164); Jefferson, NC, US: McFarland & Co.

Francis, D. B. (2018). Young black men's information seeking following celebrity depression disclosure: Implications for mental health communication. *Journal of Health Communication, 23*(7), 687–684. dio: 10.1080/10810730.2018.1506837

Gies, L. (2011). Stars behaving badly. *Feminist Media Studies, 11*(3), 347–361. doi: 10.1080/14680777.2010.535319

Gekoski, A., & Broome, S. (2014). *What's normal anyway? Celebrities own stories of mental illness.* London, UK: Constable.

Goffman, E. (1963). *Stigma: Notes on the management of spoiled identity.* New York, NY: Simon & Schuster.

Gunther, A. C., & Storey, J. D. (2003). The influence of presumed influence. *Journal of Communication, 53,* 199–215. doi: 10.1111/j.1460-2466.2003.tb02586.x

Herek, G. M. (1996). Why tell if you're not asked? Self-disclosure, intergroup contact, and heterosexuals' attitudes toward lesbians and gay men. *Out in force: Sexual orientation and the military,* 197–225.

Ho, S. S., & Yee, A. Z. H. (2017). Presumed media influence in health and risk messaging. In J. Nussbaum (Ed.), *Oxford research encyclopedia, communication.* Oxford, UK: Oxford University Press.

Hoffman, S. J., & Tan, C. (2013). Following celebrities' medical advice: Meta-narrative analysis. *BMJ: British Medical Journal, 347,* f7151. doi: 10.1136/bmj .f7151.

Hoffner, C. A., & Cohen, E. L. (2012). Responses to obsessive compulsive disorder on Monk among series fans: Parasocial relations, presumed media influence, and behavioral outcomes. *Journal of Broadcasting & Electronic Media, 56,* 650–668. doi: 10.1080/08838151.2012.732136

Hoffner, C. A., & Cohen, E. L. (2015). Portrayal of mental illness on the TV series *Monk*: Presumed influence and consequences of exposure. *Health Communication, 30,* 1046–1054. doi: 10.1080/10410236.2014.917840

Hoffner, C., & Cohen, E. L. (2018). Mental health-related outcomes of Robin Williams' death: The role of parasocial relations and media coverage in stigma, outreach and help-seeking. *Health Communication, 33,* 1573–1582. doi: 10.1080/ 10410236.2017.1384348

Hoffner, C. A., & Park, S. (in press). Carrie Fisher's mental health advocacy. In L. Mizejewski & T. D. Zuk (Eds.), *Our blessed rebel queen: Essays on Carrie Fisher.* Detroit, MI: Wayne State University Press

Holman, L., & McKeever, R. (2017). The Andrea Yates effect: Priming mental illness stereotypes through exemplification of postpartum disorders. *Health Communication, 32,* 1284–1296. doi: 10.1080/10410236.2016.1219929

Horton, D., & Wohl, R. R. (1956). Mass communication and para-social interaction. *Psychiatry, 19,* 215–229. doi: 10.1080/00332747.1956.11023049

Klin, A., & Lemish, D. (2008). Mental disorders stigma in the media: Review of studies on production, content, and influences. *Journal of Health Communication, 13,* 434–449. doi: 10.1080/10810730802198813

Lee, S. Y. (2018). The effect of media coverage of celebrities with panic disorder on the health behaviors of the public. *Health Communication.* Advance online publication. doi:10.1080/10410236.2018.1452093

Link, B. G., & Phelan, J. C. (2013). Labeling and stigma. In C. S. Aneshensel, J. C. Phelan, & A. Bierman (Eds.), *Handbook of the sociology of mental health* (2nd ed., pp. 525–541). New York, NY: Springer.

Link, B. G., Yang, L. H., Phelan, J. C., & Collins, P. Y. (2004). Measuring mental illness stigma. *Schizophrenia Bulletin, 30,* 511–541. doi: 10.1093/oxfordjournals .schbul.a007098

Maier, J. A., Gentile, D. A., Vogel, D. L. & Kaplan, S. A. (2014). Media influences on self-stigma of seeking psychological services: The importance of media portrayals and person perception. *Psychology of Popular Media Culture, 3,* 239–256. doi: 10.1037/a0034504

Martin, J. K., Pescosolido, B. A., & Tuch, S. A. (2000). Of fear and loathing: The role of "disturbing behavior," labels, and causal attributions in shaping public attitudes toward people with mental illness. *Journal of Health and Social Behavior, 41,* 208–223. doi: 10.2307/2676306

McGinty, E. E., Kennedy-Hendricks, A., Choksy, S., & Barry, C. L. (2016). Trends in news media coverage of mental illness in the United States: 1995–2014. *Health Affairs, 35,* 1121–1129. doi: 10.1377/hlthaff.2016.0011

Mental Health America. (2018). The state of mental health in America. Retrieved from: http://www.mentalhealthamerica.net/issues/state-mental-health-america

Miller, F. M., & Laczniak, G. R. (2011). The ethics of celebrity—Athlete endorsement: What happens when a star steps out of bounds? *Journal of Advertising Research, 51*(3), 499–510. doi: 10.2501/jar-51-3-499-510

Myrick, J. G. (2017). Public perceptions of celebrity cancer deaths: How identification and emotions shape cancer stigma and behavioral intentions, *Health Communication, 32,* 1385–1395. doi: 10.1080/10410236.2016.1224450

Myrick, J. G., Noar, S. M., Willoughby, J. F., & Brown, J. (2014). Public reaction to the death of Steve Jobs: Implications for cancer communication. *Journal of Health Communication, 19,* 1278–1295. doi: 10.1080/10810730.2013.872729

Noar, S. M., Willoughby, J. F., Myrick, J. G., & Brown, J. (2014). Public figure announcements about cancer and opportunities for cancer communication: A review and research agenda. *Health Communication, 29,* 445–461. doi: 10.1080/ 10410236.2013.764781

Parcesepe, A. M., & Cabassa, L. J. (2013). Public stigma of mental illness in the United States: A systematic literature review. *Administration and Policy in Mental Health, 40*(5), 384-399. doi: 10.1007/s10488-012-0430-z

Parrott, S., & Parrott, C. T. (2015). Law & disorder: The portrayal of mental illness in U.S. crime dramas. *Journal of Broadcasting & Electronic Media, 59,* 640–657. doi: 10.1080/08838151.2015.1093486

Peter, C., Rossmann, C., & Keyling, T. (2014). Exemplification 2.0: Roles of direct and indirect social information in conveying health information through social network sites. *Journal of Media Psychology, 26,* 19–28. doi: 10.1027/1864-1105/ a000103

Pettigrew, T. F., Tropp, L. R., Wagner, U., & Christ, O. (2011). Recent advances in intergroup contact theory. *International Journal of Intercultural Relations, 35*, 271–280. doi: 10.1016/j.ijintrel.2011.03.001

Pirkis, J., Blood, R. W., Francis, C., & McCallum, K. (2006). On-screen portrayals of mental illness: Extent, nature, and impacts. *Journal of Health Communication, 11*, 523–541. doi: 10.1080/10810730600755889

Price, V., Tewksbury, D., & Huang, L. N. (1998). Third-person effects on publication of a Holocaust-denial advertisement. *Journal of Communication, 48*(2), 3–26. doi: 10.1111/j.1490-2466.1998.tb02745.x

Quintero Johnson, J. M., & Riles, J. (2018). "He acted like a crazy person": Exploring the influence of college students' recall of stereotypic media representations of mental illness. *Psychology of Popular Media Culture, 7*(2), 146–163. doi: 10.1037/ppm0000121

Sanders, M. S. (2010). Making a good (bad) impression: Examining the cognitive processes of disposition theory to form a synthesized model of media character impression formation. *Communication Theory, 20*, 147–168. doi: 10.1111/j.1468-2885.2010.01358.x

Schiappa, E., Gregg, P. B., & Hewes, D. E. (2005). The parasocial contact hypothesis. *Communication Monographs, 72*, 92–115. doi: 10.1080/0363775052000342544

Sheffield, J. K., Fiorenza, E., & Sofronoff, K. (2004). Adolescents' willingness to seek psychological help: Promoting and preventing factors. *Journal of Youth and Adolescence, 33*(6), 495–507. doi: 10.1023/b:joyo.0000048064.31128.c6

Smith, R. A. (2007). Language of the lost: An explication of stigma communication. *Communication Theory, 17*, 462–485. doi: 10.1111/j.1468-2885.2007.00307.x

Tal-Or, N., Tsfati, Y., & Gunther, A. C. (2009). The influence of presumed media influence: Origins and implications of the third-person perception. In R. L. Nabi & M. B. Oliver (Eds.), *The Sage handbook of media processes and effects* (pp. 99–112). Los Angeles, CA: Sage.

Vogel, D. L., Gentile, D. A., & Kaplan, S. A. (2008). The influence of television on willingness to seek therapy. *Journal of Clinical Psychology, 64*, 276–295. doi: 10.1002/jclp.20446

Waddell, T. F., & Bailey, A. (2017). Inspired by the crowd: The effect of online comments on elevation and universal orientation. *Communication Monographs, 84*, 534–550. doi: 10.1080/03637751.2017.1369137

Wirth, J. H., & Bodenhausen, G. V. (2009). The role of gender in mental-illness stigma: A national experiment. *Psychological Science, 20*(2), 169–173. doi: 10.1111/j.1467-9280.2009.02282.x

Wong, N. C., Lookadoo, K. L., & Nisbett, G. S. (2017). "I'm Demi and I have bipolar disorder": Effect of parasocial contact on reducing stigma toward people with bipolar disorder. *Communication Studies, 68*(3), 314–333. doi: 10.1080/10510974.2017.1331928

World Health Organization. (2018). Mental disorders. Retrieved from: http://www.who.int/news-room/fact-sheets/detail/mental-disorders

Zhou, L., & Whitla, P. (2013). How negative celebrity publicity influences consumer attitudes: The mediating role of moral reputation. *Journal of Business Research, 66*(8), 1013–1020. doi: 10.1016/j.jbusres.2011.12.025

Chapter Eight

The Stigmatization of Mental Health Disclosure in the College Classroom

Student Perceptions of Instructor Credibility and the Benefits of Disclosure

Andrea L. Meluch
Shawn Starcher

One in six adults in the United States is currently living with a mental health issue, such as depression, anxiety, or post-traumatic stress disorder (National Institute of Mental Health (NIMH), 2017), with depression continuing to be one of the most common mental health issues. A national survey found that between 2013–2016, 8.1 percent of adults in the United States struggled with depression (Brody, Pratt, & Hughes, 2018). Reports of mental health issues have steadily increased in recent years among both college students and college instructors (e.g., Fowler, 2015; Hunt & Eisenberg, 2010; Gonçalves, 2017; Macaskill, 2012; Soet & Sevig, 2006). According to the American College Health Association (2013), nearly one-third of college students in the United States will struggle with depression. Rates of depression among college students are higher than the national average and garnered increased attention among administrators, faculty, and researchers in recent years (Novotney, 2014).

Researchers described several reasons for increased mental health issues experienced by undergraduate students, graduate students, and college instructors, including heavy workload, uncertainty regarding employment after graduation, and uncertainty regarding the continuation of employment after instructor contracted terms ended (Hunt & Eisenberg, 2010; Reevy & Deason, 2014). Despite understanding both contributing factors to student and faculty mental health issues and the abundance of these experiences on college campuses, stigma remains a key barrier to support for individuals on college campuses diagnosed with mental health issues, such as depression (Martin, 2010; Massuda, Anderson, & Edmonds, 2012). Many students and faculty may be hesitant to disclose their struggles with depression, anxiety, or other mental health issues because of the stigma associated with these identities. The issue may be particularly complicated for faculty members who may face professional ramifications if they disclose their struggles with mental health (Reevy & Deason, 2014). Specifically, faculty members are expected to perform the duties of their job satisfactorily, and, if mental health affects their ability to complete their work, faculty members may face negative responses from administrators, colleagues, and even students.

Recently, communication scholars called for additional research regarding instructor-student communication about mental health because of the increases in college student and instructor reports of mental health issues and the continued stigmatized nature of these experiences (Rudick & Dannels, 2018). This chapter examines student perceptions of faculty members struggling with depression. Specifically, this chapter seeks to explain the ways in which depression may influence student perceptions of instructor credibility in the classroom and whether instructor disclosures of depression are beneficial to students also struggling with depression.

DEPRESSION AND STIGMA ON COLLEGE CAMPUSES

Goffman (1963) defined stigma as an "attribute that is deeply discrediting" (p. 3). Scholars defined mental health stigma as "profoundly negative stereotypes about people living with mental disorders" (Smith & Applegate, 2018, p. 382). Stigmatized attributes take the form of both observable marks and concealable experiences (Smith, 2011). For example, an individual who lost their hair because of cancer treatment is unable to conceal their stigmatized identity, whereas an individual who is severely depressed may be able to conceal this identity from others. However, even concealable stigmas, such as mental disorders, may become internalized by the stigmatized individual and, in turn, be absorbed into the individual's identity (Rüsch, Angermeyer, & Corrigan, 2005). When others become aware of the stigmatized identity, the individual may no longer be considered human by others in the community and, thus, find themselves socially isolated (Goffman, 1963). Because stigmatized identities are based in the relationship between individuals, stigmas are social constructions (Martin, 2010). That is, stigmas are socially constructed in nature in that they are based in social beliefs about an attribute and influence the ways in which individuals interact with one another.

The stigmatization of mental health issues is a global phenomenon affecting individuals diagnosed with mental issues in an array of contexts (Sartorius, 2007; Thornicroft, 2006). People struggling with mental health issues, such as depression, often find that they are discriminated against in a wide variety of contexts, including within their families, friendships, professional lives, and experiences with healthcare providers (Thornicroft, 2006). Mainstream narratives about mental health issues in educational settings complicate this discrimination by often associating mental health conditions, such as depression and schizophrenia, with violent acts (Goldman, 2018). Thus, students may choose not to seek support and face additional barriers to support because they associate mental health issues with the mainstream narrative that casts violent acts (e.g., school shootings) as the result of mental health disorders.

Research on college students struggling with mental health issues demonstrated that students may experience discrimination because of their mental illness on campus (e.g., Eisenberg, Downs, Golberstein, & Zivin, 2009; Martin, 2010; Yamaguchi et al., 2013). For example, Martin (2010) found that the majority of college students struggling with mental health issues did not obtain necessary support resources (e.g., counseling), even when they were available on their college campus usually free of charge. Martin (2010) also explained that college students struggling with mental health issues deliberately make the choice to conceal their mental health issue from university staff (e.g., instructors) because students feared discrimination in their studies and potentially in their professional pursuits (e.g., being denied internships).

Students' choice to conceal a mental health issue from university staff and faculty may have serious consequences for the student. First, when a student conceals a mental health issue, such as depression, the student does not receive adequate resources (e.g., counseling) to help in managing the problem, which can lead to more negative health outcomes (Eisenberg et al., 2009; Martin, 2010). Second, when a student does not receive the resources to help manage a mental health issue, that individual is also likely to experience negative academic outcomes as a result of the untreated issue (Eisenberg, Golberstein, & Hunt, 2009; Stebleton & Soria, 2013). Thus, college students struggling with mental health issues who do not disclose to university staff are likely to experience worsened personal and academic outcomes when compared to their peers.

Currently, the majority of research on mental health issues in collegiate settings focuses on undergraduate student experiences alone. However, increasingly researchers have begun examining graduate students, who often teach as part of their workload, faculty experiences of mental health issues, and the potential negative outcomes associated from a faculty perspective (Levecque, Anseel, Beuckelaer, Van der Heyden, & Gisle, 2017; Reevy & Deason, 2014). In addition to peer-reviewed research, mental health issues among graduate students and faculty in academia has become increasingly discussed in academic forums (Pryal, 2017; Shaw & Ward, 2014). Thus, the crisis of mental health in higher education is not limited to undergraduate students and may be more widespread than previously acknowledged. Despite the recognition that instructors are increasingly struggling with mental health issues in higher education and need support services, faculty members struggling with mental illness continue to be vulnerable and often do not receive the right type of support on their campus (Price & Kerschbaum, 2017).

TEACHER CREDIBILITY

Teacher credibility and instructor behaviors have been examined by communication scholars for more than four decades (Finn et al., 2009). Teacher credibility is critical to developing a meaningful student-instructor relationship because students who do not find their instructors credible are unlikely to learn effectively (Myers, 2001). McCroskey and Young (1981) define credibility as "the attitude toward a source of communication held at a given time by the communicator" (p. 24). Scholars have long understood that teacher credibility is a multi-dimensional construct that can influence student learning (Finn et al., 2009; McCroskey & Young, 1981; McGlone & Anderson, 1973). The dimensions of teacher credibility examined in the research includes competence, character (or trustworthiness), and caring (Beatty, 1994; Finn et al., 2009). Although the dimensions of teacher credibility examined by scholars varied over the years, teacher competence and character are commonly used by researchers as constructs to understand student perceptions (Finn et al., 2009).

Today, interest in teacher credibility continues to be a strong area of research in instructional communication, and scholars are increasingly investigating relationships between credibility and current issues in higher education (e.g., instructor technology use) (Finn & Ledbetter, 2013; Ledbetter & Finn, 2016, 2018). Researchers examined relationships between instructor style of dress (Lightstone, Francis, & Kocum, 2011), instructor use of technology in the classroom (Finn & Ledbetter, 2013; Ledbetter & Finn, 2016, 2018; Schrodt & Turman, 2005), instructor gender (Basow & Howe, 1987; Basow & Silberg, 1987), and teacher credibility. Increasingly, researchers are interested in how instructor disclosures influence student perceptions of teacher credibility (e.g., Imlawi, Gregg, & Karimi, 2015; Klebig, Goldonowicz, Mendes, Miller, & Katt, 2016; Miller, Katt, Brown, & Sivo, 2014). For example, researchers found that instructors who disclose negative information, such as personal weaknesses, may contribute to classroom incivility (Miller et al., 2014).

COMMUNICATION PRIVACY MANAGEMENT THEORY

Communication Privacy Management Theory (CPM) (Petronio, 2002) is a communication-based theoretical framework that offers a descriptive understanding for how individuals manage their private information. Private information is defined as any information that may make an individual feel a sense of vulnerability and is determined through a rule-based management system typically influenced by gender, risk-benefit ratio, cultural expectations, context, and motivations (Petronio, 2002; Petronio & Durham, 2015). Instructors struggling with a stigmatized mental illness, such as a depression, may feel the need to effectively manage their private information regarding their illness in order to be seen as credible among students in the classroom setting. Even though instructors may feel a sense of vulnerability when disclosing their private information, Hosek and Thompson (2009) found that instructors establish rules for disclosing private information in the classroom environment and are motivated to disclose their private information when they feel it is relevant to course content or when establishing and building relationships with students. Furthermore, Martin, Myers, and Mottet (1999) posit that students appreciate an instructor's use of self-disclosure as they typically want to get to know their professors on a more personal level.

Although it may be important to consider why and when instructors may disclose their private information regarding mental health, it may be even more important to understand how that disclosure may impact the perceived credibility of the instructor, which ultimately influences learning outcomes and the likelihood that a student may then reciprocate in sharing similar information with the instructor when seeking help with their own struggles with depression. No known research has examined this type of disclosure or the impact on the perceived credibility of the instructor from the student's perspective.

When considering the disclosure from the perspective of the student, it is important to acknowledge the privacy rules that students may consider when determining whether to reveal or conceal their own struggles with depression. Similar to the work environment, students may not want to share their private information in the classroom with their instructor as the instructor will ultimately make the final determination on the student's progression through school and could also share that private information with other faculty members who may treat them differently because of their mental illness (for an example of concealment due to fear of stigma or discrimination, see Romo, 2016). In those situations, that disclosure could have ramifications for the remainder of the student's academic career and could influence how the student is perceived throughout the college.

Although researchers have not previously examined how instructor disclosures of depression can influence student perceptions and employment outcomes, researchers have investigated the outcomes of mental health disclosures in professional settings (Brohan et al., 2012). Specifically, in their systematic review of studies examining the stigmatization of mental health disclosures in employment, Brohan et al. (2012) found that the response to an individual's mental health disclosure in the workplace varies substantially by the industry (e.g., individuals diagnosed with mental health issues in social services work are less likely to receive a negative response to such disclosures when compared to the transportation or utilities industries). Thus, the disclosures in the classroom context may be different from other contexts because many students may be struggling, have struggled, or know someone who struggled with mental health issues. In addition, students struggling with mental health issues may interpret instructor disclosures of depression with understanding in contrast to students who do not also share these experiences.

Prior communication research advanced the use of CPM to examine stigmatized health issues (Petronio, 2013). Although some literature examined noted that college students do discuss mental health–related issues to their friends (Butler, 2016; Venetis, Chernichky-Karcher, & Gettings, 2018), researchers have yet to use CPM to understand disclosures of mental health issues, such as depression, among both college students and instructors. (Price, Salzer, O'Shea, & Kerschbaum, 2017). Thus, the present study seeks to apply CPM to understand whether instructor disclosures of personal experiences of depression influence student perceptions regarding instructor credibility and whether such instructor disclosures influence student decisions to disclose their own mental health issues.

RESEARCH QUESTIONS

To date, no known research has investigated student perceptions of instructor disclosures of depression. Due to the importance of establishing credibility and appearing competent in the classroom and maintaining a positive classroom environment, understanding whether instructor disclosures of depression negatively influence student perceptions of instructors is an important consideration to make before disclosing such private information. However, the many students who are also struggling with mental health issues may find instructor disclosures of mental health issues, like depression, to be helpful in lessening the stigma surrounding these issues. As such, the following research question is posed to understand students' perceptions of instructor disclosures of depression:

RQ1: How, if at all, do student perceptions of teacher credibility in the college classroom differ between professors who choose to disclose their struggles with depression and those who do not disclose?

We also seek to understand students' perceptions of whether instructor disclosures of depression would be helpful. Thus, the final research question posed is:

RQ2: How, if at all, do students find instructor disclosures of depression to be beneficial?

METHODS

Data for this analysis came from a larger study of student perceptions of mental health disclosures in the college classroom. Students enrolled in communication courses at a medium-sized Midwestern university (N = 363) participated in the survey. Participants' ages ranged from eighteen to forty-nine years (M = 20.45, SD = 3.51). One-hundred and forty-six participants self-identified as male, 211 participants self-identified as female, two participants self-identified as non-binary, one participant self-identified as queer, and three participants chose not to identify their gender. More than half of the participants self-identified as white (66.4%), 11.8 percent self-identified as Hispanic, 10.2 percent self-identified as African American, 2.8 percent self-identified as Asian, and the remaining 8.8 percent chose not to self-identify their ethnicity or listed "other." The majority of participants were first-year students (56.5%), 21.2 percent were sophomores, 10.5 percent were juniors, 10.7 percent were seniors, and 2.1 percent did not report their class standing.

Procedures and Instrumentation

To examine student perceptions of instructor disclosures of depression, the researchers created and included four vignettes (i.e., short descriptive texts) in the survey. Due to the stigmatized nature of depression and the potential risks an instructor would face if he or she disclosed their depression for a research study, the researchers employed vignette methodology to capture student perceptions of a hypothetical professor's behaviors and disclosures as opposed to using an actual instructor the student knew. Each of the vignettes consisted of a short, hypothetical story that described the hypothetical professor's behaviors.

Past researchers used vignette methodology as a quasi-experimental design to randomly assign participants to one condition (i.e., hypothetical story) and then compare differences between conditions (Alexander & Becker, 1978). In the present study, the researchers designed vignettes to describe the hypothetical professor as exhibiting behaviors that indicated an individual may be struggling with depression using the Diagnostic and Statistical Manual of Mental Disorders (DSM-5; American Psychiatric Association, 2013) as a guideline. Specifically, the vignette described the professor as tired all the time, difficulty concentrating, canceling class without explanation on multiple occasions, visibly upset when students ask about grades, and overly apologetic with students. The instructor behaviors listed in the vignettes were the same across each of the four conditions. In two of the four conditions, the professor disclosed to their class that they were struggling with depression (disclosure condition), and in the other two conditions there were no instructor disclosures (non-disclosure condition). To examine whether student perceptions varied by the gender of the professor in the condition, each of the conditions featured a different gender (i.e., female no-disclosure, male non-disclosure, female disclosure, male disclosure).

Participants first read the vignette and then completed McCroskey and Young's (1981) fifteen-item Teacher Credibility scale using the hypothetical scenario. The survey instructed the participants to indicate their evaluations of the instructor in the vignette using the scale. Teacher competence and teacher character were sub-scales measured using the instrument. Previous research demonstrated the high reliability of the scale with Cronbach's alphas from .84 to .93 (e.g., Beatty & Zahn, 1990; McCroskey & Young, 1981). In the present study, the researchers obtained a Cronbach's alpha score of .75 for the composite scale.

The survey asked several background questions related to their prior experiences with mental health issues. These questions included: (a) Have you ever personally struggled with depression or another mental health issue? (b) Have you ever had an instructor or college professor that you believed was struggling with depression? (c) Have you ever known a close family member or friend to be struggling with depression? (d) Have you ever told an instructor or professor that you were struggling with mental health issues? Finally, participants answered three open-ended questions: (a) What about a professor would allow you to feel comfortable to disclose a mental health issue?, (b) Would you disclose your struggles with depression to a professor? Why or why not?, and (c) Would you be more willing to disclose your struggles with depression to a professor who admitted to dealing with their own issues of depression? Why or why not?

Open-Ended Data Analysis

The researchers used Owen's (1984) methodology for thematic analysis to analyze the open-ended data in the present study. Two coders employed Owen's methodology for thematic analysis and compared findings. Owen's methodology follows three key steps when analyzing open-ended data: (a) recurrence, (b) repetition, and (3) forcefulness. He describes that the researcher first identifies recurring themes or similar meanings, even if they are stated differently by different participants, in the data. The researcher also must find repetition, such as repeated words or phrases, in the data. Finally, forcefulness can be observed in the data by examining emphasis of a particular idea (e.g., all capital letters used).

STUDY FINDINGS

The study asked participants to self-disclose their personal and academic experiences with depression. Almost two-thirds of participants (62.8%; n = 224) reported that they struggled with depression or another mental health issue. Only 17.6 percent (n = 62) participants reported that they had a college professor or instructor who they believed was struggling with depression. The majority of participants (85.7%; n = 308) reported that they had a close family member or friend struggling with depression. These descriptive statistics suggest that the sample surveyed was familiar with depression or other mental health issues in their personal lives.

Primary quantitative results. The first research question examined whether student perceptions of teacher credibility differed between the assigned conditions in which the hypothetical professor disclosed or did not disclose their struggle with depression. Results from a one-way ANOVA revealed a significant difference between the disclosure and non-disclosure conditions for teacher competence, $F(3, 347) = 4.590$, $p = .004$. Participants assigned to the disclosure conditions reported significantly lower levels of teacher competence (female disclosure: $M = 21.73$, $SD = 5.77$; male disclosure: $M = 22.00$, $SD = 5.77$) than participants in the non-disclosure condition (female non-disclosure: $M = 23.67$, $SD = 5.22$; male non-disclosure: $M = 24.30$, $SD = 5.17$). Post hoc tests revealed a significant difference between the male ($p = .03$) and the female ($p = .01$) disclosure conditions and the male non-disclosure condition. The researchers further conducted a 2 × 2 ANOVA to investigate whether there were any interactions between participants who struggled with depression or another mental health issue and perceptions of teacher competence among the four conditions. This analysis revealed no significant interactions ($p = .174$). Table 8.1 provides the cell means and standard deviations for each condition.

Table 8.1. Descriptive Statistics for Teacher Competence and Character by Disclosure Condition

	Female non-disclosure	Male non-disclosure	Female disclosure	Male disclosure
Teacher competence	M = 23.67 SD = 5.22 n = 83	M = 24.30 SD = 5.17 n = 87	M = 21.73 SD = 5.77 n = 91	M = 22.00 SD = 5.77 n = 87
Teacher character	M = 23.92 SD = 4.14 n = 82	M = 24.59 SD = 4.17 n = 88	M = 22.20 SD = 3.92 n = 90	M = 22.44 SD = 4.46 n = 89

Results from a one-way ANOVA revealed a significant difference between the disclosure and non-disclosure conditions for teacher character, $F(3, 348) = 6.741$, $p = .000$. Participants assigned to the disclosure conditions reported significantly lower levels of teacher character (female disclosure: $M = 22.20$, $SD = 3.92$; male disclosure: $M = 22.44$, $SD = 4.46$) than participants in the non-disclosure condition (female non-disclosure: $M = 23.92$, $SD = 4.14$; male non-disclosure: $M = 24.59$, $SD = 4.17$). Post hoc tests revealed a significant difference between the male ($p = .004$) and the female ($p = .001$) disclosure conditions and the male non-disclosure condition and a significant difference between the female disclosure ($p = .037$) and non-disclosure conditions. The researchers conducted a 2x2 ANOVA to investigate whether there were any interactions between participants who have personally struggled with depression or another mental health issue and perceptions of teacher character among the four conditions; however, no significant interactions were detected ($p = .440$). The results of the post hoc tests also revealed no significant difference between the male and female non-disclosure or the male and female disclosure conditions for teacher competence or teacher character, although the male non-disclosure and disclosure groups had slightly higher mean scores than both female conditions (See Table 8.1).

Open-ended data results. The second research question examined the possible ways in which students may find instructor disclosures of depression to be beneficial. Two researchers coded open-ended data, finding two key themes related to student perceptions of the benefits of instructors disclosing experiences of depression to students emerged from the qualitative data. The themes included: (a) students perceive instructors who also have experienced depression to be more understanding and able to relate more to student experiences, and (b) students perceive instructors who also have experienced depression will not stigmatize the student when he or she discloses their experience to the instructor. A third theme also emerged in the data related to participants' perceptions related to the appropriateness of instructor depression disclosures.

Professor understanding and relatability. The first theme that emerged was that participants perceived that instructors who also have experienced depression are more understanding and able to relate to students' experience of depression. Many participants noted that knowing their professors struggled with depression would be helpful to them because they would feel like their professor really "understands" and can "relate to" their experience. Specifically, one participant reported that if their professor had also struggled with depression he or she would be able to understand their mental health struggles because "you can't fully understand someone's struggle without going through it yourself." Other participants noted that knowing their professor has also struggled with depression lets them know that they are "not alone."

Many participants noted that having a caring and understanding instructor who struggled with depression would help them with comfortability in disclosing their own issues. For example, one participant said that knowing their professor struggled with depression would make them "feel more connected" to the professor as opposed to telling a professor who has not struggled and feeling "scared" to tell that individual because "they don't care." Although participants generally noted that their professors were not counselors and unable to provide any medical care, they did feel that comfort in telling their professor about their mental health struggles would be helpful to their academic achievement. Participants noted that talking to their professors about their mental health issues could be helpful in receiving necessary "accommodations" or "advice" to help them with their needs. In addition, some participants discussed that they had in the past tried to talk to professors about their depression, but felt like their professor did not understand. For example, a participant who had experienced mental health issues said "I feel like professors think I'm making excuses to do less work even though I'm not. I just want help. I've had negative experiences with telling professors in the past." However, this participant did feel that if the professor also had struggled with depression issues that "they would be able to relate to me." Participants' perceptions that a professor who struggled with depression better understand their struggles and can provide support suggests that some students may benefit from instructor disclosures of depression. That is, students who are struggling with depression or another mental health issue and are falling behind in their work may find an instructor's disclosure to be helpful in feeling that they are understood and can receive the accommodations necessary to them to be successful in the course.

Reduced Stigma

The second theme that emerged in the analysis related to the potential benefits of instructors disclosing their experiences of depression to students was that students perceived instructors experiencing depression will not stigmatize them when they disclose their mental health issue. Participants reported that they could be judged or treated differently on campus because of their struggles with mental health issues. For example, one participant said that telling a professor that they are struggling with depression could lead to "the professor treating me different than other students." Many participants noted that if they knew their professor also struggles with depression it would help them to feel "like I won't be judged as lazy" and that they are "not alone and it's not my fault." One participant noted:

> Sometimes my mental illness (type I bipolar) makes it hard to even get out of bed, yet alone attend class frequently or complete assignments on time and I hate that [some professors] may see it as slacking instead of struggling. [Knowing my professor also struggles make me feel like] they understand me more.

These participants' reports suggest that generally students perceive that they will be stigmatized for their mental health issue if they disclose it to their professors. However, participants believe that if their professor is also struggling with depression that the professor is less likely to treat them differently than other students.

Appropriateness of depression disclosures between instructors and students. Despite the overwhelming number of participant responses that indicated the benefits of instructor disclosures of depression to students, many participants also noted concerns related to instructors and students disclosing mental health issues in academic settings. Specifically, participants perceived that instructors may not be able to help them even if they do disclose their problems and that providing emotional support to students struggling with mental health issues is not a professor's job. Multiple participants noted that student mental health issues are "not their [professors'] problem." One participant said, "Professors have a lot to deal with besides students' mental health." Other participants felt discussions about mental health issues were "too personal" for the instructor-student relationship and belonged only in a counseling, family, or friendship context.

Instructor disclosures of depression were also not universally perceived as positive by participants. Some participants felt that knowing about their professor's struggles would change their image of the professor. For example, one participant said, "I view [professors] as leaders and beings of society to aspire to be. [Knowing that this individual struggles with depression] would destroy that image." It is interesting to note this contrast in perspective from the other two themes as the instructors may be stigmatized by students for their struggles with depression. In sum, questions of appropriateness of mental health disclosures between instructors and students was noted by some participants throughout the open-ended data. Thus, it is important to note that not all participants believed that disclosures of mental struggles were appropriate for either students or faculty.

DISCUSSION

This study examined student perceptions of instructor disclosures of depression to understand whether these disclosures affected student perceptions of instructor credibility and whether these disclosures were beneficial to students who may also be struggling with mental health issues. Examining student perceptions of instructor depressive struggles and the potential benefits of such disclosures offers practical insights to faculty in how to best manage their privacy boundaries related to mental health struggles in the classroom. Specifically, these findings highlight the complex nature of mental health disclosures in general and application in higher education contexts.

The first research question investigated whether student perceptions of teacher credibility differed between instructors who chose to disclose their struggles with depression and instructors who chose not to disclose. Overall, students' perceptions of both the instructor's competence and character were lower for the conditions in which an instructor disclosed struggles with depression. These findings suggest that student perceptions of teacher credibility may be lower if the instructors choose to disclose their depressive struggles to their students. These findings offer further evidence of the strong stigma against individuals who struggle with mental issues and the potential negative ramifications of sharing these struggles in a professional environment (Thornicroft, 2006). That is, individuals who are struggling with mental health issues may be unable to share their experiences openly in their lives (e.g., professional, personal) because of the continued stigma toward mental health issues. Although the college classroom has been regarded as a "safe space" where both instructors and students may want to share personal information, instructor credibility appeared to be damaged by the stigmatized nature of depressive disclosures. As such, it appeared that disclosures of depression in the classroom are regarded as a weakness and perceived negatively by students.

These findings also confirmed boundaries to the knowledge that students may want to know about their instructors. Students may appreciate an instructor's use of some self-disclosure to know their instructor on a more personal level (Martin et al., 1999), but disclosures about struggles with depression may be seen as inappropriate for some students. Furthermore, even though instructors may be motivated to disclose their private information because they feel it is relevant to course content or when establishing or building relationships with students (Hosek & Thompson, 2009), they may need to reconsider some of their disclosures more closely due to the impact it may have regarding student perceptions of their credibility. Instructors may have the best of intentions when attempting to share their private information with students about their depression, but students do not always share that same perception.

Findings within the open-ended data suggested that professor disclosures of depression may be beneficial to some students, especially those also struggling with mental health issues. However, these disclosures may not be universally helpful. Students perceived that instructors who also disclosed their issues with depression were more likely to be understanding toward student needs and provide students struggling with the necessary accommodations they need to be successful in their academic pursuits. However, participants also noted that if faculty disclosed their personal struggles with depression, this disclosure would change their perceptions of that faculty member. These findings are similar to other research that has indicated that instructor disclosures of personal weaknesses can create a less civil classroom environment (Miller et al., 2014).

This study illustrated the complex nature of personal disclosures and confirmed the delicate balance of revealing and concealing private information outlined in the CPM theoretical framework (Petronio, 2002). That is, while there may be benefits to sharing personal information (e.g., increased understanding, further connection), there are also drawbacks because the act of disclosure changes the nature of the relationship between individuals (Petronio, 2002). In terms of the instructor-student relationship, instructor credibility is key in establishing a positive classroom environment (Myers, 2001). Depressive disclosures did not appear to contribute in a positive way in establishing credibility or building a stronger instructor-student relationship. Instructor personal disclosures have been shown to create a more immediate environment in the classroom and make students feel closer to their instructor (Gorham, 1988; Kaufmann & Frisby, 2017). However, information that makes the individual vulnerable through stigmatization must be disclosed carefully through weighing potential drawbacks (Petronio, 2002). Thus, although there may be some benefits (e.g., reduced feelings of stigma and social isolation) to students also struggling with depression to know that their professor experienced similar struggles, the risks of divulging personal experiences of depression issues in the classroom are potentially threatening (e.g., perceptions of credibility) for faculty members.

Limitations and Future Directions

This study has several limitations that should be noted when interpreting the findings. First, the conditions used in this study were hypothetical and not based on actual instructor-student interactions. Creating conditions in which instructors disclose their experiences of depression may not be suitable for research contexts because of the potential harm to the instructor's reputation that such a disclosure could create. However, investigating student perceptions of specific instructors who have voluntarily disclosed their depression struggles individually may provide more in-depth understanding of the associated risks and benefits of these disclosures. Future research should consider the impact that disclosures of depression have on faculty advancement (e.g., promotion, tenure) and whether discrimination toward these issues impacts indicators of instructor efficacy (e.g., teaching evaluations, peer evaluations). Second, this study is limited to student experiences on one college campus. Including a national sample of college students may better capture widespread perceptions of depression disclosures in academic environments.

Practical Implications

The findings of this study offer two important practical implications for college instructors to consider in their communication about depression with students. The first practical implication is that professors should carefully consider the benefits of disclosing their personal struggles with depression to students who also are struggling with their mental health. While the classroom may not be an appropriate context for disclosing depression to students because such disclosures may directly influence student perceptions of instructor credibility, one-on-one conversations in which students first disclose their struggles may be an appropriate context for instructors to also share their personal experiences and knowledge of campus resources. The open-ended data suggest that disclosing personal depression struggles with students may be most appropriate in a one-on-one context in an effort to make the student feel more comfortable and to help provide resources to the student. College students indicated that stigma is a barrier to receiving mental health resources (Martin, 2010; Massuda et al., 2012). Thus, faculty members may be able to share their personal experiences to help reduce student perceptions of the negative associations with mental health issues and beliefs about barriers to support. In sum, instructors disclosing personal depression struggles may help students feel less isolated in their own struggles and may even aid in encouraging students to seek the mental health resources (e.g., campus counseling) that they need.

The second practical implication of the study findings is that faculty should work to create an open space in their classrooms that helps students who are struggling with mental health issues feel comfortable seeking support and care. Participant responses in the present study indicate that students perceive that faculty who are open about their own struggles with depression are less likely to treat students who also struggle with mental health issues negatively. However, a faculty member does not necessarily need to share the experience of depression to create a classroom climate that fosters open and safe communication about mental health. Smith (2007) explains that word choice can enact and create stigmatization. Thus, instructors can be careful not to use negative labels in class when discussing mental health.

Goldman (2018) explains that faculty can create a narrative in which from the first day of class they address the widespread mental health issues facing many college students, correct the negative stereotypes associated with mental health issues in educational settings, and demonstrate a caring and supportive attitude toward students who may be struggling. The open-ended data in the present study are consistent with Goldman's (2018) statements that participants reported their belief that if their college instructor was understanding toward their mental health issues, then they are more likely to feel comfortable reaching out for needed support resources. In sum, instructor communication and, in particular, personal disclosures about depression have the potential to benefit students' perceptions of stigma and barriers to resources. Thus, instructors should examine the ways in which they can create an understanding narrative about mental health in their classroom and their comfort level with sharing their experiences with students who may feel socially isolated because of their struggles with mental health issues.

REFERENCES

Alexander, C. S., & Becker, H. J. (1978). The use of vignettes in survey research. *Public Opinion Quarterly, 42*, 93–104. doi: 10.1086/268432

American College Health Association. (2013). National college health assessment. Retrieved from http://www.achancha.org/docs/achanchaii_referencegroup_executivesummary_spring2013.pdf

American Psychiatric Association. (2013). *Diagnostic and statistical manual of mental disorders* (5th ed.). Arlington, VA: American Psychiatric Publishing.

Basow, S. A., & Howe, K. (1987). Evaluations of college professors: Effects of professors' sex-type and sex, and students' sex. *Psychological Reports, 60*, 671–678. doi: 10.2466/pr0.1987.60.2.671

Basow, S. A., & Silberg, N. T. (1987). Student evaluations of college professors: Are female and male professors rated differently? *Journal of Education Psychology, 79*, 308–314. doi: 10.1037/0022-0663.79.3.308

Beatty, M. J. (1994). Personal report of communication apprehension. In R. B. Rubin, P. Palmgreen, & H. E. Sypher (Eds.), *Communication research measures: A sourcebook* (pp. 292–295). The Guilford Press: New York.

Beatty, M. J., & Zahn, C. J. (1990). Are student ratings of communication instructors due to "easy" grading practices? An analysis of teacher credibility and student-reported performance levels. *Communication Education, 39*, 275–282. doi: 10.1080/03634590009378809

Brody, D. J., Pratt, L. A., & Hughes, J. P. (2018). *Prevalence of depression among adults aged 20 and over: United States, 2013–2016* (NCHS Data Brief, Report No. 303). Centers for Disease Control and Prevention (epub). Retrieved from https://www.cdc.gov/nchs/data/databriefs/db303.pdf

Brohan, E., Henderson, C., Wheat, K., Malcolm, E., Clement, S., Barley, E. A., Slade, M., & Thornicroft, G. (2012). Systematic review of beliefs, behaviours and influencing factors associated with disclosure of a mental health problem in the workplace. *BMC Psychiatry, 12*, 1–14. doi: 10.1186/1471-244x-12-11

Butler, H. (2016). College students' disclosure of mental health counseling utilization. *Iowa Journal of Communication, 48*(1/2), 156–170

Eisenberg, D., Downs, M. F., Golberstein, E., & Zivin, K. (2009). Stigma and help seeking for mental health among college students. *Medical Care Research and Review, 66*, 522–541. doi: 10.1177/1077558709335173

Eisenberg, D., Golberstein, E., & Hunt, J. B. (2009). Mental health and academic success in college. *The B.E. Journal of Economic Analysis & Policy, 9*, 1–35. doi: 10.2202/1935-1682.2191

Finn, A. N., & Ledbetter, A. M. (2013). Teacher power mediates the effects of technology policies on teacher credibility. *Communication Education, 62*, 26–47. doi: 10.1080/03634523.2012.725132

Finn, A. N., Schrodt, P., Witt, P. L., Elledge, N., Jernberg, K. A., & Larson, L. M. (2009). A meta-analytical review of teacher credibility and its associations with teacher behaviors and student outcomes. *Communication Education, 58*, 516–537. doi: 10.1080/03634520903131154

Fowler, S. (2015). Burnout and depression in academia: A look at the discourse of the university. *European Journal for the Philosophy of Communication, 6*, 155–167. doi: 10.1386/ejpc.6.2.155_1

Goffman, E. (1963). *Stigma: Notes on the management of spoiled identity.* Englewood Cliffs, NJ: Prentice-Hall.

Goldman, Z. W. (2018). Responding to mental health issues in the college classroom. *Communication Education, 67*, 399–404. doi: 10.1080/03634523.2018.1465191

Gonçalves, F. V. (2017, August 5). Mental health in academia: What's happening and what can we do to address it. Retrieved from https://www.psychreg.org/mental-health-academia/

Gorham, J. (1988). The relationship between verbal teacher immediacy behaviors and student learning. *Communication Education, 37*(1), 40–53. doi: 10.1080/03634528809378702

Hosek, A. M., & Thompson, J. (2009). Communication Privacy Management and college instruction: Exploring the rules and boundaries that frame instructor private disclosures. *Communication Education, 58,* 327–349. doi: 10.1080/03634520902777585

Hunt, J., & Eisenberg, D. (2010). Mental health problems and help-seeking behaviors among college students. *Journal of Adolescent Health, 46,* 3–10.

Imlawi, J., Gregg, D., & Karimi, J. (2015). Student engagement in course-based social networks: The impact of instructor credibility and use of communication. *Computers & Education, 88,* 84–96. doi: 10.1016/j.compedu.2015.04.015

Kaufmann R., & Frisby, B. N. (2017). Dimensions of instructor disclosure: Implications for rhetorical and relational goals of instruction. *Communication Research Reports, 34*(3), 221–229. doi: 10.1080/08824096.2017.1286469

Klebig, B., Goldonowicz, J., Mendes, E., Miller, A. N., & Katt, J. (2016). The combined effects of instructor communicative behaviors, instructor credibility, and student personality traits on incivility in the college classroom. *Communication Research Reports, 33,* 152–158. doi: 10.1080/08824096.2016.1154837

Ledbetter, A. M., & Finn, A. N. (2016). Why do students use mobile technology for social purposes during class? Modeling teacher credibility, learner empowerment, and online communication as attitude predictors. *Communication Education, 65,* 1–23. doi: 1080/03634523.2015.1094145

Ledbetter, A. M., & Finn, A. N. (2018). Perceived teacher credibility and students' affect as a function of instructors' use of PowerPoint and email. *Communication Education, 67,* 31–51. doi: 10.1080/03634523.2017.1385821

Levecque, K., Anseel, F., Beuckelaer, A. D., Van der Heyden, J., & Gisle, L. (2017). Work organization and mental health problems in PhD students. *Research Policy, 46,* 868–879. doi: 10.1016/j.respol.2017.02.008

Lightstone, K., Francis, R., & Kocum, L. (2011). University faculty style of dress and students' perception of instructor credibility. *International Journal of Business and Social Science, 2,* 15–22.

Macaskill, A. (2012). The mental health of university students in the United Kingdom. *British Journal of Guidance and Counselling, 41,* 426–441. doi: 10.1080/03069885.2012.743110

Martin, J. (2010). Stigma and student mental health in higher education. *Higher Education Research and Development, 29,* 259–274. doi: 1080/07294360903470969

Martin, M. M., Myers, S. A., & Mottet, T. P. (1999). Students' motives for communicating with their instructors. *Communication Education, 48,* 155–164. Doi: 10.80/03634529909379163

Massuda, A., Anderson, P. L., & Edmonds, J. (2012). Help-seeking attitudes, mental health stigma, and self-concealment among African American college students. *Journal of Black Studies, 43*, 773–786. doi: 10.1177/0021934571244580

McCroskey, J. C., & Young, T. J. (1981). Ethos and credibility: The construct and its measurement after three decades. *Central States Speech Journal, 32*, 24–34. doi: 10.1080/10510978109368075

McGlone, E. L., & Anderson, L. J. (1973). The dimensions of teacher credibility. *Communication Education, 22*, 196–200. doi: 10.1080/03634527309378015

Miller, A. N., Katt, J. A., Brown, T., & Sivo, S. A. (2014). The relationship of instructor self-disclosure, nonverbal immediacy, and credibility to student incivility in the college classroom. *Communication Education, 63*, 1–16. doi: 10.1080/03634523.2013.835054

Myers, S. A. (2001). Perceived instructor credibility and verbal aggressiveness in the college classroom. *Communication Research Reports, 18*, 354–364. doi: 10.1080/08824090109384816

National Institute of Mental Health. (2017). Mental illness. Retrieved from https://www.nimh.nih.gov/health/statistics/mental-illness.shtml

Novotney, A. (2014). Students under pressure: College and university counseling centers are examining how best to serve the growing number of students seeking their services. *Monitor on Psychology, 45*, 36–41. doi: 10.1037/e522792014-013

Owen, W. F. (1984). Interpretive themes in relational communication. *Quarterly Journal of Speech, 70*, 274–287. doi: 10.1080/00335638409383697

Petronio, S. (2002). *Boundaries of privacy: Dialectics of disclosure*. Albany, NY: State University of New York Press.

Petronio, S. (2013). Brief status report on communication privacy management theory. *Journal of Family Communication, 13*, 6–14. doi: 10.1080/15267431.2013.743426

Petronio, S., & Durham, W. T. (2015). Communication privacy management theory: Significance for interpersonal communication. In D. O. Braithwaite & P. Schrodt (Eds.), *Engaging theories in interpersonal communication: Multiple perspectives* (2nd ed.) (pp. 335–347). Thousand Oaks, CA: Sage.

Price, M., & Kerschbaum, S. L. (2017). *Promoting supportive academic environments for faculty with mental illness: Resource guide and suggestions for practice*. National Institute on Disability, Independent Living, and Rehabilitation Research: Temple University Collaborative. Retrieved from http://tucollaborative.org/sdm_downloads/supportive-academic-environments-for-faculty-with-mental-illnesses/

Price, M., Salzer, M. S., O'Shea, A., & Kerschbaum, S. L. (2017). Disclosure of mental disability and university faculty: The negotiation of accommodations, supports, and barriers. *Disability Studies Quarterly, 37*(2). doi:: 10.18061/dsq.v37i2.5487

Pryal, K. R. G. (2017, December 8). On faculty mental illness. *The Chronicle of Higher Education*. Retrieved from https://www.chronicle.com/article/On-FacultyMental-Illness/242081

Reevy, G. M., & Deason, G. (2014). Predictors of depression, stress, and anxiety among non-tenure track faculty. *Frontiers in Psychology, 5*, 1–17. doi: 10.3389/fpsyg.2014.00701

Romo, L. K. (2016). How formerly overweight and obese individuals negotiate disclosure of their weight loss. *Health Communication, 31*(9), 1145–1154. doi: 10.1080/10410236.2015.1045790

Rudick, C. K., & Dannels, D. P. (2018). Yes, and . . . : Continuing the scholarly conversation about mental health stigma in higher education. *Communication Education, 67*, 404–408. doi: 10.1080/03634523.2018.1467563

Rüsch, N., Angermeyer, M. C., & Corrigan, P. W. (2005). Mental illness stigma: Concepts, consequences, and initiatives to reduce stigma. *European Psychiatry, 20*, 529–539. doi: 10.1016/j.eurpsy.2005.04.004

Sartorius, N. (2007). The health crisis of mental health stigma. *The Lancet, 387.* 1027–1028. doi: 10.1016/s0140-6736(16)00687-5

Schrodt, P., & Turman, P. D. (2005). The impact of instructional technology use, course design, and sex differences on students' initial perceptions of instructor credibility. *Communication Quarterly, 53*, 177–196. doi: 10.1080/01463370500090399

Shaw, C., & Ward, L. (2014, March 6). Dark thoughts: Why mental illness is on the rise in academia. *The Guardian.* Retrieved from https://www.theguardian.com/higher-education-network/2014/mar/06/mental-health-academics-growing-problem-pressure-university

Smith, R. A. (2007). Language of the lost: An exploration of stigma communication. *Communication Theory, 17*(4), 462–485. doi: 10.1111/j.1468-2885.2007.00307

Smith, R. A. (2011). Stigma, communication, and health. In T. L. Thompson, R. Parrott, & J. F. Nussbaum (Eds.), *The Routledge handbook of health communication* (2nd ed., pp. 455–468). New York: Routledge.

Smith, R. A., & Applegate, A. (2018). Mental health stigma and communication and their intersections with education. *Communication Education, 67*, 382–408. doi: 10.1080/03634523.2018.1465988

Soet, J., & Sevig, T. (2006). Mental health issues facing a diverse sample of college students: Results from the College Mental Health Survey. *NASPA Journal, 43*, 410–431. doi: 10.2202/0027-6014.1676

Stebleton, M. J., & Soria, K. M. (2013). Breaking down barriers: Academic obstacles of first-generation students at research universities. *The Learning Assistance Review, 17*, 7–19.

Thornicroft, G. (2006). *Shunned: Discrimination against people with mental illness.* New York: Oxford University Press.

Venetis, M. K., Chernichky-Karcher, S., & Gettings, P. E. (2018). Disclosing mental illness information to a friend: Exploring how the disclosure decision-making model informs strategy selection. *Health Communication, 33*(6), 653–663. doi: 10.1080/10410236.2017.1294231

Yamaguchi, S., Wu, S., Biswas, M., Yate, M., Aoki, Y., Barley, E. A., & Thornicroft, G. (2013). Effects of short-term interventions to reduce mental health–related stigma in university or college students. *The Journal of Nervous and Mental Disease, 201*, 490–503. doi: 10.1097/nmd.0b013e31829480df

Chapter Nine

Community-Based Mental Healthcare

A Network Analysis of Identification and Involvement in an Advocacy Group

Cameron W. Piercy
Alaina C. Zanin

According to the National Institute of Mental Health (2016), one in six adults in the United States self-identifies as living with a mental illness. While mental illness is pervasive, access to mental healthcare resources is disparate. With the onset of the deinstitutionalization movement in the last sixty years, mental healthcare in the United States shifted from a centralized institutional system to a fragmented, complex, and underfunded community-based model (Perry, 2016). This shift offers individuals living with mental illness more voice and choice in their healthcare, but this new system presents challenges. Holistically, the mental healthcare system in the United States is a complex, bureaucratic network that can make accessing scarce mental healthcare resources especially difficult (Rothbard & Kuno, 2000). Given the ubiquity of mental illness and the challenges created by the community-based model of mental healthcare, many individuals and families affected by mental illness rely on the support of volunteer, non-profit advocacy groups for support (Tsang, Tam, Chan, & Chang, 2003). Thus, the purpose of this chapter is to describe the complex network volunteer advocacy group members use to receive support under the current U.S. model of community-based mental healthcare.

DEINSTITUTIONALIZATION AND COMMUNITY-BASED MENTAL HEALTHCARE

As a result of the deinstitutionalization movement beginning in the mid-1950s, mental healthcare in the United States transformed from an in-patient, long-term model to a community-based model (Lamb & Bachrach, 2001). Led by patient-rights groups, politicians, and social justice organizations, the aims of the deinstitutionalization movement were to provide increased autonomy, care quality, and patient protection in mental healthcare. As a result of this shift, the current landscape of mental healthcare in the United States largely meets the definition of a *community-based model* for the provision of mental healthcare. This model of mental healthcare typically combines services from primary care providers with general and/or specialized mental health services, such as (a) community mental health caseworkers, (b) acute in-patient hospitalization services, (c) long-term community-based residential care, (d) work and occupation support, and (e) material resources such as food, shelter, clothing, transportation, and medical care (Thornicroft & Tansella, 2013). In sum, community-based mental healthcare requires the use of formal and informal support resources to form a network of care.

Stein and Test (1980) were among the first researchers to propose and test a comprehensive model for a community-based treatment program in comparison to conventional treatment (i.e., progressive short-term hospitalization). Their conceptual model for community-based mental healthcare provided: (a) material resources, (b) coping skills to meet the demands of community life (e.g., budgeting, preparing meals), (c) support systems to help solve problems, (d) support and education of caretakers, and (e) a caseworker that actively pursues a continuity of care among treatment agencies. The authors found that the use of this assertive skills-based community program greatly reduced the need to hospitalize patients and enhanced their community tenure. These initial proposals of community-based mental healthcare offered promising alternatives to institutionalization and long-term care facilities. In practice, however, the managed healthcare model in the United States has not been allocated the funding or organizational resources needed to implement a high-quality system of mental healthcare (Morselli, 2000).

Most U.S. states do not have a comprehensive mental healthcare program following Stein and Test's (1980) conceptual model. In fact, access to mental healthcare resources is becoming increasingly scarce. For example, one in five U.S. adults living with a mental illness reported they are not able to obtain the care and treatment they need due to systemic barriers (e.g., lack of available treatment providers and a lack of intensive community services) (SAMHSA, 2016). When available, community-based mental healthcare and support agencies are often disjointed, underfunded, and overburdened. Moreover, the provision of and access to mental healthcare services varies greatly among states and income level (Perry, 2016; Thornicroft & Tansella, 2013). The current resource and access issues relate to several structural problems within the current mental healthcare network.

In sum, while the post-deinstitutionalization model has yielded some increases in care quality and the protection of civil and human rights, the current fragmented system has also emphasized the role of diverse networks of caretakers, formal community resources, and non-profit organizations in providing mental healthcare. Still, disparities in access to networked resources exists. Several studies documented the objective and subjective burden families with a loved one living with a mental illness have had to cope with after deinstitutionalization (Potasznik & Nelson, 1984; Saunders, 2003; Thompson & Doll, 1982). For example, Plotnick and Kennedy (2016) found that 33 percent of U.S. caregivers reported that they received no community support for their loved one living with a mental illness. Given the emotional, financial, and logistical stresses associated with mental illness, many individuals and affected families utilize the social and resource networks provided by mental illness advocacy groups. Mental healthcare changes community networks. Seventy-eight percent of U.S. caregivers surveyed indicated that their own community network involvement shifted as a result of taking care of a loved one living with a mental illness (Plotnick & Kennedy, 2016).

MENTAL HEALTH ADVOCACY AND SUPPORT GROUPS

More than twenty-nine national mental illness advocacy and support organizations provide services to families and individuals living with mental illness in the United States (American Hospital Association, 2018). These groups offer a variety of services (e.g., education, applied training, advocacy for resource and policy change, hosting support groups). Membership in these groups demonstrated positive outcomes for individuals and families living with mental illness, including increased knowledge, improved morale (Pickett-Schenk, 2002), improved relational satisfaction, improved coping, and heightened resilience (Saunders, 2003). These groups offer alternative and integrative models of care and support in conjunction with the modern, industrialized managed healthcare system within the United States.

Networks and Mental Health

Social network research and theory highlight the importance of networks to mental and physical health (Bassett & Moore, 2013; Lin, 1999). Provan and Milward (1995) extensively surveyed mental health networks in four metropolitan areas with network analyses across interconnected mental health agencies. Results revealed that less dense and more centralized community networks were beneficial for those living with mental illness. Network position and layout related to the function of mental health support networks. Social support received from others related to higher well-being and better stress-coping during mental health crises (Kawachi & Berkman, 2001). The evidence is clear—increased social connection relates to decreased psychological distress and increased mental health (Levula, Harré, & Wilson, 2017). At the same time, those with mental illness often have smaller existing networks to rely on for resources (Rosenquist, Fowler, & Christakis, 2011).

One reason for these smaller networks is that mental illness is stigmatized and underreported (Bharadwaji, Pai, & Suziedelyte, 2017). Both the person with mental illness and those with whom they disclose their illness are generally aware of the attributions that go along with such disclosures (Corrigan, 2000). However, advocacy groups, like the one studied here, espouse goals of reducing stigma and lead to qualitative differences in members' behavior (Zanin & Piercy, 2018). For example, those who know others who (a) have a mental illness and (b) have sought healthcare are more likely to seek help themselves (Vogel, Wade, Wester, Larson, & Hackler, 2007). Thus, involvement in community and advocacy groups ought to both increase voice and reduce stigma. In all, we propose that mental illness stigma is reduced through increased support. Specifically, we predict:

> H1: The number of support sources reported by members will be inversely related to mental illness stigma.

Being a member of a mental illness support group also provides informational, network, and social benefits to members (Heller, Roccoforte, Hsieh, Cook, & Pickett, 1997). Membership in advocacy groups provides access to support findings resources as well as social support. The support network for those dealing with mental illness includes both the people who can assist, encourage, and help as well as important organizations that connect with others, allocate resources, and provide services (Provan & Milward, 1995). As detailed above, the U.S. mental health system is designed to work best when individuals call on a wide variety of resources (e.g., caregivers, local agencies, and community organizations). Given the importance of both individuals and organizations in providing support for those living with mental illness, we ask:

> RQ1: Are other people or organizational actors more central in the support network of volunteer advocacy members?

The position a person holds in the organizational network likely affects their associations with the organization. Using ego network data, Jones and Volpe (2011) found that those who were more connected (i.e., degree) had greater identification with their institution. In the context of mental health organizations, those who are more connected likely interact differently with other members of the organization. As Vogel et al. (2007) found, connections with others who experienced mental illness shapes behavior. Those who interact more with support sources have higher levels of well-being (Vogel et al., 2007), which is afforded by the increased social support they receive (Maulik, Eaton, & Bradshaw, 2009). Simply put, as a person increases their connections in a network, including linking others who are disconnected, they enact their role as an organizational member more frequently (Kuhn & Nelson, 2002). Thus, we posit:

H2: Strength of connection with social support sources (both frequency of interaction and identity overlap) is positively related to network centrality.

Organizational Identification

Organizational identification is defined as "the degree to which a person defines him or herself as having the same attributes that he or she believes define the organization" (Dutton, Dukerich, & Harquail, 1994, p. 239). Identification affects organizational members' decisions, choices, and actions. Social network analysis provides insight into sources of identification, increasing understanding of the identification process (Jones & Volpe, 2011). Identifications with organizations ranges from micro (e.g., identification with workgroup) to global level (e.g., identification with an industry) (Ashforth, Harrison, & Corley, 2008). Individuals often identify most closely with those whom they interact more frequently. Conversely, individuals may also identify strongly with industries, fields, or professions. However, in general, identities are "hierarchically organized such that individuals will favor a primary structure in most situations" (Kuhn & Nelson, 2002, p. 13). Studies of voluntary groups have found that group members described and enacted nested localized and macro-level identities through their membership in volunteer groups (Meisenbach & Kramer, 2014; Zanin, Hoelscher, & Kramer, 2016). Thus, we predict local identities are likely to be stronger than global identities. Specifically, we predict:

H3: Organizational identities will be stronger for the local mental health advocacy group than for the national or state entities.

Provan and Milward (1995) find that volunteer advocacy groups were most important in environments with limited funding (i.e., cities with more money relied more on state-funded resources). Studying a symphony, Ruud (1995) found that board members differed in their enacted identities from both administrators and musicians. Similarly, it is likely that the board members of a mental health organization differ in terms of both their network positions and their attitudes as compared to regular members. Given the dynamic environments mental health advocacy groups operate in, we ask:

RQ2: How, if at all, do board members and regular members differ in the context of a mental health advocacy group?

METHODS

As part of a larger program of mixed-method research on health volunteer efficacy, the authors gained access to a volunteer organization whose mission was to support community members living with mental illness (Zanin & Piercy, 2018). The current study employs a network analysis to explore the support networks of a volunteer mental illness advocacy group (Wasserman & Faust, 1994).

Research Context and Participants

The advocacy group is located in a city of one hundred thousand in the Midwestern United States. The group works closely with other community-based mental healthcare services including governmental (e.g., behavioral health court, disability services) and non-profit agencies (e.g., homeless shelters, job skills training). The depth of participation in the group varies from members who receive a monthly newsletter to members who have daily interaction with multiple board members and community services. Currently, the group has nearly three hundred members, but a much smaller proportion participate in services regularly (< 40 participate weekly). Participants were purposely selected based on their level of involvement in group activities. All current board members were included ($n = 11$) along with active non-board members ($n = 9$). Participant ages ranged from twenty-nine to seventy-five ($M = 53.41$, $SD = 13.18$). Occupations varied among participants, including police officers ($n = 2$), retired teachers ($n = 3$), social workers ($n = 1$), a lawyer ($n = 1$), non-profit workers ($n = 2$), a full-time student ($n = 1$), or individuals on federal disability ($n = 3$). Participants' tenure of CMIA membership ranged from two to twenty years ($M = 9.58$ years, $SD = 5.76$ years). Board members meet monthly and host several social events including weekly support groups, monthly classes, bi-annual workshops, and yearly attendance at state and national conferences. Some participants disclosed that they became involved with CMIA after their own mental illness diagnosis ($n = 10$), while others joined after their family member was diagnosed with a mental illness ($n = 7$). Three participants interviewed did not have a mental illness, nor a family member with a mental illness, but indicated that they had an interest in joining the group because they often interacted with individuals in their community living with a mental illness.

Data Collection

The authors collected a support network survey and interview data from all group board members and group members ($n = 20$). During interviews, participants self-reported their sources of social support. Following the interview, participants responded to a questionnaire detailing their relationship to each source they named, including both other people and organizations. This survey allowed us to construct the support network participants shared. Sources of support included local government and non-profit organizations, healthcare practitioners, a new mental health court system, and family members. A total of eighteen participants provided information about 155 relationships with eighty-five different sources ($M = 8.61$ per person). Eighty-two connections were with other people, sixty-nine with organizations, and four connections were "other" sources (i.e., cats, profession, and online sources). Table 9.1 details the categories of every node in the network.

Table 9.1.   Participants' Self-Report of Social Support Type for Mental Illness Healthcare and Rehabilitation

Support Source Type	Frequency of Source (N = 85)
Animal	1
Children	11
Churches	5
Friends and relatives	7
Government agencies	5
Healthcare professionals	3
Members	19
Online sources	2
Parents	2
Romantic Partners	7
Professional membership	1
Other support organizations	20

Note: Category were derived based on participants' qualitative interview descriptions of the source labels.

Measures

Participants completed a short survey with measures of perceived mental illness stigma and demographic information. Mental illness stigma was measured using Link and colleagues' (1989; 2015) twelve-item Perceived Devaluation and Discrimination. This is the most commonly used scale for measuring individual stigma (Livingston & Boyd, 2010). After completing these measures, participants were interviewed about the sources they turned to for support. Throughout the interview, the interviewer took note of each support source named and asked participants following the interview: "Are there any other sources you turn to for social support in addition to the people and organizations you named?"

Following the interview, participants completed a one-page network survey for each support source named. The survey asked names, gender, and age of support source (as applicable). Next, identification was measured using the inclusion of other in the self-scale (Aron, Aron, & Smollan, 1992). This single-item measure presents Venn diagrams of increasing overlap between a target (e.g., a friend, the county health services, a service organization) and the self. The scale has been cross-validated with much more comprehensive measures of closeness (Aron et al., 1992). Consistent with the original measure, this measure captures the "vicarious sharing of other's traits and abilities" or identification (Aron et al., 1992, p. 598). Participants were presented with the modified version created by Gächter, Starmer, and Tufano (2015) (reproduced under creative commons license in Figure 9.1).

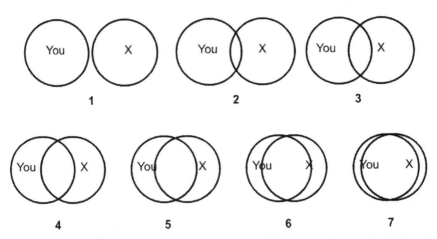

Figure 9.1.   Modified Inclusion of Other in the Self (Gächter, Starmer, & Tufano, 2015). Image provided courtesy of the author.

Participants also reported frequency of interaction with each support source on a scale ranging from daily to less than once a year. Finally, participants reported whether the source was within fifty miles of their home (131 source < 50; 24 > 50 mi) and if the source was considered a family member (46 family members; 109 non-family). Interestingly, nineteen of twenty-four sources located greater than fifty miles away were state and national branches of the same organization. Further, eighteen of the forty-six family members identified were organizations (e.g., church, the support group), not people.

For analysis, a network edgelist (displaying participant ID in one column and support source and attributes in subsequent columns; Hanneman & Riddle, 2005) was constructed and imported to the UCINET and SPSS. Visualizations were generated using the iGraph packages in R. Though this is a meager sample for statistical analysis, significance testing was conducted when possible. Given the limited sample size, tests that were significant at $p < .10$ are reported as significant (Levine, Weber, Hullett, Park, & Lindsey, 2008). As with network measures in general, these network values were skewed and kurtotic, so normalized values were used and reported (Hanneman & Riddle, 2005). A full graph depicting all participants and support sources is shown in Figure 9.2.

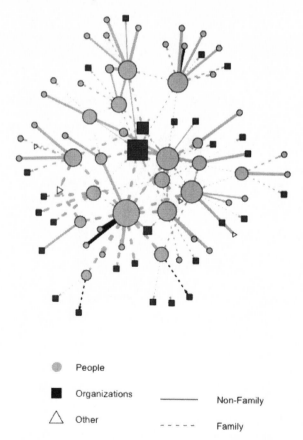

Figure 9.2. Volunteer Advocacy Group Support Network in Community-Based Mental Healthcare.
Image provided courtesy of the author.

RESULTS

RQ1

To test whether other people or organizational members were more central to the support networks reported by participants, we conducted a centrality analysis using UCINET (Borgatti, Everett, & Freeman, 2002). The resulting degree centrality and in-degree average reciprocal distance were used to evaluate participants' relative location in the network. These measures allowed researchers to understand what nodes (i.e., individuals and/or organizations) were most central and important in providing support for individuals living with mental illness within a community-based model of healthcare. Borgatti, Everett, and Johnson (2018) explain that average reciprocal distance can be superior to the traditional closeness measures because it considers and weights connections throughout the network (i.e., beyond those whom one is directly connected). This measure is appropriate with this data given that all sources of support were connected together (i.e., the members form one principle or giant component; Cunningham, Everton, & Murphy, 2016).

Next, a *t*-test was used to compare the normalized values for these centrality measures between people and organizations. Results showed a significant difference between human and organizational sources of support. In terms of degree, or number of connections, individuals ($M = 0.04$, $SD = 0.05$) had more connections than organizations ($M = 0.02$, $SD = 0.03$), $t_{corrected}$ (74.75) = -2.76, $p = .007$. However, this finding was driven by the participants' self-reported ties. A less biased comparison using in-degree (how many times a source was nominated by others) showed no significant difference between human and organizational ties, $p = .71$. Therefore, organizations and human sources had a roughly equal number of connections in this network.

Average reciprocal distance (ARD), a measure of how many connections away others are in the network on average, was computed by taking the average of all possible paths (i.e., connections) between an actor and any given partner. Values for this scale range from 0 to 1, such that 1 represents a direct connection to all other actors (Borgatti & Everett, 2006). Interestingly, the directed ARD was higher for organizations ($M = 0.06$, $SD = 0.04$) than humans ($M = 0.05$, $SD = 0.04$), $t(75) = 1.86$, $p = .067$. Restated, organizations were more connected in the support network than individuals in this context. Thus, the answer to RQ1 is although individuals and organizations are named equally, when the whole network is taken into account, organizations are more central support providers than individuals.

H1

Hypothesis 1 predicts that the number of support sources reported would be related to lower mental illness stigma. Restated in network terms, outdegree is hypothesized to negatively relate to mental illness stigma. To test this hypothesis, the correlation between stigma and outdegree was computed, but the relationships were not significant $r = .05, p = .42$. Therefore, H1 is not supported in this data. *Post hoc* examination of the self-reported stigma values were significantly lower than the scale mean of two: $M = 1.28, SD = 0.57, t(16) = -5.26, p < .001$. Therefore, interviewed members experienced relatively low levels of stigma overall, regardless of network composition.

H2

The second hypothesis proposes an individual's strength of connection to support sources related to increased network centrality. To explore this hypothesis, an average identity overlap (i.e., inclusion of other in the self) and average frequency of interaction with all connections reported was computed. These strength-of-connection measures (i.e., identity overlap and frequency of interaction) were entered in a zero-order correlation with undirected network measures (i.e., including both sources named and sources who named the participant), degree and ARD values. No relationships were present between average identity overlap and these network outcomes. Correlations were significant and large between frequency of interaction in both degree ($r = .75, p < .001$) and ARD ($r = .76, p < .001$). Thus, H2 is partially supported such that individuals who report more frequent interaction with support contacts in general are more central to the network. Restated, those who interact more frequently with their support sources are also key network actors.

RQ2

The second research question asked how, if at all, board members and regular members differed. To explore this question, identification and frequency of interaction with the organization as well as network properties of degree centrality and ARD closeness were examined between board and non-board members. Board members saw the organization as more central to their identities ($M = 6.35, SD = 0.88$) than non-members ($M = 3.57, SD = 0.53$), $t_{corrected}(14.08) = -8.06, p < .001$. Board members also interacted more with the organization ($M = 6.43, SD = 0.79$) than regular members ($M = 4.67, SD = 1.63$), $t_{corrected}(13) = -2.54, p = .027$. Members and board members did not differ in terms of network properties (degree, $p = .22$; ARD, $p = .13$) or stigma perceptions ($p = .92$). Thus, board members appear to be more closely connected and interact more frequently with the mental health support organization, but they do not differ from non-board members in terms of network properties or stigma perceptions.

H3

Hypothesis 3 predicted members would be more closely identified with the local organization than the state and national levels. A one-way ANOVA revealed participants were significantly more identified with the local organization ($M = 5$, $SD = 1.60$) than the state ($M = 3.18$, $SD = 2.04$) or national levels ($M = 2.00$, $SD = 1.79$) of the organization, $F (2, 37) = 12.73$, $p < .001$, $\eta^2 = .41$. Tests were also conducted for frequency of interaction. Participants also interacted more frequently with the local organization ($M = 3.71$, $SD = 1.27$) than the state ($M = 2.09$, $SD = 1.22$) or national levels ($M = 1.72$, $SD = 1.01$) of the organization, $F (2, 37) = 10.27$, $p < .001$, $\eta^2 = .38$. Despite the small sample size, participants clearly identified more and interacted more frequently with their local advocacy group. Figure 9.3 presents a bipartite or two-mode sociogram where line weight (thickness or width) is based on identification with the organization. As the figure shows, local identities have

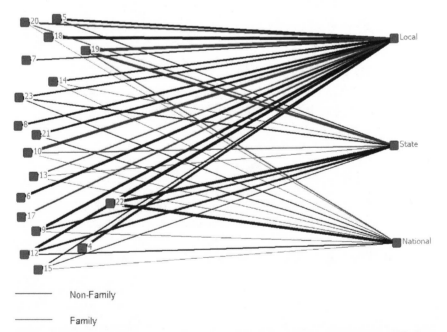

Figure 9.3. **Bipartite Network of National, State, and Local Organizational Affiliations. Modeled via UCINeT. Line thickness is based on Inclusion of Other in the Self.**
Image provided courtesy of the author.

more lines of higher width and that the local organization is more likely to be considered family. Supplemental interview data revealed nuances and depth to this finding such that participants often described organizational nodes within the network as "family" rather than naming individual actors as family. Thus, H3 was supported.

DISCUSSION

The aim of this chapter was to demonstrate the situated support roles of members in a volunteer advocacy group. Results revealed some disparities in network compositions. This study not only documents a current communicative network of a mental healthcare advocacy group, but it also provides insight into how volunteer members are co-constructing current network structures to facilitate resources and services for individuals living with mental illness in their community. As demonstrated by the results in Figure 1, the network revealed the importance of personal support from other people while also demonstrating the importance of organizations in the provision of support. At the same time, several members serve as the core of this network with many people calling on them for support. The following section discusses the implications of central network actors to providing person-centered support, the structure of layered identifications, and the relationship between voluntary membership and identification.

Centrality and Health Advocacy Group Identification

Past evidence suggests that advocacy groups serve a peripheral role in the general operations of community mental illness services (Provan & Milward, 1995). However, this study's findings suggest that for individuals in these groups, support structures were overlapped among mental health advocacy group members. Perhaps this finding is unsurprising given that macro structures, such as federal funding programs for mental healthcare, are often unable to provide meaningful person-centered support (Perry, 2016). The support networks that members rely on consist of equal proportions of other people and organizations. There were not differences in the number of people versus organizations named (i.e., no difference in overall degree) as sources of support. However, when the directed network data was considered (i.e., data focused on in-degree, excluding the organization being studied), organizations were more central to the network than other people. This finding indicates that organizations (e.g., the county health board, local churches) were at least as important as people in providing social support. Future studies of mental health and social support may find that organizations are important and that their meaningful connections are worth consideration. To apply these findings, advocacy groups could benefit from connecting with other similar community-based groups to leverage social support networks for individuals living with mental illness and extend their network reach.

Counter to past evidence demonstrating a positive relationship between degree centrality and identification (Jones & Volpe, 2011), there was no relationship between identification and degree centrality in this data. Instead, participants' identification differed in terms of frequency of interaction and hierarchical position. Individuals who were more central in the network interacted more with their sources of support. In addition, members in formal hierarchical positions interacted more with the organization in question and identified more with the volunteer organization. Previous research on social support and health advocacy groups demonstrated a relationship between membership involvement and identification, such that members enacted specific identities (e.g., illness survivor, advocate, altruistic supporter) through their participation (Irwin, LaGory, Ritchey, & Fitzpatrick, 2008). In this data, both board members and local organizations were the important (i.e., central and frequently contacted) support sources. Given these findings, a practical recommendation to increase advocacy group identification and long-term participation would be to create multiple ways for peripheral network members to become more involved in mental healthcare advocacy rather than relying on a few members to do the majority of the volunteer work. Zanin and Piercy (2018) found that this practice could provide a two-layer benefit for the organization: (a) giving community members living with mental illness opportunities for self-efficacy and involvement and (b) expanding the volunteer base to extend community outreach programs. This finding suggests that advocacy groups should provide more opportunities for involvement at the local level to increase continued participation, identification, impact, and resources over time.

Layered Identification with Network Resources

Participants identified and interacted more with the local (as compared to state and national) levels of this organization. Though all three levels of the organization were essential to the support networks on which the participants called, it appears that local identification was most salient as a result of increased participation. The organization may benefit by highlighting the shared identity of group members who live with mental illness (Dutton et al., 2006; Meisenbach & Kramer, 2014). Indeed, these findings suggest that organizations can leverage identification to foster connection among members inside and outside of the organization. Further, members in the study classified two out of every five organizations as family. Given that previous research established the importance of family in providing support to those with mental illness (Potasznik & Nelson, 1984), this could be encouraging. In this group, organizations served as meaningful supplements or proxies for social support while coping with mental illness.

Since connection with others is related to reduced distress during periods of psychological duress (Livingstone & Boyd, 2010), the localization of support could reduce stress associated with mental health crises. There were relatively few ties ($n = 4$) that were at a distance greater than fifty miles. At least for the members of this support group, localized support was more important than disparate support. This finding may signal the importance of localized support in a community-based model of mental healthcare. Only through local cooperation can mental health organizations thrive given the diffusion of resources (Provan, Isett, & Milward, 2004).

Network Structures' Relationship to Stigma and Identification

Surprisingly, there were no differences in stigma based on network position or identification; instead, stigma was universally low among members of this network. This finding may be related to members' outreach programs related to reducing stigma associated with mental illness. It is likely that through these interactions, perceptions of mental illness stigma were reduced for group members—an interesting finding given that stigma has been shown to create barriers for individuals seeking support and healthcare for their mental illness (Vogel et al., 2007). This finding suggests that participating in an advocacy group may reduce an individual's perceptions of mental illness stigma. Future studies of mental illness advocacy group membership should consider how levels of group participation affect members' perceptions of mental illness stigma or other potential barriers such as self-efficacy or agency.

Frequency of interaction within the network was related to both higher identification with peers and more connections in the network. This frequency of interaction finding is particularly meaningful as identification and frequency of interaction were strongly correlated ($r = .77, p < .001$), but each related to different outcomes. Findings about the importance of certain people (including board members) in the network reiterates the need for network interventions to adequately support those with mental illness (Anderson, Laxhman, & Priebe, 2015). In this data, members who interacted most with their support sources also had the most connections and were most central. Certain members were quite central to the network (or network stars; see Hanneman & Riddle, 2005).

These findings reiterate a well-documented network phenomena called the *Matthew Effect*, whereby those who have network resources continue to amass more network resources. As Kadushin (2012) explains, the Matthew Effect is a "scriptural truth hallowed in science . . . 'to those who hath shall be given'" (p. 69). This phenomenon may be problematic as members who have the least interaction (e.g., non-board members who primarily belong to the group for support) likely need the most support considering instances of mental health crisis. Further, the Matthew Effect posits that more central network actors are also more likely to be decision makers, a trend that also holds true in the current context with board members. Given that individuals with larger support networks are often better able to cope with difficulties and have higher ratings of well-being (Anderson, Laxhman, & Priebe, 2015), network interventions may be useful to similar groups to help cope with mental health issues. Future research should examine how strategic network interventions aimed at increasing peripheral members' network connections (e.g., mentorship programs, social mixers, etc.) might provide higher-quality support networks and increase group diversity and network reach.

Limitations and Strengths

One limitation of this research was the relatively small sample size. While we obtained data for an entire board members' network and members who were highly involved with the organization, less active members were not included in this descriptive network analysis. Extensions of this work should include more periphery members to document differences among member identification with the group. Still, considering we found relatively active members, we consider the findings discussed above to be particularly important because the less active members likely reside in similar, and possibly even less advantaged, network roles as those in the study. Given the relatively small sample size, the results presented here should be applied to other similar research contexts with care.

Participants in this study were identified as "living with mental illness," as opposed to individuals diagnosed with mental illness or family members of those diagnosed with mental illness. We believe that individuals living with mental illness include both the diagnosed and those living with the diagnosis. Future research may benefit from adopting a dynamic perspective of living with mental illness that involves all people immediately affected by the diagnoses. Complimentarily, separating analysis of those diagnosed and those who assist may lead to meaningful variation.

REFERENCES

American Hospital Association (2018). Mental Health Awareness Month. Retrieved from: https://www.aha.org/2011-02-07-national-mental-health-organizations

Anderson, K., Laxhman, N., & Priebe, S. (2015). Can mental health interventions change social networks? A systematic review. *BMC Psychiatry, 15*(1), 297. doi:/10.1186/s12888-015-0684-6

Aron, A., Aron, E. N., & Smollan, D. (1992). Inclusion of other in the self-scale and the structure of interpersonal closeness. *Journal of Personality and Social Psychology, 63*(4), 596–612. doi: 10.1037/0022-3514.63.4.596

Ashforth, B. E., Harrison, S. H., & Corley, K. G. (2008). Identification in organizations: An examination of four fundamental questions. *Journal of Management, 34*, 325–374. doi: 10.1177/0149206308316059

Assessment #10: State Mental Health Agency-Controlled Expenditures for Mental Health Services, State Fiscal Year 2013. (2014, Sept. 26). NASMHPD Research Institute. Retrieved from: https://www.nasmhpd.org/sites/default/files/Assessment%2010%20-%20Expenditures.pdf

Bassett, E., & Moore, S. (2013). Mental health and social capital: Social capital as a promising initiative to improving the mental health of communities. In Alfonso J. Rodriguez-Morales (Ed.), *Current topics in public health*, IntechOameripen, doi: 10.5772/53501.

Bharadwaj, P., Pai, M. M., & Suziedelyte, A. (2017). Mental health stigma. *Economics Letters, 159*, 57–60. doi:10.1016/j.econlet.2017.06.028

Borgatti, S. P., & Everett, M. G. (2006). A graph-theoretic perspective on centrality. *Social Networks, 28*(4), 466–484. doi: 10.1016/j.socnet.2005.11.005

Borgatti, S. P., Everett, M. G. & Freeman, L. C. (2002). *UCINET 6 for Windows: Software for Social Network Analysis.* Harvard, MA: Analytic Technologies.

Borgatti, S. P., Everett, M. G., & Johnson, J. C. (2018). *Analyzing social networks.* New York: Sage, 2013.

Corrigan, P. W. (2000). Mental health stigma as social attribution: Implications for research methods and attitude change. *Clinical Psychology: Science and Practice 7*(1), 48–67. doi: 10.1093/clipsy.7.1.48

Cunningham, D., Everton, S., & Murphy, P. (2016). *Understanding dark networks: A strategic framework for the use of social network analysis.* Lanham, MD: Rowman & Littlefield.

Dutton, J. E., Dukerich, J. M., & Harquail, C. V. (1994). Organizational images and member identification. *Administrative Science Quarterly, 39*, 239–263. doi: 10.2307/2393235

Dutton, M. A., Green, B. L., Kaltman, S. I. Roesch, D. M., Zeffiro, T. A., & Krause, E. D. (2006). Intimate partner violence, PTSD, and adverse health outcomes. *Journal of Interpersonal Violence, 21*(7). doi: 10.1177/0886260506289178

Gächter, S., Starmer, C., & Tufano, F. (2015). Measuring the closeness of relationships: a comprehensive evaluation of the "Inclusion of the Other in the Self" scale. *PloS one*, 10(6), e0129478. doi: 10.1371/journal.pone.0129478

Hanneman, R. A., & Riddle, M. (2005). *Introduction to social network methods.* Riverside, CA: University of California, Riverside.

Heller, T., Roccoforte, J. A., Hsieh, K., Cook, J. A., & Pickett, S. A. (1997). Benefits of support groups for families of adults with severe mental illness. *American Journal of Orthopsychiatry, 67*(2), 187–198. doi: 10.1037/h0080222

Irwin, J., LaGory, M., Ritchey, F., & Fitzpatrick, K. (2008). Social assets and mental distress among the homeless: Exploring the roles of social support and other forms of social capital on depression. *Social Science & Medicine, 67*, 1935–1943. doi: 10.1016/j.socscimed.2008.09.008

Jones, C., & Volpe, E. H. (2011). Organizational identification: Extending our understanding of social identities through social networks. *Journal of Organizational Behavior, 32*, 413–434. doi: 10.1002/job.694

Kadushin, C. (2012). *Understanding social networks: Theories, concepts, and findings.* Oxford University Press. Kindle Edition.

Kawachi, I., & Berkman, L. F. (2001). Social ties and mental health. *Journal of Urban Health, 78*, 458–467. doi: 10.1093/jurban/78.3.458

Kuhn, T., & Nelson, N. (2002). Reengineering identity: A case study of multiplicity and duality in organizational identification. *Management Communication Quarterly, 16*, 5–38. doi: 10.1177/0893318902161001

Lamb, H. R., & Bachrach, L. L. (2001). Some perspectives on deinstitutionalization. *Psychiatric Services, 52*, 1039–1045. doi: 10.1176/appi.ps.52.8.1039

Levine, T. R., Weber, R., Hullett, C., Park, H. S., & Lindsey, L. L. M. (2008). A critical assessment of null hypothesis significance testing in quantitative communication research. *Human Communication Research, 34*(2), 171–187.

Levula, A., Harré, M., & Wilson, A. (2017). Social network factors as mediators of mental health and psychological distress. *International Journal of Social Psychiatry, 63*, 235–243. doi: 10.1177/0020764017695575

Lin, N. (1999). Building a network theory of social capital. *Connections 22*, 28–51. doi: 10.4324/9781315129457-1

Link, B. G., Cullen, F. T., Struening, E., Shrout, P. E., & Dohrenwend, B. P. (1989). A modified labeling theory approach to mental disorders: An empirical assessment. *American Sociological Review, 54*, 400–423. doi: 10.2307/2095613

Link, B. G., Wells, J., Phelan, J. C., & Yang, L. (2015). Understanding the importance of "symbolic interaction stigma": How expectations about the reactions of others adds to the burden of mental illness stigma. *Psychiatric Rehabilitation Journal, 38*(2), 117–124. doi: 10.1037/prj0000142

Livingston, J. D., & Boyd, J. E. (2010). Correlates and consequences of internalized stigma for people living with mental illness: A systematic review and meta-analysis. *Social Science & Medicine, 71*(12), 2150–2161. doi: 10.1016/j.socscimed.2010.09.030

Maulik, P. K., Eaton, W. W., & Bradshaw, C. P. (2009). The role of social network and support in mental health service use: Findings from the Baltimore ECA study. *Psychiatric Services, 60*(9), 1222–1229. doi: 10.1176/ps.2009.60.9.1222

Meisenbach, R. J., & Kramer, M. W. (2014). Exploring nested identities: Voluntary membership, social category identity, and identification in a community choir. *Management Communication Quarterly*, *28*(2), 187–213. doi: 10.1177/0893318914524059

Morselli, P. L. (2000). Present and future role of Mental Illness Advocacy Associations in the management of the mentally ill: Realities, needs and hopes at the edge of the third millennium. *Bipolar Disorders, 2*, 294–300. doi: 10.1034/j.1399-5618.2000.20310.x

National Institute of Mental Health. (2016). *Mental Illness.* (2016 National Survey on Drug Use and Health). Retrieved from https://www.nimh.nih.gov/health/statistics/mental-illness.shtml

Perry, B. L. (2016). *50 Years after deinstitutionalization: Mental illness in contemporary communities*. Somerville, MA: Emerald.

Pickett-Schenk, S. A. (2002). Church-based support groups for African American families coping with mental illness: Outreach and outcomes. *Psychiatric Rehabilitation Journal*, *26*, 173–180. doi: 10.2975/26.2002.173.180

Plotnick, D., & Kennedy, J. (2016). Community inclusion from the perspective of caregivers of people with psychiatric disabilities. *Mental Health America*, Alexandria, VA.

Potasznik, H., & Nelson, G. (1984). Stress and social support: The burden experienced by the family of a mentally ill person. *American Journal of Community Psychology, 12*(5), 589–607. doi: 10.1176/ajp.141.4.604

Provan, K. G., Isett, K. R., & Milward, H. B. (2004). Cooperation and compromise: A network response to conflicting institutional pressures in community mental health. *Nonprofit and Voluntary Sector Quarterly*, *33*, 489–514. doi: 10.1177/0899764004265718

Provan, K. G., & Milward, H. B. (1995). A preliminary theory of interorganizational network effectiveness: A comparative study of four community mental health systems. *Administrative Science Quarterly*, 1–33. doi: 10.2307/2393698

Rosenquist, J. N., Fowler, J. H., & Christakis, N. A. (2011). Social network determinants of depression. *Molecular Psychiatry*, *16*, 273–281. doi: 10.1038/mp.2010.13

Rothbard, A. B., & Kuno, E. (2000). The success of deinstitutionalization: Empirical findings from case studies on state hospital closures. *International Journal of Law and Psychiatry*, *23*, 329–344. doi: 10.1016/s0160-2527(00)00042-x

Ruud, G. (1995). The symbolic construction of organizational identities and community in a regional symphony. *Communication Studies*, *46*, 201–221. doi: 10.1080/10510979509368452

SAMHSA. (2016). 2016 Statistical Inference Report. *Substance Abuse and Mental Health Services Administration.* Retrieved from https://www.samhsa.gov/data/report/2016-statistical-inference-report

Saunders, J. C. (2003). Families living with severe mental illness: A literature review. *Issues in Mental Health Nursing, 24*, 175–198. doi: 10.1080/01612840305301

Stein, L. I., & Test, M. A. (1980). Alternative to mental hospital treatment. *Archives of General Psychiatry, 37*, 392–397. doi: 10.1001/archpsyc.1980.01780170034003

Thompson, E., & Doll, W. (1982). The burden of families coping with the mentally ill: An invisible crisis. *Family Relations, 31*, 379–388. doi: 10.2307/584170

Thornicroft, G., & Tansella, M. (2013). The balanced care model: The case for both hospital-and community-based mental healthcare. *The British Journal of Psychiatry, 202,* 246–248. doi: 10.1192/bjp.bp.112.111377

Tsang, H. W., Tam, P. K., Chan, F., & Chang, W. M. (2003). Sources of burdens on families of individuals with mental illness. *International Journal of Rehabilitation Research, 26,* 123–130. doi: 10.1097/00004356-200306000-00007

Vogel, D. L., Wade, N. G., Wester, S. R., Larson, L., & Hackler, A. H. (2007). Seeking help from a mental health professional: The influence of one's social network. *Journal of Clinical Psychology, 63*(3), 233–245. doi:10.1002/jclp.20345

Wasserman, S., & Faust, K. (1994) *Social network analysis: Methods and applications 8.* Cambridge University Press.

Zanin, A. C., Hoelscher, C. S., & Kramer, M. W. (2016). Extending symbolic convergence theory: A shared identity perspective of a team's culture. *Small Group Research, 47*(4), 438–472. doi: 10.1177/1046496416658554

Zanin, A. C., & Piercy, C. W. (2018). The structuration of community-based mental health care: A duality analysis of a volunteer group's local agency. *Qualitative Health Research, 29*(2). doi: 1049732318786945.

Chapter Ten

When Healthcare Professionals Need Help

Nursing Burnout and Supportive Communication

Dorothy Hagmajer

Yulia A. Strekalova

In 2018, the health care system of the United States is bracing itself to care for an imminent wave of retirees. Buerhaus (2008) predicts that within the next two decades, healthcare institutions will see numbers in the nursing workforce plateau, as current nursing professionals age and seek retirement themselves, creating a dearth of nurses during a time when the demand and importance of their role is expected to increase. Researchers predict this sustained shortage of nurses will develop in the concluding half of the next decade, impeding access to healthcare, the quality of the care delivered, and inciting a spike in healthcare costs. More specifically, the demand for RNs is expected to increase at an estimated rate of 2 percent to 3 percent per year over the next twenty years, and the shortage of nurses is predicted to increase to an estimated 285,000 RNs by the year 2020, which is almost three times greater than any previous shortage documented in the United States over the past fifty years. This, in turn, is projected to expand to five hundred thousand by 2025 (Buerhaus, 2008). Now, the various members comprising what we know as the modern-day healthcare workforce—primarily health administrators, policymakers, other health professionals, and physicians—are tasked with the question of what preemptive actions may be taken to mitigate the fiscal and social consequences of the future shortage.

Fortunately, research indicates a shift in the perceptions of the nursing workforce. This is largely due to the rising amount of evidence pointing out that achieving and maintaining healthcare delivery systems of high quality has an inherently dependent relationship with the preparedness and wellness of the healthcare providers within (Buerhaus, Skinner, Auerbach, & Staiger,

2017). More specifically, research has demonstrated links between sufficient hospital nurse staffing to patient outcome. For example, hospitals that boast high numbers of patients per nurse ratios see their surgical patients experience more frequent mortality and failure-to-rescue rates despite adjusting for disparate risk factors. In addition, nurses are more predisposed to burnout and job dissatisfaction. Findings such as these have led to the development of several quality and safety initiatives, such as the nursing quality measures supported by the National Quality Forum, The Joint Commission (previously JCAHO) Agency for Healthcare Research and Quality, and the Centers for Medicare & Medicaid Services. This rising emphasis on the importance of performance measures specific to nurses is but one symptom of the benefits to incorporating a more efficient use and retention of nurses (Buerhaus, 2008). However, in order to better understand these future opportunities for retention, one must first identify the conflicts and barriers currently impeding job satisfaction and retention (e.g., burnout and the role protective factors such as social support play).

SUPPORTIVE COMMUNICATION AND MECHANISMS OF PREVENTING AND ADDRESSING BURNOUT

Among nursing professionals specifically, relationships between coworkers were characterized as providing greater "tangible assistance" in the form of resources and services than those with nonwork individuals; similarly, even emotional support offered within the work environment was deemed more effective than when offered outside of a work context (Metts, Geist, & Gray, 1994). The importance of peer support among healthcare professionals in the workplace has been identified as being of paramount importance as a coping mechanism for job-related challenges and stressors, ranging from helping one another navigate role difficulties to being the first point of contact in the aftermath of adverse medical events (Thompson, Dorsey, Parrott, & Miller, 2003; van Pelt, 2008). One study discussed the importance of support between nurse coworkers (peer-to-peer support) as a means of reducing emotional exhaustion and depersonalization, two common effects of burnout (Miller, Zook, & Ellis, 1989); this was further corroborated by a study on supportive and unsupportive communication between nurses, describing peer RNs as consistent sources of organizational support for nurses experiencing stress (Ford & Ellis, 1998).

For nurses, social support in the context of work relationships is uniquely positioned to help cope with other stressors that may amplify feelings of burnout, as peers offering support can better understand those workplace stressors than sources of support external to the healthcare work environment, such as friends and family (Jenkins & Elliott, 2004). This finding supported earlier research that found coworker relationships to be uniquely supportive due to the benefit of shared knowledge, experiences, and environment (Ray, 1987). Subsequent sections address conceptual and practical issues in social support, supportive communication, knowledge acquisition, and knowledge management as mechanisms that aid in understanding, reducing, and preventing nursing burnout.

Social Support

Social support is a topic whose importance to health has been widely explored (Arora, Finney Rutten, Gustafson, Moser, & Hawkins, 2007; Fisher et al., 2014; Gariépy, Honkaniemi, & Quesnel-Vallée, 2016; Livhits et al., 2011). With respect to burnout, research indicates that how an individual experiences burnout is highly dependent on the kind of coping resources available to them (Gray-Stanley & Muramatsu, 2011). The literature indicates that coworker support has significant effects on burnout; Maslach (1978), for example, theorized that healthcare practitioners have lower rates of burnout when they talk about their personal feelings with coworkers. While support can come in a variety of forms, such as emotional, its definition can include more practical aspects as well, such as help with a conflict at work (Sundin, Hochwälder, Bildt, & Lisspers, 2007). Goldsmith's definition of enacted social support is, quite simply, "the things people say and do for one another" and how those can aid individuals in coping with the negative effects of various stressors (Goldsmith, 2004, p. 3).

According to Kahn (1993), nurses and other primary caregivers need a high degree of caregiving themselves due to the emotional expenditures associated with their work. An absence of supportive communication from coworkers or supervisors can lead to further depletion of emotional resources, resulting in a risk of burnout. Supportive communication should, ideally, reduce perceptions of uncertainty and provide the individual in question with a sense of autonomy or control in the context at hand, making them feel equally informed as well as involved (Albrecht & Adelman, 1987). Thus, rather than social support eradicating the instance of uncertainty entirely, it provides the individual with a resource to cope with it (Thompson et al., 2003). Previous research has also demonstrated social support to be an important coping mechanism of workplace stress. For example, one study found that workers who experienced emotional or physical pressures often had poor social support in their workplaces (Lee & Ashforth, 1996). In the past, interventions intended to improve social support within the workplace focused on implementing strategies such as introducing new individuals and enhancing existing interpersonal relationships through training. This training, intended to strengthen the exchange of social support between individuals, helped individuals practice skills such as learning to efficiently request assistance, provide constructive feedback, and clear up any miscommunications (Heaney, 1991). While situations where a nurse feels in need of social support are, to some degree, unavoidable, learning how to effectively ask for help can act as a valuable first step to establishing it. Another way of conceptualizing supportive communication in the workplace uses the concept of memorable messages to identify *specific instances* of supportive and unsupportive messages, and, by extension, of supportive and unsupportive communication (Knapp, Stohl, & Reardon, 1981; Miller & Ray, 1994). Thus, in the context of nursing, nurses exemplify supportive communication by sharing tips on what to look for in patients following a particular procedure, identifying who to turn to for assistance and when, and acknowledging and affirming cases of successful conflict resolution.

Perceptions regarding how much value an organization places on supportive communication affect peer-to-peer communication between colleagues as well, leading to workers reporting feelings of personal accomplishment. Occasionally, an organization may choose to demonstrate this through a more explicitly formal instance of informational support, such as implementations of training programs for healthcare workers designed to impart stress reduction skills as a means of reducing burnout rates (Lees & Ellis, 1990; Thompson et al., 2003).

Supportive Communication

Generally, it is more realistic to improve and strengthen an individual's social support than it is to completely alleviate their exposure to stress (Cassel, 1976). Conversations provide social support and are one way of enacting it. According to Goldsmith (2004), studying the communication processes that enact support can allow researchers to be able to identify behaviors those who seek support find helpful, while also developing a set of more general principles that can "help individuals understand supportive interactions and improve their abilities to enact and negotiate social support in their close relationships" (p. 25).

Enacted social support may be defined as the things relational partners do and say with the intention of helping one another manage problems and stresses (Goldsmith & Miller, 2014; Thompson et al., 2003). Broadly speaking, enacted social support is beneficial in coping with stress. Types of enacted social support may include, but are not limited to, the following:

tangible support, emotional support, and informational support. Problem-solving support—such as informational support and emotional-focused forms of support—are helpful in different contexts. The latter possesses a larger capability of general application, whereas the helpfulness of problem-solving support is slightly more dependent on factors such as the recipient's needs and resources, the provider's expertise, and the quality of the information being offered (Thompson et al., 2003).

Research regarding the delivery of informational support has, thus, identified effective and ineffective methods of its delivery. For example, advice-giving is one of the most common iterations of social support and is intended to communicate potential solutions as well as express concern for another person's well-being. However, the act of offering advice can be negatively perceived as a form of criticism. Whether or not the support is taken well is largely dependent on the communicator's ability to acknowledge the recipient's autonomy, something generally referred to as face work. Thus, while the quality of the informational support's content is important, the way in which the support is introduced is associated with its perception as either face honoring or face threatening (Goldsmith, 1999, 2000). An instance of informational support that is interpreted as face honoring is associated with perceived helpfulness. However, whether or not the support was explicitly or implicitly requested is a factor essential to how it is taken.

Similarly, overly explicit messages of support have a tendency to lose impact over time in relational contexts where larger rewards or costs are at stake—such as health professionals in task environments. In these cases, supervisors' messages regarding innovation or novel treatment strategies are highly correlated with "global judgements of support" (Thompson et al., 2003). Similarly, one study demonstrated that trainees who described receiving high levels of organization, supervisor, and peer support (including participation in a peer support network) reported higher levels of transfer of knowledge and skills (Cromwell & Kolb, 2004). Another study regarding peer mentoring between nursing students noted that the active support from a fellow student helped to mitigate feelings of isolation by newer students in their initial clinical placements, allowing them to focus on addressing clinical challenges and reducing the factors related to attrition, facilitating opportunities for learning (Christiansen & Bell, 2010). Thus, the communication of informational support can be interpreted as one way of facilitating knowledge transfer, which can happen explicitly through instruction, demonstration, or hands-on training, as well as tacitly through things such as ongoing communication.

In summary, social support is an important component of any individual's well-being. Peer-to-peer workplace support possesses uniquely helpful attributes that can help individuals cope with workplace stressors. One way fellow coworkers, or peers, can support each other is through informational support. Although the importance of peer-to-peer support as a communicative practice has been emphasized, and different factors affecting its effectiveness are well described, the situations in which it is deemed most helpful invariably color its nature and frequency, and vary between healthcare contexts (Goldsmith, 2004). According to Goldsmith (2004), support enacted through communication is situated; meaning that what is considered by individuals involved to be an effective instance of peer-to-peer support may change between the actors and setting involved.

Types of Knowledge and Knowledge Acquisition

One of the most important tenets of communication is the imparting of knowledge from one source to another. In fact, both broad and scholarly definitions of communication center on the exchange of knowledge. A general consensus dictates that knowledge must be differentiated from data, which may be described as "raw numbers, images, words, and sounds derived from observation or measurement" and information, which identifies and rearranges the former into a meaningful pattern. For example, a patient's blood pressure measurement is just a number, or piece of data—noticing that this number is lower than the patient's accepted norm transforms this data into knowledge, or in this case an indication that something warrants further investigation.

Traditional knowledge epistemology views knowledge as something presumed to be unchanging, nonhuman, and absolute (Nonaka, 1994). When it comes to the theory of knowledge creation, however, the personal perspective and experience of an individual's knowledge may be indistinguishable from a closely held personal belief—one whose weight and credibility stem from how closely held a belief they are to the individual in the first place, rather than whether or not they are wholly truthful. Thus, in the case of knowledge creation, we acknowledge that the individual's perceptions of reality are virtually indistinguishable from their knowledge, and that this quest for a justification of personal beliefs is part of humanity's instinctive quest for truth (Nonaka, 1994). Thus, both traditional definitions and individually subjective definitions of knowledge warrant explanation, as they are capable of providing different value.

Knowledge can be restructured by communication and is called a "critical strategic resource" for good reason (Straus, Tetroe, & Graham, 2013). Studies suggest that one of the keys in nursing's strategic development as a profession lies in recognizing the importance of a "knowledge economy and the value of knowledge work," as nurses who are able to share experiences with one another can reflect on similarities and collaborate to problem-solve situations ranging from patient health to strategies for personal stress management (Linderman, Pesut, & Disch, 2015; McDonald, Jackson, Wilkes, & Vickers, 2012). Thus, it may be said that knowledge sharing is, in its way, a form of peer support, as it can provide answers to specific questions or gaps in knowledge. Knowing how to better execute a clinical task, care for a patient, or even provide guidance to another nurse, can result in a nurse's reassurance of renewed capability.

Prior to understanding how knowledge is shared, one must first make an effort to understand the ways in which an individual converts knowledge acquired in the world to something that possesses meaning to them. The conversion between tacit knowledge (knowledge that is understood to be known without necessarily requiring a statement out loud) and explicit knowledge (knowledge that is expressed and recorded as words, patterns, and other notations) can be categorized into four processes: tacit knowledge to tacit knowledge; tacit knowledge to explicit knowledge; explicit knowledge to tacit knowledge; and explicit knowledge to explicit knowledge. For example, a nurse may walk into a patient's room and feel as though something is "off"—an example of tacit knowledge, as the specific cues comprising her feeling of something being "off" are beneath her conscious assessment of the patient's condition, and not something she is immediately able to explicate in words. Acting on this assessment based on tacit knowledge, she may request a second opinion from a physician, or nursing colleague, who may then corroborate her assessment and aid her in discerning the explicit extension of her tacit knowledge—such as checking to make sure a dosage was correct, or double-checking the patient's vital signs. One of the effective ways of identifying the transfer of tacit knowledge to tacit knowledge is that it does not require language to happen—rather, it can be learned or transferred through modeling behavior, or some shared experience; this particular aspect may be referred to as socialization, as it requires two individuals to partake in the same reality or event (Nonaka, 1994). Similarly, new information can be also be obtained by transforming existing instances of information by the separation, addition, and regrouping of preexisting knowledge. This is referred to as the explicit knowledge to explicit knowledge conversation. Both processes of mixed knowledge types (i.e., explicit to tacit and vice versa) may be referred to as internalization and externalization, respectively (Nonaka, 1994).

At the same time, however, knowledge is created and maintained via social interaction, a process unavoidable in and essential to the creation of interpersonal relationships. Occasionally, consequences may arise when there is a breakdown in communication between the conversion process involving tacit and explicit knowledge (Nonaka, 1994). This is largely due to tacit knowledge's dependence on shared experiences in order to communicate it, making it difficult to share outside of highly specific contexts. Similarly, a deluge of information specific to one context can be difficult to interpret in a way that translates it into something broadly useful (Nonaka, 1994). This poses a few problems: a deficit in accurately communicating the personal meaning ascribed to individual instances of tacit information may result in a superficial externalized product. Similarly, a faulty or inconsistent internalization of information can lead to future miscommunications wherein the issue stems from the now inaccurate information. An individual whose internalization was inaccurate and did not reflect the original information's integrity results in a creation of a reality different from those operating from the original knowledge constructs. As the successful transfer of organizational values and knowledge between members is a part of maintaining and building organizational culture and communication, understanding these processes is of the utmost importance. In an ideal scenario, all four models of knowledge conversion manage to create a seamless flow of communication and facilitate knowledge management.

Knowledge Management

The broader area of knowledge management and its narrower sibling, knowledge translation, are areas with fundamental overlap to their similarity in subject. Whereas knowledge translation—especially in the context of healthcare—largely focuses on how research findings are translated into clinical practice, Lave and Wenger (1993) posit that knowledge management (KM) focuses more so on people rather than structures, and that a focus on the product of knowledge itself is less noteworthy than *how* that product is managed. Thus, he coined the term Communities of Practice, or groups of people with a common interest who interact with the purpose of bettering themselves in regard to that interest, taking place in an environment where individuals might develop knowledge by interaction with others in a place where that knowledge can be created, fostered and maintained (Wenger, 2010).

This definition illustrates the social, interactional nature of KM—the impulse in both sharing and adapting new knowledge is almost synonymous with the community members—in this case, nursing peers—and whether or not the individual feels comfortable sharing what they do know as well as, perhaps even more importantly, what they do not. This definition is less concerned with the quality or the accuracy of the information—it is not intended to evaluate the knowledge being managed. Rather, Wenger's definition of KM focused on how knowledge moved between individuals and different boundaries (Straus et al., 2013). In the context of social support, however, an individual's perceptions of the quality of information being offered have a profound effect on how effective the support being offered is in helping them cope with a problem. For example, if an individual views the advice they receive as useful and informative, it may influence their perceptions of how solvable their problem is; if they perceive the support as "uninformed, critical, condescending, or aggravating, it may undermine [their] coping and further reinforce [their] appraisal that [their] environment is stressful and threatening" (Goldsmith, 2004, p. 26). Regardless, knowledge continues to be intertwined with lived experiences (Straus et al., 2013).

Naturally, these lived experiences differ based on the individuals, organizations, and the nature of the knowledge being transferred. Similarly, so do the effects of its movement between individuals. In the context of health organizations, for example, this management and communication of knowledge, and how well this process is understood and executed, carries significant implications as a result of its relationship to patients (Straus et al., 2013). That is, because organizational culture of healthcare is patient-centered, it stands to reason that the majority of the knowledge translation and communication involved within the organization revolve around best-practices and the implementation of evidence-based patient care (Straus et al., 2013). Similarly, any instances of miscommunication and corresponding consequences are likely to affect (however directly or indirectly) the patient or standard of care provided. Nurses are integral to the providing of medical services and shoulder a significant portion of the patient's care; thus, research posits that these errors may be caused by performance deficit, a lack of expertise, and insufficient knowledge, all of which can combine to a subpar standard of care. These knowledge gaps combined with scarce knowledge sharing between nurses can lead to further opportunities of endangering patient safety. Therefore, medical error prevention necessitates "substantial knowledge sharing" among nurses (Chang, Huang, Chiang, Hsu, & Chang, 2011). Thus, one of the hallmarks of what constitutes effective knowledge use is the facilitation of volunteer groups or likeminded workers in sharing what knowledge they have learned in communities of practice, a concept not unexplored in healthcare (Werner, 1996).

John Heron's (1989, 1999) work built on Werner's to elucidate on how group facilitation can be critical in "understanding some of the processes that can influence individual and group learning and thus their ability to internalize, interpret, and act on new knowledge or innovations" (Straus et al., 2013). He places special emphasis on the importance of an experiential learning approach, or members learning via reflection on everyday experiences and considering their subsequent actions, laying the foundation for the current state of research regarding KM, that is less focused on creating an understanding including structured systems and processes to recognizing the role of "relationships between individuals and groups and how they choose to share knowledge" (Straus et al., 2013). One individual sharing knowledge with another can trigger knowledge processes, which in turn can lead to that individual's creation of their own. Then, the individual has the options of applying the knowledge, consulting with other members, or even simply recording the knowledge—the application of the knowledge may depend on a variety of factors, ranging from how sound the knowledge is perceived to be to how the individual perceives it relating to them or their situation. Thus, one common challenge in KM is identifying a way in which the greatest amount of knowledge transfer occurs, based on the assumption that the knowledge in question has already assumed to be of value and capable of positive impacting performance (Alavi & Leidner, 2001); however, there has been a growing interest in treating knowledge as a significant organizational resource. Consistent with the interest in organizational knowledge and knowledge management (KM). One concept that facilitates knowledge sharing is the identification of a shared reality between individuals or groups.

Because KM takes place between groups as well as individuals, its roots (and much of its literature) lie in organizational management. Despite its many iterations, acquisition, classification, transfer, and storage of knowledge for use are generally accepted as the holistic knowledge management processes (Doğan & Yiğit, 2014). Thus, knowledge management is viewed as one crucial means of achieving organizational success (Demir, 2006). Similarly, as KM inherently facilitates learning, it is often able to merge the individual's goals as well as that of the organization's—an individual who is well informed and comfortable sharing knowledge, as well as lack thereof, is one that can perform their tasks well within the organization (Doğan & Yiğit, 2014).

CONCLUSION

Nurses in the operating room traditionally have a high turnover rate and possess certain unique factors as a result of their work environment—namely the difference in the way they establish relationships with patients. Thus, identifying factors that contribute to this turnover, such as burnout, and exploring the nature of the social support available as to its ability in communicating effectively, can provide both short-term and long-term implications regarding the creation of a working environment conducive to nursing professionals' employment longevity as well as one that is of the utmost effectiveness in translating knowledge between peers. Although there are a significant number of studies exploring the phenomenon of burnout in medical professionals (Adriaenssens, De Gucht, & Maes, 2015; Dugani et al., 2018; Dyrbye & Shanafelt, 2016; Singh, Aulak, Mangat, & Aulak, 2016) and even nurses in particular, few have explored the function of knowledge sharing in supportive communication between peers, particularly with respect to which critical situations solicit effective communicative support from peers in a unique nursing specialty.

REFERENCES

Adriaenssens, J., De Gucht, V., & Maes, S. (2015). Determinants and prevalence of burnout in emergency nurses: A systematic review of 25 years of research. *International Journal of Nursing Studies, 52*(2), 649–661. doi:10.1016/j.ijnurstu.2014.11.004

Alavi, M., & Leidner, D. E. (2001). Review: Knowledge management and knowledge management systems: Conceptual foundations and research issues. *MIS Quarterly, 25*(1), 107–136. doi:10.2307/3250961

Albrecht, T. L., & Adelman, M. B. (1987). Communication networks as structures of social support. In T. L. Albrecht & M. R. Adelman (Eds.), *Communicating social support* (pp. 40–63). Newbury Park, CA: Sage.

Arora, N. K., Finney Rutten, L. J., Gustafson, D. H., Moser, R., & Hawkins, R. P. (2007). Perceived helpfulness and impact of social support provided by family, friends, and health care providers to women newly diagnosed with breast cancer. *Psycho-Oncology, 16*(5), 474–486. doi:10.1002/pon.1084

Buerhaus, P. I. (2008). Current and future state of the US nursing workforce. *Journal of the American Medical Association, 300*(20), 2422–2424. doi:10.1001/jama.2008.729

Buerhaus, P. I., Skinner, L. E., Auerbach, D. I., & Staiger, D. O. (2017). State of the registered nurse workforce as a new era of health reform emerges. *Nursing Economic$, 35*(5), 229–237. Retrieved from http://healthworkforcestudies.com/news/state_of_the_nursing_workforce_paper.pdf

Cassel, J. C. (1976). The contribution of the social environment to host resistance. *American Journal Public Health (66)*, 354–358. doi:10.2307/3561497.

Chang, C.-W., Huang, H.-C., Chiang, C.-Y., Hsu, C.-P., & Chang, C.-C. (2011). Social capital and knowledge sharing: Effects on patient safety. *Journal of Advanced Nursing, 68*(8), 1793–1803. doi:10.1111/j.1365-2648.2011.05871.x

Christiansen, A., & Bell, A. (2010). Peer learning partnerships: Exploring the experience of pre-registration nursing students. *Journal of Clinical Nursing, 19*(5–6), 803–810. doi:10.1111/j.1365-2702.2009.02981.x

Cromwell, S. E., & Kolb, J. A. (2004). An examination of work-environment support factors affecting transfer of supervisory skills training to the workplace. *Human Resource Development Quarterly, 15*(4), 449–471. doi:10.1002/hrdq.1115

Demir, K. (2006). School management information systems in primary schools. *The Turkish Online Journal of Educational Technology, 5*(2), 1303–6521. Retrieved from http://www.tojet.net/

Doğan, S., & Yiğit, Y. (2014). Attitudes towards knowledge management of school administrators and teachers working in Turkish schools. *Alberta Journal of Educational Research, 60*(3), 442–463. Retrieved from https://journalhosting.ucalgary.ca/index.php/ajer/issue/view/4382

Dugani, S., Afari, H., Hirschhorn, L. R., Ratcliffe, H., Veillard, J., Martin, G., . . . Bitton, A. (2018). Prevalence and factors associated with burnout among frontline primary health care providers in low- and middle-income countries: A systematic review. *Gates Open Research, 2*(4). doi:10.12688/gatesopenres.12779.3

Dyrbye, L., & Shanafelt, T. (2016). A narrative review on burnout experienced by medical students and residents. *Medical Education, 50*(1), 132–149. doi:10.1111/medu.12927

Fisher, E. B., Coufal, M. M., Parada, H., Robinette, J. B., Tang, P. Y., Urlaub, D. M., . . . Xu, C. (2014). Peer support in health care and prevention: Cultural, organizational, and dissemination issues. *Annual Review of Public Health, 35*, 363–383. doi:10.1146/annurev-publhealth-032013-182450

Ford, L. A., & Ellis, B. H. (1998). A preliminary analysis of memorable support and nonsupport messages received by nurses in acute care settings. *Health Communication, 10*(1), 37–63. doi:10.1207/s15327027hc1001_3

Gariépy, G., Honkaniemi, H., & Quesnel-Vallée, A. (2016). Social support and protection from depression: Systematic review of current findings in Western countries. *The British Journal of Psychiatry, 209*(4), 284–293. doi:10.1192/bjp.bp.115.169094

Goldsmith, D. J. (1999). Content-based resources for giving face-sensitive advice in troubles talk episodes. *Research on Language and Social Interaction, 32*, 303–336. doi:10.1207/S15327973rls3204_1

Goldsmith, D. J. (2000). Soliciting advice: The role of sequential placement in mitigating face threat. *Communication Monographs, 67*, 1–19. doi:10.1080/03637750009376492

Goldsmith, D. J. (2004). *Communicating social support*. New York, NY: Cambridge University Press.

Goldsmith, D. J., & Miller, G. A. (2014). Conceptualizing how couples talk about cancer. *Health Communication, 29*(1), 51–63. doi:10.1080/10410236.2012.717215

Gray-Stanley, J. A., & Muramatsu, N. (2011). Work stress, burnout, and social and personal resources among direct care workers. *Research in Developmental Disabilities, 32*(3), 1065–1074. doi:10.1016/j.ridd.2011.01.025

Heaney, C. A. (1991). Enhancing social support at the workplace: Assessing the effects of the caregiver support program. *Health Education Quarterly, 18*(4), 477–494. doi:10.1177/109019819101800406

Heron, J. (1989). *The facilitators' handbook*. East Brunswick, NJ: Nichols.

Heron, J. (1993). *Group facilitation: Theories and models for practice*. East Brunswick, NJ: Nichols.

Heron, J. (1999). *The facilitator's handbook*. London: Kogan Page.

Jenkins, R., & Elliott, P. (2004). Stressors, burnout and social support: Nurses in acute mental health settings. *Journal of Advanced Nursing, 48*(6), 622–631. doi:10.1111/j.1365-2648.2004.03240.x

Kahn, W. A. (1993). Caring for the caregivers: Patterns of organizational caregiving. *Administrative Science Quarterly, 38*(4), 539–563. doi:10.2307/2393336

Knapp, M. L., Stohl, C., & Reardon, K. K. (1981). "Memorable" messages. *Journal of Communication, 31*(4), 27–41. doi:10.1111/j.1460-2466.1981.tb00448.x

Lave, J. & Wenger, E. C. (1993). *Situated learning: Legitimate peripheral participation.* New York, NY: Cambridge University Press.

Lee, R. T., & Ashforth, B. E. (1996). A meta-analytic examination of the correlates of the three dimensions of burnout. *Journal of Applied Psychology, 81*(2), 123–133. doi:10.1037//0021-9010.81.2.123

Lees, S., & Ellis, N. (1990). The design of a stress-management program for nursing personnel. *Journal of Advanced Nursing, 15,* 946–961. doi:10.1111/j.1365-2648.1990.tb01951.x

Linderman, A., Pesut, D., & Disch, J. (2015). Sense making and knowledge transfer: Capturing the knowledge and wisdom of nursing leaders. *Journal of Professional Nursing, 31*(4), 290–297. doi:10.1016/j.profnurs.2015.02.004

Livhits, M., Mercado, C., Yermilov, I., Parikh, J. A., Dutson, E., Mehran, A., Gibbons, M. M. (2011). Is social support associated with greater weight loss after bariatric surgery? A systematic review. *Obesity Reviews, 12*(2), 142–148. doi:10.1111/j.1467-789X.2010.00720.x

Maslach, C. (1978). Client role in staff burnout. *Journal of Social Issues, 34*(4), 111–124. doi:10.1111/j.1540-4560.1978.tb00778.x

McDonald, G., Jackson, D., Wilkes, L., & Vickers, M. H. (2012). A work-based educational intervention to support the development of personal resilience in nurses and midwives. *Nurse Education Today, 32*(4), 378–384. doi:10.1016/j.nedt.2011.04.012

Metts, S., Geist, P., & Gray, J. L. (1994). The role of relationship characteristics in the provision and effectiveness of supporting messages among nursing professionals. In B. R. Burleson, T. L. Albrecht, & I. G. Sarason (Eds.), *Communication of social support: Messages, interactions, relationships, and community* (pp. 229–246). Thousand Oaks, CA: Sage.

Miller, K., & Ray, E. B. (1994). Beyond the ties that bind: Exploring the "meaning" of supportive messages and relationships. In B. R. Burleson, T. L. Albrecht, & I. G. Sarason (Eds.), *Communication of social support: Messages, interactions, relationships, and community* (pp. 215–228). Thousand Oaks, CA: Sage.

Miller, K. I., Zook, E. G., & Ellis, B. H. (1989). Occupational differences in the influence of communication on stress and burnout in the workplace. *Management Communication Quarterly, 3*(2), 317–340. doi:10.1177/0893318989003002002

Nonaka, I. (1994). A dynamic theory of organizational knowledge creation. *Organization Science, 5*(1), 14–37. doi:10.1287/orsc.5.1.14

Ray, E. B. (1987). Supportive relationships and occupational stress in the workplace. T. L. Albrecht & M. B. Adelman (Eds.), *Communicating and social support* (pp. 172–191). Newbury Park, CA: Sage.

Singh, P., Aulak, D. S., Mangat, S. S., & Aulak, M. S. (2016). Systematic review: Factors contributing to burnout in dentistry. *Occupational Medicine, 66*(1), 27–31. doi:10.1093/occmed/kqv119

Straus, S., Tetroe, J., & Graham, I. D. (Eds.) (2013). *Knowledge translation in health care: Moving from evidence to practice.* West Sussex, UK: John Wiley & Sons.

Sundin, L., Hochwälder, J., Bildt, C., & Lisspers, J. (2007). The relationship between different work-related sources of social support and burnout among registered and assistant nurses in Sweden: A questionnaire survey. *International Journal of Nursing Studies, 44*(5), 758–769. doi:10.1016/j.ijnurstu.2006.01.004

Thompson, T. L., Dorsey, A., Parrott, R., & Miller, K. (Eds.) (2003). *The Routledge handbook of health communication.* New York, NY: Routledge.

van Pelt, F. (2008). Peer support: Healthcare professionals supporting each other after adverse medical events. *BMJ Quality & Safety, 17*(4), 249–252. doi:10.1136/qshc.2007.025536

Wenger, E. (2010). Communities of practice and social learning systems: The career of a concept. In C. Blackmore (Ed.), *Social learning systems and communities of practice.* London: Springer.

Werner, E. (1996). How kids become resilient: Observations and cautions. *Resiliency in Action,* 1(1), 18–28.

Chapter Eleven

Managing Moral Injury Post-Deployment

Jennifer A. Samp
Andrew I. Cohen

Recent international military engagements inspired scholars and clinicians to consider the psychological impacts of military service. Increasing numbers of soldiers are returning from deployments in Iraq or Afghanistan. This particularly re-ignited interest in the psychological impacts of military service. In this chapter, we discuss the challenges of understanding and communicating about a new concept of traumatic stress: moral injury.

Moral injury is the traumatic disorientation a person experiences when she or he witnesses or is complicit in some injustice. A morally injurious experience is an "an act of transgression that severely and abruptly contradicts an individual's personal or shared expectation about the rules or the code of conduct, either during the event or at some point afterwards" (Silva, Litz, Stein, Delaney, & Maguen, 2009, p. 700). Some moral injuries involve betrayals by trusted authorities (Shay, 1995) while others involve the shame or guilt of being a witness or agent of some perceived moral transgression (Cohen, Samp, Glickstein, & Williams, 2018).

Little is known about how veterans attempt to resolve their moral injuries (Litz et al., 2009). While previous quantitative research identified cognitive processes such as negative post-trauma cognitions and maladaptive meaning-making (Currier, Holland, Drescher, & Foy, 2015; Held et al., 2018), very little is known about how veterans communicate about their moral injuries and to whom. One of the purposes of the present study was to better understand how veterans communicatively coped with their moral injuries. Given the scarcity of empirical research in this area, we utilized a qualitative, interpretive approach based on focus group conversations with veterans. Our study illuminates features of the morally injurious experience and how trauma impacts coping and communicative decisions.[1]

MORAL INJURY AND MENTAL HEALTH

Combat imposes many impairments to mental health, but warriors, scholars, and communities realize these challenges are nothing new. Surviving veterans of wars in Korea and Vietnam sometimes disclose hidden burdens that echo narratives about warriors in the *Iliad* (Shay, 1995). Letters and diaries from soldiers in the U.S. Civil War confirmed that war changes combatants (Dean, 2000). War changes warriors even in campaigns featuring considerable public support (Grinker & Spiegel, 1945). For example, Beebe and Appel (1958) observed:

> During World War II infantrymen were breaking down psychologically at such high rates in certain combat areas as to suggest to many psychiatric observers that the resistance of the average man was being exceeded, that the stress of warfare in these areas was so great that most men exposed to it long enough would break down. Such studies as could be made in wartime seemed to confirm these impressions (p. 1).

Increases in combat-related stressors sometimes provide a context for acute and chronic psychophysical breakdown (see Russell & Figley, 2017) that can last well into later life, post-deployment (Kang, Aldwin, Choun, & Spiro, 2016). Despite the rewards of serving one's country, soldiers must often grapple with the guilt, shame, resentment, and disorientation associated with combat-related violence. In turn, soldiers may lose confidence in the significance of morality and their sense of self. They may lose the ability to trust themselves and others.

Important work targeted the physical and mental health problems associated with the experience of combat. Recent empirical efforts expanded the understanding of combat-related trauma. For instance, scholars considered the health effects from cumulative exposure to war stress, examined previously classified reports on frontline psychiatry, investigated the prevalence and treatment of mental health conditions among deployed personnel, and proposed clinical models of risk and protective factors contributing to combat-related post-traumatic stress disorder (PTSD) (e.g., Battles et al., 2018; Litz et al., 2009; Russell & Figley, 2017). However, dominant clinical models do not fully capture certain forms of combat trauma and how individuals communicate about their experiences. Recent communication research provides some important insights about the dynamics of reintegration with spouses and families (e.g., Frisby, Byrnes, Mansson, Booth-Butterfield, & Birmingham, 2011; Knobloch, Ebata, McGlaughlin, & Theiss, 2013). Yet there is still much to learn about the post-deployment experiences of veterans.

Though the phenomenon of moral injury is not new, there is increasing interest by scholars, clinicians, clergy, and policymakers about the meaning and scope of such trauma. Moral injury is a concept related to, but separate from, PTSD (Kopacz et al., 2016). Current theories of PTSD can only partially explain some of the phenomena associated with moral injury. Moral injury presents with sequelae and problematic features different from those of PTSD (Currier et al., 2015; Drescher et al., 2011; Litz et al., 2009; Nash & Litz, 2013). Moral injury is a complex reaction to the perpetration, experience, or witnessing of human-generated harm (Litz et al., 2009). The signs of such injury include increased dispositions to violence, decreased ability to trust loved ones or those in authority, and an incapacitating despair, guilt, or indifference.

Many describe moral injury as a special type of trauma. A growing body of research found evidence for the experience of moral injury, particularly in the military context. In a survey of 106 professionals working at various U.S. Veteran Affairs (VA) Medical Centers, 86 percent of respondents reported that moral injury is a contributor to the health of veterans, yet only 4 percent believed the VA was doing enough to address the negative impacts of moral injury on mental health (Kopacz et al, 2018).

Samp and Cohen (2017) found preliminary evidence to support the view that moral injury is a useful interpretive lens for understanding the experiences among some of those who serve in the armed forces. One warrior who served in Vietnam reported many adjustment problems after returning home from deployment, including a broken family and homelessness. As he said, "You drop bombs from the planes, you shoot 'em from the ships, and you also shoot the 105s and the 155s and all of them. And when I saw the destruction that I held in the palms of my hands, it shook my soul" (Samp & Cohen 2018, p. 7). This sort of talk from damaged souls is common among reports of moral injury. It helps convey what many warriors, clinicians, and scholars found: the conceptual terrain associated with PTSD does not exhaust the mental health tolls of war. While PTSD includes hyperarousal and a disposition to fight or flee, moral injury manifests in problematic shame and guilt. Indeed, the features of moral injury sometimes resist clinical categories and treatments. The guilt might not be appropriate to "cure." As one speaker said, "I have felt the guilt as a Marine for all of these years. I often say to them now that I have a better understanding, that uh all of that guilt is-is-is deserved" (Cohen et al., 2018). A veteran of the Army commented, ". . . just imagine one 1,000-pound bomb. Everything within a half a mile dead or dying. Oh, it was difficult sleeping once I realized what they was [*sic*] training me to do" (Samp & Cohen, 2018, p. 8).

The recognition of moral injury can also emerge by learning about other veterans' trauma. For example, in a focus group (Samp & Cohen, 2017, p. 8), one Vietnam veteran reported the experience of a female soldier:

> I'd go down to the VA and—and it's like uh reconnecting with the, with the Marines. It's like reconnecting with facts. . . . what I did was find other people that had the problem and I sought to solve their problem, and it brought me all the way up to where we are now. Now yesterday, we—we were having our little meeting in there, and one of the young ladies who went in about twenty-five years ago, she uhm got 70% post-traumatic stress, just from filling out the papers. I said, "Now how can that be?" She wouldn't talk about it, but then when everybody else left, a few of us she motioned to—to keep behind when she was in there. That was when the service first allowed women to sleep in the same barracks as men. You had your room here, they had their room in there. She says, and she had the proof to back it up, that uhm, daily or weekly rapings was something normal, and that's what she went through. And she carried the baggage on all of that, and I started thinking that my little things with Vietnam and post-Vietnam, that's nothing compared to what the younger vet had to go through.

This example shows that moral injury may not be confined to a person committing an action, but also *witnessing* a wrongdoing. Many active, veteran, or reserve members of the armed forces are intimately familiar with guilt, shame, and remorse. Those are important *moral emotions*. They are responses to some event that violates one's sense of moral order and arise in cases where one's own agency is implicated. Sometimes these moral emotions become incapacitating, but at the same time, they might be *fitting*. They might be among the ways persons experience moral breaches in which their agency is implicated (Sherman, 2010, 2015). In this way, at least sometimes, the morally injured do not belong in the category of "victim."

COMMUNICATION ABOUT MORAL INJURY

While there is little research directly examining how veterans talk about their injurious experiences, work on coping with military-related trauma suggests that experiencing a moral injury is psychologically isolating. Individuals avoid addressing the injurious experience out of a perceived lack of social support, a reluctance to utilize available support networks, and a fear of the negative effects of disclosure (Houtsma, Khazem, Green, & Anestis, 2017). For example, in a semi-structured interview study of twenty-three veterans, Jeffreys, Leibowitz, Finley, and Arar (2010) found that veterans are often reluctant to disclose to healthcare professionals about the traumas they experienced during service out of a fear of not being believed (29%), being locked up, or labeled as "crazy" (29%), jeopardizing their careers (29%), and because of a desire to avoid discussion about the traumatic events (29%). Those who chose not to disclose a trauma to a healthcare professional voiced concerns about others thinking less of the veteran (67%) or a lack of trust in the health care provider. In an interview study of eight veterans, Held et al. (2018) found that several soldiers witnessing an atrocity spent a great deal of time ruminating, but not talking, about the experience. While not focused on the military context, a meta-analysis of thirty-nine cross-sectional studies found a relationship between greater avoidant coping in response to a potentially traumatic event and worse mental health outcomes (Littleton, Horsley, John, & Nelson, 2007). Furthermore, avoidance has been linked to poorer mental health and greater PTSD symptoms (Chawla & Ostafin, 2007).

Research on how retuning service members interact with spouses or intimate partners also suggests a pattern of avoidant communication. The cognitive dissonance generated through moral injury often brings shame, guilt, and rage, and can result in psychological and behavioral consequences such as social withdrawal, demoralization, self-handicapping, and self-injury (Dresher et al., 2011). Allen, Rhoades, Stanley, & Markman (2010) suggested that those with PTSD find it frustrating to cope with household changes while deployed and/or that the non-deployed partner cannot understand what the soldier experienced. While such coping and reintegration challenges are not distinct to the morally injured, the disorientation characteristic of moral injury can leave veterans with diminished capacities to create or navigate quotidian domestic structures. Helping with laundry may be crucial for domestic harmony, but someone returning from combat might be unable to muster the will to contribute to ordinary tasks that become increasingly meaningless in a world that permits unspeakable brutality. In a content analysis of 220 open-ended responses to topics that both returning veterans and their spouses avoided, Knobloch et al. (2013) found that returning service members avoided topics with spouses such as deployment issues (e.g.: "combat related deaths and injuries of those around me") and confidential military information (e.g. "complete details of the type and nature of work I did while [deployed]") (p. 458). Such topic avoidance corresponds with both increased stress and relationship dissatisfaction (Frisby et al., 2011).

Given the work reviewed above, it appears that one way soldiers may cope with morally injurious experiences is by avoiding communication. Thus, although the soldiers may not be directly communicating with others post-deployment, this type of avoidance likely reflects a strategic effort to manage communication, just like other more direct, verbal forms. However, it is possible that soldiers may manage their moral injuries in other ways. Therefore, we conducted focus groups of military veterans to investigate the following research question.

RQ: What themes reflect how veterans communicate (or not) about moral injury?

METHOD

Sample

A small sample (N = 3–8) of focus groups of veterans allowed for a mutually identifying, supportive experience amongst individuals of similar experience (Baker & Hinton, 1999). Veterans were recruited via Veterans of Foreign Wars (VFW), Disabled American Veterans (DAV), and American Legion posts in the southeastern United States. Those veterans interested in participating were directed to call a dedicated phone number or send a message to an email address solely used for the study. In total, fourteen veterans participated. The majority (79%) of participants served in Vietnam with the remainder deployed to Afghanistan or Iraq.

All potential participants were pre-screened by drawing on the Columbia Suicide Severity Reference Scale (Viguera et al., 2015) and the Moral Injury Questionnaire or Events Scale (Currier et al., 2015; Nash & Litz, 2013). There is a need for instrumentation that might assess morally injurious experiences (MIEs); if a respondent indicated a risk for suicide or a recent history of aggressive violence, they were thanked for their participation and that marked the end of their participation. Any pre-screened individual who showed immediate risk of self-harm was connected with mental health resources. Those who were deemed not at risk to self or others were scheduled to participate in a focus group located in a private room at a VFW, DAV post, or at a local history center. Participants were informed of procedures and their rights to refuse to answer questions or stop participating at any time. Focus groups were moderated by military veterans who were deployed to Afghanistan or various locations during the Gulf War. The moderators had been deployed multiple times and had current positions working with and counseling veterans. Veterans received $35 and a light lunch for participating.

Focus group discussions started out with low-stakes topics such as introductions. Once participants were deemed comfortable by the moderator, they were asked a series of questions to guide discussion (e.g., "Have you ever shown up to therapy to hear you've got PTSD, but you don't think it is that?"; "Do you or someone you know in the service have any feelings of guilt or shame that don't fit in PTSD?"; "What's your biggest struggle now?"; "Is there a guilt or shame that people outside the military sometimes do not understand?"). Participants were not required to address all discussion prompts to enable the participants to focus on those issues they wished to share. Discussions lasted approximately sixty to ninety minutes. Conversations were audio recorded and then transcribed by individuals unaware of the specific purpose of the study; all personal information was de-identified. These procedures were approved by the authors' Institutional Review Boards.

ANALYSIS

The content of the focus group interviews occurred in several phases, following procedures outlined by Neuendorf (2002). First, the lead author and an independent judge not aware of the purpose of the study reviewed the transcripts and analyzed each participant's message content by talk turn to identify thematic units (Krippendorff, 2004). Thus, the unit of analysis could be a word, sentence, paragraph, or sequence of paragraphs, but all based on talk turns. Coders agreed on approximately 88 percent of the thematic units. Disagreements were resolved by random selection.

Using a thematic, constant comparative method, four independent judges unaware of the purpose of the study assessed each thematic unit offered by each individual in a given focus group to identify themes related to soldiers' experiences, understandings, and communication about moral injury into mutually exclusive and exhaustive categories. Guided by Garrison, Cleveland-Innes, Koole, and Kappelman (2006), a negotiated approach was utilized, whereby coders assessed the transcripts and then actively discussed their respective codes with an aim to arrive at a final version in which most, if not all, coded messages were brought into alignment, whereby, no new codes or categories emerged. Krippendorff's (2004) alpha was used to indicate reliability; disagreements among judges were resolved by majority rule.

RESULTS

Focus group members were encouraged to discuss issues only of which they felt comfortable disclosing; all participants engaged in the majority of the focus group discussions. The fourteen participants contributed a total of 114 thematic units. The four judges achieved acceptable reliability ($\alpha = .89$). General themes identified via focus group analyses included the following.

Avoidance

This theme reflected their coping efforts to manage regret by deliberately refusing to speak or think of it (n = 41 thematic units, 35.96 percent of all thematic units, α = .87). For example, one participant explained:

> I find myself having intrusive thoughts, I usually turn and read something or study something, and put it back away, and don't deal with it in that sense. . . . No one should know what I went though. Including my kids. . . . My wife is everything. But even she does not know. And I do not want to burden her.

Another participant said:

> One of them things I think that came out of the Vietnam War, nobody wanted to talk about it. I'm talking about the people in the service. You just didn't want to talk about it. It's very hard to tell somebody what you've been through, and they don't have a clue.

In another response, a participant stated:

> Tha-that pretty much goes across the spectrum in just being available, I mean, a lot of this stuff isn't stuff that you want to share with everyone, so . . . people poking and prodding, "Oh are you okay?" and like treating you . . . like you are this completely changed person, even though you are, isn't something you really want. You just wanna . . . go ahead and live your life.

A final quote that highlights avoidance was achieved through conversation management:

> I usually just try to change the subject. I don't like talking about my experiences with anyone, just because, like . . . I know they're not gonna understand, and I don't mean that in a bad way, it just means like, when I go through it and describe it like, I know you're not gonna get it and I just wanna skip that whole part of our relationship or friendship. Let's just pretend it doesn't exist because I don't want you to look at me differently because . . . It's just like you—I know you're not gonna get it an-and I don't mean that in an offensive way, you know? That's just how I try to handle it, just try to change the dynamic. . . . That's rude to ask somebody about stuff like that, or something like that.

Hiding Concerns about Mental Illness

Participants engaged in active efforts to not reveal their feelings about or diagnoses of mental illness (n = 32 thematic units, 28.07 percent of all thematic units, α = .89). Reflective of this theme, one participant said:

If you take any exam for any job; you go down for uh, um, an application or whatever; [unclear]; one of the questions that they always ask is do you, or anybody in your family have a history of mental illness. And if you say "yeah," you're out of the job. If they find out later, you're out of the job. So this has to be suppressed as far as the individual goes. You know, especially when you have a family, and you try to, you know, make a living.

Another stated:

I guess you would say it's like any other mental illness—because it is a mental illness—um, is treated by our society differently. . . . I could go back to where they used to hide the people up in the closet, or up in the attic, and they [unclear] sanitariums, and um, mental institutions, and [unclear] like that, always shunned and put away. . . . Years ago they called it shell-shock; you could go on and on. It's been here for a long time. And people, like pain, learn to keep it low, you know, to deal with it.

As another example:

I went to the post office—the postal security first, because they were just picking up guys coming back from service. Um, if I had told them—actually I wasn't diagnosed then with PTSD—it came later. But if I had said, "I have PTSD," or showed any symptoms of being or having a mental illness, they'll put it down on paper. Wouldn't get a job. No way, shape, or form. Nobody's going to be responsible for you, or hirable for you, I'll put it that way. And this goes up until this day.

Substance Abuse

Substance abuse was identified when participants discussed substituting communication about moral injury via drugs and alcohol (n = 23 thematic units, 20.18 percent of all thematic units, α = .89). For instance, one participant said:

I work in law enforcement. You won't get a job; you won't have a gun. So you have to, I guess, keep it to yourself. You know, for 32 years I had a problem, and that problem was avoidance and drinking and alcohol.

Another respondent added that, "It's not just alcohol, you got a lot of drug addicts once they come back. Uh, you had a lot of people with problems that were hiding them." Lastly, a participant reflected that, "I think a lot of the WWII veterans self-medicated with—I know my dad did—with alcohol. And so did I."

Aggression/Anger Management

This fourth theme reflected coping efforts that related to harming themselves or others, or general expressions of anger (n = 9 thematic units, 7.89 percent of all thematic units, α = .89). One participant said, "It took me three years to adjust. Three years out of the service, I'd destroy everything I could. Put a brick through my car window and went into bars to hope I could punch somebody." Another said:

> In the moment, uh again, you really don't have any regrets or anything like that, and when I say you come back and then you start reflecting on that, that stuff is not immediate like when I got off the plane. It took a long time for my anger, like years for my anger to come down and actually think about it. It wasn't a [unclear] plan for America, oh my gosh what'll happen, you know? It's like . . . It took a long time for that anger and my reflective vision to come, at least to me. Like, it didn't happen overnight, so . . . yeah. And it wasn't—it didn't—I also say it didn't just "happen." Like, it was a lot of work and talking to my wife, and about having issues with alcohol and stuff like that. It was a long road 'til I could get there.

Personal Risk-Taking/Self-Harm

This theme reflected participants' efforts to substitute intrusive thoughts with self-harm (n = 5 thematic units, 4.39 percent of all thematic units, α = .76). One participant shared that, "when you just come out of the service, is that, if you go into another field, you look for the danger part of that field . . . law enforcement, they'll go to correction, or they'll go into uh, police department." Another said, "Oh, I continued to jump out of perfectly good airplanes even though I knew I was spinal cord injury. Uh, knowing I was spinal cord injury, I continued to jump."

Managing Fear after Deployment

The last theme highlights that veterans can have an "on guard" state or fearfulness related to their combat experiences, even post-deployment (n = 4 thematic units, 3.51 percent of all thematic units, α = .81). One respondent captured this theme, through saying,

> A lot of people get the wrong idea of what happens in combat. For the most part, it's quiet, it's tranquil, then all of the sudden—"bang." You know, something breaks out. [unclear] go two or three weeks without seeing the enemy or combat. You may never see the enemy. What is so disturbing is the anticipation.

That's what really goes and stays with you; and lingers for years and years. You think something is going to happen because all of the things that are happening around prior. Quick scenario: lightning strike. Now, normal person, they see a lightning strike, they are going to think of thunder. I see a lightning strike, light travels quicker than sound, I'm waiting for an explosion to go—and a bomb to go off. And that stays with you. The Army, trained you very well, for combat. They give you things that you can fall on in that particular incident, but they never train you to come back. And that's a big thing. No one gets how I could be afraid of lightning.

In summary, the six themes that emerged from the focus group data highlighted that veterans may cope with moral injury in a variety of ways, reflecting different level of communication. The largest percentage of themes reflected efforts to avoid talking about their time during deployment, with a lower percentage using substances to replace communicating about the moral injury. A large portion of participants expressed fear about their mental health situation being "found out," while others mentioned how to negotiate fear without support. More active communication strategies included expressing anger or risk taking.

DISCUSSION

Moral injury is a type of trauma that comes from profound challenges to fundamental values. Though veterans do not have a monopoly on the phenomenon, they offer a privileged glimpse into its meaning and impact. Improving our understanding of how military personnel maintain mental health functioning after extreme stress or trauma is critical for understanding the impacts of combat. Deepening the understanding of moral injury may be a crucial precursor to developing effective preventive interventions, amplifying people's grasp of important distinctions among types of trauma and how people variably respond to them, and helping experts and laypersons alike better appreciate what tends to cultivate resilience in the general population.

Our results indicated that there is significant overlap of management strategies veterans utilize when grappling with morally injurious experiences. But there are notable differences. People sometimes avoid because they do not know what to make of their experiences or those of others. Avoidance is a way of hiding from the unknown. Yet other people avoided discussing their moral injuries out of a fear of the negative consequences in employment or family contexts. Notably, some veterans displaced active functional communication by turning to violence or substance abuse.

If further research bears out these and related preliminary results that moral injury resists some clinical categorizations, clinicians confronting moral injury among their patients may need to reconsider traditional approaches for managing trauma. Some such traumas might not be fruitfully addressed through lenses such as treatable disorders or psychological dysfunctions. Moral injury may be evidence of an otherwise well-adjusted moral psychology that is integrating a disorienting experience with some moral challenge. As well, insights into moral injury may highlight that avoidance may be a *functional* pattern that enables some persons to cope with stressors that might otherwise be unbearable. Indeed, functional avoidance may serve as a protective pattern for individuals, as functional avoidance has been linked to a generalized autobiographical memory that reduces the negative memories individuals seek to avoid (Hallford, Austin, Raes, & Takano, 2018), as well as to harness a "calmer" brain state (Markett et al., 2013).

A different type of avoidance concerns veteran's desires to hide their perceived mental illness. Many of the attempts to hide mental issues were tied to employment issues. In other words, a veteran did not want anyone to find out about their mental issues out of a concern that they would lose their job. This is not an issue restricted to the military context, of course. Concerns about mental health can become self-stigmatic (Corrigan & Watson, 2002), leading to decisions to avoid discussion out of embarrassment or fear amongst veterans (Mittal et al., 2013).

Avoidance by communication topic shifting or ignoring bringing up a moral injury is slightly different in the case of substance abusers. Largely, those who spoke of substance abuse referred to it as a way to "escape." This is not an uncommon use of substances, but their use may have dire consequences. Marvasti and Wank (2013) reported that more than two and half million U.S. military personnel were involved in Middle East wars during the last decade, and one-third returned with PTSD, and almost one-half are suffering from psychiatric and substance use disorders. Thus, substance abuse post-deployment continues to be an important public health concern. However, some veterans deliberately committed self-harm physically through substance abuse. Some also remained fearful or anxious outside of the combat environment. Future interventions with veterans should perhaps not assume that it is the most important to talk about one's experiences of moral injury, but instead be more focused on the choices that veterans make and how such choices impact their mental well-being.

While moral injury is an important lens for understanding the complexity of war's aftermath, there is room for further work. First, investigators need to disentangle even more clearly the experiences of and coping with moral injury versus PTSD. This is a special challenge since the two phenomena are often coincidental, even though they are conceptually distinct. Second, there is room for further research that might connect with cultivating awareness among scholars and experts about the meaning of moral injury. This work my tie to the claim that military veterans define their military experience a "taboo topic" to discuss with close family members and friends (Frisby et al., 2011). Research may also explore whether some training, formal or otherwise, might reduce the incidence or impact of moral injury (Jinkerson, 2016). Our research has helped to illuminate the distinctive traumatic challenges moral injuries pose.

NOTE

1. Funding for this project was provided by the National Endowment for Humanities, RZ-249909-16, "Reparative Justice and Moral Injury among Post-Deployment Soldiers."

REFERENCES

Allen, E. S., Rhoades, G. K., Stanley, S. M., & Markman, H. J. (2010). Hitting home: Relationships between recent deployment, posttraumatic stress symptoms, and marital functioning for Army couples. *Journal of Family Psychology, 24*, 280–288. 10.1037/a0019405

Baker, R., & Hinton, R. (1999). Do focus groups facilitate meaningful participation in social research? In R. S. Barbour & J. Kitzinger (eds.), *Developing focus group research: Politics, theory and practice* (pp. 79–98). New York: Sage.

Battles, A. R., Bravo, A. J., Kelley, M. L., White, T. D., Braitman, A. L., & Hamrick, H. C. (2018). Moral injury and PTSD as mediators of the associations between morally injurious experiences and mental health and substance use. *Traumatology*, doi:10.1037/trm0000153

Beebe, G. W., & Appel, J. W. (1958). *Variation in psychological tolerance to ground combat in World War II*. Final Report Contract DA-19-007-MD-172. Washington, DC: National Academy of Sciences, National Research Council Division of Medical Sciences.

Chawla, N., & Ostafin, B. (2007). Experiential avoidance as a functional dimensional approach to psychopathology: An empirical review. *Journal of Clinical Psychology, 63*, 871–890. doi: 10.1002/jclp.20400

Cohen, A. I., Samp, J., Glickstein, R., & Williams, R. (2018, March). Refining the concept of moral injury. Paper presented at the annual meeting of the Association of Practical and Professional Ethics, Chicago, IL.

Corrigan, P. W., & Watson, A. C. (2002). The paradox of self-stigma and mental illness. *Clinical Psychology* (1), 35. Retrieved from http://proxy-remote.galib.uga .edu/login?url=http://search.ebscohost.com/login.aspx?direct=true&db=edsbl&A N=RN108772890&site=eds-live

Currier, J. M., Holland, J. M., Drescher, K., & Foy, D. (2015). Initial psychometric evaluation of the Moral Injury Questionnaire—military version. *Clinical Psychology & Psychotherapy* 22 (1): 54–63. doi:10.1002/cpp.1866.

Dean, E. T. Jr. (2000). *Shook over hell*. Cambridge: Harvard University Press.

Drescher, K. D., Foy, D. W., Kelly, C., Leshner A., Schutz, K., & Litz, B. (2011). An exploration of the viability and usefulness of the construct of moral injury in war veterans. *Traumatology*, 17(1), 8–13. doi:10.1177/1534765610395615

Frisby, B. N., Byrnes, K., Mansson, D. H., Booth-Butterfield, M., & Birmingham, M. K. (2011). Topic avoidance, everyday talk, and stress in romantic military and non-military couples. *Communication Studies*, 62(3), 241–257. doi:10.1080/1051 0974.2011.553982

Garrison, D. R., Cleveland-Innes, M., Koole, M., & Kappelman, J. (2006). Revisiting methodological issues in transcript analysis: Negotiated coding and reliability. *Internet and Higher Education*, 9(1), 1–8.

Grinker, R. R., & Spiegel, J. P. (1945). *Men under stress*. Philadelphia: Blakiston.

Hallford, D. J., Austin, D. W., Raes, F., & Takano, K. (2018). A test of the functional avoidance hypothesis in the development of overgeneral autobiographical memory. *Memory & Cognition*, 46(6): 895–908. doi: 10.3758/s13421-018-0810-z.

Held, P., Klassen, B. J., Hall, J. M., Friese, T. R., Bertsch-Gout, M. M., Zalta, A. K., & Pollack, M. H. (2018). 'I knew it was wrong the moment I got the order': A narrative thematic analysis of moral injury in combat veterans. *Psychological Trauma: Theory, Research, Practice, and Policy*. doi:10.1037/tra0000364

Houtsma, C., Khazem, L. R., Green, B. A., & Anestis, M. D. (2017). Isolating effects of moral injury and low post-deployment support within the US military. *Psychiatry Research*, 247, 194–199.

Jeffreys, M. D., Leibowitz, R. Q., Finley, E., & Arar, N. (2010). Trauma disclosure to health care professionals by veterans: Clinical implications. *Military Medicine*, 175(10), 719.

Jinkerson, J. D. (2016). Defining and assessing moral injury: A syndrome perspective. *Trumatology*, 22(2), 122–130.

Kang, S., Aldwin, C. M., Choun, S., & Spiro, A., III. (2016). A life-span perspective on combat exposure and PTSD symptoms in later life: Findings from the VA Normative Aging study. *Gerontologist*, 56, 22–32.

Knobloch, L. K., Ebata, A. T., McGlaughlin, P. C., & Theiss, J. A. (2013). Generalized anxiety and relational uncertainty as predictors of topic avoidance during reintegration following military deployment. *Communication Monographs*, 80(4), 452–477. doi:10.1080/03637751.2013.828159

Kopacz, M., Charpeid, G. L., Hollenbeck, L. A., & Lockman, J. (2018). Examining moral injury awareness in a clinical setting. *Journal of Military & Veterans' Health*, 26(1), 11–14.

Krippendorff, K. (2004). *Content analysis: An introduction to its methodology (2nd ed.)*. Thousand Oaks, CA: Sage.

Littleton, H., Horsley, S., John, S., & Nelson, D. V. (2007). Trauma coping strategies and psychological distress: A meta-analysis. *Journal of Traumatic Stress, 20*, 977–988. 10.1002/jts.20276

Litz, B. T., Stein, N., Delaney, E., Lebowitz, L., Nash, W. P., Silva, C., & Maguen, S. (2009). Moral injury and moral repair in war veterans: A preliminary model and intervention strategy. *Clinical Psychology Review, 29 (Posttraumatic Stress Disorder and the Wars in Afghanistan and Iraq)*, 695–706. doi:10.1016/j.cpr.2009.07.003

Markett, S., Weber, B., Voigt, G., Montag, C., Felten, A., Elger, C., & Reuter, M. (2013). Intrinsic connectivity networks and personality: The temperament dimension harm avoidance moderates functional connectivity in the resting brain. *Neuroscience, 240*, 98–105. https://doi-org.proxy-remote.galib.uga.edu/10.1016/j.neuroscience.2013.02.056

Marvasti, J. A., & Wank, A. A. (2013). Suicide in US veterans. *American Journal of Forensic Psychology, 31*(4), 27–54. Retrieved from http://proxy-remote.galib.uga.edu/login?url=http://search.ebscohost.com/login.aspx?direct=true&db=psyh&AN=2013-39041-002&site=eds-live

Mittal, D., Drummond, K. L., Blevins, D., Curran, G., Corrigan, P., & Sullivan, G. (2013). Stigma associated with PTSD: Perceptions of treatment seeking combat veterans. *Psychiatric Rehabilitation Journal, 36*(2), 86–92. https://doi-org.proxy-remote.galib.uga.edu/10.1037/h0094976

Nash, W. P., & Litz, B. T. (2013). Moral injury: A mechanism for war-related psychological trauma in military family members. *Clinical Child and Family Psychology Review* 16 (4), 365–75. doi:10.1007/s10567-013-0146-y.

Neuendorf, K. A. (2002). *The content analysis guidebook*. Thousand Oaks, CA: Sage.

Russell, M. C., & Figley, C. R. (2017). Is the military's century-old frontline psychiatry policy harmful to veterans and their families? Part three of a systematic review. *Psychological Injury and Law, 10*(1), 72–95.

Samp, J. A., & Cohen, A. I. (2017, April). Toward a theory of moral injury and relational framing among post-deployment soldiers in close relationships. Paper presented at the annual meeting of the Southern States Communication Association, Greenville, SC.

Samp, J. A., & Cohen, A. I. (2018, September). *Managing moral injury post-deployment: Mental health implications*. Presented at the 23nd International Summit of the Institute on Violence, Abuse and Trauma, La Jolla, CA.

Shay, J. (1995). *Achilles in Vietnam: Combat trauma and the undoing of character*. Simon & Schuster.

Sherman, N. (2010). *The Untold War: Inside the Hearts, Minds, and Souls of Our Soldiers*. New York: W. W. Norton & Company, 2010.

Sherman, N. (2015). *Afterwar: Healing the Moral Wounds of Our Soldiers*. New York, NY: Oxford University Press, 2015.

Silva, C., Litz, B. T., Stein, N., Delaney, E. & Maguen, S. (2009). Moral injury and moral repair in war veterans: A preliminary model and intervention strategy. *Clinical Psychology Review, 29*(8), 695–706.

Viguera, A. C., Milano, N., Laurel, R., Thompson, N. R., Griffith, S. D., Baldessarini, R. J., & Katzan, I. L. (2015). Original research reports: Comparison of electronic screening for suicidal risk with the patient health questionnaire item 9 and the Columbia Suicide Severity Rating Scale in an outpatient psychiatric clinic. *Psychosomatics, 56*, 460–469. doi:10.1016/j.psym.2015.04.005

Chapter Twelve

Combating Mental Health Stigma in Underserved Black Communities

A Three-on-Three Basketball Tournament Intervention

Brett Ball
Yulia A. Strekalova

In the book *Black Pain: It Looks Like We Are Not Hurting*, Williams (2008) contextualizes Black Americans' salient reasons for resisting mental health assistance by addressing the legacy of pain and depression from years of slavery. He wrote, "How does suffering from living with addiction, incarceration, dirty neighborhoods, HIV, hypertension, violence, racism, and class discrimination make us vulnerable to depression in the Black community" (p. 256)?

The disparities in the health care system have created yet another barrier for Black Americans seeking help (American Psychological Association, 2014, para. 2). Blacks are underrepresented among American psychologists and psychiatrists, which results in racial incongruence between health practitioners and patients, and barriers to issues of medical mistrust and cultural conflicts. As a result, many practitioners are not equipped to treat the needs of their Black patients (Alvidrez, Snowden, & Kaiser, 2008; American Psychological Association, 2014), which can lead to misdiagnoses and inadequate use of mental health services.

Research has shown that Black Americans dismiss depression signs as "crazy" in their social circles and deem the discussion of mental health a stigmatized, taboo topic (Williams, 2011). Although religion, spirituality, and the church have been the centerfold for African Americans and provided hope for African American during treacherous times, some literature suggests religion has become a barrier for some African Americans who have a stigma toward mental health professionals (Holt & McClure, 2006). Moreover, the mass incarceration of Black men has disrupted Black families, placing more mental strains on a mother's mental health and social relationships (Wilde-man, Wakefield, & Turney, 2013).

This chapter proses a three-on-three basketball tournament intervention supported by literature on sport-for-development and social theories as one way to address mental health disparities and destigmatize mental health stigma within Black communities. Health disparities as it related to under-served Black communities is such a complex issue, so this chapter focuses on just a few barriers such as stigma, medical mistrust, and religion as it relates to the context of this intervention. Then it justifies the intervention from literature and the intervention protocol. While mental health stigma is a macro-level issue and the proposed intervention is a micro level and novel way to address the problem through increasing mental health literacy, it can change attitudes about mental health stigma and increase intentions to seek professional help.

BACKGROUND

Stigma

Stigma has been identified as one of the primary barriers to help-seeking behaviors (Corrigan, 2004), especially among young adults (Blaine, 2000). Goffman is credited for his early work on stigma. Goffman (1963) defined stigma as "an attribute that is deeply discrediting from a whole and usual person to a tainted discounted one" (p. 3). Alternative definitions of stigma include the recognition of differences and devaluations due to a given characteristic (Dovidio, Major, & Crocker, 2000). For example, Vogel, Wade, & Haake (2006) defined stigma as "the perception of being flawed because of a personal or physical characteristic that is regarded as socially unacceptable" (p. 325). Link and Phelan (2001) defined stigma as a moral experience because stigma is a social process. It is essential to note the distinction between societal stigma and local social network (Vogel, Wade, & Ascheman, 2009). The distinction is necessary because individuals are highly influenced by those whom they have the most interaction (Vogel et al., 2009). Research has shown that individuals are more likely to consult with a close friend before seeking professional services, which will often determine their help-seeking decision (Vogel, Wade, & Hackler, 2007; Vogel et al. 2009).

Furthermore, Smith's (2007) explication of stigma communication argued that specific content in stigma communication bear elements that evoke stigmatizing attitudes, which can lead to sharing the stigmatized message. In a qualitative study on low-income Black mental health consumers, partici-pants expressed their experience with mental health problems and treatment

(Alvidrez et al., 2008). This study found that 62 percent admitted to being reluctant to seek help because of the lack of conversation about the topic, which led to denial of the need for services and fear of judgment. One of the participants, a fifty-nine-year-old man said, "A lot of people they, they don't even know. I didn't know I was, I was suicidal. I just thought that this is the way you're supposed to be" (p. 882). A twenty-nine-year-old man expressed a similar hesitation:

> I felt about that, me getting a psychiatrist . . . I felt shame, that people would know that. Well, I felt shame over what I thought other people would think . . . I am thinking like that they'd prejudge me on that like they would prejudge on me having HIV. And that's the big reason that was stopping me from getting the mental health services that I need (p. 883).

Participants admitted growing up in an environment that valued strength in the face of adversity. They recalled avoiding topics concerning mental health and a desire for keeping personal business within the family. Williams (2008) suggested that similar characteristics to keep quiet are imprints of the survival mechanism of slavery, and have a lingering impact on Blacks. Consequently, most underserved Black community members go untreated for years causing other mental and physical health problems.

Medical Mistrust and Religion

Historical medical specific tragedies, such as the Tuskegee Syphilis study, has created mistrust in medical institutions and public health among African Americans. However, Gamble (1997) argued that the mistrust goes beyond Tuskegee and dates back to racial inequities in medical decision making. Literature has shown underserved Black communities' distrust of medical professionals and therefore they are more likely to turn to another member of the community for advice (Guadagnoio et al., 2009; Jacobs, Rolle, Ferrans, Whitaker, & Warnecke, 2006) and that community members may hold similar stigmas causing the cycle to continue for generations (Guadagnoio et al., 2009; Jacobs et al., 2006). Moreover, medical mistrust has also been linked to the deficiencies in the delivery of mental health services because of the lack of cultural trust among African Americans (Whaley, 2001). An adequate cultural representation in the profession allows for more efficient communication and understanding of clients' background (Sue et al., 1991) and decreases the chances for misdiagnosis.

To better understand religion's role and its influence on Black's attitudes and help-seeking decisions, the role of the Black church must be assessed. According to Williams (2008), the Black church is founded on principles of self-help. We had to educate our-selves, inform ourselves and one another, and build forms of social change and fighting back—all from inside the church. This is why when we feel oppressed . . . we often turn to the place we know best—the church (p. 201).

According to Pew Research (2009), most African Americans in the United States belong to a religious institution and reported that faith allowed them to connect with a consciousness outside of themselves that gives meaning to life-threatening illnesses. For centuries, the Black church served as a sacred form of personal identity and provided a physical and abstract sanctuary for many African Americans (Williams, 2008) and served as an informal social service provider (Blank, Mahmood, Fox and Guterbock, 2002).

Sports psychologists have identified ways religion and athletic perfor-mance intersect (Balague, 1999; Hoffman, 1992), including guidance and humility (Atchley, 1989), hope and security (Hoffman, 1992), and coping strategies (Gould, Udry, Bridges, & Beck, 1997; Koeing, 1994). Storch and colleagues (2001) suggest the four possible explanations as to how an athlete's religious beliefs correlate to performance: direction and humility, optimism and security, reassurance during uncertainty, and relief of com-petition anxiety. Although other barriers are instrumental in Blacks seeking professional help stigma, medical mistrust and religion were highlighted for the context of the proposed intervention.

Significance

Therefore, this chapter proposes a practical intervention of a three-on-three basketball tournament framed and supported by theoretical concepts as one way to address mental health disparities in underserved Black communi-ties. For decades, sports have played an important role in Black culture. From Jack Johnson breaking racial barriers in boxing to LeBron James and Miami Heat's photo-op of hooded players to support justice for Trayvon Martin—an unarmed teen that was killed—sports have been the platform in which Black athletes could unapologetically speak to a mass audience (Lamb, 2016). Although some have seen the sports industry as using Black athletes as gladiators for entertainment, athletes, like John Carlos, Tommie Smith, Arthur Ashe, and many others, have used sports as a change agent to disrupt the status quo and dismantle negative stereotypical messages to the masses. Sports as a change agent is the mechanism used for repackaging messages in a believable fashion (Berkowitz, 2004) in underserved Black communities.

Today, in the United States, sports have been commercialized into a multi-billion-dollar industry. Edwards (2000) recognized and debated the phenomenon that Black youth framed their potential for success through media representation and commercialization of Black sports figures. Despite the criticism, the suggested intervention in this chapter does not intend to reinforce Black youth athlete stereotypes in sports but instead introduce a traditionally stigmatized topic in a familiar domain.

For this chapter, underserved communities constitute vulnerable populations such as "low-income individuals, uninsured persons, immigrants, racial and ethnic minorities, and the elderly" (Silow-Carroll, Alteras, & Stepnick, 2006, p. 9). Conceptually, the chapter will draw from the social norm, social cohesion, and community-based participatory research (CBPR), but the practical application is through the sport-for-development literature.

Sport-for-Development Model

The symbolic power of sports to reconcile and reunite is evident from sports and social history dating back to the Olympic Games. From Nelson Mandela's wearing of a hat of Springbok—the South African Rugby team—1995 victory in the Rugby World Cup (Schulenkorf, 2012) to Colin Kaepernick kneeling to the national anthem to protest police brutality in 2016, sports have become a catalyst for some societal discourse to promote tranquility, equality, or mobilize nations. Schulenkorf (2012) referred to change agents as "external parties that help [communities] establish contact, open negotiations and develop projects for cooperation and sustainable development" (p. 4). In Figure 12.1, sport(s) (i.e., a three-on-three basketball tournament intervention) is the Sport-for-Development (S4D) project intervention between community members in the underserved area (micro) and the long-term social outcomes (macro).

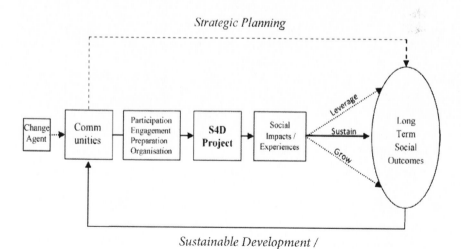

Figure 12.1.   Schulenkorf (2012) Sport-for-Development.
Image provided courtesy of the author.

The S4D model is the most appropriate framework because it provides strategic guidelines and a model for practical research for (inter-)community development and empowerment and is sports specific (Schulenkorf, 2012). Schulenkorf (2012) noted how the model describes an ex-ante approach toward understanding and guiding the strategic planning, investigation, and evaluation of sport and event development projects by integrating and visualizing the social processes generated through participatory sports activities. The S4D Framework should be understood as a loose frame toward sustainable "community and/or inter-community empowerment" (Schulenkorf, 2012, p. 7). Moreover, community capacity, which is a described as "means of effective implementation of community health development" (Labonte & Laverack, 2001, p. 7), has played a vital role in supporting and promoting community-level health and has gained recent attention by public health researchers and practitioners (Edwards, 2015). Edwards's (2015) review confirmed evidence that community capacity through sports for development practices can effectively facilitate dimensions of community capacity when executed in culturally specific ways and address community-specific needs. The inherited benefit of the S4D approach is physical activity. However, in Berg and colleague's (2015) qualitative study on the public health perspective on leisure time and physical activity, participants suggested that social interaction is the most overlooked yet primary benefit for participation in leisure sports. S4D is a holistic approach that considers cultural heterogeneity in underserved communities but is not without criticism. Sporting events are associated with competitiveness and can be a site for confrontation, prejudice, and anti-social behavior (Dimeo & Kay, 2004) where social group identity and ingroups prevail (Tomlison, 2003), reinforcing prejudicial stereotypes (Schulenkorf, 2012). Therefore, strategic planning for a conducive intergroup environment that is specific to a mental health cause is imperative.

CONCEPTUAL FRAMEWORK

The conceptual framework of this intervention is based on social norms, social cohesion theories, and community-based participatory research. These theories have implications for health promotion and prevention (Berkowitz, 2004). A culturally sensitive approach to addressing mental health among Blacks is grounded in social norms and social cohesion theories through community-based participatory research (CBPR) (see Figure 12.2).

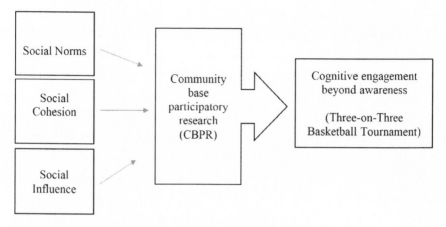

Figure 12.2.   A theoretical model for the sports intervention.
Image provided courtesy of the author.

Social Norms and Social Cohesion Theories

The Social Norms Theory, advanced by Berkowitz (2004), suggests that our behaviors are influenced by incorrect perceptions about how other members of the group think or act and suggest that we misjudge ourselves as a minority whenever our issues are contradictory to social norms when in fact it could potentially be a problem of the majority. Our behaviors are influenced by incorrect perceptions about how other members of the group thinks or acts (Berkowitz, 2004). Borsari and Carey (2003) found that peer influence has the most significant impact on beliefs in the health behaviors of youth. Thus, Berkowitz (2004) concluded that by repackaging correct information about peer norms in a believable fashion is hypothesized to reduce peer pressure and increase the likelihood of expressed health promoting beliefs and behaviors that were outside their social norms. Therefore, within this chapter, peers denote underserved Black community members and mental health communication at the three-on-three tournament is the repackaged information presented in a way that is familiar to that community. According to Berkowitz (2004), as a result, community members are more likely to have fruitful conversations about pre-existing beliefs among one another (Berkowitz, 2004).

Moreover, researchers have suggested a correlation between social cohesion, health (Wilkinson, 1999), and empowerment (Speer et al., 2001). The idea of the Social Cohesion Theory incorporates the notion of trust, participation, connectedness, and civic engagement (Speer et al., 2001). Social norms and social cohesion theories are relevant to the study because social norms are foundational to stigma development due to the human need for social acceptance. Social norms literature was consistent with stigma literature and the importance of social support as a buffer against mental illness in general (Mueller et al., 2006).

Community Based Participatory Research (CBPR)

Researchers Berge, Mendenhall, and Doherty (2009) suggested that CBPR is a viable approach to addressing health disparities in communities and fostering active engagement between researcher and community members that participate in the research. Such collaborative efforts provide researchers with proper tools and information to create tailored and appropriate services for a community (Heslop, Elsom, & Parker, 2000; Kovacs, 2000). In the last decade, CBPR has become the transformative research paradigm for translational social science and used for effective intervention strategies across diverse communities (Wallerstien & Duran, 2010). CBPR is "the prevailing paradigm to facilitate health [*sic*] goals by promoting a mutual transfer of expertise and power-sharing in decision making and data ownership across community and academic partners" (Jones & Wells, 2007, p. 407). This approach fosters active engagement between researcher and community members in locations where constituents are being studied (Israel et al., 2010).

Moreover, activities and guest speakers evoke cognitive involvement by participants. Krugman (1965) introduced the concept of involvement, suggesting that it is critical in determining how messages will be perceived. Studies show that people who process information more deeply can become more highly involved with the topic, especially in health communication where risks are negotiated. Involvement is highly correlated to knowledge, behavior, and attitude change (Chaffee & Roser, 1986); hence this basketball tournament will be an effective persuasive message for mental health communication messages. Social cohesion and influence literature legitimize the need for guest speakers with whom community members are familiar. Association cues of a noticeable person advocating mental health destigmatization can increase the likelihood of involvement behaviors (Kapitian & Silvera, 2016).

The Perspective

The proposed intervention aligned with personal experience and understanding the importance of science translation. Reflexivity, which addresses any bias and established values (Creswell & Poth, 2018), is often used in qualitative studies to inform the reader of how the researcher is situated in the study. As a former student-athlete, I understand sports as a powerful communication channel and its ability to evoke social change. From conversations with opinion leaders, assessing community needs, I desire to investigate further and reduce the mental health stigma in rural and underserved Black communities. Personal experiences situated me in a unique position to investigate social norms and mental health stigma. As the issue of mental health disparities has been established in the literature as mentioned earlier, I am proposing a different way to address the issue in this community through a three-on-three basketball tournament intervention.

THE INTERVENTION PROTOCOL

The main goals of this intervention are to:
1. Qualitatively assess the communities' current knowledge regarding social norms of mental health stigma through a community-engagement partner organization
2. Intervention: Three-on-Three Basketball Tournament for Mental Health Awareness
3. Evaluate the qualitative and quantitative assessment of community participant's feedback.

Methods and Procedure

Goal 1: To assess, qualitatively, communities' current knowledge regarding social norms of mental health stigma within Gainesville and Alachua, Florida, through a community-engagement partner organization.

This intervention is designed to have theoretical and practical implications for multiple locations of underserved Black communities. However, this proposed intervention is for those areas that are considered underserved and have mental health disparities in Alachua County in Gainesville, Florida.

Approach

A mixed methods approach is the best approach to develop a comprehensive analysis of mental health stigma in underserved Black communities. According to Creswell and Clark (2011), an Exploratory Sequential Design (qualitative-quantitative), qualitative data should be analyzed in phase one, which leads to the development of quantitative measures in phase two. Mixing occurs through the creation of phase two and during the analysis and discussion (Creswell & Clark, 2011). Qualitative data is initially collected, followed by quantitative data in order to explore the themes found in the qualitative data based on interesting findings or different patterns. This method requires analysis of the qualitative data first, thus shaping the development of quantitative components. Both data results will be used collectively in the final analysis. Nevertheless, an exploratory sequential design is the best approach for such intervention, but it can also be time-consuming and non-absolute because the design occurs in phases that are sequentially dependent on each other (Creswell & Clark, 2011).

Creswell (2007) defines qualitative research to be "an inquiry process of understanding based on a distinct methodological tradition of inquiry that explores a social or human problem where the researcher builds a complex, holistic picture, analyzing words, reports detailed views of informants and conducts the study in a natural setting" (p. 37). Preliminary qualitative assessment from community members will provide insights to identify culturally sensitive factors in the community and other potential solutions for combatting the stigma. Emerging themes and significant findings from interviews will be used to frame messages for the three-on-three basketball tournament. Qualitative insights will provide direction for the type of activities and education provided at the tournament. Moreover, the qualitative approach in phase one intends to provide insight into the community's basic knowledge about mental health stigma and could provide parameters for phase two of quantitative surveys.

Participants will be recruited through the University of Florida's (UF) community-engagement partner, Health Street, and asked questions regarding their perceptions, experience, and attitudes toward mental health stigma and help-seeking behaviors. In 2011, the University of Florida established Health Street as a resource to assess community health needs by recruiting community members through Community Health Workers (CHW) to join the Health Street registry (Health Street, 2018, para 1). According to UF Health Street (2018) website, Health Street "is a community engagement model that seeks to reduce disparities in health research and access to care. Community Health Workers engage community members in discussions at barbershops, beauty shops, parks, bus stops, community agencies, churches, neighborhood associations, healthcare facilities, sports venues, grocery stores, laundromats, nail salons, fitness centers, college health fairs, and other places people congregate" (para 1). Registration with the program includes a thirty-minute IRB-approved health assessment, including a blood pressure reading and opportunities to participate in health research. Health Street is a model for community engagement and translational research and is supported by the University of Florida National Institute for Health, UF College of Public Health and Health Profession, and NIDA (Health Street, 2018, para 1). However, it is understood that not everyone has access to resources and recruitment sites such as Health Street. However, CBPR can still be conducted through direct contact with community leaders and influencers. The sample size for Health

Street participants' qualitative phase depends upon interviewer's experience and judgment of the quality of information gathered (Sandelowski, 1995).

Goal 2: Intervention Three-on-Three Basketball Tournament for Mental Health Awareness

Purpose

According to the aforementioned social norms literature, the three-on-three tournament is a way to repackage a stigmatized message in a natural environment. Mental health stigma in underserved Black communities is a normative problem being answered by a practical solution through this intervention.

Location

The Three-on-Three Tournament for Mental Health Awareness will take place in Gainesville, Florida, and surrounding cities and towns will have an invitation to participate.

Time

The tournament will occur for an average of six hours depending on the number of participating teams. It is also contingent upon the availability of the host site space.

Participants

There will be a junior league for participating teams under eighteen years of age and a big league for participating teams over eighteen years of age. The teams will be co-ed. After registration, each team will be emailed a registration packet with official game rules and expectation of the tournament.

2 Courts

The games will be played on two courts labeled court number one and court number two.

Referees

Referees will be acquired through the community network of volunteers.

Games

Teams will be guaranteed three games. Additional games are tentative and depend on the number of teams registered to participate. For example, there will be seven open team spots. If an additional three teams show interest in participating, one guaranteed game will be eliminated for time and schedule efficiency. Tournament brackets will be created and contingent up the number of teams registered. Guest speakers for the event are encouraged to play.

Guest Speaker(s)

Guest speakers will include notable Floridians of color and others who are athletes (current and former), politicians, community leaders, psychologists, counselors, or entertainers whom are avid mental health awareness advocates or support the cause. Guest speakers will be encouraged to participate in at least one three-on-three game. Their speaking schedule will be determined within the layout of the games, which will be determined once all team participation is finalized. With qualitative insights in mind, guest speakers will be advised on what specific themes to address in conjunction with their personal story of becoming an advocate for mental health or why they support the cause.

On-Site Resources

On-site resources include booths varying from educational resources, counseling consultations, chiropractic adjustments, and sampling table of healthy snacks. Such booths will include UF Health, Health Street registry, Pinnacle Point Chiropractor, Project 375, National Institute of Mental Health, and because these entities support mental health advocacy on a local and state level.

Goal 3: Evaluate the qualitative and quantitative assessment of community participants' feedback

Approach

The project is to be evaluated on two levels: the reliability of the study and the achievement of stated goals. Quantitative data will be collected during the event at the check-in and check-out kiosk. Insights from the qualitative study will be used to create the survey in addition to attitude and knowledge retention scales. While on site and after attendees have registered, they will be asked to participate in the voluntary survey and will also indicate if they permit to be contacted for a separate quantitative Qualtrics survey, which will be used during check-in and check-out of the event, to measure their experience, knowledge gained from the event, and additional feedback using primarily Likert scales. An example of a question that would be asked in the check-out survey would be, "Was the information you received today regarding mental health help to you?" [beneficial, somewhat helpful, helpful, not helpful, NA] and/or "How likely are you after today to have more conversations about mental health in your community? [Very likely, somewhat likely, likely, not likely, NA]. The check-out survey will prompt the participant to opt in for a follow-up interview regarding their three-on-three tournament experience. The purpose of the follow-up interview is to measure attitudes and knowledge retention up to six weeks after the tournament intervention to test the "sleeper effect" on participant's attitudes about mental health stigma and literacy. Kleinnijenhuis, Van Hoof, & Oegema (2006) defined "sleeper effect" as "when the persuasiveness of the (an impress of) message increases with the passage of time" on participants attitudes about mental health awareness (p. 87). Once all quantitative data have been collected, check-in and check-out responses will be analyzed and evaluated.

Sample Size

According to The Audience Agency (2011), estimating the attendance of an event or festival is vital during the planning process, especially when there are no previous events in the area to compare. Although research methods vary by event, the literature suggests benchmarking as an excellent tool for things as unpredictable as outdoor events and festivals. Therefore, a 50 percent benchmark or more attendees of the tournament to complete the survey is most appropriate for this proposal (The Audience Agency, 2011). Due to the complexity in administering surveys at community events and festivals, the survey data can be challenging to obtain. However, this intervention proposes to employ attendee traffic control by designating a check-in and check-out tent or table at the tournament where personal information is not collected but provides an opportunity for attendees to complete the survey.

Outcomes

The intended outcomes for the intervention are an increase about mental health literacy, ability to identify local- and state-level mental health resources, change in attitudes toward mental health stigma, and increase in behavioral intentions to seek professional mental health help. According to the Audience Agency (2011), "Evaluation is about assessing whether your festival achieved its intended aims" (p. 7). Evaluation of these outcomes will be measured during the check-in and check-out survey before participants leave the tournament site. The intended overall impact of this intervention is to improve overall mental health awareness in underserved Black communities where mental health disparities are the most prevalent. Lastly, results from the intervention will be packaged for dissemination to stakeholders after data analyzation.

CONCLUSION

In conclusion, community-level interventions have been recognized as one of the most favorable practices in public health because of its ability to unify community insight with the researcher and practitioner's expertise to address community-specific needs (Wallerstein & Duran, 2010). This chapter discussed mental health disparities in the black community, proposed a three-on-three basketball tournament intervention for Alachua County in Gainesville, Florida, and discussed the intended outcomes. The intervention proposed is for underserved Black communities that experience mental health disparities. The practical intervention was justified through the sport-for-development (S4D) model and was supported by conceptual frameworks of social cohesion, social norms, and community participatory research literature. Despite the success or failures of other interventions to decrease health disparities, this intervention tailors an established sport-for-development model based on the needs of the community and seeks not to solve the entire mental health epidemic, but sheds a light on the issue hoping to foster future research inquires.

The idea of development through sport (Coalter, 2007) utilizes sports as a channel for change for worldwide social issues such as health promotion (Edwards & Casper, 2012) and crime and obesity reduction (Houlihan & White, 2002). Berg and colleagues' (2015) study on how to position sports within the public health agenda found that the typical narrative of its health benefits and better physical appearance is unlikely to change behavior or increase participation (Berg et al., 2015, p. 27). However, while physical benefits are implied in sports participation, it was the socialization opportunity and hedonic rewards that were most relevant to participants (Berg et al., 2015). Moreover, this intervention includes social cohesion literature that supports the importance and need for social interaction and its impact on health. The aforementioned social cohesion literature and Green's (2005) suggestion to cater to multiple motivations when promoting community-based programs aligns with the marketing intention of the proposed intervention.

The sport-for-development model has been successfully executed and assessed in Khayelitsh Township, Cape Town, South Africa for an interactive football-based health education program for sixth- and seventh-graders (Whitley, Coble, & Jewell, 2016). In addition, the Coach Across America program in New Orleans, Louisiana, used the S4D and showed an increase in nutritional knowledge and high-impact attitudes (i.e., well-being, discipline) through a quasi-experimental design (Whitley et al., 2016). Based on the literature on health disparities in underserved Black communities, sports, and public health, the proposed intervention is expected to start the conversation around mental illness and be replicated in other communities with similar characteristics.

As with any approach, the sport-for-development is not without criticism. It can be misinterpreted as the development of sport, which refers to sports for the sake of sports (Collins, 2010) and development through sports (Coalter, 2007), which leverages sports participation for character building. However, a component of the former—development through sport—is criticized by Coakley's (2011) study on what constitutes positive development in youth sports. He argued that sports enthusiasts claim that sports provide young people attributes to succeed and promotes positive development, yet there remains a lack of understanding of the conditions that breed such outcomes. He suggested that a combination of factors such as type of sport played, norms associated with the sport, and sport experiences determine the outcomes of effective sport development.

As for any scientific inquiry, including the proposed intervention, limitations are expected to be present. However, established literature on health disparities and the Black community alone, but more specifically mental health literature, provides enough support for the need and anticipated success of this intervention. Although health disparities in underserved Black communities is a macro-level issue, it is comprised of the micro-level disparities. While the proposed three-on-three basketball intervention seeks to address health disparities on a local level, its contribution to literature is essentially just one step in dealing with the mental health disparities that continue to plague underserved Black communities.

REFERENCES

Alvidrez, J., Snowden L. R., & Kaiser, D.M. (2008). The experience of stigma among black mental health consumers. *Journal of Health Care for the Poor and Underserved, 19*(3), 874–893. doi:10.1353/hpu.0.0058.

American Psychological Association. (2014). Demographic characteristics of APA members by membership characteristics. Retrieved from: http://www.apa.org/workforce/publications/14-member/table-1.pdf.

Atchley, R. C. (1989). A continuity theory of normal aging. *Gerontologist, 29*, 183–190. doi: 10.1093/geront/29.2.183

Balague, G. (1999). Understanding identity, value, and meaning when working with elite athletes. *The Sport Psychologist, 11*, 379–399. doi: 10.1123/tsp.13.1.89

Berg, B. K., Warner, S., & Das, B. M. (2015). What about sport? A public health perspective on leisure-time physical activity. *Sport Management Review, 18*(1), 20–31. doi: 10.1016/j.smr.2014.09.005

Berge, J. M., Mendenhall, T. J., & Doherty, W. J. (2009). Using community–based participatory research (CBPR) to target health disparities in families. *Family Relations, 58*(4), 475–488. doi: 10.1111/j.1741-3729.2009.00567.x

Berkowitz, A. (2004). The social norms approach: Theory, research and annotative bibliography. www.alanberkowitz.com.

Blaine, B. E. (2000). *The psychology of diversity: Perceiving and experiencing social difference.* Mountain View, CA: Mayfield Publishing.

Blank, M. B., Mahmood, M., Fox, J. C., & Guterbock, T. (2002). Alternative mental health services: The role of the Black church in the South. *American Journal of Public Health, 92*(10), 1668–1672. doi: 10.2105/ajph.92.10.1668

Borsari, B., & Carey, K. B. (2003). Descriptive and injunctive norms in college drinking: A meta-analytic integration. *Journal of Studies on Alcohol, 64*(3), 331–341. doi:10.15288/jsa.2003.64.331.

Chaffee, S. H., & Roser, C. (1986). Involvement and the consistency of knowledge, attitudes, and behaviors. *Communication Research,* 13(3), 373–399. doi: 10.1177/009365086013003006

Coakley, J. (2011). Youth sports: What counts as "positive development?" *Journal of Sport and Social Issues, 35*(3), 306–324. doi: 10.1177/0183723511417311

Coalter, F. (2007). *A wider social role for sport.* London: Routledge.

Collins, M. (2010). From 'sport for good' to 'sport for sport's sake'–not a good move for sports development in England?. *International Journal of Sport Policy and Politics,* 2(3), 367–379.

Corrigan, P. (2004). How stigma interferes with mental health care. *American Psychologist, 59*(7), 614–625. doi: 10.1037/0003-066x.59.7.614

Creswell, J. W. (2007). *Qualitative inquiry and research design: Choosing among five approaches.* 2nd Ed. Sage Publications. Thousand Oaks, CA.

Creswell, J. W., & Clark, V. L. P. (2007). *Designing and conducting mixed methods research.* Thousand Oaks, CA: Sage.

Creswell, J. W., & Clark, V. L. (2011). Choosing a mixed methods design. *Designing and conducting mixed method research, 2,* 53–106.

Creswell, J. W., & Poth, C. N. (2018). *Qualitative inquiry and research design: Choosing among five approaches.* (4th ed.) Thousand Oaks, CA: Sage.

Dimeo, P., & Kay, J. (2004). Major sports events, image projection and the problems of' semi-periphery: A case study of the 1996 South Asia Cricket World Cup. *Third World Quarterly, 25*(7), 1263–1276. doi: 10.1080/0143659042000281267

Dovidio, J. F., Major, B., & Crocker, J. (2000). Stigma: Introduction and overview. In T. F. Heatherton, R. E. Kleck, M. R. Hebl, & J. G. Hull (Eds.), *The social psychology of stigma* (pp. 1–28). New York, NY: Guilford.

Edwards, H. (2000). Crisis of Black athletes on the eve of the 21st century. *Society,* 37(3), 9. doi: 10.1007/bf02686167

Edwards, M. B. (2015). The role of sport in community capacity building: An examination of sport-for-development research and practice. *Sport Management Review, 18*(1), 6–19. doi: 10.1016/j.smr.2013.08.008

Edwards, M. B., & Casper, J. M. (2012). Sport and health. In G. B. Cunningham & J. D. Singer (Eds.), *Sociology of sport and physical activity* (2nd ed., pp. 69–98). College Station, TX: Centre for Sport Management Research and Education.

Gamble, V. N. (1997). Under the shadow of Tuskegee: African Americans and health care. *American Journal of Public Health, 87*(11), 1773–1778. doi: 10.2105/ajph.87.11.1773

Goffman, E. (1963). *Stigma.* Englewood Cliffs, NJ: Spectrum.

Gould, D., Udry, E., Bridges, D., & Beck, L. (1997). Cope with season-ending injuries. *The Sport Psychologist, 11*(4), 379–399. doi: 10.1123/tsp.11.4.379.

Green, B. C. (2005). Building sport programs to optimize athlete recruitment, retention, & transition: Toward a normative theory of sport development. *Journal of Sport Management, 19*(3), 233–253. doi: 10.1123/jsm.19.3.233

Guadagnoio, B. A., Cina, K., Helbig, P., Molloy, K., Reiner, M., Cook, E. F., & Petereit, D. G. (2009). Medical mistrust and less satisfaction with health care among native Americans presenting for cancer treatment. *Journal of Health Care of Poor and Underserved, 20*(1), pp. 210–226. doi: 10.1353/hpu.0.0108.

Health Street. (2018). Retrieved from: http://healthstreet.program.ufl.edu/.

Heslop, L., Elsom, S., & Parker, N. (2000). Improving continuity of care across psychiatric and emergency services: Combining patient data within a participatory action research framework. *Journal of Advanced Nursing, 31*(1), 135–143. doi: 10.1046/j.1365-2648.2000.01251.x

Hoffman, S. J. (1992). Religion in sport. In S.J. Hoffman (Ed.), *Sport and religion* (pp. 213–225). Champaign, IL: Human Kinetics.

Holt, C. L., & McClure, S. M. (2006). Perceptions of the religion-health connection among African American church members. *Qualitative Health Research, 16*(2), 268–281. doi: 10.1177/104932305275634

Houlihan, B., & White, A. (2002). *The politics of sports development: Development of sport or development through sport?* London: Routledge.

Israel, B. A., Coombe, C. M., Cheezum, R. R., Schulz, A. J., McGranaghan, R. J., Lichtenstein, R., . . . & Burris, A. (2010). Community-based participatory research: A capacity-building approach for policy advocacy aimed at eliminating health disparities. *American Journal of Public Health, 100*(11), 2094–2102. doi: 10.2105/ajph.2009.170506.

Jacobs, E. A., Rolle, I., Ferrans, C. E., Whitaker, E. E., & Warnecke, R. B. (2006). Understanding African Americans' view of the trustworthiness of physicians. *Journal of General Internal Medicine, 21*(6), 642–647. doi: 10.1111/j.1525-1497.2006.00485.x.

Jones, L., & Wells, K. (2007) Strategies for academic and clinician engagement in community-participatory partnered research. *Jama, 297*(4), 407–410. doi:10.1001/jama.297.4.407.

Kapitan, S., & Silvera, D. H. (2016). From digital media influencers to celebrity endorsers: Attributions drive endorser effectiveness. *Marketing Letters, 27*(3), 553–567. doi: 10.1007/s11002-015-9363-0

Kleinnijenhuis, J., Van Hoof, A. M., & Oegema, D. (2006). Negative news and the sleeper effect of distrust. *Harvard International Journal of Press/Politics, 11*(2), 86–104. doi: 10.1177/1081180x06286417

Koeing, H. G. (1994). *Aging and God: Spiritual pathways to mental health in midlife and later years.* New York: The Haworth Pastoral Press.

Kovacs, P. J. (2000). Participatory action research and hospice: A good fit. *The Hospice Journal, 15*(3), 55–62. doi: 10.1080/0742-969x.2000.11882957

Krugman, H. (1965). The impact of television advertising: Learning without involvement. *Public Opinion Quarterly, 29*(3), 349–356. doi: 10.1086/2673

Labonte, R., & Laverack, G. (2001). Capacity building in health promotion. Part 1: For whom? And for what purpose? *Critical Public Health, 11*(2), 111–127. doi: 10.1080/09581590110039838.

Lamb, C. (Ed.). (2016). *From Jack Johnson to Lebron James: Sports, media, and the color line.* University of Nebraska Press.

Link, B. G., & Phelan, J. C. (2001). Conceptualizing stigma. *Annual Review of Sociology, 27,* 363–385. doi: 10.1146/annurev.soc.27.1363

Mueller B., Nordt, C., Lauber, C., Rueesch, P., Meyer, P. C., & Roessler, W. (2006). Social support modifies perceived stigmatization in the first years of mental illness: A longitudinal approach. *Social Sciences & Medicine, 62*(1), 39–40. doi: 10.1016/j.socscimed.2005.05.014

Pew Research (2009). A religious portrait of African-Americans. Retrieved from: https://www.pewforum.org/2009/01/30/a-religious-portrait-of-african-americans/

Sandelowski, M. (1995). Sample size in qualitative research. *Research in Nursing & Health, 18*(2), 179–183. doi: 10.1002/nur.4770180211

Schulenkorf, N. (2012). Sustainable community development through sport and events: A conceptual framework for Sport-for-Development projects. *Sport Management Review, 15*(1), 1–12. doi: 10.1016/j.smr.2011.06.001

Silow-Carroll, S., Alteras, T., & Stepnick, L. (2006). *Patient-centered care for underserved populations: Definition and best practices* (pp. 1–43). Washington, DC: Economic and Social Research Institute.

Smith, R. A. (2007) Language of the lost: An explication of stigma communication. *Communication Theory, 17*(4). 462–485. doi:10.1111/j.1468-2885.2007.00307.x.

Speer, P. W., Jackson, C. B., & Andrew Peterson, N. (2001). The relationship between social cohesion and empowerment: Support and new implications for theory. *Health Education Behavior, 28*(6), 716–732. doi:10.1177/109019810102800605.

Storch, E. A., Kolsky, A. R., Silvestri, S. M., & Storch, J. B. (2001). Religiosity of elite college athletes. *The Sport Psychologist, 15*(3), 346–351. doi: 10.1123/tsp.15.3.346

Sue, S., Fujino, D. C., Hu, L. T., Takeuchi, D. T., & Zane, N. W. S. (1991). Community mental health services for ethnic minority groups: A test of the cultural responsiveness hypothesis. *Journal of Consulting and Clinical Psychology, 59*(4), 533–540. doi:10.1037/0022006X.59.4.533.

The Audience Agency: Researching Audiences at Outdoor Events and Festivals (2011). Retrieved from: http://culturehive.co.uk/wp-content/uploads/2013/06/BL_Researching-audiences-at- outdoor-events-and-festivals.pdf.

Tomlinson, M. (2003). Lifestyle and social class. *European Sociological Review*, *19*(1), 97–111. doi: 10.1093/esr/19.1.97

Vogel, D. L., Wade, N. G., & Ascheman, P. L. (2009). Measuring perceptions of stigmatization by others for seeking psychological help: Reliability and validity of a new stigma scale with college students. *Journal of Counseling Psychology*, *56*(2), 301–308. doi: 10.1037/a0014903

Vogel, D. L., Wade, N. G., & Haake, S. (2006). Measuring the self-stigma associated with seeking psychological help. *Journal of Counseling Psychology*, *53*(3), 325–337. doi: 10.1037/002-0167.53.3.325

Vogel, D. L., Wade, N. G., & Hackler, A. H. (2007). Perceived public stigma and the willingness to seek counseling: The mediating roles of self-stigma and attitudes toward counseling. *Journal of Counseling Psychology*, *54*(1), 40–50. doi: 10.1037/0022-0167.54.1.40

Wallerstein, N. B., & Duran, B. (2010). Using community-based participatory research to address health disparities. *Health Promotion Practice*, *7*(3), 312–323. doi: 10.1177/1524839906289376.

Whaley, A. L. (2001). Cultural mistrust and mental health services for African Americans: A review and meta-analysis. *The Counseling Psychologist*, *29*(4), 513–531. doi: 10.1177/0011000001294003

Whitley, M. A., Coble, C., & Jewell, G. S. (2016). Evaluation of a sport-based youth development programme for refugees. *Leisure, 40*(2), 175–199. doi: 10.1080/14927713.2016.1219966

Wildeman, C., Wakefield, S., & Turney, K. (2013). Misidentifying the effects of parental incarceration? A comment on Johnson and Easterling (2012). *Journal of Marriage and Family*, *75*(1), 252–258. doi: 10.1111/j.1741-3737.2012.01026.x

Williams, M. T. (2011). Why African Americans avoid psychotherapy. *Psychology Today*. Retrieved from: https://www.psychologytoday.com/us/blog/culturally-speaking/201111/why-african-americans-avoid-psychotherapy.

Williams, T. (2008). *Black Pain: It Just Looks Like We're Not Hurting.* New York, NY: Scribner.

Wilkinson, R. G. (1999). Income inequality, social cohesion, and health: Clarifying the Theory-A reply to Muntaner and Lynch. *International Journal of Health Services*, *29*(3), 525–543. doi:10.2190/3QXP-4N6T-N0QG-ECXP

Section 4

MENTAL HEALTH IN CRITICAL RELATIONSHIPS: THE ROLE OF FAMILY

Chapter Thirteen

Mental Illness, Ambiguous Loss, and Communicative Resilience in Families

Elizabeth A. Craig
Jessica Moore

Mental illness is one of the most prevalent health issues worldwide with approximately one in five adults experiencing symptoms of mental illness each year (National Alliance on Mental Illness, 2018). Just as mental illness can substantially alter a person's cognitive, emotional, and behavioral patterns, it can also prompt changes in how individuals relate to themselves and within family systems (e.g., shifts in individual and family identities, roles, and planning). As the individual suffering from mental illness loses their ability to function in ways that they had prior to the development of illness, debilitating experiences of grief and loss can follow. Such grief might not only occur for the person suffering from mental illness, but can extend to enduring close relationships (e.g., children, parents, siblings, spouses). Understanding how mental illness can rouse ambiguous loss, a type of complicated and disruptive grief that is difficult to resolve, is essential for researchers, health practitioners, and families. Moreover, understanding the communicative processes through which families develop resilience in the face of such affective experiences is paramount to the development of practices that can support and promote family health.

This chapter includes a theoretical conversation about mental health, ambiguous loss, and resilience, utilizing therapeutic and communication perspectives. We begin with an overview of mental health in families and turn to discuss how mental illness can lead to ambiguous loss.

Next, we argue that resilience theories from the fields of clinical and marriage therapy (Boss, 2006) and communication studies (Buzzanell, 2010) be integrated to best serve individuals and families dealing with ambiguous loss related to mental illness. Though research on resilience suggests that families can "bounce back" from such experiences, this chapter explicates how persisting with and through disruptions in life is not simply an individual act, but a co-constructed, communicative act. Just as Boss (2006) noted ambiguous loss as a "relational disorder" (p. 144), Buzzanell (2010) argued that communicative theorizing on resilience is "fundamentally grounded in messages, d/Discourse, and narratives" (p. 2). Subsequently, we articulate how these communicative processes are transferable to health practitioners, individuals, and families affected by mental illness. We conclude by emphasizing how research on ambiguous loss and resilience might serve individuals and families living with mental illness and discussing future directions for clinical as well as communication research.

MENTAL ILLNESS IN FAMILIES

Mental illness is one of the most prevalent health issues worldwide. According to the National Alliance on Mental Illness (2018), one in five adults will experience symptoms of mental illness (e.g., fatigue and anxiety to extreme mood changes and suicidal thoughts) each year, and one in four will experience a mental illness that substantially disrupts or limits major components of their day-to-day lives (e.g., work performance, family functioning, social activities). Mental illness can lead to idiosyncratic or unilateral changes in cognition, emotion, motivation, and behavior, all of which may take significant mental and physical tolls on a person. Seemingly simple routines such as eating and sleeping, for example, can be negatively impacted by a mental disorder, possibly leading to fatigue, changes in cognitive function, or an increase in allostatic load (American Psychiatric Association, 2013; Barlow, Durand, & Hofmann, 2018). Such stressors are not only challenging psychologically and physiologically, but they can also be taxing socially (Raglan & Schulkan, 2014). That is, the reach of mental illness often extends beyond individuals to destabilize social systems (Zautra, 2014), including the partners, children, and family members of those coping with illness (Boss, 2010). Simply stated, a family's equilibrium is vulnerable to the dynamic ambiguities that often accompany mental illness.

Just as families are each somewhat unique, so too are mental illnesses. Some mental illnesses are dysthymic (i.e., persistent) and appear with homeostatic features, thereby making certain diseases somewhat "predictable" for some individuals and their allies in care. For example, persistent depressive disorder (i.e., dysthymia) is a continuous and long-term disorder that may vary in intensity over time, but is typically characterized by persistent symptoms that are relatively predictable on a day-to day basis (Barlow et al., 2018). Other mental illnesses, however, may be more dynamic or occur with comorbidities (i.e., occur as a cluster of illnesses) (Prince et al., 2007). For example, bipolar 1 disorder is characterized by episodes of extreme highs and lows, which are often difficult to predict and manage (Barlow et al., 2018). Pragmatically speaking, this means that mental illness management can be relatively predictable for some and extremely unpredictable for others, existing on a continuum of cognitive, emotional, and behavioral dysfunction (APA, 2013). According to Johnstone (2001), the intensity of symptoms affects how functioning and behaviors change, which indicates that breadth and depth of symptomology ultimately impacts an individual's ability to sustain healthy roles, routines, relationships, and self-care.

Of central importance is that mental illnesses can: 1) materialize for a variety of reasons (e.g., biological, psychological, social, contextual, circumstantial), 2) be characterized by a variety of presenting features (e.g., cognitive, affective, and behavioral symptoms), and 3) change subtly or dramatically, sometimes without clear warnings (APA, 2013; Barlow et al., 2018). This makes diagnosing, treating, and managing mental illnesses challenging for both healthcare professionals and the individuals and families living with these illnesses.

Mental Illness and Ambiguous Loss in Families

Every aspect of an individual's life can be affected by mental illness. As previously stated, mental illness can prevent a person from successfully navigating their daily functions at home, work, or in the community. These changes in functionality can be quite painful, oftentimes leading to significant stress and feelings of loss (Boss, 2006, 2010; Boss, Bryant, & Mancini, 2017). Just as one may experience loss from losing functionality of their physical body (e.g., arms, legs), so too might one experience loss from deteriorating cognitive, affective, or behavioral functionality due to mental illness. Such losses might not only affect the individual suffering from mental illness but also their children, partners, spouses, and family members. That is, mental illness often results in people feeling "not themselves" and those around them noticing that loved ones are "no longer as they once were." Such losses might be additional, unpredictable disruptions for those living with mental illness and their families (Boss, 2010).

Every individual and family experiences loss at some point, but some losses can be more difficult to process than others. In particular, research indicates that ambiguous loss can be particularly devastating. According to Boss (2006; 2010), ambiguous loss is one that includes a lack of information, clarification, or validation of the loss. Boss extends her articulation of ambiguous loss by articulating two specific types—physical and psychological. Physical ambiguous loss occurs when the physical manifestation of a person is absent while psychological presence persists. For example, one might experience the disappearance of a family member due to kidnapping, war, or unexplained disappearance. In such cases, the loss is ambiguous because a physical body is missing while a psychological presence persists. One might also experience physical ambiguous loss after unsuccessful family planning or a miscarriage, a situation in which a psychological narrative persists that no longer aligns with a physical reality. Just the opposite of physical ambiguous loss is psychological—a physical body is present concomitant with a disruption or lack of psychological presence. Family members of patients with dementia often experience this kind of loss wherein their loved one's body is intact but cognitive functioning has changed such that they may seem "absent" altogether. Individuals and family members of those suffering from mental illness might also experience a psychological ambiguous loss because the illness often affords a physical presence in the midst of significant changes in cognitive, emotional, or behavioral functioning that can sometimes make a person feel like they are "missing" or "not themselves." In fact, some mental illness might result in ambiguities that can occur both physically (e.g., physical absences related to a disorder such as hospitalization or unexplained disappearance) and/or psychologically (e.g., dissociative identity disorder or behavior that routinely violates expectations and relational norms).

For individuals and families, ambiguous loss associated with mental illness is not always apparent and immediate. Mental illness for many is progressive in nature, moving from subtle symptoms and non-chronic disruptions to more significant symptomology and persistent disruptions (Barlow et al., 2018). However, even for those whose losses may be evident or occur suddenly, the understanding and/or acceptance of such losses can take time for individuals as well as their significant others (Boss, 2010; Panksepp, 2014). Additionally, the ability for individuals and families to effectively cope with the ambiguous losses associated with mental illness can necessitate emotional and cognitive flexibility, already strained resources for those facing illness and loss. Whether losses are physical or psychological in nature, what is clear is that they often result in significant changes in identities, affecting roles and relationships within families (Boss, 2006; Boss & Yeats, 2014).

Some of the most challenging losses to navigate can be attributed to shifts in identity (Boss, 2006, 2010; Boss & Yeats, 2014). People who once saw themselves as independent, motivated, strong, and resilient may no longer feel this way. Self-efficacy and self-esteem are particularly vulnerable in people living with depression (Maciejewski, Prigerson, & Mazure, 2000; Tennen & Herzberger, 1987); the disorder itself might significantly alter individuals' perceptions of themselves and their beliefs about what they are capable of accomplishing. For instance, a person who once felt like an expert in her profession, a capable mother, and a supportive friend may now view herself as an imposter at work, a failing caregiver to her children, or a friend with too much baggage. Given the social stigmas associated with mental illness, it is not uncommon for individuals to go through stages of stigmatizing themselves or labeling themselves with inappropriate and/or inaccurate identities (Corrigan, Watson, & Barr, 2006; Maciejewski et al., 2000; Tennen & Herzberger, 1987). Such stigmatizing and labeling can result in temporary or chronic changes in identity that can often feel like a significant loss—one that feels void of clarity and validation (Boss, 2006). Thus, people living with mental illness and their families must be wary of developing negative identities and/or labels. Communication that normalizes these identity shifts over the lifespan could positively impact long-term health and well-being.

In summary, ambiguity may arise from losses of daily functioning, employment, personal worth, changes in identity, and dreams for the future, among other things. What one person grieves another may not, and what one person sees as a relationship lost another might see as an opportunity gained. Just as disorders might manifest for different people in different ways, so too do people respond differently to disorders. These responses might make all the difference when considering resilience. Below we discuss the importance of integrating the theory and practice of resilience. Integrating Boss's (2006) work on building resilience in families affected by ambiguous loss and Buzzanell's (2010) framework on communicative resilience could inform therapeutic strategies for clinical treatment while concomitantly extending the scope of communicative resilience beyond its current contextual domain.

Ambiguous Loss, Communication, and Resilience

Losses related to mental illness can require complex adaptive processes; however, the process of navigating these challenges can be enriching when accompanied by guidance and support. Therapeutic recommendations for coping with ambiguous loss have been offered for individuals and their families. Boss (1999, 2006, 2010) offers six guiding tenets aimed at building resilience in families wanting to mitigate disruptions caused by ambiguous loss—finding meaning, tempering mastery, reconstructing identity, normalizing ambivalence, revising attachment, and discovering hope. Buzzanell (2010) offers a theoretically complementary framework for the construction of resilience after severe life disruptions where families might engage in five processes—crafting normalcy, affirming identity anchors, maintaining and using communication networks, putting alternative logics to work, and legitimizing negative feelings while foregrounding positive action. Communicative resilience is based on developmental and ecological approaches

(Lucas & Buzzanell, 2012) where resilience is embedded in everyday talk, cultivated through practice and experience, throughout the lifespan (Beck & Socha, 2015; Buzzanell & Houston, 2018). Just as Boss (2006) notes ambiguous loss as a "relational disorder" (p. 144), Buzzanell (2010) argues that communicative theorizing on resilience is "fundamentally grounded in messages, d/Discourse, and narratives" (p. 2), where resilience is cultivated in relationships (Afifi, 2018). Scholars agree that resilience is not an individual trait or simple tool for disruption repair (Boss, 2002; Buzzanell & Houston, 2018), but instead a process where adaptation is ongoing, systemic, and concomitantly influenced by characteristics of the disrupting event(s), namely, whether it is a) permanent or not permanent, b) a singular or accumulated event(s), and c) unexpected or forecasted (Buzzanell, 2018).

Resilience, then, is not for families to return to what they once were, but to engage in transformational processes in which they find meaning from the distress through communication messages, symbols, and processes (Buzzanell, 2018). Persisting with and through disruptions in life is not simply an individual act, but a relational one, spanning one's life (Buzzanell, 2018) in which families create new stories and rituals, identities, find agency, and discover new modes of being (Boss, 2006; Walsh, 2003). However, with this view of resilience, communication is not simply a skill or something backgrounded to other processes, but communication is constitutive of resilience (Lucas & Buzzanell, 2012). Below we address Boss's (1999; 2006) tenets and Buzzanell's (2010) processes to provide an integration of theory and practice on mental illness, ambiguous loss, and resilience in families.

Finding Meaning and Crafting Normalcy

Boss (2006) begins the conversation about navigating ambiguous loss by discussing the notion of finding meaning. Finding meaning, she suggests, is simply akin to being able to make sense of a situation or event. For some people coping with mental illness might simply mean being able to properly name their illness (e.g., bipolar depression, double depression, schizophrenia, anxiety disorder) or understand how their illness functions (e.g., insomnia, negative affect, disassociation, delusions of grandeur), but, for most families, finding meaning will extend beyond these boundaries. That is, finding meaning may come from dialectical thinking, often materialized as "both/and" thinking (p. 88). A person can be both depressed and stable, both manic and kind, both ill and yet capable of doing great things for themselves and members of their community. Finding meaning may also emerge from doing good work or sustaining/building healthy rituals. Of importance in finding meaning is that this goal can be achieved in as many ways as there are individual belief systems for families living with mental illness. What has meaning for one person may or may not situate ambiguity and cultivate resilience in another. Thus, finding meaning requires a willingness for people with mental illness and their families to be curious about the beliefs, places, rituals, and/or conversations through which meaning will be discovered. Finding meaning, then, is a co-constructed process that unfolds over a life course in order to navigate ambiguous loss and build resilience.

One of the ways that families might find meaning when experiencing ambiguous loss is by crafting normalcy through communication processes and messages. Buzzanell (2010) and Boss (2002; 2006) both describe the desire for families to "get back to normal" after severe disruptions in life have occurred. This is difficult to do with the ambiguous nature of loss associated with certain mental illnesses where routines, relationships, and daily functioning can be impeded, and can persist throughout the lifespan. Using communication to frame one's world with a sense of consistency becomes important for families to explicitly and implicitly cultivate systems that help them hold on to the mundane, or the normal, of life. Buzzanell and Turner (2003) found that among families that had experienced job loss, despite significant changes in emotions and routines, they insisted that things were normal. That is, they talked normalcy into being (Buzzanell, 2010) through rituals and routines. Establishing new routines and rituals or reframing existing ones are opportunities for families to centralize patterned talk, create messages and narratives around the loss, and/or manage ambiguity related to the loss through communication. Narrative sense making (Koenig Kellas & Kranstuber Horstman, 2015; see also ch. 10 in this volume) is one way that families might focus on constructing shared narratives around mental illness and ambiguous loss. Through joint storytelling, families can validate perspectives, create rituals, establish new identities, and cope with stress through interpersonal engagement, turn taking, perspective taking, and narrative coherence (Koenig Kellas & Trees, 2006; Trees & Koenig Kellas, 2009).

Reconstructing and Affirming Identities

Ambiguous loss can also cause the loss of identity for individuals, families, and even communities. When significant others are absent in body or mind, people become understandably confused about identities and their accompanying roles. Therefore, reconstructing identities is helpful in the development and maintenance of resilience (Boss, 1999; 2006).

Implicitly embedded with the reconstruction of identities is the need to rely on family members to help in the negotiation of these transformations. Buzzanell (2010) notes that identity anchors are "a relatively enduring cluster of identity discourses upon which individuals and their familial, collegial and/ or community members rely on when explaining who they are for themselves and in relation to each other" (p. 4). As loss might heighten ambiguity related to the enactment of one's identity (i.e., the person living with the disorder or the family member), communication messages and d/Discourses might interact to enhance the affirmation of important identities, the adaptation of current identities, and/or the formation of new identities (Buzzanell, 2010). With mental illness, roles that family members might typically perform may need shifting (Boss, 2006). However, specific communication messaging that can assist family members in acknowledging and accepting the fluidity of these new roles and conflict associated with roles is paramount for the health of the family. A man whose wife has succumbed to the darkness of major depressive disorder, for example, might benefit from revising his expectations of his wife as a lover, daughter, or church leader.

Part of this process might include recognizing certain identities that no longer exist, developing new scripts for talking about identities, or understanding that sometimes people hide identities for safety. This might also include redefining family roles and responsibilities tied to family or community events. Communication on and around identity anchors, like reaffirming an identity in times of distress through self-talk, might also be helpful for those living with depression. Relying on religious and spiritual thoughts or enacting other positive identities might move one away from unhelpful labels, such as depressed, sick, or unwell, toward more positive ways of thinking and talking about oneself.

Tempering Mastery of Ambivalent or Negative Feelings

Over the course of a relationship, ambivalence about one's partner is likely to surface. The course of managing a mental illness is also likely to produce a similar ambivalence. Creating space for resilience to manifest means, in part, recognizing and labeling ambivalent feelings "in order to manage them and thereby avoid harmful behaviors that will be regretted later" (Boss, 2006, p. 145). Normalizing ambivalence might be enacted by bringing ambivalent feelings out into the open, admitting negative feelings without accepting negative actions, seeing conflict as a birthplace for positive outcomes, and valuing diverse ways of managing ambivalence.

Though normalizing ambivalence can be helpful in building resilience, it is not uncommon for people to embrace normalizing with the goal of solving their problems or mastering their situations. When it comes to illness, however, a longing for absolute mastery, or having a feeling that one controls their own life (Pearlin & Skaff, 1995, p. 12), is likely to result in disappointment.

Mental health disorders, by definition, deviate from expectations for what is both individually and socio-culturally normative (APA, 2013; Barlow et al., 2018). The supposition of tempering mastery requires a releasing of control accompanied by an understanding that we are not always able to predict the changes associated with mental illness or, moreover, how people in our families will respond to our specific disease or idiosyncratic symptoms over time. Boss (2002; 2006) suggests individuals might temper mastery by softening the negative attributions they make about themselves and others, identifying past competencies, decreasing self-blame, and increasing the identification of success experiences. Taken together, these tactics might ease the grief of ambiguity and allow flexibility and adaptability to reign when "the preferred solution is impossible" (p. 103). Whether its ambivalence about our partner, or the negative attributions we make about ourselves, communication can help us reframe our thoughts and actions.

In a communicative framework, we might see the benefit that legitimizing negative feelings while foregrounding positive action (Buzzanell, 2010) can have for family members and those living with mental illness. Verbal and nonverbal messages that acknowledge the sad, angry, and sometimes devastating feelings that come with loss are essential in this process of legitimizing lived experiences. The recognition that these negative feelings are present, yet not the focal point of all interaction within families, provides an opportunity to engage in positive action (Buzzanell, 2010). Here, to recognize the importance of normalizing ambivalence, one can begin to accept that ambivalence is a part of the process. Consequently, some relief might come as one begins to temper their mastery, no longer striving for absolute mastery, but learning how to reasonably manage their inside worlds when their outside worlds seem unmanageable in the presence of illness, grief, or loss. This might look like a child confessing to a depressed father that she simply wants him to be present for her sporting events despite his ambivalence about attending. This confession, while it might be expressed as a negative feeling, might serve a number of goals related to positive action: a) outwardly expressing the hurt or sadness she might feel around his ambivalence (i.e., normalizing ambivalence), b) verbalizing her desire for a continued relationship with her father, even though she has no control over his response to her (i.e., tempering mastery), and/or c) communicating hope for a day when her father might be able to respond differently to her request. This process might also empower family members to be proactive, not reactive, communicators. Families might then see that they have not gained a sense of mastery over the illness, but a sense of mastery around making it through difficult times and the efficacy to be able to do so again when strain reoccurs (Boss, 2002; Lucas & Buzzanell, 2012; Theiss, 2018). According to Boss (2006), bringing ambivalent and/or negative feelings into the light serves to prevent families from entering cycles of silence and shame, which can often compound feelings of isolation, grief, and loss.

Revising, Reframing, or Reconstructing Cognition and Communication

People who are closely attached (i.e., bonded) yet become separated as a byproduct of ambiguous loss are said to endure grief and loss that far outweighs a confirmed death (Boss, 2006). Thus, revising attachment allows families to place hope for a return or recover alongside the uncertainty or unlikelihood of that happening. Putting alternative logics to work describes the lived contradictions that are reframed due to situations that are difficult to navigate (Buzzanell, 2010). Many times, systems or structures impede resilience processes; for example, binary thinking would lead us to believe that our family member is either well or sick. Families seek creative responses— or reframe situations, organizations, or messages—to manage this binary when they are unable to make sense of why their experience deviates.

Creative messaging might allow families to circumvent the discourse of this sick/well binary, a system that does not match with their lived experience. For example, individuals and families might engage in a softening of attachment over certainty through particular messages to loved ones (e.g., we will do everything we can to heal versus we will beat depression this year), create space for the presence of hope alongside closure rituals through intrapersonal communication processes (e.g., maintaining positive attitude about returning to health while making peace with the existing version of one's self), and/or embrace dialectical tensions through interaction with loved ones (e.g., my loved one can be emotionally distant and love me at the same time). By revising attachments and putting alternative logics to work, one might cognitively and communicatively choose protest over passivity and place hope for health and well-being alongside the uncertainties that often accompany illness.

Building and Sustaining Networks and Support

According to Butterworth and Rodgers (2008), couples with at least one partner living with mental illness are more likely to experience marital strain than couples where both partners are healthy. For example, consider a couple with one partner living with depressive disorder with a bipolar II comorbidity. In this case, the partner with mental illness might cycle through periods of extreme depressive and manic symptoms, which could necessitate an ongoing redistribution of roles and responsibilities in the relationship. It might also result in the healthy partner taking on the role of caretaker or feeling compelled to oversee their partner's pharmaceutical regimen.

Moreover, the up and down cycles and intense behaviors that often accompany bipolar depression, when not well managed, could fatigue support provided by family and friends over time. Over time, this could result in the couple feeling isolated, alienated, or experiencing loss for the extra-dyadic roles and relationships that once surrounded them. Significant stressors, like mental illness and ambiguous loss, are important contexts for understanding supportive communication and supportive networks (Burleson, 2009). Maintaining and using communication networks can be an invaluable way to access the support needed to address individual, relational, family, and community resilience (Buzzanell, 2010; Buzzanell & Houston, 2018). For example, the theory of resilience and relational load (TRRL) argues that when individuals validate their partner through positive relational maintenance strategies, they build emotional reserves that protect the relationship. These protections are conferred for couples, in particular, that have a more unified or relational approach to stressors (Afifi, Merrell, & Davis, 2016).

Theiss (2018) outlines the importance of the parent-child relationship in constructing strength and adaptability during difficult times, through responsive parent communication to assist children in emotion regulation and coping. Hall (2018) also found that among a sample of marginalized family members (i.e., people perceived to be the black sheep of the family), seeking support from communication networks was imperative to enacting resilience. An adult living with mental illness, for example, might benefit from seeking support from one's parent as well as one's psychological family (e.g., friends, close colleagues, proximal/intimate neighbors). In conclusion, friends, families, and communities are relational spaces that provide opportunities for communal coping, unified messages of support, and a way for individuals and families to know that they are not alone. These environments are essential to one's ability to look toward the future, plan, or find hope during distressing times.

Hope for Families Living with Mental Illness

The process of finding meaning, tempering mastery, reconstructing identity, normalizing ambivalence, and revising attachment culminate in discovering hope according to Boss (2006). "Without meaning, there is no hope. Without hope, there is no meaning" (p. 177). Simply stated, hope may be found in spiritual or religious practice and for others it might be raised by laughing at the absurdity of life, finding forgiveness for self and others, developing patience, and imagining or reimagining options. As a reminder, what works for one individual or family might not work for everyone. For a couple needing family and community support, it may be that restarting attendance to a religious service provides hope for rebuilding a community that has felt missing. Alternatively, for a person feeling guilty about the way she treats her friends and family in the throes of a manic episode, she might forgive herself with the hope that forgiveness will be extended to her.

Communication scholars have also forwarded similar ideas on hope, framing hope as a communication process (Beck & Socha, 2015). Spark, Hefner, and Rogeness (2015) contend that with such high rates of depression among those diagnosed with cancer, messages of hope must be nuanced, as to meet the emotional needs of those diagnosed and their families in order to assist decision-making efforts related to their illness. What hope is not is wishful thinking in the midst of abuse, such as hoping that a spouse with mental illness will stop being abusive once the medication takes hold. It is also not a parent spending all of her time surfing the web for a nonexistent cure while her terminally ill daughter slips away in the next room. Discovering hope is situated in living well in the present and being curious about the transformative possibilities ahead. Discovering hope is about looking for connections that were severed, finding new symbols and languages to co-create bonds that cannot be broken, and finding meaning in one's experiences that can be used to help others find meaning in theirs.

Discussion and Future Directions

How do I let go of what I cannot control? What do I do with my conflicted feelings? Who am I now that my loved one has changed? How do I find hope in an ongoing loss that has no closure? These questions, among others, are important ones being asked by people experiencing ambiguous loss as a result of their own mental illness or the mental illness of a family member. Fortunately, research on resilience from the fields of clinical and marriage therapy (Boss, 2006) as well as communication studies (Buzzanell, 2010) provides guidance that can serve individuals and families pursuing answers to these questions. As previously stated, families are capable of persisting with and through such disruptions in life and can do so, in part, communicatively (Boss, 2010; Buzzanell, 2010). As discussed in this chapter, constructing new norms, managing identities, accepting negative feelings, reframing, seeking and accepting support from communication networks, and maintaining hope are processes through which resilience can be cognitively and communicatively constructed at individual, dyadic, and familial (i.e., systems) levels.

Researchers agree that finding meaning through both/and thinking and crafting normalcy via talk in the midst of upheaval can ease the intensity of mental illness–induced grief or loss. This orientation and communicative approach also allows for the management and anchoring of identities, whether those are identities of past, present, or future. Throughout this process, researchers argue, legitimizing and accepting the presence of negative feelings while foregrounding positive and productive logics can be helpful, particularly during periods when one may feel ambivalent about doing so. Additionally, using alternative logics and reframing intrapersonal, interpersonal, and extra-dyadic attachments allows for the celebration of what remains while grieving what or who may be lost. Consequently, the more comfortable people become living with and accepting ambiguity, the freer they are to imagine and discover new courses of hope (Boss & Yeats, 2014).

In addition to the contributions of clinicians and clinical researchers, communication research and scholarship is crucial in understanding family resilience. For example, scholarship on the influence of positive communication on health and well-being (Albada & Moore, 2013; Pitts & Socha, 2013) as well as communicative resilience (Buzzanell, 2010; Beck & Socha, 2015) demonstrate the importance that communicative frameworks can have for those examining significant life disruptions. Resilience is not an individual trait, where one is either resilient or not (Masten, 2014), but something that can be cultivated through relational and family communication throughout the lifespan. Consequently, the loss and grief associated with the ambiguity of living with mental illness calls for communication of both competencies and theories, namely, theories on communicating resilience (Houston & Buzzanell, 2018), supportive communication frameworks (Burleson, 2009), and narrative sense-making (Koenig Kellas & Krastuber Hortsman, 2015).

One such framework, the theory of resilience and relational load (TRRL), might be used to identify communal coping processes among partners that function as protections in relationships (Afifi, Merrill, & Davis, 2016). Afifi and colleagues suggest that partners that have more of a communal mindset toward stressors are more likely to appraise stressful situations with a more positive mindset, less likely to blame their partners, and more likely to protect them and the relationship. The theory of resilience and relational load could be used to predict threatening appraisals in couples living with mental illness and communication patterns leading to excessive relational load and impeding adaptation processes.

Relational and family resilience process can also be influenced by other systems. Multi-level resilience processes (e.g., individual, relational, family, community, organizational, and national) are poised for communication interventions (Buzzanell & Houston, 2018), prompting scholarship from diverse epistemological and ontological traditions. In other contexts, researchers might examine how communities and organizations that offer mental health services are prepared for the multifaceted effects of ambiguous loss, have the structures needed to promote resilience processes, or have secured the resources a community might need to bring greater awareness to loss related to the ambiguities of mental illness. Also, with a long history of stigmatization of mental illness, more critical scholarship might question the ways resilience is framed within the context of mental illness (Houston & Buzzanell, 2018; Bean, 2018). For example, researchers could consider who and what is considered resilient and by whom (e.g., framing, societal narratives on mental health, structures such as health care systems and access to resources that might disrupt or impede adaptation processes, historical issues that would limit ways of communicating about resilience). A closer look at these issues might reveal systemic inequities regarding the care of persons "with" mental illness, the types of ambiguous losses they might incur, and the ability to adapt to such losses. Finally, researchers might more fully explore resilience conceptually across research contexts. How resilience is conceptually delineated alongside neural plasticity, self-efficacy, or determination, for example, may be of import for those studying resilience in the context of mental health.

The application of this work is just emerging, yet there is so much to be done. Within the context of mental health and well-being, scholars should continue to, a) explore social connections and support as integral components of constructing resilience in individuals, relationships, families, organizations, communities, and nations, b) question the ways resilience is framed, challenging structures and resources (i.e., historical issues or systemic inequities) that would limit ways of communicating about resilience, and 3) create resilience activities, programs, and interventions developed and tested to fully realize how multilevel resilience is fostered (Buzzanell & Houston, 2018). "Caring for family members who [may be] partially present and partially absent is confusing work and a demanding task" (Boss, 2006, p. 209). However, there is hope for the study of symbols, messages, meaning, and communicative processes to forge pathways toward better health and relating for individuals and families living with mental illness.

REFERENCES

Afifi, T. (2018). Individual/relational resilience. *Journal of Applied Communication Research, 46*, 5-9. doi: 10.1080/00909882.2018.1426707

Afifi, T., Merrill, A., & Davis, S. (2016). The theory of resilience and relational load (TRRL). *Personal Relationships, 23*, 663–683. doi: 10.1111/pere.12159

Albada, K., & Moore, J. (2013). Moving from positive thinking to positive talk. In M. Pitts & T. Socha (Eds.), *Positive communication in health and wellness* (pp. 117–132). New York: Peter Lang Publishing. ISBN 978-1-4331-1446-5

American Psychiatric Association. (2013). Diagnostic and statistical manual of mental disorders. doi:10.1176/appi.books.9780890425596

Barlow, D. H., Durand, V. M., & Hofmann, S. G. (2018). *Abnormal psychology: An integrative approach.* Boston, MA: Cengage Learning.

Bean, H. (2018). National resilience. *Journal of Applied Communication Research, 46,* 23–25. doi: 10.108000909882.2017.1426691

Beck, G., & Socha, T. (Ed.) (2015). *Communicating hope and resilience across the lifespan.* New York: NY. Peter Lang Publishing. doi: 10.3726/978-1-4539-1520-2

Boss, P. (1999). *Ambiguous loss: Learning to live with unresolved grief.* Cambridge, MA: Harvard University Press. doi: 10.4135/9781412972031.n12

Boss, P. (2002). *Family stress management: A contextual approach* (2nd ed.). Thousand Oaks, CA: Sage. doi: 10.4135/9781452233895

Boss, P. (2006). *Loss, trauma, and resilience: Therapeutic work with ambiguous loss.* New York: W.W. Norton & Company.

Boss, P. (2010). Trauma and complicated grief of ambiguous loss. *Pastoral Psychology, 59,* 137–145. doi: 10.1007/s11089-009-0264-0

Boss, P., Bryant, C. M., & Mancini, J. A. (2017). *Family stress management: A contextual approach.* Los Angeles: SAGE. doi:10.4135/9781506352206

Boss, P., & Yeats, J. (2014). Ambiguous loss: A complicated type of grief when loved ones disappear. *Bereavement Care, 33*(2), 63–69. doi: 10.1080/02682621.2014.933573

Burleson, B. (2009). Understanding the outcomes of supportive communication: A dual-process approach. *Journal of Social and Personal Relationships, 26,* 21–38. doi: 10.1177/0265407509105519

Buzzanell, P. (2010). Resilience: Talking, resisting, and imagining new normalcies into being. *Journal of Communication, 60,* 1–14. doi:10.1111/j.1460-2466.2010.01469.x

Buzzanell, P. (2018). Organizing resilience as adaptive-transformational tensions. *Journal of Applied Communication Research, 46,* 14–18. doi: 10.1080/00909882.2018.1426711

Buzzanell, P., & Houston, J. (2018). Communication and resilience: Multilevel applications and insights. *Journal of Applied Communication Research, 46,* 1–4. doi: 10.1080/00909882.2018.1412086

Butterworth, P., & Rodgers, B. (2008). Mental health problems and marital disruption: Is it the combination of husbands and wives' mental health problems that predict later divorce? *Social Psychiatry and Psychiatric Epidemiology 44*(9), 758–763. doi:10.1007/s00127-008-0366-5

Buzzanell, P., & Turner, L. H. (2003). Emotion work revealed by job loss discourse: Backgrounding-foregrounding of feelings, construction of normalcy and (re)instituting of traditional masculinities. *Journal of Applied Communication Research, 31,* 27–57. doi: 10.1080/00909880305375

Corrigan, P., Watson, A., & Barr, L. (2006). The self-stigma of mental illness: Implications for self-esteem and self-efficacy. *Journal of Social and Clinical Psychology, 25,* 875-884. doi: 10.1521/jscp.2006.25.8.875

Hall, E. (2018). The communicative process of resilience for marginalized family members. *Journal of Social and Personal Relationships, 35*, 307–328. doi: 10.1177/0265407516683838

Houston, J. & Buzzanell, P. (2018). Communication and resilience: Concluding thoughts and key issues for future research. *Journal of Applied Communication Research, 46*, 26–27. doi: 10.108000909882.2017.1426691

Johnstone, M. (2001). Stigma, social justice and the rights of the mentally ill: Challenging the status quo. *Australian and New Zealand Journal of Mental Health Nursing, 10*(4), 200–209. doi:10.1046/j.1440-0979.2001.00212.x

Koenig Kellas, J., & Kranstuber Horstman, H. (2015). Communicated narrative sense-making: Understanding family narratives, storytelling, and the construction of meaning through a communicative lens. In L. Turner & R. West (Eds.), *The Sage handbook of family communication* (pp. 76–90). Thousand Oaks, CA: Sage. doi: 10.41359781483375366.n5

Koenig Kellas, J., & Trees, A. (2006). Finding meaning in difficult family experiences: Sense-making and interaction processes during joint family storytelling. *Journal of Family Communication, 6*, 49–76. doi: 10.1207/s15327698jfc0601_4

Lucas, K., & Buzzanell, P. (2012). Memorable messages of hard times: Constructing short- and long-term resiliencies through family communication. *Journal of Family Communication, 12*, 189–208. doi: 10.1080/15267431.2012.687196

Maciejewski, P., Prigerson, H., & Mazure, C. (2000). Self-efficacy as a mediator between stressful life events and depressive symptoms: Differences based on history of prior depression. *British Journal of Psychiatry, 176*(4), 373–378. doi:10.1192/bjp.176.4.373

Masten, A. S. (2014). Ordinary magic: Resilience in development. *American Psychologist, 56*(3), 227–238. doi: 10.1037/0003-066X.56.3.227

National Alliance on Mental Illness (2018). *Mental health by the numbers.* Retrieved from https://www.nami.org/learn-more/mental-health-by-the-numbers. May 15, 2018.

Panksepp, J. (2014). Seeing and loss in the ancestral genesis of resilience, depression, and addiction. In M. Kent, M. Davis, & J. Reich (Eds.), *The resilience handbook: Approaches to stress and trauma* (pp. 3–14). New York: Routledge. ISBN: 9780203135303

Pearlin, L. I., & Skaff, M. M. (1995). Stressors and adaptation in late life. In M. Gatz (Ed.), *Emerging issues in mental health and aging* (pp. 97–123). Washington, DC, US: American Psychological Association. http://dx.doi.org/10.1037/10179-004

Pitts, M., & Socha, T. (Ed.) (2013). *Positive communication in health and wellness.* New York: Peter Lang Publishing. ISBN: 978-1-4331-1446-5

Prince, M., Patel, V., Saxena, S., Maj, M., Maselko, J., Phillips, M. R., & Rashman, A. (2007). No health without mental health. *The Lancet, 370*(9590), 859–877. doi: 10.1016/501406-736(08)61238-0

Raglan, G., & Schulkan, J. (2014). Introduction to allostasis and allostatic load. In M. Kent, M. Davis, & J. Reich (Eds.), *The resilience handbook: Approaches to stress and trauma* (pp. 44–52). New York: Routledge. ISBN: 9780203135303

Spark, L., Hefner, V., & Rogeness, A. (2015). The state of cancer care communication across the lifespan: The role of resilience, hope and decision-making. In G. Beck & T. Socha (Ed.), *Communicating hope and resilience across the lifespan.* New York: Peter Lang Publishing. doi: 10.3726/978-1-4539-1520-2

Tennen, H., & Herzberger, S. (1987). Depression, self-esteem, and the absence of self-protective attributional biases. *Journal of Personality and Social Psychology, 52*(1), 72–80. doi:10.1037//0022-3514.52.1.72

Theiss, J. (2018). Family communication and resilience. *Journal of Applied Communication Research, 46,* 10–13. doi: 10.1080/00909882.2018.1426706

Trees, A., & Koenig Kellas, J. (2009). Telling tells: Enacting family relationship in joint storytelling about difficulty family experiences. *Western Journal of Communication, 73*, 91–111. doi: 10.1080/10570310802635021

Walsh, F. (2003). Family resilience: A framework for clinical practice. *Family Processes, 42*, 1–18. doi: 10.1111/j.1545-5300.2003.00001.x

Zautra, A. (2014). Resilience is social after all. In M. Kent, M. Davis, & J. Reich (Eds.), *The resilience handbook: Approaches to stress and trauma* (pp. 185–196). New York: Routledge.

Chapter Fourteen

Conflict Communication in Families and Mental Health Outcomes for Parents

Examining Mother and Father Reports of Depressive and Anxiety Symptoms, Verbal Aggression, and Constructive Conflict

Timothy Curran

Kristina M. Scharp

Mental health problems are pervasive in the United States and deeply affect all members of the family system. For example, Pratt and Brody (2014) reported that from 2009 to 2012 more than 7 percent of people over the age of twelve in the United States suffered from depression. A family member's mental illness could be, as Segrin and Flora (2011) contend, "profoundly distressing and painfully debilitating" (p. 295). Given the importance of mental health in families, researchers previously examined how family communication patterns and characteristics predict mental health outcomes for children (e.g., Curran & Arroyo, 2018; Smokowski et al., 2015). An abundance of research shows a strong link between mental health factors and conflict communication (Segrin & Flora, 2016). Familial conflicts are vital to well-being because positive conflict interactions improve relational qualities, whereas destructive conflict communication, such as verbal aggression, predicts numerous negative outcomes including cognitive impairments, depressive symptoms, anxiety, and early mortality (Curran & Arroyo, 2018; Segrin & Flora, 2016).

Although family conflicts are important to well-being, they are complex and often difficult to manage. As such, family members exhibiting higher levels of conflict communication skills likely experience fewer psychological problems. Existing research suggests that people are particularly vulnerable to developing psychosocial problems (e.g., depression and anxiety) when they lack communication skills (Segrin & Flora, 2000). Despite the robust linkages between negative parent conflict behaviors and child mental health, less research examines how family conflict (particularly parent-child conflict) relates to parental psychological health. Thus, the goal of this chapter is to examine the relationship between mother and father reports of family conflict communication and their own depressive and anxiety symptoms. Further, this study focuses on the prevalence of mental health symptoms in a non-clinical sample of parents. Given that families are interdependent systems, examining how parent-child conflict communication predicts mental health factors for parents extends both the theoretical and practical implications of conflict in families.

In this chapter, we focus on two of the communicative behaviors that serve as markers of communication (in)competence: constructive conflict management and verbal aggression. Specifically, we examine how parental reports of both communication behaviors with their co-parent and their young adult child relate to their anxiety and depressive symptoms. First, we outline how parent-child conflict communication should predict parental depressive and anxiety symptoms. Next, we argue for the links between interparental conflict communication and parental depressive and anxiety symptoms before presenting our results and interpretations.

CONSTRUCTIVE PARENT-CHILD CONFLICT AND MENTAL HEALTH

We contend that parent reports of constructive conflict communication with adult children should negatively predict their anxiety and depressive symptoms. We conceptualize constructive conflict as a communicative process of negotiation, collaboration, and/or brainstorming to obtain a mutually satisfying goal (Rinaldi & Howe, 2003). According to the National Institute of Mental Health (2018), depressive symptoms include factors such as increased irritability, difficulties concentrating, sad and hopeless moods, and feelings of worthlessness and pessimism. On the other hand, anxiety symptoms are characterized by persistent and excessive worry that interferes with daily activities (Hallford & Mellor, 2017). These symptoms should negatively relate to familial conflict given that constructive conflict communication can help families to grow, solve problems, and increase understanding between members (Sillars & Canary, 2013). Family members showing support during conflict tend to have higher levels of relational and family satisfaction (Cummings & Davies, 2010). As Laursen and Hafen (2010) argue, constructive conflict in families can promote more supportive and close relationships. These positive outcomes associated with constructive family conflict suggest that parents may experience less psychological distress when they enact constructive conflict. Family cohesion and closeness is particularly important for parents when their children are young adults, given that the generational stakes hypothesis claims that parents' desire increased family cohesion during this time (Bengston & Kuypers, 1971; McLaren & Sillars, 2014). Laursen and Hafen (2010) also argue that constructive conflict can enhance mental well-being through expressing individual ideas and beliefs and negotiating family roles to improve overall family functioning. Thus, parents who use constructive conflict communication with their adult children likely feel less negative after a parent-child conflict and worry less about future conflicts. As such, we pose the following hypotheses:

H1: Mother reports of constructive conflict communication with their adult child will negatively relate to mother depressive symptoms (H1a), and generalized anxiety symptoms (H1b).

H2: Father reports of constructive conflict communication with their adult child will negatively relate to father depressive symptoms (H2a), and generalized anxiety symptoms (H2b).

PARENT-CHILD VERBAL AGGRESSION
AND MENTAL HEALTH

Compared to constructive conflict behaviors, verbal aggression is one of the hallmarks of destructive conflict, which often includes verbal threats and attacks. Parents who express destructive conflict communication tend to experience distress and negative emotions (Irvine et al., 1999). Moreover, research suggests that hostile and combative martial conflict is related to poor mental and physical health outcomes in adults (Segrin & Flora, 2016). According to Infante (1995), verbal aggressiveness is linked to deficits in conflict communication skills. In other words, those who enact verbal aggression often lack the skills needed to reason with children or partake in problem-solving communication. Consistent with social skills are vulnerability models of depression (Segrin & Flora, 2000); verbal aggressiveness should predict mental health problems. In fact, familial verbal aggression is related to increased depressive and anxiety symptoms in young adults (Curran & Arroyo, 2018). Yet, no prior research examined this link for parents. Verbal aggression is related to poor social outcomes such as taking conflict personally and conflict escalation, which are indications of mismanaged family conflict (Hample & Dallinger, 1995; Lorber, Felton, & Reid, 1984). This is particularly relevant considering that child perceptions of mismanaged family conflict predict lower levels of parental mental health (Segrin, Burke, & Dunivan, 2012).

Overall, verbal aggression is a maladaptive conflict strategy that likely results in a more distressing social environment. For example, adult children's perceptions of parental verbal aggression are linked to lower levels of perceived parental responsiveness and insecure attachment styles in young adults (Roberto et al., 2009). In fact, trait verbal aggression is related to an increased risk of child abuse (Wilson et al., 2006). As such, family members may be vulnerable to mental health issues such as anxiety and depressive symptoms. Given that depressive symptoms are partly characterized by increased irritability, increased verbal aggressiveness would predict increased depressive symptoms. Verbal aggression may result in ruminating negative thoughts about familial conflict, which, in turn, could make individuals vulnerable to increased anxiety and depressive symptoms. With this argument in mind, we pose the following hypotheses:

H3: Mother reports of verbal aggression with their adult child will positively relate to mother's depressive symptoms (H3a) and generalized anxiety symptoms (H3b).

H4: Father reports of verbal aggression with their adult child will positively relate to father depressive symptoms (H4a) and generalized anxiety symptoms (H4b).

INTERPARENTAL CONFLICT AND MENTAL HEALTH

In addition to examining parent-child conflict communication and parental mental health, we also examine how parent reports of interparental conflict predicts their anxiety and depressive symptoms. Research shows that interparental conflict marked by hostility, criticism, and anger predict damaging mental and physical health effects for adults (Segrin & Flora, 2016). For example, poor marital conflict management is related to cardiovascular and immune functioning issues as well as mental distress (Segrin & Flora, 2016). Even for parental dyads who are not married, their conflict communication is associated with mental health indicators including depression, self-esteem, and life satisfaction (Symoens, Colman, & Bracke, 2014). Specifically, interparental aggression and confrontation are related to poor mental health for both men and women (Symoens et al., 2014). On the other hand, couples who minimize negativity and focus on problem solving can experience physical health benefits (Graham et al., 2009). Likewise, couples who exhibit positive behaviors during and after conflict experience decreased depressive symptoms (Ellison et al., 2016). Thus, aligned with this research we posit the following:

> H5: Mother reports of verbal aggression with their child's father will positively relate to mother depressive symptoms (H5a) and generalized anxiety symptoms (H5b).

> H6: Father reports of verbal aggression with their child's mother will positively relate to father depressive symptoms (H6a) and generalized anxiety symptoms (H6b).

> H7: Mother reports of constructive conflict communication with their child's father will negatively relate to mother depressive symptoms (H7a) and generalized anxiety symptoms (H7b).

> H8: Father reports of constructive conflict communication with their child's mother will negatively relate to father depressive symptoms (H8a) and generalized anxiety symptoms (H8b).

METHOD

Procedures

The data analyzed in this study were part of a project focused on family communication and mental health. The data collection for this project occurred in 2016. The researchers first recruited young adult participants from introductory communication studies courses at a large university in the Southeastern United States. Participants who were eighteen years or older and had two living parents were eligible to participate. The research opportunity was posted to a research forum where students can sign up for research participation in exchange for course credit. Young adults who wished to participate were asked to email the researchers with their expressed interest and provided both of their parents' email addresses. The researchers then asked the parents to complete surveys via email. Parents received emails that briefly outlined the purpose of the study and provided them a link to their respective survey. Parents were explicitly told that their participation was optional. Young adult children received course credit regardless of parent participation to ensure validity. Surveys asked each parent to report on their conflict communication with their child as well as their depressive symptoms, anxiety symptoms, and variables not included in this study, such as their tendency to take conflict personally. The IRB approved surveys took roughly fifteen minutes to complete.

Participants

In total, 134 fathers and 150 mothers completed surveys. Mothers ranged in age from forty to sixty-one ($M = 50.02$; $SD = 4.43$), and fathers ranged in age from forty-two to sixty-five ($M = 51.67$; $SD = 5.01$). For mothers, 120 reported White/Caucasian, 13 reported Asian/Pacific Islander, 5 reported Hispanic/Latinx, 10 reported Black/African American, and 2 reported Other. For fathers, 108 reported White/Caucasian, 9 reported Asian/Pacific Islander, 6 reported Hispanic/Latinx, 5 reported Black/African American, and 4 reported Other.

Constructive Conflict

To measure parent perceptions of their own constructive conflict, we used the Negotiation Subscale of the Revised Conflict Tactics Scale (CTS2) (Straus et al., 1996). Parents completed this five-item measure (e.g., "During conflict with my child/spouse I say we can work out a problem.") on a 5-point Likert scale (1 = *almost never true of me* to 5 = *almost always true of me*). Higher scores indicated higher levels of constructive conflict. The following descriptive statistics are for parent reports of constructive communication with their adult child ($M = 4.00$, $SD = .63$, $\alpha = .82$ for mothers; $M = 3.92$, $SD = .75$, $\alpha = .85$ for fathers). The following descriptive statistics are for interparental reports of constructive communication ($M = 3.78$, $SD = .62$, $\alpha = .82$ for mothers; $M = 3.80$, $SD = .56$, $\alpha = .79$ for fathers).

Verbal Aggression

We measured verbal aggression using the four-item version of the Verbal Aggressiveness Scale (Beatty, Pascual-Ferra, & Levine, 2015; Infante & Wigley, 1986). We phrased items such that parents reported their verbal aggressiveness in conflict interactions with their adult child (e.g., "If I am trying to influence child/spouse and she/he really deserves it, I attack her/his character"). The items utilized a five-point Likert scale (1 = *almost never true* to 5 = *almost always true*). Beatty et al. (2015) argued that this four-item scale has higher levels of construct validity. Higher scores indicated higher levels of verbal aggression. The following descriptive statistics are for parent reports of verbal aggression with their adult child ($M = 1.50$, $SD = .61$, $\alpha = .80$ for mothers; $M = 1.49$, $SD = .65$, $\alpha = .80$ for fathers). The following descriptive statistics are for interparental reports of verbal aggression ($M = 1.65$, $SD = .75$, $\alpha = .91$ for mothers; $M = 1.58$, $SD = .67$, $\alpha = .80$ for fathers).

Depressive Symptoms

We used Santor and Coyne's (1997) Revised Center of Epidemiologic Studies Depression Scale (CES-D) to measure depressive symptoms for parents. These eight items (e.g., "I felt depressed," "I felt sad.") measured the regularity of depressive symptoms over the past week. We used a four-point Likert scale to rate the items ($1 = $ *less than 1 day* to $4 = $ *5–7 days*). Higher scores indicated higher levels of depressive symptoms ($M = 1.37$, $SD = .56$, $\alpha = .91$ for mothers; $M = 1.34$, $SD = .72$, $\alpha = .93$ for fathers).

Anxiety

We used The Generalized Anxiety Disorder (GAD) scale to measure parent's anxiety (Spitzer et al., 2006). This seven-item scale (e.g., Felt nervous or on edge.") assessed the frequency of anxiety symptoms from the past two weeks. The items utilized a four-point Likert scale ($1 = $ *not at all* to $5 = $ *nearly every day*). Higher scores indicate higher levels of anxiety symptoms ($M = 1.28$, $SD = .62$, $\alpha = .91$ for mothers; $M = 1.43$, $SD = .55$, $\alpha = .90$).

RESULTS

The first hypothesis claiming that mother reports of constructive conflict communication with their adult child will negatively relate to the mother's generalized anxiety symptoms and depressive symptoms was partially supported. The hypothesis was tested using a series of simple linear regressions given that the hypotheses claim linear relationships among the variables. The mother's reports of constructive conflict communication with her child was negatively related to mother anxiety ($\beta = -.18$, $t = -2.17$, $p < .05$). However, the analysis showed a nonsignificant relationship between mother reports of constructive conflict communication with her child and mother depressive symptoms ($\beta = -.07$, $t = -.82$, $p = ns$).

Our second hypothesis predicted the father's reports of constructive conflict communication with their adult child would negatively relate to father depressive symptoms and generalized anxiety symptoms. The results from the regression analyses showed no support for H2. Specifically, the father's reports of constructive conflict communication with their adult child did not relate to their anxiety symptoms ($\beta = .08$, $t = .93$, $p = ns$) or their depressive symptoms ($\beta = .03$, $t = .34$, $p = ns$).

The third hypothesis tested the mother's reports of verbal aggression with an adult child and their generalized anxiety and depressive symptoms. The results revealed full support for H3. Specifically, the mother's reports of verbal aggression with their adult child positively associated with their generalized anxiety symptoms (β = .24, t = 3.04, p < .01). The mother's verbal aggressiveness also positively predicted their depressive symptoms (β = .21, t = 2.60, p < .05).

The fourth hypothesis tested the father's reports of verbal aggression with an adult child and their generalized anxiety and depressive symptoms. The results showed that the father's verbal aggressiveness did not predict their own mental health outcomes. As seen, the father's reports of verbal aggression with their adult child were not significantly associated with their generalized anxiety symptoms (β = .02, t = .27, p = ns). The father's verbal aggressiveness was also not significantly related to their depressive symptoms (β = .07, t = .81, p = ns).

The remaining four hypotheses (H5–H8) tested interparental conflict communication and parent mental health outcomes. Relational status between parents was controlled in the remaining hypotheses. H5 predicted that the mother's reports of verbal aggression with her child's father would positively predict her depressive and anxiety symptoms. The results showed a positive association between the mother's verbal aggression and both the mother's depressive (β = .29, t = 3.63, p < .001) and anxiety symptoms (β = .32, t = 4.15, p < .001).

H6 examined the father's reports of verbal aggression with his child's mother and their own depressive and anxiety symptoms. The father's verbal aggressiveness with mothers was positively associated with anxiety (β = .19, t = 2.13, p > .001) but not depressive symptoms (β = .11, t = 1.27, p = .001).

The last two hypotheses (H7 and H8) tested parental reports of constructive conflict communication with their co-parent and their own depressive and anxiety symptoms. For mothers, constructive conflict communication with fathers was negatively associated with anxiety (β = –.34, t = –4.48, p < .001) but not depressive symptoms (β = –.11, t = –1.32, p = .001). For fathers, constructive conflict communication with mothers was not significantly associated with either depressive (β = –.05, t = –.56, p = .001) or anxiety symptoms (β = –.02, t = –.21, p = .001).

DISCUSSION

Conflicts are an expected part of family life. Handling conflict constructively can increase intimacy, understanding, and mental health among family members (Sillars & Canary, 2013). On the other hand, destructive family conflict predicts mental health issues such as depressive symptoms (Lewinsohn et al., 2000). The goal of this research was to test parent reports of conflict communication with their child and co-parent as predictors of their own depressive and anxiety symptoms. Although scholars traditionally conceptualize mental health factors as the antecedent of negative conflict communication from parents, we reasoned that low conflict communication skills can, theoretically, manifest in a negative and stressful family environment, which increases one's risk of mental health problems. Conversely, high conflict communication skills should theoretically predict decreased mental health issues. The data reported here clearly show that the sample was generally well adjusted, given they reported low levels of verbal aggression and low levels of depressive and anxiety symptoms. However, the results did show that for mothers, constructive conflict communication with both their adult child and co-parent was negatively associated with their anxiety symptoms (but not depressive symptoms). The mother's reports of verbal aggressiveness with both family members was also associated with increased depressive and anxiety symptoms. The results for fathers were quite different compared to mothers. The father's depressive and anxiety symptoms were not predicted by any positive or negative conflict communication with an adult child. In fact, the positive relationship between the father's verbal aggressiveness with their co-parent and their own anxiety symptoms was the only significant finding. Overall, these results suggest that the mother's conflict communication with her adult child and co-parent may be more closely associated to mental health symptoms compared to fathers. The following paragraphs elaborate on the implications of these results.

The results indicate that the mother's reports of verbal aggression related to increased anxiety and depressive symptoms. The generational stakes hypothesis (Bengtson & Kuypers, 1971) offers a sound theoretical framework for understanding these results. Verbal aggressiveness towards adult children may predict maternal psychological health problems because parents tend to desire closeness and cohesion in their family of orientation; yet verbal aggressiveness likely creates distress and hostility in the parent-child relationship. Likewise, the mother's verbal aggressiveness towards a co-parent also related to depressive and anxiety symptoms. These findings are consistent with past research showing that dysfunctional interparental conflict is linked to increased mental and physical health problems (Segrin & Flora, 2016).

These results also support the social skills vulnerability model, which posits that individuals are at risk for psychological distress when they lack social skills (Segrin & Flora, 2000). Verbal aggression is a maladaptive conflict management strategy that is related to distressing and abusive social environments (Wilson et al., 2006). Thus, lacking the communication skills to effectively manage family conflict appears to be associated with elevated risks of depressive and anxiety symptoms for mothers. Again, it is important to note that this sample of mothers reported relatively low levels of verbal aggression with their family members. Thus, it is difficult to discern what the impact of verbal aggression would be on mental health issues for a sample with higher levels of aggressiveness. That said, these results do indicate that, for relatively well-adjusted mothers, verbal aggressiveness predicted increased psychological problems.

Interestingly, the father's reports of verbal aggression with adult children did not significantly relate to the father's depressive or anxiety symptoms, and verbal aggression with a co-parent only related to increased anxiety. Mothers may be more prone to experiencing psychological distress from verbal aggressiveness in family conflict because of intensive mothering and cultural expectations of women in close relationships. Intensive mothering is a cultural belief that childrearing is the most critical responsibility in a woman's life (Douglas & Michaels, 2004). According to Douglas and Michaels (2004) mothers are expected to devote the majority of their time and energy into childrearing, and view childrearing as a positive experience. Verbal aggression towards an adult child deviates from this cultural assumption about motherhood. Thus, mothers who are verbally aggressive may experience increased feelings of parenting inadequacy and psychological distress. Given that verbal aggression toward an adult child only predicted mother depression, these results imply that cultural ideologies of parenthood, such as intensive mothering, may adversely affect women's psychological well-being. Moreover, women are also expected to be skilled at problem solving in close adult relationships—given that conflict is a relationally focused activity (Canary & Wahba, 2006). Thus, because of cultural expectations placed on women, they may experience more distress when conflict with a co-parent is verbally aggressive, for an example of cultural expectations of mothers (Moore, 2018). It is important to understand these results within the context of intensive mothering. Cultural expectations to both attain and maintain positive family environments could potentially increase one's chronic stress and lower mental well-being. Although positive family environments are clearly important to family functioning and human development, it is important to consider which family members are predominantly held responsible for creating such environments. Overall, these findings highlight the importance of future interdisciplinary research regarding parenthood and mental health.

Furthermore, constructive conflict communication with both an adult child and co-parent related to decreased anxiety symptoms for mothers. Thus, it appears that conflict communication that focuses on problem solving is beneficial to mothers beyond the outcome of the conflict itself. This is a significant finding given that anxiety is related to reduced quality of life (Olatunji, Cisler, & Tolin, 2007). Moreover, this finding builds upon past research showing that anxiety symptoms are related to one's capacity to manage complex social interactions (e.g., Bekker & Croon, 2010). For example, Bekker and Croon (2010) found that individuals who could not manage new social situations had higher levels of anxiety. Thus, this research suggests that enhancing competent communication skills in complex circumstances such as conflicts or new social situations could reduce anxiety symptoms.

Practical Implications

Conflict communication skills interventions aimed at increasing constructive communication could serve to improve the overall family climate and reduce parental psychological problems. Specifically, acceptance commitment therapy (ACT) (Hayes, Strosahl, & Wilson, 1999), aimed specifically at helping avoid verbal aggression and communicate with collaboration and compromise, could potentially yield positive benefits for parents. The purpose of ACT is to enhance cognitive flexibility when dealing with distressing events (Hayes et al., 1999). For example, ACT has been shown to help parents cope with stressful parenting experiences such as coping with a child's life-threating illness (Burke et al., 2014). As Burke et al. (2014) explain, ACT aids individuals in developing an "ability to remain fully present to emotions and thoughts while engaging in behavior that is in the service of personally chosen values" (p. 123). ACT treatment has been shown to be effective for treating negative behaviors. For example, in a randomized controlled trial, ACT treatment reduced physical and physiological acts of aggression in interpersonal relationships.

ACT is based on six steps aimed to increase psychological flexibility and reduce negative behaviors: acceptance, diffusion, self as context, contact with the present moment, values, and committed action (Hayes & Strosahl, 2004). These six steps are aimed at increasing one's ability to think and experience emotions without judgement. Hayes and Strosahl (2004) argued that the six ACT steps involve letting go of the impulse to control events and act in a way that aligns with one's values (Hayes & Strosahl, 2004). In the context of the current project, ACT could be used to help parents who are verbally aggressive in family conflict. ACT could help parents avoid verbal aggression and reframe conflicts to communicate more positively. In doing so, reduced verbal aggression and increased constructive conflict communication could help alleviate parental psychological distress, particularly for mothers.

Limitations and Future Directions

The current study has several limitations that should be noted when making conclusions based on these results. The data is cross-sectional, which impedes our ability to observe or make causal conclusions among the variables in this study. Certainly, longitudinal data is needed to examine the causal link between conflict communication skills and parental mental health. Also, both mothers and fathers reported relatively low levels of depression and anxiety. A more distressed sample may produce different results. The convenience sample also limits our ability to generalize these results to a broader population. This study also examined mother-father dyads as parents. Many families have different family structures (e.g., same-sex couple families, single parent families) that could influence the relationship between conflict communication and mental health, particularly given the potential effect of gender and parenting roles in the relationship between family conflict and psychological problems.

Despite these limitations, the current study adds to research on the links between family conflict and parental psychological health. A robust body of literature shows that destructive family conflict predicts mental health issues for children. The results reported here broaden our understanding of conflict communication and mental health by showing links between verbal aggression, constructive conflict and depressive and anxiety symptoms. Moving forward, research should continue to examine the family communication dynamics that predict psychological health factors for all family members.

REFERENCES

Beatty, M. J., Pascual-Ferra, P., & Levine, T. R. (2015). Two studies examining the error theory underlying the measurement model of the verbal aggressiveness scale. *Human Communication Research, 41*(1), 55–81. doi:10.1111/hcre.12039

Bekker, M. H. J., & Croon, M. A. (2010). The roles of autonomy-connectedness and attachment styles in depression and anxiety. *Journal of Social and Personal Relationships, 27*(7), 908–923. https://doi.org/10.1177/0265407510377217

Bengtson, V. L., & Kuypers, J. A. (1971). Generational difference and the developmental stake. *Aging and Human Development, 2*, 249–260.

Burke, K., Muscara, F., McCarthy, M., Dimovski, A., Hearps, S., Anderson, V., & Walser, R. (2014). Adapting acceptance and commitment therapy for parents of children with life-threatening illness: Pilot study. *Families Systems & Health, 32*(1), 122–127.

Canary, D., & Wahba, J. (2006). Do women work harder than men at maintaining relationships? In K. Dindia & D. Canary (Eds.), *Sex differences and similarities in communication* (2nd ed., pp. 359–377). Mahwah, NJ: Erlbaum.

Cummings, E. M., & Davies, P. T. (2010). *Marital conflict and children: An emotional security perspective.* New York, NY: Guilford Press.

Curran, T., & Arroyo, A., (2018). Emulating parental levels of taking conflict personally: Associations with behavioral and mental health outcomes in young adult children. *Journal of Family Communication 18*, 171–184. doi https://doi.org/10.1 080/15267431.2018.1450254

Douglas, S. J., & Michaels, M. W. (2004). *The mommy myth.* New York: Free Press. ISBN: 9780743260466

Ellison, J. K., Kouros, C. D., Pap, L. M., Cummings, E. M., & Papp, L. M. (2016). Interplay between marital attributions and conflict behavior in predicting depressive symptoms. *Journal of Family Psychology, 30*, 286–295. doi:10.1037/fam0000181

Graham, J. E., Glaser, R., Loving, T. J., Malarkey, W. B., Stowell, J. R., & Kiecolt-Glaser, J. K. (2009). Cognitive word use during marital conflict and increases in proinflammatory cytokines. *Health Psychology, 28*, 621–630. doi: 10.1037/a0015208

Hallford, D. J., & Mellor, D. (2017). Autobiographical memory specificity and general symptoms of anxiety: Indirect associations through rumination. *International Journal of Mental Health, 46*(2), 74–88. doi:10.1080/00207411.2017.1294968

Hample, D., & Dallinger, J. M. (1995). A Lewinian perspective on taking conflict personally: Revision, refinement, and validation of the instrument. *Communication Quarterly, 43*, 297–319. doi:10.1080/01463379509369978

Hayes, S. C., & Strosahl, K. D. (Eds.). (2004). *A practical guide to acceptance and commitment therapy.* New York: Springer-Verlag.

Hayes, S. C., Strosahl, K., & Wilson, K. G. (1999). *Acceptance and commitment therapy: An experiential approach to behavior change.* New York, NY: Guilford Press.

Infante, D. A. (1995). Teaching students to understand and control verbal aggression. *Communication Education, 44*, 51–63.

Infante, D. A., & Wigley, C. J. (1986). Verbal aggressiveness: An interpersonal model and measure. *Communication Monographs, 53*, 61–69. doi:10.1080/03637758609376126

Irvine, A. B., Biglan, A., Smolkowski, K., & Ary, D. V. (1999). The value of the Parenting Scale for measuring the discipline practices of parents of middle school children. *Behaviour Research and Therapy*, 37, 127–142. doi:10.1016/S0005-7967(98)00114-4

Laursen, B., & Hafen, C. A. (2010). Future directions in the study of close relationships: Conflict is bad (except when it's not). *Social Development*, 859–872. Retrieved from http://proxy-remote.galib.uga.edu/login?url=http://search.ebsco-host.com/login.aspx?direct=true&db=edsbl&AN=RN279319850&site=eds-live

Lewinsohn, P., Rohde, P., Seeley, J., Klein, D., & Gotlib, L. (2000). Natural course of adolescent major depressive disorder in a community sample: Predictors of recurrence in young adults. *American Journal of Psychiatry, 157*(10), 1584–1591.

Lorber, R., Felton, D., & Reid, J. B. (1984). A social learning approach to the reduction of coercive processes in child abusive families: A molecular analysis. *Advances in Behavior Research and Therapy, 6*, 29–45.

McLaren, R., & Sillars, A. (2014). Hurtful episodes in parent–adolescent relationships: How accounts and attributions contribute to the difficulty of talking about hurt. *Communication Monographs, 81*:3, 359–385. doi: 10.1080/03637751.2014.933244

Moore, J. (2018). From "I'm never having children" to motherhood: A critical analysis of silence and voice in negotiations of childbearing face. *Women's Studies in Communication, 41*(1), 1–21. doi: 10.1080/07491409.2017.1421282

National Institute of Mental Health (2018). *Depression*. Retrieved from https://www.nimh.nih.gov/health/topics/depression/index.shtml

Olatunji, B. O., Cisler, J. M., & Tolin, D. F. (2007). Quality of life in the anxiety disorders: A meta-analytic review. *Clinical Psychology Review, 27*, 572–581. http://dx.doi.org/10.1016/j.cpr.2007.01.015.

Pratt, L. A., & Brody, D. J. (2014). *Depression in the U.S. household population, 2009–2012.* Hyattsville, MD: U.S. Dept. of Health and Human Services, Centers for Disease Control and Prevention, National Center for Health Statistics.

Rinaldi, C. M., & Howe, N. (2003). Perceptions of constructive and destructive conflict within and across family subsystems. *Infant and Child Development, 12*, 441–459. doi:10.1002/icd.324

Roberto, A., Carlyle, K., Goodall, C., & Castle, J. (2009). The relationship between parents' verbal aggressiveness and responsiveness and young adult children's attachment style and relational satisfaction with parents. *Journal of Family Communication 9*, 90–106. doi: 10.1080/15267430802561659

Santor, D. A., & Coyne, J. C. (1997). Shortening the CES-D to improve its ability to detect cases of depression. *Psychological Assessment, 9*(3), 233–243. doi:10.1037/1040-3590.9.3.233

Segrin, C., Burke, T. J., & Dunivan, M. (2012). Loneliness and poor health within families. *Journal of Social and Personal Relationships, 29*, 597–611. doi: 10.1177/0265407512443434

Segrin, C., & Flora, J. (2000). Poor social skills are a vulnerability factor in the development of psychosocial problems. *Human Communication Research, 26*, 489–514. doi:10.1111/j.1468-2958.2000.tb00766.x

Segrin, C., & Flora, J. (2011). *Family communication.* New York, NY: Routledge. ISBN:9780203857830

Segrin, C., & Flora, J. (2016). Family conflict is detrimental to physical and mental health. In J. A. Samp (Ed.), *Communicating interpersonal conflict in close relationships* (pp. 207–224). New York, NY: Routledge.

Sillars, A., & Canary, D. (2013). Conflict and relational quality in families. In *The Routledge handbook of family communication* (pp. 338–356). New York, NY: Routledge.

Smokowski, P. R., Bacallao, M. L., Cotter, K. L., & Evans, C. B. R. (2015). The effects of positive and negative parenting practices on adolescent mental health outcomes in a multicultural sample of rural youth. *Child Psychiatry & Human Development, 46*, 333–345. doi:10.1007/s10578-014-0474-2

Spitzer R., Kroenke, K., Williams, J., & Löwe, B. (2006). A Brief Measure for Assessing Generalized Anxiety Disorder: The GAD-7. *Arch Intern Med. 166*(10): 1092–1097. doi:10.1001/archinte.166.10.1092

Straus, M. A., Hamby, S. L., Boney-McCoy, S., & Sugarman, D. B. (1996). The revised Conflict Tactics Scales (CTS2): Development and preliminary psychometric data. *Journal of Family Issues, 17*, 283–316.

Symoens, S., Colman, E., & Bracke, P. (2014). Divorce, conflict, and mental health: How the quality of intimate relationships is linked to post-divorce well-being. *Journal of Applied Social Psychology, 44*, 220–233. doi:10.1111/jasp.12215

Wilson, S. R., Hayes, J., Bylund, C., Rack, J. J., & Herman, A. P. (2006). Mothers' trait verbal aggressiveness and child abuse potential. *Journal of Family Communication, 6*, 279–296. doi: 10.1207/s15327698jfc0604_3

Chapter Fifteen

"Warrior Moms"

Stigma Management Communication and Advocacy on Postpartum Progress Concerning Maternal Mental Health Concerns

Sarah Smith-Frigerio

According to the National Institute of Mental Health (NIMH), 20 percent of American adults had a diagnosable mental illness in 2016 (NIMH, 2016). The World Health Organization (WHO) announced in 2017 that depression has become the leading cause of disability in women and children throughout the world, and the organization has initiated a focused effort on addressing mental illness globally in their 2013 to 2020 action plan (WHO, 2019). Specific focus on maternal mental illness—a term used by the WHO to encompass the mental health concerns many women encounter during pregnancy and the postpartum period—has also increased with this amplified focus on depression.

Maternal mental health concerns (MMHC) encompass more than the "baby blues" during the first several days postpartum, and can include depression, anxiety, panic disorders, obsessive compulsive disorder, post-traumatic stress disorder (typically following the experience of a traumatic birth), and, rarely, postpartum psychosis (Postpartum Support International, 2009). Postpartum Support International (PSI) (2009) has catalogued prevalence studies dating from 1987 through 2008 and determined that maternal mental health concerns can appear "in women of every culture, age, income level, and race" (p. 1). Prevalence rates for postpartum anxiety and depression (PPD) are the highest, with PPD affecting around 15 percent to 20 percent of women giving birth worldwide with an average of 11.5 percent of mothers in the United States experiencing it. Prevalence rates of postpartum psychosis are the lowest, at a rate of one to two per one thousand births. Maternal mental health concerns do not resolve themselves, as is commonly believed with the "baby blues"; these health concerns require treatment. Treatment of maternal mental health concerns has been highly effective (Rahman et al., 2013). Without treatment interventions, MMHC can have severe impacts on both the woman experiencing them as well as their child/children and other family members.

Many individuals who experience any variety of mental health concerns do not receive treatment—even if easily managed—and many scholars believe much of this has to do with the stigmatization of these mental health concerns. Stout, Villegas, and Jennings (2004) found that depictions of mental health concerns in broadcast and print media exhibit negative themes, typifying individuals with mental health concerns as dangerous and criminal, as people to be avoided. Wahl's (1992) analysis of the literature on media depictions of mental health concerns found similar results; depictions of individuals with mental health concerns are biased, inaccurate, and label most people with mental health concerns as unlikeable, unpredictable, and dangerous. For instance, anecdotal evidence of such negative and stigmatizing themes exists in media coverage of women allegedly experiencing a MMHC who harmed their children, such as the more recent more publicized cases of Andrea Yates, Susan Smith, and Romechia Simms. In each of these instances, news media focused extensively on the horrific nature of the deaths and speculated on the mental health of the mothers. Oftentimes these claims were made without verification and with incorrect diagnoses (e.g., stating Yates and Smith had postpartum depression, where Yates was actually diagnosed with psychosis and schizophrenia, and Smith was diagnosed with major depression and a personality disorder; similarly, it was stated that Simms had postpartum psychosis when she was actually diagnosed with schizophrenia). There was minimal coverage involving the small prevalence rates of such diagnoses, how unlikely it is that a woman experiencing a MMHC will harm her children, how treatable MMHCs are, or how to obtain access to additional information for those who think they may be experiencing a MMHC.

Corrigan (1998) demonstrated how this stigma negatively affects individuals with mental health concerns as well as those without. From this work, Corrigan established that individuals dealing with a mental health crisis are likely to suffer in silence for fear of stigmatization, discrimination, and loss of economic and social opportunities. Those fears appear well grounded as Corrigan's (2000) work also described how Western societies uphold stigmatizing media messages about mental health concerns and how this can lead to fear, prejudice, and discriminatory behaviors against those who manage a mental health crisis. When those individuals with a mental health concern suffer in silence for fear of stigmatization or societal scorn, they significantly inhibit their ability to enter recovery and lead successful and fulfilling lives, and significantly increase their chances of dying prematurely (Smith & Applegate, 2018; WHO, 2017).

Societal expectations of motherhood further complicates the stigmatization of maternal mental health concerns. Heisler and Ellis (2008) explored societal messages females receive about motherhood and the face-work (see Goffman, 1967) respondents engaged in to present themselves as a "good mother." In their study, they found the most prevalent message theme was that motherhood becomes the primary identity for a woman. Many messages regarding the social construction of motherhood were unidimensional and focused exclusively on the wonderful, meaningful, and rewarding aspects of motherhood, and appeared to exclude how challenging parenting can be. Finally, Heisler and Ellis (2008) found that sacrificing personal needs was one of the main ways that mothers engaged in face-work and enacted a "good mother" face. They did so in order to gain the acceptance and approval of others. Wardrop and Popadiuk (2013) found similar themes in their investigation of societal scripts for motherhood in women experiencing postpartum anxiety, along with feelings of isolation and the societal demands to do everything "right," despite a lack of social support. In a recent *Healthy Women* survey of women, aged eighteen to forty-nine, who were pregnant or planning to become pregnant in the near future, 91 percent of approximately one thousand women stated PPD may be underdiagnosed due to stigma, based on the "societal pressure on mothers to hide the struggles, anxieties and sadness that may accompany motherhood" (Sizensky, n.d.). Alarmingly, most females surveyed did not recognize the causes or symptoms of PPD, more than half thought that PPD was preventable, and nearly one-third of women surveyed thought that PPD was untreatable (Sizensky, n.d.). Social expectations that women remain quiet about the "ugliness" (Wardrop & Popadiuk, 2013) of motherhood, combined with the stigmatized nature of mental health concerns, are preventing women from understanding what MMHCs are, how they are diagnosed, and how easily they can be treated.

While scholars have an understanding of how media messages, particularly in traditional media, lead to inaccurate understandings of mental health concerns and stigmatization, there has been limited scholarly attention to the role of online media, in either the depiction of mental health crises or the effects of online media on mental health concerns (Fisher et al., 2012; Klin & Lemish, 2008; Stout, Villagas, & Jennings, 2004). With the opportunity for more interactivity (Jenkins, 2006) and content production online (Bird, 2011), there is the possibility for audiences to challenge stigmatizing content or create non-stigmatizing content. There is also room for more research in the field of audience reception of media messages concerning mental health concerns within the United States. How do audiences of online content understand and make meaning from messages about mental health concerns? This study, in part, aimed to address these gaps.

Additionally, research into how stigma surrounding mental health concerns may be reduced or managed is certainly warranted and was incorporated into this study. Stigma is communicatively constructed, according to Smith (2007, 2009), and stigma management is communicative as well (Meisenbach, 2010). In this chapter, I describe the stigma management communication model (SMC), which proposes several strategies that can be employed to manage public stigma as well as the perception that stigma applies to one's self. I applied SMC better to understand how users of Postpartum Progress (n.d.)—a popular online site concerned with maternal mental health—come to use the site and employ stigma management communication both online and offline. The SMC strategies present in this study provide health communication practitioners with opportunities to incorporate similar strategies in their messaging campaigns, and this study provides theoretical recommendations for incorporating organizing/advocacy into the construction of stigma management communication. First, it is important to describe the current understanding of mental health messaging online and how it relates to the most popular maternal mental health website, Postpartum Progress (PPP), before turning to a detailed discussion of stigma management communication techniques.

MENTAL HEALTH MESSAGING ONLINE AND POSTPARTUM PROGRESS

Scholars interested in mitigating mental health stigma online demonstrated that online mental health messaging allows individuals to anonymously seek information online (Rains, 2014; Zhu, Smith, & Parrott, 2017), potentially leading to online self-disclosure (Rains, 2014) and group support and organizing and advocacy work (Zhu, Smith, & Parrott, 2017). Moreover, Rains and Keating (2011, 2015) found that blogging about health concerns allows individuals to decrease their uncertainty about their health concerns and can give individuals who post regularly and receive comments from readers a sense of well-being and purpose in life. Thompson (2012) found that journaling on a mental health social support site allowed users to construct their self-identity, make sense of their mental health concerns, and begin the individual healing process by using discursive techniques and coherence systems. Valenzuela, Park, and Kee (2009) stated that social capital exists online and can likely be created or augmented online when addressing health concerns. Still, not enough is known about the capacity of mental health messaging online to create opportunities for audiences to do more than seek information anonymously, self-disclose, or participate in support groups—namely, to engage in stigma management communication and advocacy work. In addition, none of the aforementioned research has addressed sites associated with MMHC. This is why investigation into users' experiences of the site Postpartum Progress was an avenue worthy of exploration.

In 2004, Katherine Stone, a mother of two who identifies as a survivor of postpartum depression and postpartum obsessive-compulsive disorder, founded Postpartum Progress (PPP),. With a background in journalism and corporate marketing, Stone started the site first as a blog, relating stories and information about MMHC, and expanded its mission throughout the years. Postpartum Progress became a 501c3 non-profit organization in 2011 and incorporated a wide array of informational materials for women and health care professionals, semi-private forums for peer support, and opportunities for offline advocacy work (e.g., fundraising events, book clubs, and conferences). The site boasted two million unique visitors annually in 2016, and it continues to be the most read blog concerning maternal mental health in the world (Postpartum Progress, n.d.). Stone received of several awards for her work through PPP. Additionally, the site strived to raise awareness and decrease stigmatization of MMHC across society. While information and peer-support were large parts of how PPP sought to achieve its mission, the site took an interesting step, actively appealing to users to engage in offline events and become part of the "Warrior Mom Battalion": a group of survivors willing to share their personal stories of MMHC, the site and its resources to non-users. Showcasing "Warrior Moms" became a large part of the mission of the organization once users were willing and able to take on an advocacy role.

Unfortunately, in early 2017, Stone and PPP faced serious public allegations of mistreating women of color working for the organization, and these allegations appeared to be well-founded (Drozd, 2017; Seabrook, 2017). In lieu of addressing the concerns of women of color within the organization, PPP elected to close its non-profit arm in February 2017. While the blog, social media presence, and informational materials still exist online, the private forums, conferences, fundraising efforts and other advocacy efforts have either been transferred to other organizations, or no longer exist in their original form. Nevertheless, it is important to investigate PPP, in order to better understand how users interacted with the site, transitioned that into online and offline advocacy work, and potentially employed stigma management communication strategies.

STIGMA COMMUNICATION AND STIGMA MANAGEMENT COMMUNICATION

In Smith's (2007) explication of stigma communication, she described stigma as "social constructions serving social functions" (p. 467). Building off the work of scholars like Goffman (1963) and Link and Phelan (2001), Smith (2009) conceptualized stigma as inherently communicative. She argued that stigma possessed four distinct components: marking an individual as having a specific trait, labeling those individuals who possess that trait as a group distinct from one's own group, attributing responsibility for the marked trait to the individuals who possess it, and determining that those who possess the marked trait are perilous or dangerous (Smith, 2007). She stated that these components must be present to constitute communication that is stigmatizing.

The idea that communicative acts construct stigma and that stigma serves social functions dovetails with Foucault's (1977) understanding of how discourse operates in the world. According to Foucault (1977), discourse creates one's world, generates what one determines to be knowledge and truth, and communicates about the people who speak (and perhaps, those who do not) within socially embedded networks of power. The interplay of discourse and the stigmatization of mental health concerns can be seen in Foucault's (1965) *Madness and Civilization.* Here Foucault detailed how "madness" is discursively constructed to control the unwanted behaviors of some individuals within society by labeling these behaviors as abnormal, unexplainable, irrational, and deviant. Not only does the threat of being labeled in this way control the unwanted behaviors of some individuals, but these discourses also instruct others in how to respond to individuals expressing unwanted behaviors. In Foucault's work on the role of discourse, particularly as it relates to mental health concerns, one can clearly see Smith's (2007) components of marking and labeling, as well as distinct hints of attributing responsibility and determining the perilousness of a behavior.

Building from Smith's (2007) work, Meisenbach (2010) proposed a model of stigma management communication (SMC) based on a typology of strategies individuals might employ when experiencing stigma or the effects of stigma (e.g., prejudice, discrimination, etc.). As Meisenbach (2010) posited, SMC can "address vulnerability and resilience to stigma communication by focusing on how individuals encounter and discursively react to perceived stigmas" (p. 269). Given the presence of stigma communication, the type of stigma attributed to an individual, the individual's attitude toward perceived public stigma, and the applicability of that stigma to one's self (for examples and further discussion, see Goffman, 1963), an individual may choose one of several communicative strategies to manage that stigma. These strategies incorporate several tenets of Benoit's (1997) image restoration work: accepting, avoiding, evading responsibility, reducing offensiveness, denying, and ignoring/displaying. According to Meisenbach (2010), different strategies could result in different outcomes, and further inquiry into both strategy use and outcomes is warranted.

Meisenbach's (2010) strategies are grouped into four larger categories based on whether the individual accepts or challenges that there is public stigma and/or accepts or challenges that the stigma is applicable to self. Specifically, if one accepts both the public stigma and the applicability of that stigma to one's self, individuals are likely to use accepting strategies. If they accept the public stigma but not the applicability to self, individuals will likely use avoiding strategies. If individuals challenge the public stigma but accept that the stigma does apply to self, then they may use the strategies of evading responsibility and reducing offensiveness. If individuals challenge both the public stigma and its applicability to self, then they may choose to use denying or ignoring/displaying strategies.

According to Meisenbach (2010), most strategies have sub-strategies associated with them. For instance, accepting may take the form of passive acceptance, displaying/disclosing the stigma, apologizing, using humor to ease comfort, blaming stigma for negative outcomes, isolating self, and bonding with others who are stigmatized. Avoiding may include sub-strategies of hiding/denying the stigma, avoiding stigma situations, stopping stigma behaviors, distancing self from the stigma, or making favorable social comparisons to others. Evading responsibility includes sub-strategies of demonstrating provocation, defeasibility and unintentionality of the stigma. Reducing offensiveness includes the sub-strategies of bolstering/refocusing, minimizing, and transcending/reframing. One may deny the stigma's existence and applicability to self either simply or logically, by providing evidence and information, discrediting those who would discredit the individual with the attribution of the stigma, and highlighting any logical fallacies associated with the stigma. Ignoring/displaying the stigma differs from displaying/disclosing the stigma based on the intent, where the former challenges both the public understanding of the stigma and applicability to self, the latter accepts both the public stigma and applicability to self.

In essence, there are a variety of strategies and sub-strategies one may use to manage stigma communicatively, and they could lead to different outcomes. It is important to explore how these strategies are employed online, given the extent to which individuals are going online, perhaps in lieu of using interpersonal or traditional media channels. As previously noted, communication involving MMHC has not received as much attention from scholars as is warranted. To that end, the following two research questions about SMC strategies were posited:

RQ1: What SMC strategies and sub-strategies, if any, of stigma management are described by users of Postpartum Progress?

RQ2a: Do there appear to be common SMC strategies or sub-strategies?

RQ2b: Is there a common pattern or path of strategy use employed by users of Postpartum Progress?

METHOD

This study employed an audience studies–based interpretive approach to deepen the understanding of the stigma management communication strategies individuals may use online, particularly as they relate to MMHC. This is a different methodological approach than is typically seen in effects-based health communication research. Most research on mental health communication has focused on content analysis or effects research on media messages. Ruddock (2007) explained how incorporating interpretative approaches to communication research, such as audience studies, provides more than knowledge of what messages do to audiences; interpretative approaches help researchers better understand what messages mean to audiences, and what audiences do with those messages in return. Furthermore, Meisenbach (2010) called for further interpretive study of SMC, and Zoller and Kline (2008) have recommended more critical and interpretive work in health communication overall.

After appropriate IRB approval, respondents were recruited on PPP social media. Semi-structured interviews were conducted over the phone with audience members ($N = 21$) of Postpartum Progress who responded to social media requests posted by the PPP editorial team to their Facebook page and Twitter feed. Interviews were conducted until theoretical saturation was reached. The interviews took place during March and April 2015 and ranged in duration from approximately fifteen to forty-five minutes, with most interviews being about thirty minutes long. Transcriptions and notes from these interviews resulted in nearly 135 single-spaced pages of text for analysis. Respondents were predominantly female ($n = 20$), and Caucasian ($n = 19$), with two respondents identifying as Latina/Hispanic. The ages of respondents ranged from twenty-six to sixty-one years of age, with the mean age of 38.5 years old. Twenty participants identified as heterosexual, and one identified as bisexual. Respondents lived in every geographical region of the United States: Northeast, South, Midwest, Southwest, and the West Coast. Time spent participating on the Postpartum Progress site ranged from one month to over seven years, with the mean time spent interacting with the site just under two and a half years.

Nearly all respondents self-identified in various states of treatment and recovery from MMHC, despite this not being a question included in the interview protocol. The researcher elected not to seek information about any diagnosis or perceptions of self-stigma in the study as to avoid labeling something as stigmatizing or reifying any existing stigma associated with MMHC. Respondents often stated the need to be open and honest about their diagnosis in order to reduce shame and stigma, particularly with an eye toward other women who may be struggling silently with MMHC. The disorders mentioned by respondents were postpartum depression, postpartum anxiety and postpartum obsessive-compulsive disorder. Additionally, the researcher did not include specific questions about public stigma associated with mental health concerns to not stigmatize respondents' experiences or reify any existing stigma. The questions asked respondents to describe how their social networks (offline and online) and viewed media (news and entertainment) communicate about mental health concerns, if they thought this communication was accurate or not, and what should be done about communication or content involving MMHC. Other questions included in the interview protocol asked respondents how they became aware of and used the site, and how they used information and resources from the site to communicate about MMHC in other aspects of their lives (both online and offline), among others. It is important to note that the nature of semi-structured interviews allows room for respondents to direct the interview to points they feel are most important to cover. Therefore, although each question of the interview protocol was covered in the interviews, respondents were also encouraged to discuss items not related to interview questions in order to ensure that the researcher privileged the voices and understandings of the respondents.

After transcription was complete, the author began a reiterative, line-by-line open coding process in accordance with constant comparative analysis as first described by Glaser and Strauss (1967) in grounded theory and methodology, and expanded upon by Fram (2013). Open coding allows researchers to revisit data points multiple times throughout data analysis, to ensure that all emerging codes are captured. Axial coding, or coding focused specifically on SMC strategies and sub-strategies present in both online communication and inspired offline communication (e.g., sharing printed materials with doctor's offices, sharing the website with offline social networks), also occurred, but open coding allowed for codes and themes not present in SMC to emerge. Additionally, axial coding was used to identify connections between categories identified during the open coding process, which was important in answering the second research question. Codes were then collapsed into larger constructs, or themes. Incorporating axial and open coding techniques, as well as a reiterative approach to coding, can ensure validity in qualitative research. An additional check of validity in qualitative research included the use of thick description, or rich detail of the strategies present in the interviews, as well as the incorporation of respondents' own language, in the analysis itself.

RESULTS

The first research question asked if stigma management communication strategies and sub-strategies were present in users of Postpartum Progress, and interviews with respondents demonstrated several strategies were present. These included the acceptance of sub-strategies of isolation and bonding, evasion of responsibility through defeasibility, the reducing offensiveness of sub-strategies of minimization and transcendence, the denying sub-strategy of providing information and evidence, and the strategy of ignoring/displaying. Analysis and evidence of these strategies are described below.

Accepting Public Stigma and Its Applicability to Self

Accepting

When describing how they came to be users of PPP, respondents demonstrated acceptance of the public stigma and its applicability to self primarily through descriptions of initial isolation, moving into bonding once they began to engage with the site.

Isolation

Nearly every respondent detailed how they came to be users of PPP by first describing how isolated they felt when they realized they might be struggling with MMHC. Many isolated themselves to avoid unwanted questions or reactions from others (e.g., ranging from noting differences post-pregnancy, to the perceived threat of having one's child(ren) removed from their care). Some, such as Tia (28, PPP user for less than one month) noted that others did not understand how to help: "Nobody was there to help me . . . and I felt very alone." By engaging with PPP content, they were able to recognize that they were isolating themselves. Anna (29, PPP user for two years) described reading the blog and "realizing that you're not weird; that you're not the only person who has the thoughts that you have, or that goes through the things that you go through." In fact, 90 percent of users specifically mentioned being drawn to stories of other women's experiences on the blog; the stories of others' experiences with MMHC and recovery were very important to users of the site. Natasha (37, user for six years) noted the sense of solidarity she received from reading other women's narratives of struggle and recovery:

> The stories that are shared on that site, and that page are just . . . they hit home! I can relate to a lot of them, and it just helps to . . . even though I'm six years out, it's just nice to know that I'm not alone.

Bonding

Nearly all respondents in the study noted that once they began using the site, they bonded with other users by actively engaging with them, both online and offline. All respondents mentioned following the site's Facebook page, and 38 percent also participated in the private Facebook groups associated with the site. Fifty-two percent of the respondents followed on Twitter, and some even followed other audience members or members of the editorial team on social networking sites. Respondents made friends with other site users, both in person (57%) and online (62%). Anna (29, user for two years) described the online connections she made as based on shared experiences:

> Of course, it started out with just reading the blog and getting to know things. When I heard about the Climb Out of the Darkness [annual national fundraising event similar to other fundraising walks/runs], then I met a few of the moms there. When we all see each other post, and we talk to each other like you would a friend and someone you can go and . . . you have experience with, even though a lot of us have not met each other, directly. But, we have that connection through our—like I said before, that joint experience.

Many times, respondents discussed how these relationships not only helped them with their day-to-day struggles with MMHC or their quest for recovery, but also allowed users to organize their advocacy efforts outside of the site, including events like the Climb Out of the Darkness and the Warrior Mom Conference (a patient-centered annual national educational conference focused exclusively on MMHC). These organizing/advocacy efforts will be described in fuller detail below.

Challenging Public Stigma While Accepting Applicability to Self

With the exception of the sub-strategy of transcendence, most respondents did not discuss employing the evading responsibility or reducing offensiveness strategies, but some did mention the sub-strategies of defeasibility and minimization. Transcendence, however, was a common sub-strategy of reducing offensiveness.

Evading Responsibility

The most common sub-strategy of evading responsibility was defeasibility. This took the shape of medicalizing MMHC, or considering them as illnesses or diseases like cancer or diabetes, though this was not a common sub-strategy overall. Put more simply, some respondents felt that individuals experiencing mental health concerns should not be viewed as responsible for those issues. While not always overtly expressed by respondents, it also appeared there was an undercurrent of unintentionality in their responses. Experiencing a MMHC was not something they sought out, and if they could avoid the experience, they likely would. They did not view themselves or one another as culpable for the onset of any MMHC. As Saundra (35, user for five years) stated, "Postpartum depression, and pregnancy depression, and all the mood and anxiety disorders, they don't discriminate. They are not your fault. This is a medical condition." Defeasibility certainly worked to challenge public stigma surrounding MMHC while accepting that this stigma did apply to respondents' experiences of MMHC.

Reducing Offensiveness

The main sub-strategies present under reducing offensiveness were minimization and transcendence. As mentioned before, there was not much discussion of minimization among respondents, but when it did occur, it took the form of acknowledging that the stigma did once apply to them, but no longer, as they had moved past their MMHC and entered a stage of recovery. Now, one might conflate this with distancing self from the stigma, a sub-strategy associated with avoiding, falling under the typology of accepting public stigma while challenging applicability to self. However, the tone of respondents was more in line with the idea that the public stigma is what should be challenged—and not their prior experience with MMHC—given that MMHC could be treated, has a high rate of recovery, and there is no reason for public stigma to persist. Language speaking to minimization often was embedded within other contexts, such as when Jamie (36, user for three years) described how her use of the site has changed:

> So now what's happened since I am now recovered, I use the website a little bit differently . . . I'm really looking now for any new research that's come out, and I really like looking at the mom's stories, the firsthand accounts from the mothers. It's a really good representation of things that change on that front, is not happening fast enough, and mothers are still are not getting treatment, and not getting diagnosed like they should be. Transcendence, on the other hand, was a common sub-strategy of reducing offensiveness.

Being a Warrior Mom was a badge of honor, recovery was celebrated online and having experienced MMHC often led to helping others online and offline. Respondents felt a sense of purpose in sharing their stories and knowledge; 90 percent of respondents stated that they shared stories and resources online, and 86 percent of respondents stated they shared the same in face-to-face interactions. Maddie (26, user for one year) summed it up perfectly in her response to the question of motivation to share:

Just knowing how I was feeling—and I felt pretty alone for a while—and so if I can help anybody by pointing them in that way, then I definitely want to try! When I meet other moms, who are still dealing with it, I tell them that it's not just me that's recovered; there's lots of others and support them in that way!

The pride and sense of purpose apparent in transcendence appeared to segue into the work of challenging both the public stigma and applicability to self through the sub-strategies of denying and ignoring/displaying.

Challenging Both Public Stigma and Applicability to Self

Denying and Ignoring/Displaying

Most respondents challenged public stigma and the applicability of the stigma to self by providing information/evidence to others, a form of logically denying the stigma. As mentioned before, nearly all respondents shared information online and offline, and this occurred in a variety of ways. Sharing included organizing events like the Climb Out of the Darkness and the Warrior Mom Conference. In addition, participants discussed their other endeavors: starting personal blogs, personal YouTube channels, book clubs, and local support groups. One participant created a documentary, which has been released and is currently being shown at institutions to foster conversation among health-care professionals most likely to identify MMHC in their patients. Finally, a few participants mentioned that the ties they made to other users of the site allowed them to coordinate their efforts in visiting obstetricians and pediatricians to provide the free informational materials Postpartum Progress offers for distribution, as well as scheduling time to speak with legislators in the states where they live. Sharing evidence and information in such public ways coincides with the ignore/display strategy to challenge public stigma and applicability to self. Respondents were not simply sharing information with people they knew or interacted with; they sought to share information more broadly while disclosing their own experience with MMHC.

More than half of respondents stated that the site's mission to raise awareness also mirrored their own personal mission to raise awareness and support women who are struggling with MMHC. Andrea (37, user for two years), discussed how Postpartum Progress' mission to raise awareness matches her own and other site users' missions:

When she [Katherine Stone] feels strongly about something, and something needs to be done about it, there's a thousand people willing to jump on board and help out with the right message. Because, working—like I said—in mental health, the more you talk about it, the less shame people feel about it. And I feel like that's important, and all of that comes through in their underlying message.

The second and most surprising reason respondents felt the drive to share information and resources as widely as they did is related to the perceived inadequacies of healthcare professionals and traditional media outlets to provide such information and resources. Many respondents expressed that their healthcare providers were under informed about maternal mental health and had failed them in their time of need, despite the fact that this was not a line of questioning on the interview guide. Rebecca (42, user for one year)—who was quick to point out that she raised the topic herself when she wasn't screened as part of her postpartum checkup—discussed her disappointment with her midwife group:

> I was with midwives, which you would think they, they would be more, you know, aware, and, I don't know, nicer about it? But I felt really dismissed when I brought it up, in my appointments after I had the baby. They were like, "Well, okay, here's a prescription for Zoloft. This may or may not be okay if you're breastfeeding. And we're very pro-breastfeeding, so it's not okay to stop. And, um, you know, go handle this with a therapist. We can't really do anything for you."

Jamie (36, user for three years), took on the subject of the failings of healthcare practitioners further in a documentary project:

> I think it's ownership. Who will take ownership of this? Who is that going to be? And I think it's interesting because actually, in our film, the villain of our film is an OB practice, and we really want to get a showing in an OB practice, like going into the lion's den, like "We want to show you! This is what's happening because you don't require your OBs to screen!"

Providing evidence/information and ignoring/displaying are both strategies that seek to challenge public stigma and applicability to self, and Meisenbach (2010) stated these strategies are proactive, and even include opportunities for protest, (re)education, and increased interaction with individuals facing mental health concerns (see Corrigan & Penn, 1999). That being said, some of this outreach and awareness raising work (organizing/advocacy) appears to go well beyond the challenging strategies currently listed in stigma management communication. Respondents often described engaging in organizing/advocacy work once they felt they were in an adequate space in their recovery from MMHC, and some of the organizing/advocacy work appears to have occurred in the absence of stigma communication messages. It may be prudent to consider if organizing/advocacy constitutes its own strategy under challenging public stigma and applicability to self, akin to how Goffman

(1963) conceptualized how those who were stigmatized may organize/advocate to remove the negative associations surrounding the marked attribute that led to their stigmatization.

From Isolation to Bonding to Providing Evidence/Information and Ignoring/Displaying

The second research question sought to determine if there were common strategies or sub-strategies among users of the PPP site, and if these strategies might follow any type of pattern or pathway. The answer to both parts of this research question is yes. The most common SMC sub-strategies described by respondents were those of isolation in the beginning, and then once use of the PPP site began, bonding with other users, both online and offline. The denying sub-strategies of evidence/information sharing and ignoring/displaying became evident when respondents felt comfortable enough in their own recovery and their bonding with other site users to pursue these opportunities. Engaging in these sub-strategies appeared to reinforce the sub-strategy of transcendence, where respondents were able to justify their experiences with MMHC as providing them with the opportunity to raise awareness and help others, thereby giving them a sense of purpose and pride in their recovery and stigma management communication endeavors. Respondents did not fall into one specific typology and remain static in their strategy use within that typology. They employed a variety of strategies at different stages of their recovery from MMHC and site use.

It is also important to note that this appears to demonstrate a specific progression through strategy typologies. Respondents generally moved from accepting both the public stigma and applicability to self in the beginning of the PPP site use (isolation, bonding), to challenging the public stigma while accepting the applicability to self (evading responsibility, reducing offensiveness), to then challenging both the public stigma and applicability to self (providing evidence/information, ignoring/displaying). No other progression from one strategy typology to another was present in the interviews with respondents. It is important to note that sub-strategy of transcendence sticks out somewhat in this progression, as typified as a reducing offensiveness strategy in the SMC typology. Perhaps transcendence, with respondents feeling a sense of purpose and pride in their experiences with MMHD, shared commonalities with ignoring/displaying; this certainly warrants further investigation. Nevertheless, there were popular SMC strategies and sub-strategies employed by PPP users who were interviewed, and these strategies appear to follow a specific progression.

DISCUSSION

The analysis above revealed that respondents used several strategies in SMC, namely those of accepting, evading responsibility, reducing offensiveness, denying, and ignoring/displaying. The participating respondents did not use every sub-strategy available to them under these strategies, but typically described themselves managing stigma through isolation, then bonding, providing evidence/information and ignoring/displaying as well as transcendence. This is in line with Meisenbach's (2010) work: not all strategies should be expected to be employed, but only certain strategies, under specific conditions, leading to possibly different outcomes. It is quite possible that other groups studied would exhibit different strategies altogether, and this is certainly an avenue for future studies to explore.

There appears to be a progression in typologies from acceptance of public stigma and applicability to self to challenging both the public stigma and applicability to self. It is important to note the absence of the avoiding strategy in this study, although perhaps individuals who accept the public stigma of MMHC but challenge the applicability to self are not using PPP because they do not view themselves as having an MMHC in need of addressing. It is also possible that the interview protocol did not adequately provide the opportunity to address avoiding sub-strategies, or perhaps MMHC prompt a type of stigmatization—harkening back to moral, physical, and social, as well as discreditable and discredited (Meisenbach, 2010)—that makes it more difficult to challenge the applicability to self.

Isolation, bonding, transcendence, providing evidence/information and ignoring/displaying were the most common sub-strategies, and this is not unanticipated, as these were primary functions of the PPP site. It is interesting to point out that isolation was a theme present in Wardrop and Popadiuk's (2013) more general work on the social construction of motherhood. Also, these are common reasons why individuals seek out information about mental health concerns online (Rains, 2014; Rains & Keating, 2015; Zhu, Smith & Parrott, 2017). It would be prudent for communication professionals charged with creating messages about MMHC, and mental health in general, to explore how they may incorporate these SMC sub-strategies in their work, particularly as it relates to guiding audiences from isolation to bonding, and then to subsequent strategies. There also appears to be other practical opportunities, with the sub-strategies of defeasibility, unintentionality and minimization in mind, that professionals may wish to pursue.

Theoretically, this study contributes to the call to further explore SMC through interpretive inquiry, and suggests future research consider whether to include organizing/advocacy as its own sub-strategy. While aspects of organizing/advocacy present in this study certainly fall under providing evidence/information and ignoring/displaying, it appears there may be times when respondents engaged in organizing/advocacy in the absence of direct stigma communication. This warrants further empirical investigation. It would also be interesting to investigate how such organizing and advocacy work may advance messages about motherhood that move beyond the ideas that motherhood takes priority over all other identities for females, where being a "good mother" is enacted through sacrificing personal needs for the needs of others (Heisler & Ellis, 2008). Organizing and advocacy work may allow women experiencing MMHC to conduct face-work demonstrating that a "good mother" also takes care of herself and helps other mothers take care of themselves. The study also suggests individuals may move through stigma communication management strategies as they experience stigma shifts and variance in degree (Meisenbach, 2010), possibly leading individuals to move from accepting public stigma and its applicability to self to challenging both.

While PPP has scaled back significantly since early 2017, study of the users' experiences with stigma management communication remains important. The site continues to be the most-read content concerning MMHC online. Other organizations (e.g., Postpartum Support International, Mental Health on The Mighty) have incorporated aspects featured on the PPP site into their own online presences. The opportunities for stigma management communication provided by the site before closure of the non-profit arm were substantial and are now being used by other organizations. For instance, the Climb out of the Darkness fundraising endeavors have now been transferred to Postpartum Support International. Some respondents did hint at concerns in reaching persons of color and individuals who possess lower socioeconomic status (SES) during their interviews. When asked what PPP could do to improve, some respondents stated there needed to be more women of color writing on the site, and that revamping the functionality of the mobile app to accommodate those who did not have routine access to a computer would help those who might come from low SES backgrounds. These are important suggestions for both scholars and communication professionals.

There are, of course, limitations to this research. One could argue that without asking directly about diagnoses or perceptions of stigmatization, one must speculate that both apply to respondents in this study. However, nearly all respondents openly disclosed their diagnosis and current mental health status without being asked to do so. In addition, nearly all respondents mentioned perceptions of public stigma and its applicability to self without prompting. Another potential limitation to this study is that Postpartum Progress may still be a unique case, and further data, method, and researcher triangulation would go far in demonstrating transferability and theoretical generalization regarding SMC and MMHC.

Future research should seek to explore a variety of online sites on a variety of topics, all the while remaining cognizant of ways in which to avoid attributing or reifying stigma in respondents. Finally, there is a possibility that findings may be different with varied recruitment methods. For example, those who were very willing to be interviewed may be more likely to engage in strategies that challenge both public stigma and applicability to one's self. Opportunities to engage the SMC research with methods such as participant observation should be pursued. Despite the limitations present in the current study, this research contributes to the body of work in SMC in important ways. It also demonstrates how online content concerning mental health concerns may counteract stigmatizing news and entertainment content on more traditional platforms, particularly as it relates to MMHCs and the propensity of news coverage to paint women experiencing MMHCs as criminals who harm their children. Finally, the study provides insights for mental health communicators working to manage or reduce stigma associated with maternal mental health concerns.

REFERENCES

Benoit, W. L. (1997). Image repair discourse and crisis communication. *Public Relations Review*, *23*(2), 177–186. doi: 10.1016/S0363-8111(97)90023-0

Bird, S. E. (2011). Are we all produsers now? Convergence and media audience practices. *Cultural Studies*, *25*(4–5), 502–516. doi: 10.1080/09502386.2011.600532

Corrigan, P. (1998). The impact of stigma on severe mental illness. *Cognitive and Behavioral Practice*, *5*, 201–222. 10.1016/S1077-7229(98)80006-0

Corrigan, P. (2000). Mental health stigma as social attribution: Implications for research methods and attitude change. *Clinical Psychology: Science and Practice*, *7*(1), 48–67. doi: 10.1093/clipsy.7.1.48

Corrigan, P. W., & Penn, D. L. (1999). Lessons from social psychology on discrediting psychiatric stigma. *American Psychologist*, *54*(9), 765. doi: 10.1037/0003-066x.54.9.765

Drozd, M. (2017). The fall of Postpartum Progress: Who will help the warrior moms? *Chicago Now*. Retrieved from http://www.chicagonow.com/stable-mable/2017/03/the-fall-of-postpartum-progress-who-will-help-the-warrior-moms/

Fisher, C. L., Goldsmith, D., Harrison, K., Hoffner, C. A., Segrin, C., Wright, K., & Miller, K. (2012). Communication and mental health: A conversation from the CM Café. *Communication Monographs*, *79*(4), 539–550. doi: 10.1080/03637751.2012.727284

Foucault, M. (1965). *Madness and civilization* (trans. Richard Howard). New York: Pantheon.

Foucault, M. (1977). *The archaeology of knowledge.* London: Tavistock.

Fram, S. M. (2013). The constant comparative analysis method outside of grounded theory. *The Qualitative Report, 18*(1), 1–25. Retrieved from https://nsuworks.nova.edu/tqr/vol18/iss1/1

Glaser, B. G., & Strauss, A. L. (1967). *Discovery of grounded theory: Strategies for qualitative research.* New York: Aldine Publishing.

Goffman, E. (1963). *Stigma: Notes on a spoiled identity.* New York: Jenkins, JH & Carpenter.

Goffman, E. (1967). *On face-work.* Garden City, NY: Anchor Books.

Heisler, J. M., & Ellis, J. B. (2008). Motherhood and the construction of "mommy identity": Messages about motherhood and face negotiation. *Communication Quarterly, 56*(4), 445–467. doi:10.1080/01463370802448246

Jenkins, H. (2006). *Convergence culture: Where old and new media collide.* New York: NYU Press.

Klin, A., & Lemish, D. (2008). Mental disorders stigma in the media: Review of studies on production, content, and influences. *Journal of Health Communication, 13*, 434-449. doi:10.1080/10810730802198813

Link, B. G., & Phelan, J. C. (2001). Conceptualizing stigma. *Annual Review of Sociology, 27*(1), 363–385. doi:10.1146/annurev.soc.27.1.363

Meisenbach, R. J. (2010). Stigma management communication: A theory and agenda for applied research on how individuals manage moments of stigmatized identity. *Journal of Applied Communication Research, 38*(3), 268–292. doi: doi:10.1080/00909882.2010.490841

National Institute of Mental Health. (2016). *About.* Retrieved from https://www.nimh.nih.gov/health/statistics/mental-illness.shtml

Postpartum Progress. Retrieved from: http://www.postparumprogress.com

Postpartum Support International. (2009). Perinatal mood and anxiety disorders fact sheet. Retrieved from http://www.postpartum.net/wp-content/uploads/2014/11/PSI-PMD-FACT-SHEET-2015.pdf

Rahman, A., Fisher, J., Bower, P., Luchters, S., Tran, T., Yasamy, M. T., Saxena, S., & Waheed, W. (2013). Interventions for common perinatal mental disorders in women in low-and-middle-income countries: A systematic review and meta-analysis. *Bulletin of the World Health Organization, 91*(8), 593–601I. doi:10.2471/blt.12.109819

Rains, S. A. (2014). The implications of stigma and anonymity for self-disclosure in health blogs. *Health Communication, 29*(1), 23–31. doi:10.1080/10410236.2012.714861

Rains, S. A., & Keating, D. M. (2011). The social dimension of blogging about health: Health blogging, social support, and well-being. *Communication Monographs, 78*(4), 511–534. doi:10.1080/03637751.2011.618142

Rains, S. A., & Keating, D. M. (2015). Health blogging: An examination of the outcomes associated with making public, written disclosures about health. *Communication Research, 42*(1), 107–133. doi:10.1177/0093650212458952

Ruddock, A. (2007). *Investigating audiences.* Thousand Oaks, CA: Sage.

Seabrook, G. (February 24, 2017). The weight of the last straw. *Medium*. Retrieved from https://medium.com/@graeme_59025/the-weight-of-the-last-straw-852ceada5d70

Sizensky, V. (n.d.). Why aren't women speaking up about postpartum depression? *Healthy Women*. Retrieved from https://www.healthywomen.org/content/article/why-arent-women-speaking-about-postpartum-depression

Smith, R. A. (2007). Language of the lost: An explication of stigma communication. *Communication Theory, 17*(4), 462–485. doi:10.1111/j.1468-2885.2007.00307.x

Smith, R. A. (2009). Stigma communication. In S. W. Littlejohn & K. A. Foss (Eds.), *Encyclopedia of communication theory* (Vol. 1, pp. 931–934). Thousand Oaks, CA: Sage.

Smith, R. A., & Applegate, A. (2018). Mental health stigma and communication and their intersections with education. *Communication Education, 67*(3), 382–393. doi:10.1080/03634523.2018.1465988

Stout, P., Villegas, J., & Jennings, N. (2004). Images of mental illness in the media: Identifying gaps in the research. *Schizophrenia Bulletin, 30*(3), 543–561. doi:10.1093/oxfordjournals.schbul.a007099

Thompson, R. (2012). Screwed up, but working on it: (Dis)ordering the self through e-stories. *Narrative Inquiry. 22*(1), 86–104. doi:10.1075/ni.22.1.06tho

Valenzuela, S., Park, N., & Kee, K. F. (2009). Is there social capital in a social network site? Facebook use and college students' life satisfaction, trust, and participation. *Journal of Computer–Mediated Communication, 14*(4), 875–901. doi:10.1111/j.1083-6101.2009.01474.x

Wahl, O. F. (1992). Mass media images of mental illness: A review of the literature. *Journal of Community Psychology, 20*, 343–352. doi: 10.1002/1520-6629(199210)20:4<343::AID-JCOP2290200408>3.0.CO;2-2

Wardrop, A. A., & Popadiuk, N. E. (2013). Women's experiences with postpartum anxiety: Expectations, relationships, and sociocultural influences. *The Qualitative Report, 18*(3), 1–24. Retrieved from https://nsuworks.nova.edu/tqr/vol18/iss3/2

World Health Organization. (2017). "Depression: let's talk" says WHO, as depression tops list of causes of ill health. Retrieved from http://www.who.int/en/news-room/detail/30-03-2017--depression-let-s-talk-says-who-as-depression-tops-list-of-causes-of-ill-health.

World Health Organization. (2019). Mental health action plan: 2013–2020. Retrieved from: http://apps.who.int/iris/bitstream/10665/89966/1/9789241506021_eng.pdf

Zhu, X., Smith, R. A., & Parrott, R. L. (2017). Living with a rare health condition: The influence of a support community and public stigma on communication, stress, and available support. *Journal of Applied Communication Research, 45*(2), 179–198. doi:10.1080/00909882.2017.1288292

Zoller, H. M., & Kline, K. N. (2008). Theoretical contributions of interpretive and critical research in health communication. *Annals of the International Communication Association, 32*(1), 89–135. doi:10.1080/23808985.2008.11679076

Section 5

COMMUNICATING ABOUT MENTAL HEALTH: LOOKING BACK AND MOVING FORWARD

Chapter Sixteen

Biopolitical Rationalities

The Changing Face of Mental Illness

Maryam El-Shall

Contemporary understanding of the brain and its chemistry have reconstituted ideas about the self, personhood and identity. These now form the "ethical substances"—neurochemistry, genetics and biological predispositions—that one relates to and works upon—however artificially—in the course of daily life. In this regard, psycho-pharmaceutical treatments of mental illness intersect with and underscore a host of contemporary self-care practices linking the brain, the body and the self: yoga, acupuncture, hypnosis, psychotherapy, are now regarded as norms of healthy living. In addition, patients struggling with mental illness incorporate their mental illness status into their identities while also treating their illnesses as conditions separate from them-selves. The illness is simultaneously a health condition that must be managed and treated as well as a facet of the self that can, if left untreated or poorly managed, overtake the self. This chapter explores this dynamic as a mode of self-government and self-creation stemming from a broader biopolitical rationality emphasizing (individual) health and wellness and personal responsibility.

Before I begin, I would like to first clarify what I mean by the term *biopolitical rationality*. The arguments I develop here were prompted by two crucial moments in the work of Michel Foucault. The first of these can be found in the first volume of the *History of Sexuality* (1979) in which Foucault first formulates his theory of biopower and biopolitics. In a passage that has since generated much critical attention, Foucault distinguishes modern humans from ancient humans through the former's distinct relationship to life: "For millennia man remained what he was for Aristotle: a living being with an additional capacity for political existence; modern man is an animal whose politics calls his existence as a living being into question" (p. 143). In this short passage, Foucault marks the formation of modern humans through a novel conceptualization of life as power. Biopower, as Foucault came to call this form of power, concerned the "phenomena characteristic of a group of living human beings constituted as a population: health, sanitation, birthrate, longevity [and] race"; biopolitics, in this formulation, is the study of "what brought life and its mechanisms into the realm of explicit calculations and made knowledge-power an agent of transformation of human life" (p. 143). Crucially, the population problem addressed by the biopolitical apparatuses of the state in its early formation justified the existence of a government that already "governs too much." Beginning in the eighteenth century, then, the physician became an essential figure in liberal government. This brings us to the second moment in Foucault's work in which he analyzes biopolitics in relationship to liberalism. In *The Birth of Biopolitics* Foucault (2008) defines liberalism as a governmental rationality that exercises power through freedom. In Foucault's account, liberalism exists in a symbiotic relationship with bio-power to produce biopolitics, what one might say has given birth to contemporary techniques, technologies, experts, disciplines and apparatuses for the care and administration of life at both the level of the populace and, crucially for this chapter, the self and discourses of identity. The effect of the doctor-patient relationship represents the constitution of a regime of power developed through the permanent knowledge of the individual—pinned in a given space and followed by a potentially continuous gaze—as a patient, which individuals then use to communicate their identities and life experiences.

With this as background, I employ the term "biopolitical rationality" a lens to examine the ways in which medical languages of health and illness come into association with and inform contemporary discourses of identity and citizenship in contemporary popular culture. In this respect, biopolitics designates a dialectical relationship between the prevailing techniques of self and understandings of personhood—identity claims, discourses, practices and their attendant cultural technologies—and biological life—the body, illness and health. This chapter offers a discourse analysis of popular mental illness memoirs as a case study of biopolitical rationalities in communication about mental health/illness.

POPULARIZATION

In a 2003 issue of *Society*, Nikolas Rose asks, "How did we in the developed Western world become neurochemical selves? How did we come to think about our sadness as a condition called depression caused by a chemical imbalance in the brain and amenable to treatment by drugs that would 'rebalance these chemicals?'" (p. 46). Rose traces the conception and ongoing production of neurochemical beliefs to pharmaceuticals. Over the last fifty years, health care practices in developed, liberal democracies (e.g., Europe, the United States and Japan) have become increasingly dependent on commercially produced pharmaceuticals for the treatment of psychiatric conditions (p. 46). Because of their reliance on pharmaceutical treatment for illnesses which are thought to affect both the body and the brain, these societies constitute what Rose aptly terms "psychopharmacological societies," where the medical modification of thought, mood and conduct is more or less routine (p. 46). Rose traces the origins of this formation to the 1950s when pharmaceuticals were being formulated and marketed on claims that they produced specific effects on particular symptoms of certain psychiatric conditions (p. 46). Despite their popularity and the favorable publicity about "happy pills" and "aspirin for the soul" (as well as the growing awareness among some government regulators and physicians that these new classes of drugs were also addictive and likely were the cause of Parkinson-like symptoms in patients taking them—symptoms that would later be attributed to the drugs' neurotoxic reactions and the consequential development of a condition called Tardive Dyskinesia) (p. 46), it was not until the 1970s and the advent of Valium that the neurochemical beliefs characterizing today's psychiatry would become part of popular discourses about the self.

The significance of Valium in popular understandings of the "neurochemical self" in the 1970s and into the 1980s was underscored by the emergence of a number of popular books, films and television shows in which characters routinely referred to the pharmaceutical for its calming, sedating effects. Patty Duke's *Call Me Anna* (2011) ushered in the genre of memoir corresponding to today's psychiatric biopolitics in which author-subjects utilize both specialized psychiatric discourse as well as their own experiential authority to talk about themselves as mental illness patients and as advocates/lay-expert for the cause of mental illness. In these memoirs, author-patients also interrogate themselves and document their struggles with their mental illness conditions in biomedical terms. Today, the mental illness narrative has also become its own genre of autobiography (Couser, 2009).

However, the theory of the neurochemical self-entered the mainstream with the 1997 FDA decision to allow pharmaceutical manufacturers to market their pharmaceuticals directly to consumers. With ads for everything from Prozac to Viagra, this decision opened the way for the popularization of medical modifications to self. With the proliferation of magazine ads, information pamphlets, and memorable television commercials for pharmaceuticals with names which seem to symbolize their effects—*Pro*zac for depression, *Cym*balta, *Serequal* and *Well*butrin, for both depression and General Anxiety Disorder—the neurochemical itself became, not only the basis upon which to construct mental illness but, rather, constituted the way many understand the self itself. Viewers came to understand that persistent feelings of sadness or fear are not normal responses to a troubling context but are rather biologically encoded manifestations of the self that must be managed pharmacologically.

The proliferation of pharmaceuticals also began to play a dominating role in the diagnostic process. What psychiatrists look for in patients depends to a great degree on available medications (Kramer, 2006). That a particular form of mental illness—depression, for example—is accompanied by characteristics of compulsiveness, it became of interest to psychiatrists since this might be an indicator of something that can be treated with new psychotropic drugs. Who a patient is—whether fully functional with personal problems such as marital conflict or slightly handicapped by a neurochemical imbalance—is a function of pharmaceutical development. This presents new ethical questions for psychiatrists since prescription psychotropic pharmaceuticals have the power not only to alleviate the symptoms of mental disorder but also to reshape personality (Kramer, 2006, p. 34).

MENTAL ILLNESS MEMOIRS

As a genre, the mental illness memoir is significant in thinking about today's psychiatry because it constitutes a novel form of authority based in experience. The mental illness memoir brings together older forms of authority based in medical-knowledge-power with experiential authority of psychic pain. Relations with medical authority or, "psychiatric power," mutate. These mutations shape the way in which psychiatric patients perceive themselves and plan their lives. Thus, Elizabeth Wurtzel writes toward the end of *Prozac Nation*: "Every so often I find myself with the urge to make sure people know that I am not just on Prozac, but on lithium too, that I am a real sicko, a depressive of a much higher order than all these happy-pill poppers with their low-level sorrow" (Fraser, 2001, p. 74). And Andrew Solomon (2001) writes "I will be in treatment for depression for a long time. I wish I could say how it happened. I have no idea how I fell so low, and little sense of how I bounced up or fell again, and again, and again. . . . After all that, I do what I have to do to avoid further disturbances. Every morning and every night, I look at the pills in my hand: white, pink, red, turquoise" (p. 30).

Mental illness memoirs are therefore perhaps the best representation of self-making through mental illness. The mental illness memoir is characterized by the obligation to speak the truth about mental illness for the self and for others similarly afflicted with mental illness. This is often the expressed purpose for writing. In her memoir documenting her struggle with manic-depression, Kay Redfield Jamison, author of an *Unquiet Mind* (1997), writes,

> the major clinical problem in treating manic-depressive illness is not that there are not effective medications—there are—but that patients refuse to take them [. . .] Manic depression distorts moods and thoughts, incites dreadful behaviors, destroys the basis of rational thought and too often erodes the will to live [. . .] Because of this, I have in turn tried, as best I could, to use my experiences of the disease to inform my research, teaching, clinical practice and advocacy. Through writing and teaching I have hoped to [. . .] change public attitudes about psychiatric illnesses in general and manic-depressive illness in particular. (pp. 6–7).

But by documenting the self's descent into mental illness and its salvation through psychotropic drugs and/or hospitalization, these memoirs also document a manifestly biopolitical understanding of the self grounded in medical truth. Mental illnesses are, says Jamison (1995), biological in their origins but are felt psychologically in their experience (p. 6).

Andrew Solomon's *The Noonday Demon: An Atlas of Depression* (2001), William Styron's *Darkness Visible: A Memoir of Madness* (1990), Lewis Wolpert's *Malignant Sadness: The Anatomy of Depression* (1999), Elizabeth Wurtzel's *Prozac Nation: Young and Depressed in America* (1998) and Lauren Slater's *Prozac Diary* (1999) are representative of the most popular depression narratives as well as the most biopolitically driven in that they ascribe biomedical causes for mental illness and advocate biomedical treatment for mental distress in the form of antidepressant prescription drugs.

Most generally, however, the mental illness memoir is a genre of autobiography that follows a more or less regular pattern of development following the disease course. Like earlier practices of confession and diary writing, illness memoirs are techniques of self, entailing the disclosure of personal experiences and thoughts according to particular rules, values and forms of authority. In the mental illness memoir, the primary technique is biographical narration beginning with first manifestation of illness, which often takes place in adolescence or early adulthood, to diagnosis, to treatment and coping. Through narration, authors of mental illness memoirs develop a language to reflect upon themselves through their illnesses. This is accomplished through the eventual identification of self with mental illness and a reshaping of personhood in psychiatric terms. Through psychiatric languages and pharmacological adjustments, author-patients strategize their options for caring for themselves and managing their lives. In this respect, the mental illness diagnosis becomes a resource through which individuals think and fashion themselves and construct their autobiographies.

THE BATTLE AGAINST THE SELF

The central conflict in mental illness is self's battle against itself and involves questions regarding identity, agency and freewill. While the diagnosis of mental illness provides a biomedical rationale for the inexplicable pain of the psyche, it also produces new dilemmas about resolving one's prior conceptions of oneself as free and independent with one's mental illness condition. In this respect, the listings in the *Diagnostic Statistical Manual* (*DSM)* represent an important technology by which the authors of mental illness memoirs come to conceive and relate to themselves as subjects of biological conditions. The characteristics of depression or bipolar disorder listed in the *DSM* provide a means not only for the professional assignment of illness, but they also provide a vocabulary for those who experience the symptoms of mental illness to describe and reflect upon psychic pain, the self and identity in biomedical terms.

Prior to the diagnosis of mental illness, authors give priority to "traditional" identity positions within society—gender, familial and/or occupational roles and age-related experiences— offering a view of the self-filtered through the socio-cultural technologies bestowed by social institutions. At this stage of the narrative, experiences of emotional pain are rendered in a discourse of sadness and despair, loss and self-loathing and what can be considered essentially existential problems rather than being reflective of biomedical conditions. In this first movement, truth is produced via an attachment to experience through an in-depth interrogation of feelings and the ambiguity of emotions. Authors pose philosophical questions about the purpose of life and the meaning of suffering. The diagnosis of mental illness, however, institutes a new truth regime in relation to the self, emotional pain and life experience. In the course of the narrative, the mental illness diagnosis can be thought to represent a moment of truth, a sort of dramatic climax within the narrative and in the battle of the self with itself. The mental illness diagnosis provides psychological relief and resolution to the existential quandaries created by mental illness and hope for future relief. In the memoir, this is accomplished through neurochemical languages of thought, emotion and behavior. The diagnosis answers the questions about the truth of the self-generated by the self's assault on itself in the throes of depression or mania through neurochemical terms. Through a discourse of science, genetics and disease, the soul's anguish is reduced to the brain's neurochemical imbalance.

While the mental illness diagnosis resolves the existential questions emerging in the throes of measureless psychic pain associated with depression and other mental disorders sharing depression's primary characteristics (e.g., hopelessness, sadness and overwhelming feelings of guilt and self-loathing), it also introduces new questions about identity and the source and meaning of life. "Let us make no bones about it," writes Solomon (2001), "We do not really know what causes depression . . . We do not really know how depression made it through the evolutionary process. We do not know why one person gets depression from circumstances that do not trouble another. We do not know how will operates in this context" (p. 29). The revelations of psychiatry and biomedical truth can leave individuals newly isolated and newly alienated.

Following the diagnosis, one can see a new pattern of discourse in which life events and painful emotions are explained in psychiatric terms. The prior existential battle of the self against itself described in scenes of self-destruction finds resolution in neurochemical answers. According to Slater (1999), "behind every crooked thought . . . lies a crooked molecule" (p. 108). According to Solomon (2001), depression, though a consequence of chemistry, also "frequently destroys the power of mind over mood . . . the complex chemistry of loss and love may lead to the chemistry of depression" (p. 23). The materiality of the brain and its chemical fluctuations reshape authors' thoughts about pain, the self and identity. The effect of psychotropic medications in the treatment of mental illness then reinforces neurochemical theories of the self. Prozac, Zoloft and Paxil provide chemical relief for the anxieties produced by what were otherwise inchoate feelings of sadness or the bizarre drives of mania. Thus Slater (1999) writes toward the end of *Prozac Diary* that "Prozac's view" had become her own and that "history is meaningless . . . the person, a mere concoction of chemicals, programmed from birth. Pure beast" (p. 114). However, for some, things are not resolved so easily. Following the diagnosis of illness, identity is once again thrust into conflict. The narrative follows one of two courses: individuals struggle to find ways to reconcile their new identity in the specific terms of the mental illness while others reject the diagnosis altogether. In his study of depression, Solomon (2001) notes that mental illnesses have two diametrically opposite effects on patients. For some, it brings resolution and relief while for others it "often reveals the dreadful side of someone" (p. 23). The period of indecision authors characterize following their diagnoses is, however, eventually met with the precision of psychotropic drugs. From their medication response, those who initially reject their mental illness status are able to infer their disease and properly care for themselves and manage their lives in light of the mental health status. "In the long run," says Solomon, psychiatric illness "makes good people better; it makes bad people worse. It can destroy one's sense of proportion and give one paranoid fantasies and a false sense of helplessness; but it is also a window onto truth" (p. 23).

RELATION TO EXPERTISE

In the mental illness memoir, psychiatry informs and reshapes how individuals perceive themselves. In offering treatment for the biomedical causes for mental illness, psychiatry plays a vital role in how individuals formulate life objectives and plan their futures. The literary achievement of the mental illness memoir reflects psychiatry's primary biopolitical achievement: the subjectification of the responsible and insightful mental illness patient. In the pattern of the narrative, the diagnosis opens the way for the author to express new self-modalities in biomedical terms. The narrative tone shifts from being interrogatory and apprehensive to being assertive and pedagogic as authors take on new forms of responsibility vis-à-vis their mental illness conditions. Authors become survivor-advocates for new biomedical techniques in managing psychic pain and for the sociopolitical cause of educating the public about both the reality of mental illness and treatment possibilities. Almost all authors end their stories with a kind of return to the "normal self" instituted through psychiatric therapies and psychotropic drugs.

The psychiatric evaluation is a dynamic process in which both doctor and patient have a role to play. Power relations between psychiatric patients and doctors today are shared and involve shared decision-making, non-directive counseling and cooperation. But for Jamison (1995), a professor of psychiatry, the psychiatric evaluation, at least initially, is awkward and difficult. Jamison's mental illness diagnosis is complicated by her own professional presumptions about her mental health. Although countless mood swing episodes convince her that things are not quite right, she remains, up until the moment of her diagnosis, convinced that her emotional battles were the consequence of stress, lack of sleep or poor eating habits and not due to mental illness. When confronted by a colleague with the possibility that she could be manic-depressive, Jamison is combative, defiant and suspicious. Sitting in the reception area waiting to be seen by her psychiatrist for the first time, Jamison admits to being "terrified" and "deeply embarrassed" and is shocked at "finding [her]self with the roles reversed" (1995, p. 85). Being a psychiatric patient rather than a psychiatric professional, Jamison admits, shatters her sense of self-confidence, "which had permeated every aspect of [her] life for as long as [she] could remember," and which, as a result of finding herself a patient in a psychiatrist's office, "had taken a very long and disquieting holiday" (p. 85).

But if the prospect of being diagnosed mentally ill is frightening and embarrassing, the diagnosis itself represents a death blow to her identity. Jamison recalls "flailing against the sentence" and being "bitterly resentful" toward her doctor for delivering it (p. 87). On learning that she needed to take lithium in order to stabilize her moods, Jamison admits to reacting violently: "I was wildly agitated, paranoid and physically violent" (p. 87). In fact, Jamison describes this period as the worst of her illness not just because her depressions were deeper and longer and her manic episodes more complex and precipitous than ever before (signs she says she later recognized as evidence of her worsening condition), but also because, confronted with the severity of her illness, she had begun to realize that she no longer recognized her own mind. A scholar, writer and teacher, Jamison is devastated by the possibility that the same mind upon which she depended to make a living and with which she had achieved so much could also be the source of so much destruction, pain and uncertainty in her life. Waiting to be seen by her psychiatrist for the first time, Jamison realizes that she could no longer trust herself. Thus, the decision to seek professional help and, later, to take lithium consistently despite its at times debilitating side-effects—cloudy thinking, confusion, hallucinations, lethargy and weakness—came only after much insistent and gentle persuasion on the part of Jamison's doctor and Jamison's own realization that she had no other options: "I had completely, but completely, lost my mind. If I didn't get professional help, I was quite likely to lose my job, my already precarious marriage and my life as well" (p. 84). Freedom from the control imposed by medication, says Jamison, "loses its meaning when the only alternatives are death and insanity" (p. 6).

The sinking feeling Jamison describes while waiting to be evaluated is quickly replaced with reassurance and hope when Jamison meets her doctor: "He was tough, disciplined, knew what he was doing and cared very much about how he did it. He loved being a doctor" (p. 83). Upon opening the door to greet her, Jamison recalls his calm and assuring manner and says that throughout that first session he "sat there, listening forever, it seemed," as she, in a fit of mania and nerves, sat "rambling, unstrung and confused" (p. 85). After a series of questions about her sleep habits, her moods, her energy levels and her spending sprees, Jamison, as if a novice, realizes that she was "on the receiving end of a very thorough psychiatric history and examination," and finds, even as the setting and questions are familiar, that the tasks of being a patient—answering questions, providing background information and asking questions of her own—were "unnerving and confusing" (p. 86). Yet at the end of that first session, Jamison recalls "gaining a new respect for psychiatry and professionalism" (p. 86) and leaving the office with a sense of relief. The session, in fact, had proven to be therapeutic. Her doctor "listened patiently" to all of her "convoluted, alternative explanations for her breakdown," while remaining "firm in his diagnosis," and making it "unambivalently clear that he thought [she] had manic-depressive illness and that [she] was going to need to be on lithium probably indefinitely" (p. 87).

Over the years, Jamison says, her relationship with her psychiatrist became vital to her livelihood: "He saw me through madness, despair, wonderful and terrible love affairs, an almost fatal suicide attempt, the death of a man I greatly loved, and the enormous pleasures and aggravations of my professional life—in short he saw me through the beginnings and endings of virtually every aspect of my psychological and emotional life" (p. 87). Throughout their sessions, Jamison says, he treated her "with respect, a decisive professionalism, wit, and an unshakeable belief in [her] ability to get well" (p. 88). In the course of her treatment, Jamison not only learns about the nature and course of her own illness and how to effectively manage it by balancing stress and properly taking her medication, but she also learns a valuable lesson about the meaning and fragility of human subjectivity itself: "[H]e taught me by example, for my own patients, the total beholdenness of the brain to the mind and the mind the brain . . . The challenge was in learning to understand the complexity of this mutual beholdenness and in learning to distinguish the roles of lithium, will, and insight in getting well and leading a meaningful life" (p. 88).

CONCLUSION

They say that only those who have themselves experienced the pain of depression can understand the distress associated with its development. William Styron (1990) describes it as a dimension of experience wholly unknown to normal life when even language fails. Freud's formulation of suicide is as a murderous impulse toward the self (Freud, 1953). In this sense, the pain of mental illness can only be represented through associations with death. In Abraham and Torok's theory (1994; as quoted in Schwab, 2010), suicide is the brain-body speaking of internal trauma: "it can hurt itself to speak the pain; it can waste away to speak the wish to die" (p. 46). From the point of view of subjectivity there is no way to represent the experience of psychic pain except through destruction of the self. In this sense, as easily as one can read mental illness as a manifestation of biological dysfunctions in the brain, one can also conceive of it as the death of the self in life. At the height of her illness, suicide for Jamison seemed an act not of selfishness, but the only reasonable option in light of insurmountable mental pain: "Nothing alive and warm could make its way through my carapace. I knew my life to be a shambles and I believed—incontestably—that my family, friends, and patients would be better off without me" (1999, p. 39). In *Night Falls Fast* (1999), Jamison's masterful book on suicide, she catalogues countless techniques for killing oneself: drinking boiling water, pushing boom handles down the throat, thrusting darning needles into the abdomen, gulping down leather and iron, jumping into volcanoes, placing the neck in a vise and arranging for self-decapitation, among other means (pp. 133–134). In the United States, the most common methods of suicide are the obvious ones: guns, drugs, hanging and jumping (Solomon, 2001).

Foucault's achievement in *Madness and Civilization* (2006) was showing the similitude between madness and death in the history of insanity:

> In a general way madness was not linked to the world and its subterranean forms, but rather to man, his weaknesses and his illusions. . . . madness no longer waits for mankind but insinuates itself within man; or rather it is a subtle rapport that man maintains within himself (p. 23).

In spite of the changing nature of madness, its twists and turns from the labyrinths of a Christian hell to the confines of the asylum and now, in its organic formulations in the discourse of contemporary psychiatry where it resides in the neurochemistry of the brain, the relationship between madness and death has remained stable: the pain associated with mental illness is often described as death's embodiment in life. Within the discourse of psychiatry, death is always present with mental illness in the form of suicide. For those suffering from mental illness, suicide is the choice that looms on the horizon as the ready and final solution to the problem of interminable and inexplicable psychic pain. From both a philosophical and a scientific perspective, it is thought that the culmination of mental illness's truth lies in this battle with life. The desire to die announces the truth of mental illness once and for all. The death wish stands in diametric opposition to one's presuppositions about human beings and the will to live. Suicide in this respect is the price humans pay for self-consciousness. The desire to die strips the mask from the face of human civilization.

REFERENCES

Birke, L. (1986). *Women, feminism and biology: The feminist challenge.* Brighton, UK: Wheatsheaf Books.

Burr, V., and Butt, T. (2000). "Psychological distress and postmodern thought." *Pathology and the postmodern: Mental illness as discourse and experience.* Ed. Dwight Fee. London, UK: Sage.

Couser, T. (2009). *Signifying bodies: Disability in contemporary life writing.* Ann Arbor, MI: University of Michigan Press.

Delueze, G., and Guattari, F. (2004). *Anti-Oedipus: Capitalism and schizophrenia.* Trans. Robert Hurley, Mark Seem, and Helen R. Lane. London, UK and New York, NY: Continuum.

Duke, P. (2011). *Call Me Anna.* New York, NY: Bantam.

Foucault, M. (1975). *The birth of the clinic: An archeology of medical perception.* New York, NY: Vintage Books. Print.

Foucault, M. (1979). *The history of sexuality: An introduction volume one.* New York, NY: Vintage.

Foucault, M. (1991). "Governmentality." *The Foucault effect: Studies in governmentality.* Trans. Rosi Braidotti and revised by Colin Gordon, Graham Burchell, Colin Gordon and Peter Miller. Chicago, IL: University of Chicago Press.

Foucault, M. (1994). *The history of sexuality: The care of the self volume three.* New York, NY: Vintage Books.

Foucault, M. (2004). *Abnormal: Lectures at the Collège de France, 1974–1975,* Eds. Valerio Marchetti and Antonella Salomoni. Trans. Graham Burchell. New York, NY: Picador.

Foucault, M. (2005). *The Hermeneutics of the subject 1981–1982.* Ed. Arnold I. Davidson. Trans. Graham Burchell. New York, NY: Palgrave Macmillan.

Foucault, M. (2006). *Psychiatric power: Lectures at the College de France, 1973–1974.* Trans. Graham Burchell. New York, NY: Palgrave McMillan.

Foucault, M. (2006). *Madness and civilization: A history of insanity in the age of reason.* London, United Kingdom: Routledge.

Foucault, M. (2008). *The birth of biopolitics: Lectures at the collège de France, 1978–1979.* Ed. Michel Senellart. Trans. Graham Burchell. New York, NY: Palgrave Macmillan.

Foucault, M. (2010). *The government of self and others 1982–1983.* Ed. Arnold I. Davidson. Trans. Graham Burchell. New York, NY: Palgrave Macmillan.

Fraser, M. (2001). The nature of Prozac. *History of the Human Sciences, 4,* 56–84. https://doi.org/10.1177/095269510101400303.

Freud, S. (1953–1974). Morning and melancholia. *The standard edition of the complete psychological works of Sigmund Freud.* London, England: Hogarth Press.

Healy, D. (1997). *The antidepressant era.* Cambridge, MA and London, UK: Harvard University Press.

Illouz, E. (2008). *Saving the modern soul: Therapy, emotions and the culture of self-help.* Berkley and Los Angeles, CA: University of California Press.

Jamison, K. R. (1995). *An unquiet mind: A memoir of moods and madness.* New York, NY: Vintage.

Jamison, K. R. (1999). *Night falls fast.* New York, NY: Alfred A. Knopf.

Kramer, P. (2006). *Listening to Prozac: The landmark book about and the remaking of the self.* New York, NY: Penguin.

Lury, C. (1998). *Prosthetic culture: Photography, memoir and identity.* London, UK and New York, NY: Routledge.

Rajan, K. S. (2006). *Biocapital: The constitution of post-genomic life.* Durham, NC: Duke University Press.

Rose, N. (1999). *Powers of freedom: Reframing political thought.* Cambridge, UK: Cambridge University Press.

Rose, N. (2003). Neurochemical selves. *Society, 4*(1), 46–59. https://doi.org/10.1007/BF02688204.

Schwab, G. (2010). *Haunting legacies: Haunting legacies and transgenerational trauma.* New York, NY: Columbia University Press.

Slater, L. (1999). *Prozac diary.* London, United Kingdom: Hamish Hamilton.

Solomon, A. (2001). *The noonday demon: An atlas of depression.* New York, NY: Scribner.

Styron, W. (1990). *Darkness visible: A memoir of madness.* New York, NY: Random House.

Turner, B. (1995). *Medical power and social knowledge.* Thousand Oaks, CA: Sage.

Wolpert, L. (1999). *Malignant sadness: Anatomy of depression.* New York, NY: Free Press.

Wurtzel, E. (1998). *Prozac nation: Young and depressed in America, a memoir.* London, England: Quartet.

Chapter Seventeen

Dangerous and Disturbed

Media Misportrayals of Mental Illness

Dylan M. McLemore

When Russian president Vladimir Putin invaded the Crimean Peninsula, the Polish edition of *Newsweek* (2014) placed a photo illustration of a rabid Putin in a straightjacket on its cover. When mass shootings occurred across the United States, news media have been quick to blame mental illness, even when such details are unknown or even demonstrably incorrect (Kolenic, 2009; McGinty et al., 2016). Even Sheldon Cooper, the comically eccentric genius on *The Big Bang Theory*, is described as someone who should not be provoked because he is "one lab accident away from being a supervillain" (Prady, Doyle, & Cendrowski, 2008). It seems that around the world, whether serious news or entertainment, mental disorders are readily associated with the threat of violence. It is one of many misconceptions about mental illness documented in media narratives. Concerned with the effect this could have on public sentiment and behavior toward people with mental illness and the healthcare providers seeking to provide treatment, academics from a wide variety of disciplines have approached the topic. Though originating from diverse research traditions, the literature is lacking in terms of theoretical footing. This is particularly apparent from a mass communication perspective, where the media effects paradigm offers rich theoretical explanations.

This chapter summarizes media portrayals of mental illness compared to reality and with public perceptions to see whether the public shares the view of mental illness proffered by mass media, and more importantly, if media portrayals play a role in public perceptions. Through an examination of research goals and methodologies, existing studies are presented in terms of popular theories in mass communication in an attempt to synthesize the diverse body of literature and provide theoretically grounded directives for future research.

MEDIA PORTRAYALS OF MENTAL ILLNESS

Mental health in media became a point of interest for scholars in the late 1950s. Taylor (1957) conducted a content analysis of print and broadcast media and found mental health to be a daily topic, though one with disturbing tendencies. Taylor observed that most references to mental disorders in both drama and news had to do with crime. People with mental illness were set apart in appearance and behavior and were frequently seen as being dangerous. This was occurring even during a time of heightened television censorship, as the three major broadcast networks at the time all had policies against using mental disabilities "for shock or comic effects" (Gerbner, 1959, p. 294).

Mental illness remains a frequent topic in modern media (Chapman, Shankar, Palmer, & Laugharne, 2017; Diefenbach, 1997; Rose, 1998), especially children's programming. Lawson and Fouts (2004) found most Disney animated films included an average of five verbal references to mental illness, and that 21 percent of characters could readily be identified as having a mental illness. Mental illness is referenced in 46 percent of children's television (Wahl et al., 2007), 80 percent of children's cartoons (Wilson et al., 2000), and a quarter of all G/PG-rated films, many of which are at least partially aimed at children (Wahl, 2003).

Homicidal Maniacs and Inevitable Criminals

The content of these depictions also align with Taylor's (1957) seminal findings. Across print, broadcast, and film, people with mental illnesses are consistently portrayed as dangerous, unpredictable criminals (Coverdale, Nairn, & Classen, 2002; Fennell & Boyd, 2014; Guarniero, Bellinghini, & Gattaz, 2017; Hyler, Gabbard, & Schneider, 1991; McGinty et al., 2014; Parrott & Parrott, 2015; Razali, Sanip, & Sa'ad, 2018; Rose, 1998; Wahl et al., 2007; Wahl & Roth, 1982; Wahl, Wood, & Richards, 2002). Hyler, Gabbard, and Schneider (1991) refer to this phenomenon as the "homicidal maniac" stereotype and find it to be perpetuated more by media than any other stigma source regarding mental illness. Signorielli (1989) reported that 72 percent of mentally ill characters on primetime television physically harmed or killed others. Almost a decade later, Diefenbach (1997) found that one-third of mentally ill characters committed serious violent crimes (e.g., murder, rape), while including lesser violent crimes (e.g., manslaughter, kidnapping) raised the number to 44 percent. More recently, Parrott and Parrott (2015) observed a disproportionate number of criminally violent characters with mental illness in crime dramas.

News coverage tells a similar story. Two-thirds of people with a mental illness on television news in the U.K. are reported to have committed acts of violence (Philo, 1996; Rose, 1998), while more than half of mental health coverage in U.S. and German media depicts violence (Angermeyer & Schulze, 2001; McGinty et al., 2016). This is not to say that news media breathlessly manufacture hysteria over violent crime by mentally ill perpetrators—they rarely receive more coverage than "normal" perpetrators (Kalucy et al., 2011). However, this pattern of violence and crime accounts for the majority of coverage one hears about mental illness through news media, producing "a representation of individuals with mental health problems as almost inevitable criminals" (Foster, 2006, p. 294).

Victimhood and Favorable Portrayals

Gerbner (1980) suggested that "the mentally ill are most likely to be both violent and victimized in the world of television" (p. 20). At least two studies since have observed similarly frequent depictions of violence and victimhood (Parrott & Parrott, 2015; Signorielli, 1989). Unfortunately, data about victimhood is sparse, possibly because it is being lumped into broader categories of sympathetic portrayals rather than discussed separately (see Philo, 1996).

However, there are examples of sympathetic to favorable media portrayals of people with mental disorders. Content analyses have found that positive or sympathetic framing of mental illness represent anywhere from 18 percent to a quarter of content (Coverdale et al., 2002; Philo, 1996), with higher proportions for specific conditions, such as post-traumatic stress disorder (Wu, 2017). Some studies of specific character portrayals of those with mental illness have noted favorable references to intelligence, friendliness, and grooming (Hoffner & Cohen, 2015; Wahl & Roth, 1982; Wahl et al., 2007). However, determining "positive" portrayals can become the subject of debate among researchers. Numerous films and television shows portray characters with mental disorders as savants, capable of brilliance in particular arenas (e.g., John Nash in *A Beautiful Mind*, the eponymous detective in *Monk*, Dr. Shaun Murphy in *The Good Doctor*, or an implied disorder, such as Cooper in *The Big Bang Theory*, or Sherlock Holmes in the modern-day BBC series). While these depictions are heralded by some, they are criticized by others who view them as diminishing of the person as a whole to only their illness (see Pirkis et al., 2006 for a review).

Lack of Identity

The short supply of favorable depictions may be part of a larger theme of media portrayals—that people with mental illness have no identity outside of their disorder. News programming often forgoes background on individuals with mental illnesses, and almost never includes interviews with people who actually have the disorder (Guarniero et al., 2017; McGinty et al., 2014; Wahl et al., 2002). Mentally ill characters in fictional content are disproportionately white and male (Fennell & Boyd, 2014; Parrott & Parrott, 2015), but little else is typically revealed about their background. Most do not have a stated occupation or marital status, and, for those who do, they are almost always single and without any apparent relatives (Signorielli, 1989; Wahl & Roth, 1982; Wahl et al., 2007), though this may be changing in more recent dramas (Parrott & Parrott, 2015).

Lawson and Fouts (2004) note that mental illness is used to "set apart and denigrate" characters who "serve as objects of derision, fear, or amusement" (pp. 312–313). Contextual, behavioral, and even visual depictions of those with mental illness as different and disconnected from society have been noted from the earliest studies (Taylor, 1957) to the present (Cross, 2010; Fennell & Boyd, 2014; McGinty et al., 2014; Wahl, 2003; Wahl et al., 2007; Wilson et al., 2000). Not surprisingly, the quality of life for these characters (e.g., socioeconomic status, happiness, quality of interpersonal relationships) is worse than any other subgroup (Diefenbach, 1997; Signorielli, 1989), leading Diefenbach (1997) to conclude that "according to television, it is better to be a victim of violent crime, or a violent criminal than mentally ill if one is to have a better quality of life" (p. 298).

Explanations and Experts

Interestingly, this emphasis on mental illness at the exclusion of virtually every other element of a persona does not translate into detailed information about the illness. McGinty and colleagues (2014) found that less than 10 percent of news stories about mental illness provided even the most basic facts to help understand the disorder. Combining news and entertainment television, Rose (1998) found only 6 percent of references to mental illness included any explanation for the disorder. Further, only one mental health professional appeared in the two-month sample to discuss a disorder. A study of Brazilian news media observed "diagnoses" often being delivered by non-experts (Guarniero et al., 2017). With such limited explanation of past and present circumstances, perhaps it is not surprising that most media portrayals of mental illness are attributed to stress in the external environment as opposed to biological causes (Wilson et al., 2000), and media jump to conclusions in attributing negative actions to mental illness (Carmichael & Whitley, 2019). This lack of detail may also account for the misapplication of mental health labels to behaviors that are simply unconventional or unpopular (see Wahl, 2003).

While appeals to the legitimate expertise of mental health professionals are limited, that does not mean the professional roles as characters are not utilized at all. Rose's study (1998) observed three additional appearances of professionals in dramatic programming: one was a fraud and the other two were moonlighting as criminals. Fennell and Boyd (2014) noted instances of characters with obsessive-compulsive disorder victimized by unscrupulous healthcare professionals. Gabbard and Gabbard (1999) studied over four hundred films depicting psychologists, psychiatrists, therapists, and other mental health professionals. They found a trove of sinister villains with ulterior motives who regularly violated ethical codes. Therapists engaged in practices like memory "de-repression," a great narrative tool for drama, but a technique Freud abandoned more than a century ago. Medicine, on the other hand, was not presented as an effective treatment in a single film, though it had negative repercussions on more than one occasion. These Hollywood misportrayals are evident in news as well, with only 14 percent of stories about treatment describing successful interventions (McGinty et al., 2016). Perhaps not surprisingly, mental health professionals exhibit distrust toward media (Chapman et al., 2017), which could exacerbate their lack of representation.

DISCONNECTED FROM REALITY

At the same time that Taylor (1957) began quantifying and categorizing media mentions of mental disorders, Nunnally (1957) observed that these media depictions differed greatly from the views of mental health professionals. Indeed, media portrayals of people with mental illness starkly contrast reality. From a sheer numerical perspective, mental illness is underrepresented in media compared to its prevalence in the real world (World Health Organization, 2001). More importantly, available representations are consistently negative and misleading. While there are correlations between violence and severe mental disorders, such as schizophrenia (Munkner et al., 2003), these patients make up a very small portion of people with a mental illness, and even then, they are still largely nonviolent (Crisp et al., 2000). Researchers are skeptical of a causal link between mental illness and violence due to confounding variables that severely weaken the relationship (Arboleda-Florez, 1998). What is demonstrable is that those with mental illnesses are more likely to be victims of violent crime than perpetrators (Choe, Teplin, & Abram, 2008). Yet the violent crime rate for persons with mental illness seen in media content are ten times greater than the most liberal real-world estimates (Diefenbach, 1997).

Explaining the Disconnect

Why do differences exist between the representations of mental illness seen in media and the real world? The need of media, both news and entertainment, to simplify stories and present familiar points of reference invites stereotypes that are formed through repetition over time. The long history of negative stereotypes surrounding mental illness, then, might well explain their endurance in today's narrative construction (Foster, 2006). The appeal of the bizarre can lead to an overemphasis on the most outlandish and shocking members of a group without consideration of representativeness. The prominence of the crazed killer in news and entertainment has been documented for decades (Diefenbach & West, 2007; Steadman & Cocozza, 1977), while Gabbard and Gabbard (1999) suggest that on-screen mental health professionals in cinema serve as little more than plot devices to advance a story or shock audiences with cruel and unusual treatments.

While stigma-reinforcing portrayals of mental illness remain prevalent, a corrective trend might be developing, particularly in entertainment, where diversification has encouraged breaking formulaic molds of scripted dramas and "prestige dramas" focus on deep character development (Cross, 2010; Fennell & Boyd, 2014; Parrott & Parrott, 2015). Still, positive—or at least less negative—representations have a long way to go to catch the legacy of stigma and stereotype that media have built over decades.

Public Perceptions of Mental Illness

The public views mental illness in much the same way media portray it. Studies spanning five continents report a consistent belief that those with mental illnesses are dangerous, violent, and unpredictable (Angermeyer & Dietrich, 2006). People are generally poor at recognizing mental illnesses and understanding psychiatric terms (Jorm, 2012), and any mental distinctions made between the severity of various disorders dissipate when it comes to behavioral reactions (Crant, 2018; Crisp et al., 2000; Pescosolido et al., 1999). The public attributes mental illnesses largely to environmental factors. Link and colleagues (1999) found that stress was the most common cause assigned to every mental illness on their survey. This misperception of causation could fuel the belief that a change of scenery is all that is needed to vanquish a mental illness (Jorm, 2012).

The same negative stereotypes assigned to those with mental illness are held by people with more education, specific knowledge about aspects of mental health, and direct exposure to someone with a mental illness (Crisp et al., 2000; Granello, Pauley, & Carmichael, 1999; Philo, 1996; contra

Pescosolido et al., 1999). Even mental health professionals have been found to hold negative stereotypes (Sartorius, 2002).

The public also holds negative stereotypes of mental health professionals and their treatments. Jorm (2012) found that many people fear professional help for mental disorders and often delay treatment for years, even decades. Instead, informal conversations with friends are seen as better alternatives, even though those friends likely hold many of the inaccurate beliefs reported in these very studies. Medicinal treatments are viewed even more negatively (Angermeyer & Dietrich, 2006; Jorm, 2012), leading people to try natural remedies or "miracle cures."

These stigmas are also harmful to the socialization of people with mental illness. The exclusion seen in media content plays out in real social behaviors. Numerous studies find that negative perceptions of people with mental illness led to a desire to distance oneself from the "other," whether by social exclusion or by physical space (Angermeyer & Dietrich, 2006; Angermeyer & Schulze, 2001; Crisp et al., 2000; Cross, 2010; Diefenbach & West, 2007; Link et al., 1999).

Media's Role in Public Perceptions of Mental Illness

Naturally, researchers notice the similarities between erroneous public perceptions and the misportrayals of mental illness in media. Media content analyzers and health literacy pollsters have long speculated that a link must exist between the two (Crisp et al., 2000; Gabbard & Gabbard, 1999; Steadman & Cocozza, 1977; Wahl et al., 2007). The families of people with mental illness consider media to be the greatest contributor to stigma (Wahl & Harman, 1989). Even the United States government put forth the idea of a persuasive mass media through the President's Commission on Mental Health (1978).

There is a substantial and growing body of literature that suggests the relationship between media depictions of mental illness and public perceptions is indeed a real and powerful one. Media serve as the primary information source about mental health for about a third of Americans (Chapman et al., 2017; Granello et al., 1999; Granello & Pauley, 2000), and the messages they convey have been shown to override direct experience with the mentally ill (Granello et al., 1999; Philo, 1996). Philo's team of researchers (1996) found that both factual news items and fictional dramatic depictions could independently—and oftentimes collectively—form negative perceptions of mental illness in the receiver's mind.

Studies using survey or experimental techniques linked negative perceptions about mental illness and desired distance from mentally ill people to consuming media content on the topic through film (Domino, 1983; Wahl &

Lefkowits, 1989), television (Hoffner & Cohen, 2012, 2015; Granello & Pauley, 2000; Turner et al., 2014), and newspapers or online news (Angermeyer & Schulze, 2001; Dietrich et al., 2006; McGinty, Webster, & Barry, 2013; Thornton & Wahl, 1996; Wilson, Ballman, & Buczek, 2016). Similarly, unflattering portrayals of psychologists on television correlated with unfavorable perceptions of mental health services (Vogel, Gentile, & Kaplan, 2008).

Research also suggests that these media effects could correct public misconceptions, if only the content was designed as such. Thornton and Wahl (1996) successfully primed participants in an experiment with factual information about mental health and media depictions and saw a reduction in negative sentiments toward the mentally ill. Hoffner and Cohen (2012, 2015) found less stigmatizing portrayals of OCD in the television show *Monk* reduced desired social distance and increased willingness to disclose and seek treatment of a mental disorder. Crant (2018) showed participants video of a person with schizophrenia functioning effectively as an educator, and observed an increase in perceived cognitive abilities and a decrease in perceived dangerousness. A number of mental health literacy campaigns have involved media to transmit their messages (e.g., Pirkis et al., 2006). There is, however, understandable skepticism. In the wake of the overwhelmingly negative portrayals currently in print and on screen, the great purveyor of stigma has not been viewed favorably as a venue to conquer it (Chapman et al., 2017; Wahl & Harman, 1989). For instance, when an Irish soap opera agreed to let researchers write a character to realistically exhibit schizophrenia, viewers came away more knowledgeable about treatment options, but saw no difference in recognizing symptoms and surprised researchers by expressing *greater* desire for social distance than before seeing the program (Turner et al., 2014).

THEORETICAL FRAMEWORKS

In order to determine the nature of this relationship between public perceptions and media portrayals, research must employ rigorous methods firmly grounded in theory. The existing literature originates from a wide range of disciplines, employing various (a)theoretical and methodological approaches. These can be sorted by rare explicit uses of mass communication theories, as well as research questions and designs that implicitly associate with such theories. More specifically, the study of effects has used cultivation and social cognitive theories to explain survey and experimental data, while framing theory has been used to interpret content analyses. The following sections consider these approaches in light of their ability to contribute to an understanding of media effects on perceptions of mental health.

Cultivation Theory

Many atheoretical studies of media depictions of mental illness attribute a great deal of influence to mass media (Gabbard, 2001; Granello & Pauley, 2000). This view of media as powerful shapers of attitudes, beliefs, and behaviors is reminiscent of early media effects scholarship, and perhaps best represented among modern approaches by cultivation theory. According to cultivation theory, the world portrayed by media becomes the world outside peoples' homes and away from their screens (Gerbner & Gross, 1976; Gerbner et al., 1980).

A distinctive characteristic of cultivation is that it is not concerned with selective exposure. The original researchers argued that television programming lacked variety, especially in prime viewing hours when the largest audience was available (Gerbner & Gross, 1976). Therefore, the themes seen by heavy consumers would be similar, even if their specific program preferences did not align exactly. As cable, satellite, and online television providers entered the market, the number of programs skyrocketed, which could lead to niche audiences presented with distinctly different messages. Nevertheless, cultivation researchers look at a larger picture, maintaining that, over time, certain "commonalities and consistencies" (Morgan, Shanahan, & Signorielli, 2009, p. 37) will emerge across otherwise diverse media content, and that those themes are embedded in one's perceptions of the world.

Cultivation theory is not concerned with the fact or fiction of media content so much as its realism in the receiver's eyes. As one recalls messages, these mediated facts and fictions blend into observations that form attitudes about the world. Indeed, Philo (1996) observed this exact phenomenon occurring in focus groups about media representations of mental illness.

Signorielli (1989) concluded her content analysis of mental health portrayals in primetime television by suggesting that the overwhelmingly negative depictions were "likely to contribute to the cultivation of ignorance and neglect" (p. 330). Wahl (2003; Wahl et al., 2007) shares this concern, especially in light of the pervasive stigma in programming targeted at children developing their understanding of society. In one of the rare studies to define explicitly the theoretical framework, Diefenbach and West (2007) documented a cultivation of stigma toward people with mental illness.

Social Cognitive Theory

Social cognitive theory (Bandura, 1986) explains the development of social behaviors. It is vast in scope, extending to all manner of social behaviors learned from all manner of information sources, including media. Like cultivation theory, social cognitive theory points to the capability of audiences to obtain and employ useful information from media sources. However, whereas cultivation theorists assert that the picture of reality offered by media is so pervasive as to shape the meaning of human identity, social cognitive theory gives weight to human agency and the formation of unique identities based upon how the media message fits within an existing schema.

Social cognitive theory presents a model of observational learning. This mostly occurs in one's surrounding environment, with friends, family, and colleagues. However, for those contexts not experienced in an immediate social environment, media representations provide behavioral models for decision making in unfamiliar situations (Bandura, 2009).

Should this unfamiliar situation be an encounter with a person with a mental illness? Media depictions overwhelmingly present distancing as the appropriate behavior. Some studies, outside of the social cognitive arena, nevertheless point to this behavior being adopted into real-life situations (Angermeyer & Schulze, 2001; Diefenbach & West, 2007). Should the unfamiliar situation be considering medical treatment for a mental illness? Instances where media depictions of sinister doctors and medication gone wrong provide reason to avoid treatment. Social cognitive theory is seen as the theoretical backbone to the health belief model, which predicts whether people with a medical condition will seek professional help (Rosenstock, Strecher, & Becker, 1988). Applying the health belief model, negative media depictions of treatment lessen perceived benefits and enhance perceived barriers, presumably making it less likely to seek treatment.

Rose (1998) uses the closely related theory of social representations (Moscovici, 1984) to assume that television depictions of mental illness become cognitive anchors by which people make sense of unfamiliar conditions. Many content analyses of children's media content point to the potential of an exacerbated media effect on children who are developing their cognitive maps of the world (see especially Wilson et al., 2000). These studies use variations of social cognitive theory to assume media effects, rather than testing the theories by directly measuring media effects. Proper measurement could help differentiate the pervasive perceptual effects of heavy media consumption consistent with cultivation from the moderated adoption of behaviors observed through media consistent with social cognitive theory.

Framing

Inherent in the perceptual and behavioral predictions of cultivation and social cognitive theories is the notion that media messages present information in distinctly tailored ways. Stakeholders do not bear hostilities toward media simply for portraying mental illness, but rather for the way in which it is portrayed. Framing provides solid theoretical footing upon which to examine these media portrayals.

Framing theory finds its roots in psychology (Goffman, 1974) and appears in virtually every branch of the social sciences and humanities. Mass communication scholars have contributed a great deal to the theory's development and conceptualization. Entman (1993) examined the use of framing across disciplines and defined it as the selecting of "some aspects of a perceived reality and mak[ing] them more salient in a communicating text" (p. 52). Gitlin (1980) suggested that media select frames that present a desired reality, emphasize frames to increase public salience, and exclude some aspects of a reality entirely, diminishing their public salience. Framing, then, attributes significant power to the producers and gatekeepers of media content. However, frame building is only part of the process. To have an effect, the frame must "set" in the audience's minds. This frame setting will only occur when the salience cue of emphasizing a frame is recognized and accepted through an individual's personal interpretation of the message (Entman, 1993).

Once again, the atheoretical nature of the media-mental health relationship avoids many explicit references to the theory (see Parrott & Parrott, 2015 for an exception), but the methods and findings of many studies hint strongly at its influence. Before Goffman (1974) and Entman (1993), Taylor's (1957) content analysis noted "themes" of media portrayals of mental illness—commonalities of physical appearance, behavior, emotion, and even the underlying causes of the illness. Numerous works since have continued this approach (e.g., Coverdale et al., 2002; Hyler et al., 1991; Philo, 1996; Wahl & Roth, 1982).

Sieff (2003) recognized the similarities between existing media-mental illness research and framing theory, suggesting that Entman's (1993) four functions of framing had already been observed. First, the research defined the problem: people with mental illness are dangerous and unpredictable. Second, there was a diagnosed cause: it is the mental illness, borne of external events, which makes people dangerous and unpredictable. Third, there were judgments about the causal agents: people with mental illnesses cannot handle their circumstances or take care of themselves. Fourth, there were remedies offered: people with mental illnesses should be hospitalized or otherwise removed from external stress and the "normal" population.

The collective argument could be that media content producers build frames that exaggerate a problem, misdiagnose the cause, appropriate false characteristics, and arrive at flawed remedies to solve a problem largely of their own design. Experimental studies have observed these stigmatizing frames "set" in the receiver's mind, increasing fears of danger and desire for distance as the solution (McGinty et al., 2013; Reavley, Jorm, & Morgan, 2016; Thornton & Wahl, 1996; Wilson et al., 2016).

Framing would explain the extent of mental illness stereotypes in media through the degree to which the topic is discussed episodically or thematically (Iyengar, 1991). As mental illness tends to serve as a plot twist more than a central motif, Sieff (2003) reasons that most media framing of mental illness is episodic—limited in time, frequency, and thus, elaboration. Thematic frames form over multiple elaborate presentations. They are significantly more detailed, and thus, typically more representative of the complexities of a particular topic (Iyengar, 1991). Such frames have a better chance of accurately portraying mental illness (McGinty et al., 2014) and are more likely to be seen from media outlets with significant resources to devote to the topic, such as national newspapers (Wu, 2017). More cognitively demanding content has historically struggled to win over the average media consumer (Sieff, 2003), though the complex characters of television's new golden age offer a compelling retort.

METHODOLOGICAL APPROACHES

Content Analysis

The most common approach to studying media portrayals of mental illness is content analysis. Through systematic coding of stimuli, researchers can observe frequencies of certain types of content across various conditions. Scholars have carried out content analyses in this research context in a number of ways.

Studies often focus on a particular medium, sampling from a collection of films, television programs, newspapers or online news sources that reflect general consumption such as primetime television (Diefenbach & West, 2007) or high-circulation newspapers (Carmichael & Whitley, 2019; McGinty et al., 2014). Sometimes studies focus on specific genres such as children's films (Lawson & Fouts, 2004) or crime dramas (Parrott & Parrott, 2015). Common sampling periods range from one week (Diefenbach & West, 2007; Wilson et al., 2000) to one month (Carmichael & Whitley, 2019; Coverdale et al., 2002), though some longitudinal studies spanned more than a decade (e.g., McGinty et al., 2014, 2016; Signorielli, 1989; Wu, 2017).

Researchers utilized a number of different units of analysis, sometimes within the same design. Studies noted the number of publications within a sample that mention mental illness (e.g., Lawson & Fouts, 2004; Wilson et al., 2000), the number of characters with a mental illness (e.g., Diefenbach & West, 2007; Parrott & Parrott, 2015; Wilson et al., 2000), or the number of references to mental illness (e.g., Lawson & Fouts, 2004; Philo, 1996; Wahl et al., 2007). A few studies observed visual frames within larger content analyses (Philo, 1996; Rose, 1998; Wilson et al., 2000); however, operational definitions for coding were lacking.

These surface-level tally counts offer little insight. In fact, Philo (1996) cautions against them, noting how they artificially inflated the appearance of positive media content buried in back pages of newspapers, as opposed to front-page headlines, which were almost entirely unfavorable depictions of mental illness. Similarly, while studies analyzing both news and entertainment usually separate the two, few studies make further divisions among genres of entertainment, where differences seem likely. For instance, Diefenbach (1997) found that mentally ill characters were far more likely to be portrayed as criminals in dramas than sitcoms.

Fortunately, most research employs depth beyond simple frequency counts. Many content analyses also examine specific frames of mental health depictions. Common frames emphasized traits of people with mental illnesses, such as dangerousness (to self and others), criminality, unpredictability, vulnerability, aggression, and intelligence (Coverdale et al., 2002; Hyler et al., 1991; Philo, 1996; Wahl & Roth, 1982). Other framing techniques include separating impressions and actions from causes and treatments (Philo, 1996; Taylor, 1957).

The greatest discrepancies among content analyses are the operationalizations of "mental illness" and "violence." The scope of these definitions can have a dramatic impact on the results of a content analysis. Some researchers require the illness to be stated explicitly (Signorielli, 1989; Wahl et al., 2007; Wahl & Roth, 1982), or even clinically diagnosed (Kalucy et al., 2011), while others note implicit depictions of mental illness based upon symptoms (Diefenbach & West, 2007). Terms like "crazy" could be interpreted colloquially, or as a direct reference to mental illness (see Cross, 2010 for a critical review). Further, some forms of mental illness are disputed—mainly whether or not substance abuse is perceived as a mental health issue (Diefenbach & West, 2007; Wahl & Roth, 1982). A lack of clear coding guidelines has been regularly lamented by researchers facing reliability problems (Philo, 1996; Pirkis et al., 2006; Wahl & Roth, 1982).

Yet rigid operationalizations might fail to measure fully the variable in question. By only considering violence in terms of crimes committed (Diefenbach & West, 2007; Kalucy et al., 2011), researchers achieved better reliability than those who adopted a more nebulous definition of physical harm (Signorielli, 1989). Such strict coding likely underestimates the extent of violence involving characters with mental illness, which increases falsifiability for hypothesis testing, but obviously falls short of an encompassing conceptualization of violence.

Survey

To measure the effects of media content on public perceptions, researchers utilized both surveys and experiments. Surveys offer convenience to participants, often resulting in larger sample sizes than experimental research. Absent manipulations and laboratory settings, they also capture a more generalizable image of how people think and behave in the real world. However, that same lack of experimental control can make it difficult to untangle covariance and determine causal mechanisms (Cook & Campbell, 1979).

Sampling techniques in this area run the gamut, from towns (Diefenbach & West, 2007; Steadman & Cocozza, 1977) to college campuses (Granello et al., 1999; Granello & Pauley, 2000), to purposive samples of healthcare practitioners (Chapman et al., 2017) or the families of people with mental illnesses (Wahl & Harman, 1989). Representative national samples remain relatively rare (Angermeyer & Schulze, 2001; McGinty et al., 2013).

Most surveys utilized the Community Attitudes toward the Mentally Ill (CAMI) scale (Taylor & Dear, 1981). The scale consists of four ten-item subscales all measured along five-point Likert scales. *Authoritarianism* refers to the belief that those with mental illness require decisions to be made for them, particularly regarding hospitalization. *Benevolence* invokes the idea that society should be sympathetic and helpful to those with mental illness. *Social restrictiveness* measures perceptions of people with mental illness being dangerous and support for distancing. *Community mental health ideology (CMHI)* measures support for institutional and community-based mental healthcare and incorporates the idea of distancing. The scale is often interpreted in terms of tolerance, with high scores on the benevolence and CMHI subscales being representative of an acceptance of people with mental illness, and high scores on the authoritarianism and social restrictiveness scales representing fear and avoidance.

CAMI scores were then compared across other variables for differences. Most pertinent to media studies is the relationship between CAMI scores and some measure of media consumption or general information seeking behaviors regarding mental illness, with different forms of media being among the choices (Granello et al., 1999; Wahl & Harman, 1989).

Experiment

Experimental designs permit the most confident estimations of causal relationships between variables. The basic experimental design to measure the effect of media depictions of mental illness on audience perceptions is to randomly divide a sample into two groups, exposing one to media content reflective of the stereotypical portrayals found in content analysis, while exposing a control group to media content unrelated to mental health (e.g., Crant, 2018). Experimenters often modify this design to test specific hypotheses.

Some add an experimental group in which participants are primed regarding the inaccuracies of media depictions of mental illness, sometimes serving to reduce or eliminate perceived stigma (Dietrich et al., 2006; Thornton & Wahl, 1996), while the misportrayals overpowered the prime in at least one instance (Wahl & Lefkowits, 1989).

Experiments focusing on the link between mental illness and gun violence have presented articles about mass shootings with or without references to mental illness or proposed regulations that would affect all gun owners versus only those with mental illness. Those studies found that the tie between mental illness and mass shootings is so strong that negative stereotypes persist even when mental illness is not mentioned, or the focus of regulation is shifted elsewhere (McGinty et al., 2013; Wilson et al., 2016).

Finally, some researchers have used the release of relevant media content to conduct natural experiments. Domino (1983) collected student attitudes about mental illness prior to the theatrical debut of *One Flew over the Cuckoo's Nest*. Three weeks after the film released, he had the same students complete the instrument again. He found that exposure to the film correlated with less positive attitudes toward mental health professionals, patients, and facilities.

DIRECTIVES FOR FUTURE RESEARCH

After six decades of research into media depictions of mental illness, a solid foundation of literature exists. However, many questions remain unanswered, and approaches to the topic remain disjointed. At minimum, future research should explicitly test hypotheses within existing theory and avoid findings limited to descriptive, atheoretical interpretations. Links to cultivation, social cognitive, and framing theories can be gleaned from previous research. The investigation of media effects on public perceptions may also benefit from incorporating more theoretical frameworks from the mass communication discipline. Agenda setting, for example, considers the ability of media to bring issues to the public's attention (McCombs & Shaw, 1972). Combined with framing, media could increase the saliency of mental health and particular attributes therein to explain why certain events occur. This approach seems appropriate for investigating the linkage between mental health and violent crime purported by media and the effect it has on public attitudes.

Additionally, there seems to be an overstatement of media effects from some researchers from other disciplines (e.g., Gabbard, 2001; Granello et al., 1999). The idea of media as an unstoppable, powerful shaper of attitudes and behaviors has been greatly diminished by decades of research. The prevailing paradigm is that media can indeed be persuasive, but that the extent of that influence is dependent on many other individual and social factors. Those studying the effects of mediated portrayals of mental illness should similarly look to incorporate elements like involvement and social identity, as well as perceptual effects theories like third-person effect (Diefenbach & West, 2007) or perceived media influence (Hoffner & Cohen, 2012; Hoffner et al., 2017). These studies may help to determine whether the broad and deep media effects observed in some studies point to something unique about depictions of mental illness, or if differences in effect strength are present among people with differing characteristics.

While content analyses provide an abundant look at the messages that are presented through media, there is little to no media sociology research investigating the selection of those media messages by content producers and gatekeepers. Does media coverage change over time and, if so, what is influencing those changes? Gerbner (1959) asked these questions in the infancy of the topic's investigation, but little has been done since to provide answers. Speculation is widespread—stereotypical portrayals are easier for dramatic producers or more comfortable for audiences; news organizations have a similar bent toward salaciousness or journalists do not know enough about mental illness—but thorough investigation remains absent.

Certain contexts could also benefit from further exploration. While news and entertainment are well defined in previous literature, different types of entertainment are rarely subdivided. There seems to be a modern emergence of implicit mental disorders in comic roles, while the same eccentricities of the emotionless, asexual, compulsive savant serve as comic relief in dramas. These portrayals, while not as negative as the "homicidal maniac," still present inaccuracies that could heighten social distancing, among other potential effects.

Finally, variations in existing study designs allow for some observations and suggestions for future research. First, definitions are important. Content analyses have been plagued by poor intercoder reliability, likely because studies appear to work under the assumption that one will know mental illness when one sees it. While many address potential judgment calls regarding ambiguous terms like "crazy" or "mad," only one study in the literature review mentioned having a pre-determined list of words and phrases to assist coders (Lawson & Fouts, 2004). Emphasis should be placed on careful operationalization of concepts to improve reliability between coders and across studies.

Definitions matter in survey and experimental designs as well. People do not perceive all mental illnesses equally. While most people do a poor job of identifying disorders, they do realize that depression is not synonymous with schizophrenia. Link et al. (1999) avoided the generic "mental illness" label, and even went beyond "substance abuse," measuring perceptions of a person addicted to cocaine. The result was extreme attitudes that were not consistent with other studies with more abstract identifiers. Specificity increases the likelihood of measuring real attitudes, and the complexity of interpretation that must be accepted as part of that exchange.

Experimental research is lacking. Diefenbach (1997) notes an abundance of covariance in surveys attempting to correlate media with perceptions of mental health. While there are exceptions to this (e.g., Granello et al., 1999; Granello & Pauley, 2000), even the strongest survey designs will struggle to move from correlation to causation. Content analyses have exhibited that media misportray mental illness. Surveys have found correlations between media usage and adherence to these stereotypes. Controlled experiments with sound conceptualization and measurement can satisfy even the harshest critic of this relationship, and will likely contribute greatly to understanding the ways in which media affect the way people think, feel, and act toward those living with mental illness, and the healthcare practitioners who strive to help them.

REFERENCES

Angermeyer, M. C., & Dietrich, S. (2006). Public beliefs about and attitudes towards people with mental illness: A review of population studies. *Acta Psychiatrica Scandinavica, 113*, 163–179. doi: 10.1111/j.1600-0447.2005.00699.x

Angermeyer, M. C., & Schulze, B. (2001). Reinforcing stereotypes: How the focus on forensic cases in news reporting may influence public attitudes toward the mentally ill. *International Journal of Law and Psychiatry, 24*, 469-486. doi:10.1016/s0160-2527(01)00079-6

Arboleda-Florez, J. (1998). Mental illness and violence: An epidemiological appraisal of the evidence. *Canadian Journal of Psychiatry, 43*, 989-996. doi:10.1177/070674379804301002

Bandura, A. (1986). *Social foundations of thought and action: A social cognitive theory*. Englewood Cliffs, NJ: Prentice-Hall.

Bandura, A. (2009). Social cognitive theory of mass communication. In J. Bryant & M. B. Oliver (Eds.), *Media effects: Advances in theory and research* (pp. 94–124). New York: Routledge.

Carmichael, V., & Whitley, R. (2019). Media coverage of Robin Williams' suicide in the United States: A contributor to contagion? *PLoS ONE, 14*(5), 1–13.

Chapman, B., Shankar, R., Palmer, J., & Laugharne, R. (2017). Mental health professionals and media professionals: A survey of attitudes toward one another. *Journal of Mental Health, 26*(5), 464–470.

Choe, J. Y., Teplin, L. A., & Abram, K. M. (2008). Perpetration of violence, violent victimization, and severe mental illness: Balancing public health concerns. *Psychiatric Services, 59*(2), 153–164. doi:10.1176/ps.2008.59.2.153

Cook, T. D., & Campbell, D. T. (1979). *Quasi-experimentation: Design & analysis issues for field settings.* Boston, MA: Houghton Mifflin.

Coverdale, J., Nairn, R., & Classen, D. (2002). Depictions of mental illness in print media: A prospective national sample. *Australian and New Zealand Journal of Psychiatry, 36*, 697–700. doi:10.1046/j.1440-1614.2002.00998.x

Crant, J. (2018). The relationship between media portrayal of schizophrenia and attitudes toward those with schizophrenia. *Journal of the Indiana Academy of the Social Sciences, 21*, 192–198.

Crisp, A. H., Gelder, M. G., Rix, S., Meltzer, H. I., & Rowlands, O. J. (2000). Stigmatisation of people with mental illnesses. *British Journal of Psychiatry, 177*, 4–7. doi:10.1192/bjp.177.1.4

Cross, S. (2010). *Mediating madness: Mental distress and cultural representation.* London: Palgrave Macmillan.

Diefenbach, D. L. (1997). The portrayal of mental illness on prime-time television. *Journal of Community Psychology, 25*(3), 289–302. doi: 10.1002/(SICI)1520 6629(199705)25:3%3C289::AID-JCOP5%3E3.0.CO;2-R

Diefenbach, D. L., & West, M. D. (2007). Television and attitudes toward mental health issues: Cultivation analysis and the third-person effect. *Journal of Community Psychology, 35*(2), 181–195. doi:10.1002/jcop.20142

Dietrich, S., Heider, D., Matschinger, H., & Angermeyer, M. C. (2006). Influence of newspaper reporting on adolescents' attitudes toward people with mental illness. *Social Psychiatry and Psychiatric Epidemiology, 41*, 318–322. doi:10.1007/s00127-005-0026-y

Domino, G. (1983). Impact of the film, "One Flew over the Cuckoo's Nest," on attitudes towards mental illness. *Psychological Reports, 53*, 179–182. doi: 10.2466% 2Fpr0.1983.53.1.179

Entman, R. M. (1993). Framing: Toward clarification of a fractured paradigm. *Journal of Communication, 43*(1), 51–58. doi:10.1111/j.1460-2466.1993.tb01304.x

Fennell, D., & Boyd, M. (2014). Obsessive-compulsive disorder in the media. *Deviant Behavior, 35*(9), 669–686. doi:10.1080/01639625.2013.872526

Foster, J. L. H. (2006). Media presentation of the mental health bill and representations of mental health problems. *Journal of Community & Applied Social Psychology, 16*(4), 285–300. doi:10.1002/casp.863

Gabbard, G. (2001). Psychotherapy in Hollywood cinema. *Australasian Psychiatry, 9*(4), 365–369. doi: 10.1046/j.1440-1665.2001.00365.x

Gabbard, K., & Gabbard, G. O. (1999). *Psychiatry and the cinema* (2nd ed.). Washington, DC: American Psychiatric Press.

Gerbner, G. (1959). Mental illness on television: A study of censorship. *Journal of Broadcasting, 3*, 293–303. doi:10.1080/08838155909385890

Gerbner, G. (1980). Dreams that hurt: Mental illness in the mass media. In R. C. Baron, I. D. Rutman, & B. Klaczynska (Eds.), *The community imperative* (pp. 19–23). Philadelphia: Horizon House.

Gerbner, G., & Gross, L. (1976). Living with television: The violence profile. *Journal of Communication, 26*(2), 172–194. doi:10.4324/9781315086613-10

Gerbner, G., Gross, L., Morgan, M., & Signorielli, N. (1980). The "mainstreaming" of America: Violence profile No. 11. *Journal of Communication, 30*(1), 37–47. doi:10.1111/j.1460-2466.1980.tb01987.x

Gitlin, T. (1980). *The whole world is watching: Mass media in the making & unmaking of the New Left.* Berkeley, CA: University of California Press.

Goffman, E. (1974). *Frame analysis: An essay on the organization of experience.* New York: Harper & Row.

Granello, D. H., & Pauley, P. S. (2000). Television viewing habits and their relationship to tolerance toward people with mental illness. *Journal of Mental Health Counseling, 22*(2), 162–175.

Granello, D. H., Pauley, P. S., & Carmichael, A. (1999). Relationship of the media to attitudes toward people with mental illness. *Journal of Humanistic Counseling, Education and Development, 38*, 96–110. doi:10.1002/j.2164-490x.1999.tb00068.x

Guarniero, F. B., Bellinghini, R. H., & Gattaz, W. F. (2017). The schizophrenia stigma and mass media: A search for news published by wide circulation media in Brazil. *International Review of Psychiatry, 29*(3), 241–247.

Hoffner, C. A., & Cohen, E. (2012). Responses to obsessive compulsive disorder on *Monk* among series fans: Parasocial relations, presumed media influence, and behavioral outcomes. *Journal of Broadcasting & Electronic Media, 56*, 650–668. doi:10.1080/08838151.2012.732136

Hoffner, C. A., & Cohen, E. L. (2015). Portrayal of mental illness on the TV series *Monk*: Presumed influence and consequences of exposure. *Health Communication, 30*, 1046–1054. doi:10.1080/10410236.2014.917840

Hoffner, C. A., Fujioka, Y., Cohen, E. L., & Atwell Seate, A. (2017). Perceived media influence, mental illness, and responses to news coverage of a mass shooting. *Psychology of Popular Media Culture, 6*(2), 159–173. doi:10.1037/ppm0000093

Hyler, S. E., Gabbard, G. O., & Schneider, I. (1991). Homicidal maniacs and narcissistic parasites: Stigmatization of mentally ill persons in the movies. *Psychiatric Services, 42*(10), 1044–1048. doi:10.1176/ps.42.10.1044

Iyengar, S. (1991). *Is anyone responsible?* Chicago: University of Chicago Press.

Jorm, A. F. (2012). Mental health literacy: Empowering the community to take action for better mental health. *American Psychologist, 67*(3), 231–243. doi:10.1037/a0025957

Kalucy, M., Rodway, C., Finn, J., Pearson, A., Flynn, S., Swinson, N., Roscoe, A., Cruz, D. D., Appleby, L., & Shaw, J. (2011). Comparison of British national newspaper coverage of homicide committed by perpetrators with and without mental illness. *Australian & New Zealand Journal of Psychiatry, 45*(7), 539–548. doi:10.3109/00048674.2011.585605

Kolenic, A. J. (2009). Madness in the making: Creating and denying narratives from Virginia Tech to Gotham City. *Journal of Popular Culture, 42*(6), 1023–1039. doi:10.1111/j.1540-5931.2009.00720.x

Lawson, A., & Fouts, G. (2004). Mental illness in Disney animated films. *Canadian Journal of Psychiatry, 49*(5), 310–314. doi:10.1177/070674370404900506

Link, B. G., Phelan, J. C., Bresnahan, M., Stueve, A., & Pescosolido, B. A. (1999). Public conceptions of mental illness: Labels, causes, dangerousness, and social distance. *American Journal of Public Health, 89*, 1328–1333. doi:10.2105/ajph.89.9.1328

McCombs, M. E., & Shaw, D. L. (1972). The agenda-setting function of mass media. *Public Opinion Quarterly, 36*(2), 176–187. doi:10.1075/asj.1.2.02mcc

McGinty, E. E., Kennedy-Hendricks, A., Choksy, S., & Barry, C. L. (2016). Trends in news media coverage of mental illness in the United States: 1995–2014. *Health Affairs, 35,* 1121–1129. doi:10.1377/hlthaff.2016.0011

McGinty, E. E., Webster, D. W., & Barry, C. L. (2013). Effects of news media messages about mass shootings on attitudes toward persons with serious mental illness and public support for gun control policies. *American Journal of Psychiatry, 170*(5), 494–501. doi:10.1176/appi.ajp.2013.13010014

McGinty, E. E., Webster, D. W., Jarlenski, M., & Barry, C. L. (2014). News media framing of serious mental illness and gun violence in the United States, 1997–2012. *American Journal of Public Health, 104*(3), 406–413. doi:10.2105/ajph.2013.301557

Morgan, M., Shanahan, J., & Signorielli, N. (2009). Growing up with television: Cultivation processes. In J. Bryant & M. B. Oliver (Eds.), *Media Effects: Advances in Theory and Research* (pp. 34–49). New York: Routledge.

Moscovici, S. (1984). The phenomenon of social representations. In R. M. Farr & S. Moscovici (Eds.), *Social Representations* (pp. 3–70). Cambridge: Cambridge University Press.

Munkner, R., Haastrup, S., Joergensen, T., & Kramp, P. (2003). The temporal relationship between schizophrenia and crime. *Social Psychiatry and Psychiatric Epidemiology, 38*, 347–353. doi:10.1007/s00127-003-0650-3

Newsweek (2014, March). *Wydania Newsweeka.* Retrieved from http://www.newsweek.pl/wydania/1566

Nunnally, J. (1957). The communication of mental health information: A comparison of the opinions of experts and the public with mass media presentations. *Behavioral Science, 2*(3), 222–230. doi: 10.1002/bs.3830020305

Parrott, S., & Parrott, C. T. (2015). Law & disorder: The portrayal of mental illness in U.S. crime dramas. *Journal of Broadcasting & Electronic Media, 59*, 640–657. doi:10.1080/08838151.2015.1093486

Pescosolido, B. A., Monahan, J., Link, B. G., Stueve, A., & Kikuzawa, S. (1999). The public's view of the competence, dangerousness, and need for legal coercion of persons with mental health problems. *American Journal of Public Health, 89,* 1339–1345. doi: 10.2105/AJPH.89.9.1339

Philo, G. (1996). *Media and mental distress.* London: Longman.

Pirkis, J., Blood, R. W., Francis, C., & McCallum, K. (2006). On-screen portrayals of mental illness: Extent, nature, and impacts. *Journal of Health Communication, 11*(5), 523–541. doi:10.1080/10810730600755889

Prady, B., Doyle, T. (Writers), & Cendrowski, M. (Director). (2008). The panty piñata polarization. In C. Lorre (Producer), *The big bang theory.* Los Angeles, CA: Warner Bros.

President's Commission on Mental Health (1978). *Task panel reports submitted to the President's Commission on Mental Health.* Washington, DC: U.S.G.P.O.

Razali, Z. A, Sanip, S., & Sa'ad, R. A. (2018). Mental illness portrayal in media: A summative content analysis of Malaysian newspapers. *International Journal of Business and Society, 19*(2), 324–331.

Reavley, N. J., Jorm, A. F., & Morgan, A. J. (2016). Beliefs about dangerousness of people with mental health problems: The role of media reports and personal exposure to threat or harm. *Social Psychiatry and Psychiatric Epidemiology, 51*(9), 1257–1264. doi:10.1007/s00127-016-1215-6

Rose, D. (1998). Television, madness and community care. *Journal of Community & Applied Social Psychology, 8*, 213–228. doi: 10.1002/(SICI)1099 1298(199805/06)8:3%3C213::AID-CASP449%3E3.0.CO;2-C

Rosenstock, I. M., Strecher, V. J., & Becker, M. H. (1988). Social learning theory and the health belief model. *Health Education & Behavior, 15*(2), 175–183. doi:10.1177/109019818801500203

Sartorius, N. (2002). Iatrogenic stigma of mental illness begins with behavior and attitudes of medical professionals, especially psychiatrists. *British Medical Journal, 324*, 1470–1471. doi:10.1136/bmj.324.7352.1470

Sieff, E. M. (2003). Media frames of mental illnesses: The potential impact of negative frames. *Journal of Mental Health, 12*(3), 259–269. doi:10.1080/0963823031000118249

Signorielli, N. (1989). The stigma of mental illness on television. *Journal of Broadcasting & Electronic Media, 33*(3), 325–331. doi:10.1080/08838158909364085

Steadman, H. J., & Cocozza, J. J. (1977). Selective reporting and the public's misconceptions of the criminally insane. *Public Opinion Quarterly, 41*, 523–533. doi: 10.1086/268412

Taylor, S. M., & Dear, M. J. (1981). Scaling community attitudes toward the mentally ill. *Schizophrenia Bulletin, 7*(2), 225–240. doi.org/10.1093/schbul/7.2.225

Taylor, W. L. (1957). Gauging the mental health content of the mass media. *Journalism Quarterly, 34*, 191–201. doi:10.1177/107769905703400203

Thornton, J. A., & Wahl, O. F. (1996). Impact of a newspaper article on attitudes toward mental illness. *Journal of Community Psychology, 24*(1), 17–25. doi: 10.1002/(sici)1520–6629(199601)24:1%3C17::aid-jcop2%3E3.0.co;2-0

Turner, N., Foley, S. R., Kinsella, A., O'Callaghan, E., & Clarke, M. (2014). Putting television's portrayal of schizophrenia into reverse: An evaluation of the impact on public opinion. *Early Intervention in Psychiatry, 83*, 66–374. doi: 10.1111/eip.12056

Vogel, D. L., Gentile, D. A., & Kaplan, S. A. (2008). The influence of television on willingness to seek therapy. *Journal of Clinical Psychology, 64*, 276–295. doi:10.1002/jclp.20446

Wahl, O. F. (2003). Depictions of mental illnesses in children's media. *Journal of Mental Health, 12*(3), 249–258. doi: 10.1080/0963823031000118230

Wahl, O., Hanrahan, E., Karl, K., Lasher, E., & Swaye, J. (2007). The depiction of mental illnesses in children's television programs. *Journal of Community Psychology, 35*(1), 121–133. doi:10.1002/jcop.20138

Wahl, O. F., & Harman, C. R. (1989). Family views of stigma. *Schizophrenia Bulletin, 15*(1), 131–139. doi:10.1037/t12716-000

Wahl, O. F., & Lefkowits, J. Y. (1989). Impact of a television film on attitudes toward mental illness. *American Journal of Community Psychology, 17*(4), 521–527. doi:10.1007/bf00931176

Wahl, O. F., & Roth, R. (1982). Television images of mental illness: Results of a metropolitan Washington media watch. *Journal of Broadcasting, 26*(2), 599–605. doi:10.1080/08838158209364028

Wahl, O. F., Wood, A., & Richards, R. (2002). Newspaper coverage of mental illness: Is it changing? *Psychiatric Rehabilitation Skills, 6*, 9–31. doi:10.1080/10973430208408417

Wilson, C., Nairn, R., Coverdale, J., & Panapa, A. (2000). How mental illness is portrayed in children's television: A prospective study. *British Journal of Psychiatry, 176*, 440–443. doi: 10.1192/bjp.176.5.440

Wilson, L. C., Ballman, A. D., & Buczek, T. J. (2016). News content about mass shootings and attitudes toward mental illness. *Journalism & Mass Communication Quarterly, 93*(3), 644–658. doi:10.1177/1077699015610064

World Health Organization (2001). *Outline of the World Health Report* (pp. 1–160). Geneva, Switzerland: World Health Organization.

Wu, L. (2017). US media representation of post-traumatic stress disorder: A comparative study of regional newspapers and national newspapers. *Journal of Mental Health, 26*(3), 225–231.

Chapter Eighteen

Depression in Romantic Relationships

Integrating Social Constructionist Perspectives

Amy L. Delaney

Erin D. Basinger

Depressive symptoms influence the way people live their day-to-day lives. These symptoms influence how they feel, think, eat, work, and relate to others (National Institute of Mental Health, 2018). Nearly 8 percent of adults in the United States suffer from some form of depressive disorder (Centers for Disease Control and Prevention, 2014), with more than sixteen million reporting at least one major depressive episode every year (National Institute of Mental Health, 2017). Beyond its individual challenges, depression is also problematic for relationships. As Rehman, Gollan, and Mortimer (2008) note, "Depression has interpersonal causes, is interpersonally mediated, and interpersonal factors can predict depression relapse" (p. 180). Coyne's work in the 1970s (e.g., Coyne, 1976a, 1976b) first focused an interpersonal lens on the experience of depression, but a contemporary emphasis on cognitive and biological influences often overshadows the study of relationship factors (Segrin, 2000). The Mayo Clinic (2018) recognizes that interpersonal and family relationships are especially likely to be burdened by depression, and relational processes can predict depressive episodes (Davila, 2001). Thus, examining depression from an interpersonal perspective is crucial for understanding its causes and consequences (Segrin, 2000).

Substantial scholarly attention has been devoted to describing and explaining the relational challenges associated with one or both partners' depressive symptoms (e.g., Beach, Sandeen, & O'Leary, 1990; Davila, 2001; Hames, Hagan, & Joiner, 2013; Whisman, 2013). Existing research identifies rejection, dissatisfaction, decreased intimacy, and sexual difficulties as processes influencing partners living with depression (Braithwaite & Holt-Lunstad, 2017; Coyne, 1976a; Delaney, in press; Fowler & Gasiorek, 2017; Hames et al., 2013). Individuals with depression also perceive a variety of barriers (e.g., financial strain, stigma) that keep them from entering and preserving romantic partnerships (Boucher, Groleau, & Whitley, 2016). Couples coping with depression encounter unique communication difficulties, such as increased conflict, criticism, emotional responses, difficulties providing support, excessive reassurance seeking, topic avoidance, demand-withdrawal, and hostility (Davila, 2001; Delaney & Sharabi, in press; Duggan & LePoire, 2006; Fowler & Gasiorek, 2017; Holley et al., 2017; Knobloch et al., 2016; Kouros & Cummings, 2011). Social scientific theories rooted in the study of depression (e.g., marital discord model of depression) and theories of communication in relationships (e.g., relational turbulence theory) have provided useful lenses for delineating associations among depressive symptoms and relational qualities and processes.

The purpose of this chapter is to encourage communication scholarship that complements the predictive and post-positivist findings outlined above with an emphasis on interpretive and critical approaches to understanding communication in couples coping with depression. We start by overviewing the dominant theoretical perspectives in the study of depression in romantic relationships. We then advocate for a more subjectivist approach to investigating communication in the context of depression, proposing that communication scholars can make unique contributions to the depression literature by returning to the roots of social constructivism, and examining how the lived experience of depression shapes and is shaped by interpersonal forces. We specifically invite scholarship that investigates the meaning-making functions of communication, adopts a dyadic view of relational processes, and captures the intersectional experiences and identities reflected in individuals and couples coping with depression.

THEORETICAL PERSPECTIVES

A variety of theories are currently used to explicate the relationship dynamics associated with depression in romantic partnerships. Five commonly used theories in fields focused on depression, interpersonal communication, and relationships include: a) social skills deficit theory, b) interactional theory of depression, c) integrative interpersonal theory, d) marital discord model of depression, and e) relational turbulence theory.

Social Skills Deficit Theory

Segrin's (2000, 2001) social skills deficit (SSD) perspective asserts that there are basic differences in social behaviors between depressed and non-depressed individuals, and interpersonal difficulties may be a result of those differences (Joiner & Timmons, 2009). Social skills elicit positive reinforcement from others, so a deficit in those skills will be aversive to others (Segrin, 2000, 2001). Segrin (2000) defines social skills as "the ability to interact with other people in a way that is both appropriate and effective" (p. 382) and explains that such skills can be conceptualized as either a state or as a trait. Depressive symptoms can make people less effective at generating and processing messages and can create struggles in expressing oneself nonverbally through facial expressions, eye contact, posture, gesturing, and rate of speech (Joiner & Timmons, 2009; Segrin, 2000). SSD theory argues that depressed individuals' diminished social skills make it challenging for them to obtain positive reinforcement from others and to avoid negative reinforcement (Segrin, 2001). Those social skills become further depleted as the severity of depression increases (Segrin, 1990). SSD theory, then, points to ineffective social behaviors as the culprit for relationship challenges for those suffering from depression.

Interactional Theory of Depression

Coyne's (1976a, 1976b) interactional theory suggests that depressed individuals are rejected by others through a cyclical process of reassurance seeking and increased negative affect (Hames et al., 2013; Joiner & Metalsky, 1995). Specifically, the theory argues that depressed individuals are likely to a) seek reassurance and support from others, b) question the sincerity of those reassuring messages, and then c) seek further reassurance (Hames et al., 2013; Joiner & Metalsky, 1995). The interactional perspective additionally includes a focus on the experiences of the non-depressed partner by assuming that it is irritating and frustrating to interact with a depressed person and, therefore, claiming that depressed people may produce symptoms of depression in their partners (Segrin, 2001). Interactional theory postulates that persistent reassurance seeking can both exacerbate depression and elicit rejection.

Integrative Interpersonal Theory

Integrative interpersonal theory (IIT) refines Coyne's interactional theory by a) asserting that excessive reassurance seeking (ERS) is the particular behavior that leads to rejection and b) additionally highlighting negative feedback-seeking (NFS) as a rejection-inducing interpersonal behavior (Hames et al., 2013; Joiner & Metalsky, 1995). ERS is the "relatively stable tendency to excessively and persistently seek assurances from others that one is lovable and worthy, regardless of whether such assurance has already been provided"

(Hames et al., 2013, p. 359), and NFS is the "tendency to actively solicit criticism and other negative interpersonal feedback from others" (Hames et al., 2013, p. 361). IIT claims that depressed individuals engage in these two types of feedback seeking, yet ERS and NFS have different and conflicting goals: ERS seeks self-enhancement, and NFS seeks self-verification. These behaviors' combined effects tend to elicit rejection (Hames et al., 2013). Although most individuals engage in these two behaviors occasionally, individuals with depression do so "persistently and repeatedly," even after the assurance and feedback have been offered by relational partners (Knobloch, Knobloch-Fedders, & Durbin, 2011, p. 438). IIT expands on the work initiated by Coyne by specifically pointing to two behaviors driving the processes of rejection in relationships marked by depression.

Marital Discord Model of Depression

The marital discord model of depression (MDD) (Beach & O'Leary, 1993; Beach et al., 1990) suggests that marital relationships play a role in the development and maintenance of depressive symptoms. The MDD acknowledges the intricate link between relationships and depression, claiming that marital discord triggers depression by reducing support and increasing stress and hostility (Beach et al., 1990; Fincham et al., 1997; Rehman et al., 2008). Research guided by the MDD has attempted to move beyond documenting an association between marital distress and depression to uncover causal and mediating relationships (Fincham et al., 1997). According to the MDD, there are six facets of social support that can be reduced in discordant couples: couple cohesion, acceptance of emotional expression, actual and perceived coping assistance, self-esteem support, spousal dependability, and intimacy and confiding (c.f. Beach et al., 1990). Additionally, the MDD points to five stress-producing patterns that link marital discord to depressive symptoms: verbal and physical aggression, threats of separation and divorce, spousal criticism, disruption of scripted routines, and major marital stressors (c.f. Beach et al., 1990). The theory further posits that the presence of marital discord and severe marital stressors may precipitate a major depressive episode and that depressed individuals are prone to heightened reactivity to stress (Beach et al., 2003; Beach & O'Leary, 1993). Consequently, the MDD asserts that the link between marital trouble and depression is driven by an increase in negative behaviors and a decrease in positive behaviors in the relationship.

Relational Turbulence Theory

Relational turbulence theory (RTT) (Solomon et al., 2016), an update and extension of the relational turbulence model (RTM) (Knobloch, 2007; Solomon & Knobloch, 2004), explains that romantic partners can perceive their relationships as chaotic when in flux because they are experiencing uncertainty about the relationship and interference from their partners in their daily routines. Relational uncertainty is the degree of confidence individuals have in their perceptions of the relationship and their own and their partners' feelings about the relationship (Solomon & Knobloch, 2004). Relational uncertainty contributes to turmoil in relationships because it makes it challenging for partners to make sense of their relationships (Knobloch & Theiss, 2010). Interference from partners is the degree to which a partner disrupts an individual's ability to achieve their day-to-day goals (Solomon & Knobloch, 2004). RTT posits that interference from a partner associates with intensified emotions (Solomon et al., 2016). Research drawing on the tenets of RTT has produced evidence that it serves as a valuable framework for examining the experience of depression in romantic relationships (Knobloch & Delaney, 2012; Knobloch et al., 2011; Knobloch, Sharabi et al., 2016; Knobloch & Knobloch-Fedders, 2010; Sharabi, Delaney, & Knobloch, 2016). Beyond investigations specifically in the context of depression, a turbulence perspective provides a lens for investigating processes involving depressive symptoms and mechanisms of turbulence in the context of other relational transitions, such as reintegration after a military deployment (Knobloch et al., 2017; Knobloch et al., 2016). In the context of mental health, RTT is a theory that both illuminates relational processes related to depression and examines depressive symptoms as a relevant variable within relational transitions.

Together, these theories guide research on depression in romantic partnerships to examine antecedents and consequences of depressive symptoms and relationship variables. In highlighting social skills, specific communication processes, and perceptions of the relationship, these frameworks take primarily post-positivist or subjective (critical realistic) stances in describing and explaining the dynamics of depressed partnerships. The body of research drawing on these theories has produced significant insight, both theoretical and practical, into the effects of a depressive illness on people's relationships.

USING A SOCIAL CONSTRUCTIONIST LENS TO INVESTIGATE DEPRESSION IN RELATIONSHIPS

Historically, work in interpersonal communication has utilized post-positivist approaches, which "explore inherent meanings that might be found in a person, object, or idea; or that focus on a person's interpretation of people, objects, or idea" (Manning & Kunkel, 2014, p. 435). Although much is known about relationship troubles experienced by couples struggling with depression, a vast majority of the depression theory and research reviewed in the previous sections adopts the same set of ontological and epistemological assumptions. Specifically, existing work operates from the standpoint that ontologically, romantic partners managing depression live in a tangible, knowable world. Epistemologically, such research takes an objectivist viewpoint, which assumes that it is possible to know and explain the world. The theories summarized above, indeed, offer significant description and explanation of depression in romantic partnerships. Social constructionist approaches, however, allow researchers to capture the complexity and nuance of communication by focusing on meaning making as a "reflexive, complex, and continuous process" (Manning & Kunkel, 2014, p. 435). Our argument in the remainder of this chapter is that research on depression would benefit from alternative ways of thinking. Namely, we suggest that a social constructionist, subjectivist viewpoint would enhance scholarly work on depression by adopting the stance that experiences are best understood from the point of view of the individuals involved because reality is constructed through social and interpersonal communication.

Our position is somewhat reflective of a shift from a biomedical model to a biopsychosocial model of health, which accounts for "human experiences as well as disease abstractions" (Engel, 1977, p. 131). Embedded in the assumptions of the biopsychosocial approach to illness is the idea that disease is not purely physiological, but also simultaneously psychological, social, and emotional. A more interpretive approach to research on communication in romantic relationships affected by depression aligns with the biopsychosocial approach by underscoring people's social and emotional processes in depression and elucidating their lived experiences as part of their health and illness trajectory. We organize our argument around three suggestions for communication scholars investigating depression. Specifically, we propose that researchers should a) investigate communication as a meaning-making process, b) adopt a view of depression as a dyadic experience, and c) take an intersectional approach.

Conceptualizing Communication as a Meaning-Making Process

First, we suggest that communication should be viewed as a meaning-making process in couples with depression. Some scholars have suggested that because relationships are constructed, transformed, and sustained through communication (Baxter, 2004; Manning & Kunkel, 2014; Moore, 2017), we ought to study communication as a meaning-making process in which "communication is not a mere tool for expressing social reality but is also a means of creating it" (Manning, 2014, p. 432). Viewing communication as a means of social construction offers a broader understanding of scholars' phenomena of interest than more traditional lenses (Braithwaite, 2014). Thus, this type of work can illuminate how communication around depression constructs romantic relationships. Indeed, investigations in other health-related contexts (e.g., cardiac events, HIV/AIDS, cancer) have framed communication through this lens, and that work has enhanced understanding how communication shapes interpersonal relationships (see Brashers, Neidig, & Goldsmith, 2004; Goldsmith, Lindholm, & Bute, 2006; Goldsmith & Miller, 2015). Unfortunately, research on depression lacks this perspective, often focusing instead on the individual or clinical implications of the diagnosis. Here, we describe ways that communication scholars can adopt an approach that privileges the meaning-making functions of communication.

One way to study communication as a meaning-making process is to employ critical theory, which is "a lens through which to critique and work toward changing unjust operations of power" (Moore, 2017, p. 2). A hallmark of critical perspectives is that they account for the power structures that shape individual identity. Often, such work entails the examination of cultural and social influences. Communication scholars, however, are poised to investigate how power emerges more locally in discourse, even at the level of the dyad (Baxter, 2011; Baxter & Asbury, 2015). Couples may create, reinforce, and sustain power structures in their communication with one another (Moore, 2017), and, specific to depression, there can be power differences in couples where one partner is affected by depression, given that health is a source of power and privilege. Critical theory would help scholars to be attentive to communication and discourse as constitutive of that power (Baxter & Asbury, 2015; Moore, 2017), and it can therefore be an important tool for investigating how communication makes meaning.

Moore (2017) argued that multiple pathways exist for incorporating critical theory into interpersonal relationship research. One option is to use theories that have meaning making as a cornerstone of the processes they explore. One such example in communication research is the normative approach (Goldsmith, 2004; Goldsmith & Fitch, 1997). The normative approach is rooted in the multiple goals perspective, which explains that individuals are constantly attending to potentially competing objectives in conversation (Clark & Delia, 1979). This approach focuses heavily on meaning, in that communication goals are not reached by the simple presence of communicative acts, but by the meaning ascribed to those acts (Goldsmith & Fitch, 1997). In other words, effective communication occurs when participants are able to attend to multiple (potentially competing) goals (Goldsmith, 2004). For example, a non-depressed partner may face competing goals in a conversation in wanting to validate and understand the partner's depression (a relational goal), but also encourage the partner to make more contributions with household duties (a task goal). A normative perspective is well suited to highlight how communication constructs meaning in partnerships affected by depression.

Another option for using a critical approach in depression research is to integrate existing critical theories with interpersonal theories (Moore, 2017). It is possible to ask critical questions based on the assumptions of the aforementioned theories, and a critical perspective would highlight how communication is socially constructive in romantic relationships. For example, social skills deficit theory suggests that those with depression are lacking in interpersonal skills (Segrin, 2000, 2001); using a critical approach, researchers may ask how such a deficiency a) shows up in discourse and b) creates or sustains power struggles in the partnership. Integrative interpersonal theory focuses on two communication behaviors: excessive reassurance seeking and negative feedback seeking (Hames et al., 2013; Joiner & Metalsky, 1995).

Finally, scholars may explore communication as meaning making through the use of novel methodological choices. Presently, some interpersonal communication research adopts post-positivist methods. Although valuable, the use of such methods has left understandings of communication phenomena "impoverished because of the lack of diverse perspectives and vocabularies" (Moore, 2017, p. 2). In work about depression, communication is often operationalized via open- or closed-ended self-reported frequency of particular acts. For instance, participants may indicate how often they avoid topics (e.g., Knobloch et al., 2016), seek reassurance or negative feedback (e.g., Knobloch et al., 2011), criticize their partner (Trombello, Post, & Smith, 2018), or engage in conflict (Ellison et al., 2016). Although such work is, of course, valuable, it primarily conceptualizes communication as a tool for exchanging information or transmitting content, rather than highlighting its socially constructive functions. We contend that both interpretive and critical analyses are needed in scholarly conversations regarding depression to add nuance and depth of understanding. Whereas interpretive analysis can shed light on what actions mean, critical analysis can disrupt and examine power in communication (Braithwaite, Moore, & Abetz, 2014). Using such methods would allow scholars to pose research questions that highlight depression as creating meaning. For instance, instead of asking how depression shows up in communication in romantic relationships, they could ask how depression is constructed through talk or how power structures are perpetuated locally in discourse. Adding these questions to the repertoire of those already being asked could "enhance the scholarly conversation" (Baxter & Asbury, 2015, p. 198).

Considering Depression Dyadically

Second, we argue that scholarship on depression in romantic relationships should take a dyadic approach, explicitly accounting for the co-construction of depression in romantic partnerships. A dyadic approach is necessary for capturing the communication processes that unfold between romantic partners. Prioritizing the dyad in research on depression in romantic relationships means focusing on how partners communicate to create their social context (Manning & Kunkel, 2014). Psychologists and communication scholars have dedicated significant scholarly attention to studying communication in people with depression. For example, recent studies have examined avoidance of conversations about the relationship and about the depression (Knobloch et al., 2016), engagement in relationship maintenance behaviors (Fowler & Gasiorek, 2017), and associations between conflict behaviors and later depressive symptoms (Ellison et al., 2016). As research reveals that depressive symptoms and relationship dynamics are cyclically related, such that depression hurts relationships and relationship troubles amplify depressive symptoms for both partners (Davila, 2001; Kouros & Cummings, 2011), uncovering the dyadic patterns that drive these associations is necessary.

A dyadic focus would shift the scholarly emphasis from individuals in the relationship occupying "patient" and "partner" roles to instead treating the dyad as a unit that is interdependently impacted by depression, particularly because depressive symptoms may not be isolated to only one partner. Coyne's (1976a) work first brought scholarly attention to the possibility of emotional contagion, defined as "the tendency to automatically mimic and synchronize expressions, vocalizations, postures, and movements with those of another person's, and consequently, to converge emotionally" (Hatfield, Cacioppo, & Rapson, 1992, pp. 153–154). In other words, in interactions with a person with depression, a partner may imitate her/his mode of speaking, facial expressions, etc., and then experience similar depressive symptoms. Although the existence of emotional interplay between partners is well established (e.g., Joiner & Katz, 1999), less is known about the *communicative* mechanisms that drive the link between one partner's depressive symptoms and the other partner's symptoms.

An individualized approach to the study of depression in relationships also discounts the experiences of dual diagnosed couples. Several recent studies (e.g., Ellison et al., 2016; Holley et al., 2017) have documented statistically significant associations between partners' levels of depressive symptoms. Moreover, in the sample analyzed in Knobloch et al. (2016), 28 percent of couples included two partners who reported having been professionally diagnosed with a form of depression. Much work on emotional contagion comes from the perspective of social psychologists, who surmise that it may be mimicry or feedback that transmit negative emotion from one person to another (Hatfield, Cacioppo, & Rapson, 1993). Communication scholars, however, might illuminate the meaning making processes and the co-constructed reality that drive negative emotions between partners coping with one or both members' depressive symptoms. Accordingly, a dyadic approach softens the emphasis on diagnosis and roles as patient/partner, and instead attends to the dyad as a unit affected by depression.

Prioritizing a qualitative approach to examining depression dyadically would allow scholars to theorize about the constitutive and meaning-making functions of communication between relational partners (Manning & Kunkel, 2015). From an interpretive perspective, scholarship emphasizing the dyad would illustrate ways that couples communicate to construct their relationship, their understanding of depressive symptoms within that relationship, and their means for navigating mental health challenges. Eisikovits and Koren (2010) argue for treating the dyad as a qualitative unit of analysis to capture a "wider and deeper" theoretical picture of the phenomena in which scholars are interested and to increase trustworthiness of qualitative studies (p. 1652). Scholars looking to investigate depression through a qualitative and dyadic lens have multiple methods at their disposal. Manning and Kunkel (2015) overview several, ranging from thematic analysis to more sophisticated methods such as contrapuntal analysis (Baxter, 2011) and affective analyses. Grounded theory methods (Corbin & Strauss, 2008) also allow for theory building through inductive analyses of qualitative data and can be applied to dyadic data. Recent investigations of couples grappling with health challenges, including depression, have adopted a qualitative approach to amplify the lived experiences of couples (Alves et al., 2018). In the context of couples coping with breast cancer, couples may experience disconnection within the partnership, negotiation of relational and health challenges, and both partners' needs for support (Keesing, Rosenwax, & McNamara, 2016). Interpretive studies of depression have also revealed rich insight into couples' struggles. Östman (2008) investigated effects of depression on couples' sexual relationships, discovering both distal and proximal factors in challenges regarding sexuality for both patients with severe depression and their partners. Sharabi and colleagues (2016) described the effects of depression in partners' own words, also evaluating areas of agreement and complementarity in partners' accounts.

In short, to answer the call for research and theorizing that integrates a communication lens into the study and treatment of depression, research must adopt a dyadic approach that captures the intricate connections between partners and constructive functions of communication within and surrounding the partnership. Bodenmann and Randall (2013) conceptualize depression as systemic and interpersonal, advocating for a couples' approach to treatment. A systemic approach to treatment can come from a dyadic approach to investigations of dyads affected by depression. To better treat couples coping with depression, research and theory must examine the dyad as the unit of analysis.

Approaching Depression Intersectionally

Finally, we advocate for investigations into communication in depression that acknowledge and appraise the intersectional systems of privilege and oppression that shape how patients and partners experience the illness. Unfortunately, most existing communication research on depression is not poised to examine identity given the characteristics of its samples. For example, both early (e.g., Beach & O'Leary, 1993) and contemporary (e.g., Knobloch et al., 2016) studies of depression in romantic relationships include primarily white couples, and existing research overwhelmingly focuses on different-sex couples, even when the racial make-up of the sample is more diverse (e.g., Holley et al., 2017). These homogenous samples are particularly problematic because public health data demonstrate that they are not representative of the individuals most likely to receive a depression diagnosis: Women, Black/African American people, individuals who report two or more races, LGBTQ+ youth, and gay or bisexual men are all more likely to deal with depression (Centers for Disease Control and Prevention, 2016, 2017; National Alliance on Mental Illness, 2018a; National Institute of Mental Health, 2017). Unfortunately, existing research on depression in relationships does not give voice to the experiences of people who are often disproportionately affected by mental illness.

Taking a critical approach means, by definition, looking at power structures. For communication researchers, this must include looking at marginalized, under-resourced, and under-represented communities and intersectional identities. Crenshaw (1989) coined the term "intersectionality" as a lens for examining the junctions of systems of power and privilege. An intersectional approach evaluates how intersecting effects of race, class, gender, and other marginalized characteristics can impact health (Seng et al., 2012). Bowleg (2012) identifies three tenets of an intersectionality framework that are useful for examining health and illness. First, social identities are not independent and additive, but instead intersect and overlap to shape experiences. Second, people who belong to historically disenfranchised groups are the starting point for an intersectional approach, and research should examine their experiences from their vantage point, not just as a deviation from the experiences of majority groups (e.g., white, heterosexual, middle-class individuals). Third, Bowleg (2012) argues that both micro-level identities (e.g., race and sexual identity) and macro-level social structures (e.g., systems of racism and heterosexism) intersect to frame people's health and illness experiences. In short, an intersectional approach to investigating depression in romantic relationships must acknowledge the complex systems of intersecting individual and societal structures that influence people's mental health across the illness trajectory.

Some existing research has acknowledged the value of an intersectional framework in studying mental health, including depression. Seng and colleagues (2012) took a quantitative approach to modeling multiple levels of identity (interpersonal, contextual, and structural) and identified marginalized identities and frequency of discrimination as statistically significant predictors of post-traumatic stress disorder. Kohn and Hudson (2002) argued that an intersectional approach that emphasizes gender identity and racial identity would help address gaps in knowledge about the experience of depression for African American females. Aranda et al. (2015) built on existing research that identified negative correlations between coming out and mental health outcomes for lesbian females by evaluating how that association may vary by racial identity. They found that in this context, living with multiple minority identities (race and sexual identity) did influence disclosure and the link between disclosure and depression. Together, these studies shine some light on how multiple intersecting social identities position individuals' experiences with depression in relationships. This work, however, does not integrate a communication perspective. The studies cited here are rooted in fields of public health, psychology, social work, nursing, and gender studies. Intersectionality is all about interconnecting identities, and communication is an enacted element of identity (Goffman, 1959; Hecht, 2015). By adopting an intersectional and critical framework, communication scholarship will add valuable insight to literature on diverse people living with depressive illnesses.

Additionally, it is not just the presence or absence of identity markers that matters in adopting an intersectional approach; rather, it is prioritizing the lived experience of inhabiting one or more marginalized identities. For example, the National Alliance for Mental Illness (2018b) asserts, "LGBTQ individuals are almost 3 times more likely than others to experience a mental health condition such as major depression or generalized anxiety disorder. This fear of coming out and being discriminated against for sexual orientation and gender identities, can lead to depression, post-traumatic stress disorder, thoughts of suicide and substance abuse." In other words, the social and cultural forces that shape the LGBTQ experience broadly are also tied to individuals' mental health. As an additional example, social structures such as stigma, medical mistrust, provider bias, and access to treatment also disproportionately affect Black/African Americans' mental health (National Alliance for Mental Illness, 2018a). A focus on these lived experiences will give voice to the challenges associated with relating interpersonally in the context of a depressive illness or individuals and couples who inhabit non-majority standpoints.

To illuminate power structures in the experience of depression, we recommend that researchers make concerted efforts to diversify the perspectives represented in their research by recruiting samples that include people of color, diverse gender and sexual identities, and multiple socioeconomic brackets. Of course, an intersectional approach does not just mean more diverse samples; it also means integrating discussions of the social-structural systems that shape individuals' and couples' experiences of depression. Scholars must evaluate and consider the interlocking systems of privilege and oppression that operate systemically and are lived individually. For example, existing research often recruits participants through treatment outlets (e.g., couples in therapy, individuals who take antidepressant medication), but such recruitment efforts presume that healthcare access is available. Evaluating more structural barriers to mental health care should also be part of examining the depression experience holistically. Giving voice to marginalized populations necessitates the interpretive and critical approach advocated for in this chapter. To understand the experiences of individuals, couples, and communities, the lived experiences of those patients and partners should be prioritized alongside the more deductive approaches already used to understand depression.

CONCLUSION

In sum, depression is a formative and deeply impactful disease for both those diagnosed with the illness and their romantic partners. Research on depression is rich with theory; however, some important questions remain unanswered in work about the disease in part because most work on depression takes an objective epistemological and ontological stance. We argue for a social constructionist approach to supplement this existing approach, advocating for three specific ways to implement such a stance. First, we argue that communication should be conceptualized as socially constructive. Second, we propose that scholars should view the romantic couple as the unit of analysis. Finally, we suggest that depression should be viewed intersectionally. Heeding these suggestions would advance research, but more importantly, it would aid in treatment for couples coping with depression.

REFERENCES

Alves, S., Martins, A., Fonseca, A., Canavarro, M. C., & Pereira, M. (2018). Preventing and treating women's postpartum depression: A qualitative systematic review on partner-inclusive interventions. Journal of Child & Family Studies, 27(1), 1–25. doi: 10.1007/s10826-017-0889-z

Aranda, F., Matthews, A. K., Hughes, T. L., Muramatsu, N., Wilsnack, S. C., Johnson, T. P., & Riley, B. B. (2015). Coming out in color: Racial/ethnic differences in the relationship between level of sexual identity disclosure and depression among lesbians. Cultural Diversity and Ethnic Minority Psychology, 21(2), 247–257. doi: 10.1037/s0037644

Baxter, L. A. (2004). A tale of two voices: Relational dialectics theory. Journal of Family Communication, 4(3–4), 181–192. doi: 10.1080/15267431.2004.9670130

Baxter, L. A. (2011). Voicing relationships: A dialogic perspective. Thousand Oaks, CA: Sage.

Baxter, L. A., & Asbury, B. (2015). Critical approaches to interpersonal communication: Charting a future. In D. O. Braithwaite & P. Schrodt (Eds.), Engaging theories in interpersonal communication: Multiple perspectives (pp. 189–201). Thousand Oaks, CA: Sage.

Beach, S. R. H., Katz, J., Kim, S., & Brody, G. H. (2003). Prospective effects of marital satisfaction on depressive symptoms in established marriages: A dyadic model. Journal of Social and Personal Relationships, 20(3), 355–371. doi: 10.1177/0265407503020003005

Beach, S. R. H., & O'Leary, K. D. (1993). Marital discord and dysphoria: For whom does the marital relationship predict depressive symptomatology? Journal of Social and Personal Relationships, 10(3), 405–420. doi: 10.1177/0265407593103007

Beach, S. R. H., Sandeen, E. E., & O'Leary, K. D. (1990). Depression in marriage: A model for etiology and treatment. New York, NY: Guilford Press.

Bodenmann, G., & Randall, A. K. (2013). Close relationships in psychiatric disorders. Current Opinion in Psychiatry, 26(5), 464–467. doi: 10.1097/YCO.0b013e3283642de7

Boucher, M., Groleau, D., & Whitley, R. (2016). Recovery and severe mental illness: The role of romantic relationships, intimacy, and sexuality. Psychiatric Rehabilitation Journal, 39(2), 180–182. doi: 10.1037/prj0000193

Bowleg, L. (2012). The problem with the phrase women and minorities: intersectionality—an important theoretical framework for public health. American Journal of Public Health, 102(7), 1267–1273. doi: 10.2105/AJPH.2012.300750

Braithwaite, D. O. (2014). "Opening the door": The history and future of qualitative scholarship in interpersonal communication. Communication Studies, 65(4), 441–445. doi: 10.1080/10510974.2014.927295

Braithwaite, D. O., Moore, J., & Abetz, J. S. (2014). "i need numbers before I will buy it": Reading and writing qualitative scholarship on close relationships. Journal of Social and Personal Relationships, 31(4), 490–496. doi:10.1177/0265407514524131

Braithwaite, S., & Holt-Lunstad, J. (2017). Romantic relationships and mental health. Current Opinion in Psychology, 13, 120–125. doi: 10.1016/j.copsyc.2016.04.001

Brashers, D. E., Neidig, J. L., & Goldsmith, D. J. (2004). Social support and the management of uncertainty for people living with HIV or AIDS. *Health Communication, 16*(3), 305–331. doi:10.1207/S15327027HC1603_3

Centers for Disease Control and Prevention (2014). *Depression in the U.S. household population, 2009–2012.* Retrieved from https://www.cdc.gov/nchs/data/databriefs/db172.htm

Centers for Disease Control and Prevention (2016). *Gay and bisexual men's health: Mental health.* Retrieved from https://www.cdc.gov/msmhealth/mental-health.htm

Centers for Disease Control and Prevention (2017). *Lesbian, gay, bisexual, and transgender health: LGBT youth.* Retrieved from https://www.cdc.gov/lgbthealth/youth.htm

Clark, R. A., & Delia, J. G. (1979). TOPOI and rhetorical competence. *Quarterly Journal of Speech, 65*(2), 187–206. doi: 10.1080/00335637909383470

Corbin, J., & Strauss, A. (2008). *Basics of qualitative research: Techniques and procedures for developing grounded theory* (3rd ed.). Thousand Oaks: CA: Sage.

Coyne, J. C. (1976a). Depression and the response of others. *Journal of Abnormal Psychology, 85*(2), 186–193. doi: 10.1037/0021-843X.85.2.186

Coyne, J. C. (1976b). Toward an interactional description of depression. *Psychiatry, 39*(1), 28–40. doi: 10.1080/00332747.1976.11023874

Crenshaw, K. (1989). Demarginalizing the intersection of race and sex: A black feminist critique of antidiscrimination doctrine, feminist theory and antiracist politics. *University of Chicago Legal Forum, 1989*(1), 139–167. Retrieved from https://chicagounbound.uchicago.edu/cgi/viewcontent.cgi?article=1052&context=uclf

Davila, J. (2001). Paths to unhappiness: The overlapping courses of depression and romantic dysfunction. In S. R. H. Beach (Ed.), *Marital and family processes in depression: A scientific foundation for clinical practice* (pp. 71–87). Washington, DC: American Psychological Association.

Delaney, A. L., & Sharabi, L. S. (in press). Relational uncertainty and interference from a partner as predictors of demand/withdraw in couples with depressive symptoms. *Western Journal of Communication.*

Duggan, A. P., & Le Poire, B. A. (2006). One down, two involved: An application and extension of inconsistent nurturing as control theory to couples including one depressed individual. *Communication Monographs, 73*(4), 379–405. doi: 10.1080/03637750601024149

Eisikovits, Z., & Koren, C. (2010). Approaches to and outcomes of dyadic interview analysis. *Qualitative Health Research, 20*(12), 1642–1655. doi: 10.1177/1049732310376520

Ellison, J. K., Kouros, C. D., Papp, L. J., & Cummings, E. M. (2016). Interplay between marital attributions and conflict behavior in predicting depressive symptoms. *Journal of Family Psychology, 30*(2), 286–295. doi: 10.1037/fam0000181

Engel, G. L. (1977). The need for a new medical model: A challenge for biomedicine. *Science, 196*(4286), 129–136. doi: 10.1126/science.847460

Fincham, F. D., Beach, S. R. H., Harold, G. T., & Osborne, L. N. (1997). Marital satisfaction and depression: Different causal relationships for men and women? *Psychological Science, 8*(5), 351–356. doi: 10.1111/j.1467-9280.1997.tb00424

Fowler, C., & Gasiorek, J. (2017). Depressive symptoms, excessive reassurance seeking, and relationship maintenance. *Journal of Social and Personal Relationships, 34*(1), 91–113. doi: 10.1177/0265407515624265

Goffman, E. (1959). *The presentation of self in everyday life.* Garden City, NY: Anchor.

Goldsmith, D. J. (2004). *Communicating social support.* New York, NY: Cambridge University Press.

Goldsmith, D. J., & Fitch, K. (1997). The normative context of advice as social support. *Human Communication Research, 23*(4), 454–476. doi: 10.1111/j.1468-2958.1997.tb00406

Goldsmith, D. J., Lindholm, K. A., & Bute, J. J. (2006). Dilemmas of talking about lifestyle changes among couples coping with a cardiac event. *Social Science & Medicine, 63*(8), 2079–2090. doi: 10.1016/j.socscimed.2006.05.005

Goldsmith, D. J., & Miller, G. A. (2015). Should I tell you how I feel? A mixed method analysis of couples' talk about cancer. *Journal of Applied Communication Research, 43*(3), 273–293. doi: 10.1080/00909882.2015.1052832

Hames, J. L., Hagan, C. R., & Joiner, T. E. (2013). Interpersonal processes in depression. *Annual Review of Clinical Psychology, 9*(1), 355–377. doi: 10.1146/annurev-clinpsy-050212-185553

Hatfield, E., Cacioppo, J. T., & Rapson, R. L. (1992). Primitive emotional contagion. In M. S. Clark (Ed.), *Review of personality and social psychology, Vol. 14 Emotion and social behavior* (pp. 151–177). Thousand Oaks, CA: Sage.

Hatfield, E., Cacioppo, J. T., & Rapson, R. L. (1993). Emotional contagion. *Current Directions in Psychological Science, 2*(3), 96–100. doi: 10.1111/1467-8721.ep10770953

Hecht, M. L. (2015). Communication theory of identity. In D. O. Braithwaite & P. Schrodt (Eds.), *Engaging theories in interpersonal communication: Multiple perspectives* (pp. 175–188). Thousand Oaks, CA: Sage.

Holley, S. R., Haase, C. M., Chui, I., & Bloch, L. (2017). Depression, emotion regulation, and the demand/withdraw pattern during intimate relationship conflict. *Journal of Social and Personal Relationships, 35*(3), 408–430. doi: 10.1177/0265407517733334

Joiner, T. E., & Katz, J. (1999). Contagion of depressive symptoms and mood: Meta-analytic review and explanations from cognitive, behavioral, and interpersonal viewpoints. *Clinical Psychology: Science and Practice, 6*(2), 149–164. doi: 10.1093/clipsy.6.2.149

Joiner, T. E., & Metalsky, G. I. (1995). A prospective test of an integrative interpersonal theory of depression: A naturalistic study of college roommates. *Journal of Personality and Social Psychology, 69*(4), 778–788. doi: 10.1037/0022-3514.69.4.778

Joiner, T. E., & Timmons. K. A. (2009). Depression in its interpersonal context. In I. H. Gotlib & C. L. Hammen (Eds.), *Handbook of depression* (pp. 322–339). New York, NY: Guilford Press.

Keesing, S., Rosenwax, L., & McNamara, B. (2016). A dyadic approach to understanding the impact of breast cancer on relationships between partners during early survivorship. *BMC Women's Health, 16*(1), 57–70. doi: 10.1186/s12905-016-0337-z

Knobloch, L. K. (2007). Perceptions of turmoil within courtship: Associations with intimacy, relational uncertainty, and interference from partners. *Journal of Social and Personal Relationships, 25*(3), 467–495. doi: 10.1177/0265407507077227

Knobloch, L. K., & Delaney, A. L. (2012). Themes of relational uncertainty and interference from partners in depression. *Health Communication, 27*(8), 750–765. doi: 10.1080/10410236.2011.639293

Knobloch, L. K., & Knobloch-Fedders, L. M. (2010). The role of relational uncertainty in depressive symptoms and relationship quality: An actor-partner interdependence model. *Journal of Social and Personal Relationships, 27*(1), 137–159. doi: 10.1177/0265407509348809

Knobloch, L. K., Knobloch-Fedders, L. M., & Durbin, C. E. (2011). Depressive symptoms and relational uncertainty as predictors of reassurance-seeking and negative feedback-seeking in conversation. *Communication Monographs, 78*(4), 437–462. doi: 10.1080/03637751.2011.618137

Knobloch, L. K., Knobloch-Fedders, L. M., Yorgason, J. B., Ebata, A. T., & McGlaughlin, P. C. (2017). Military children's difficulty with reintegration after deployment: A relational turbulence model perspective. *Journal of Family Psychology, 31*(5), 542–552. doi: 10.1037/fam0000299

Knobloch, L. K., Mcaninch, K. G., Abendschein, B., Ebata, A. T., & Mcglaughlin, P. C. (2016). Relational turbulence among military couples after reunion following deployment. *Personal Relationships, 23*(4), 742–758. doi: 10.1111/pere.12148

Knobloch, L. K., Sharabi, L. L., Delaney, A. L., & Suranne, S. M. (2016). The role of relational uncertainty in topic avoidance among couples with depression. *Communication Monographs, 83*(1), 25–48. doi: 10.1080/03637751.2014.998691

Knobloch, L. K., & Theiss, J. A. (2010). An actor-partner interdependence model of relational turbulence: Cognitions and emotions. *Journal of Social and Personal Relationships, 27*(5), 595–619. doi: 10.1177/0265407510368967

Kohn, L. P., & Hudson, K. M. (2002). Gender, ethnicity and depression: Intersectionality in mental health research with African American women. *African American Research Perspectives, 8*(1), 174–184. https://digitalcommons.iwu.edu/psych_scholarship/6

Kouros, C. D., & Cummings, E. M. (2011). Transactional relations between marital functioning and depressive symptoms. *American Journal of Orthopsychiatry, 81*(1), 128–138. doi: 10.1111/j.1939-0025.2010.01080

Manning, J. (2014). A constitutive approach to interpersonal communication studies. *Communication Studies, 65*(4), 432–440. doi: 10.1080/10510974.2014.927294

Manning, J., & Kunkel, A. (2014). Making meaning of meaning-making research: Using qualitative research for studies of social and personal relationships. *Journal of Social and Personal Relationships, 31*(4), 433–441. doi: 10.1177/0265407514525890

Manning, J., & Kunkel, A. (2015). Qualitative approaches to dyadic data analyses in family communication research: An invited essay. *Journal of Family Communication, 15*(3), 185–192. doi: 10.1080/15267431.2015.1043434

Mayo Clinic (2018). *Depression (major depressive disorder)*. Retrieved from https://www.mayoclinic.org/diseases-conditions/depression/symptoms-causes/syc-20356007

Moore, J. (2017). Where is the critical empirical interpersonal communication research? A roadmap for future inquiry into discourse and power. *Communication Theory, 27*(1), 1–20. doi: 10.1111/comt.12107

National Alliance on Mental Illness (2018a). *African American mental health.* Retrieved from https://www.nami.org/Find-Support/Diverse-Communities/African-Americans

National Alliance on Mental Illness (2018b). *LGBTQ*. Retrieved from https://www.nami.org/Find-Support/LGBTQ

National Institute of Mental Health (2017). *Major depression.* Retrieved from https://www.nimh.nih.gov/health/statistics/major-depression.shtml

National Institute of Mental Health (2018). *Depression.* Retrieved from https://www.nimh.nih.gov/health/topics/depression/index.shtml

Östman, M. (2008). Severe depression and relationships: The effect of mental illness on sexuality. *Sexual and Relationship Therapy*, *23*(4), 355–363. doi: 10.1080/14681990802419266

Rehman, U. S., Gollan, J., & Mortimer, A. R. (2008). The marital context of depression: Research, limitations, and new directions. *Clinical Psychology Review, 28*(2), 179–198. doi: 10.1016/j.cpr.2007.04.007

Segrin, C. (1990). A meta-analytic review of social skill deficits in depression. *Communication Monographs, 57*(4), 292–308. doi: 10.1080/03637759009376204

Segrin, C. (2000). Social skills deficits associated with depression. *Clinical Psychology Review, 20*(3), 370–403. doi: 10.1016/S0272-7358(98)00104-4

Segrin, C. (2001). *Interpersonal processes in psychological problems.* New York, NY: Guilford Press.

Seng, J. S., Lopez, W. D., Sperlich, M., Hamama, L., & Meldrum, C. D. R. (2012). Marginalized identities, discrimination burden, and mental health: Empirical exploration of an interpersonal-level approach to modeling intersectionality. *Social Science & Medicine, 75*(12), 2437–2445. doi: 10.1016/j.socscimed.2012.09.023

Sharabi, L. L., Delaney, A. L., & Knobloch, L. K. (2016). In their own words: How clinical depression affects romantic relationships. *Journal of Social and Personal Relationships, 33*(4), 421–448. doi: 10.1177/0265407515578820

Solomon, D. H., & Knobloch, L. K. (2004). A model of relational turbulence: The role of intimacy, relational uncertainty, and interference from partners in appraisals of irritations. *Journal of Social and Personal Relationships, 21*(6), 795–816. doi: 10.1177/0265407504047838

Solomon, D. H., Knobloch, L. K., Theiss, J. A., & McLaren, R. M. (2016). Relational turbulence theory: Explaining variation in subjective experiences and communication within romantic relationships. *Human Communication Research, 42*(4), 507–532. doi: 10.1111/hcre.12091

Trombello, J. M., Post, K. M., & Smith, D. A. (2018). Depressive symptoms, criticism, and counter-criticism in marital interactions. *Family Process.* Advance online publication. doi: 10.1111/famp.12349

Whisman, M. A. (2013). Relationship discord and the prevalence, incidence, and treatment of psychopathology. *Journal of Social and Personal Relationships, 30*(2), 163–170. doi: 10.1177/0265407512455269

Index

About the Editors

Daniel Cochece Davis (PhD, University of Southern California) is currently a faculty member in Illinois State University's School of Communication. His research interests include the intersection of neuroscience and human communication, especially as this is expressed across effective and sustainable organizational communication, health communication, relational communication and intercultural communication. Over the last thirty-four years, he consulted with governmental, educational, public safety, nonprofit and manufacturing organizations to help them improve their leadership and organizational effectiveness. He teaches health communication, organizational communication, and leadership communication courses at the graduate level, and a host of human communication and research methods courses at the undergraduate level. He is excited to be part of the editorial team bringing mental health communication into print.

Robert D. Hall (MA, Illinois State University) is currently a PhD student at the University of Nebraska-Lincoln. His research interests include the intersections of interpersonal, family, and health communication with a focus on mental and chronic health issues. He has received awards for both his research and teaching. He has taught interpersonal communication, family communication, intercultural communication, and served as the assistant basic course director at two separate universities.

Lance R. Lippert (PhD, Southern Illinois University, Carbondale) is currently a professor in the School of Communication at Illinois State University since 2000 where he has been recognized for his teaching, research, and service. He is the program coordinator for the Communication Studies Program in the School of Communication. His research interests include effective workplace communication, health communication, organizational culture, civic engagement pedagogy, and appropriate and therapeutic humor use. Lance has published on topics in the areas of organizational, health, and instructional communication. Over the last twenty-five years, he has consulted for various public, private, and governmental organizations including health care, small business, large and small corporations, education (higher education and K–12), and non-profits to help them improve organizational effectiveness. Presently, he teaches health communication, organizational communication, leadership communication, training & development, and qualitative research methods.

Aimee E. Miller-Ott (PhD, University of Nebraska-Lincoln) is an associate professor in the School of Communication at Illinois State University where she teaches graduate and undergraduate courses in interpersonal and family communication, human communication and aging, and the dark side of interpersonal communication. Her research interests center on the ways that people manage identity and information through their communication, including in the contexts of family health and non-normative family types. Her major line of research in interpersonal communication focuses on co-present cell phone use in romantic relationships, friendships, and families.

About the Contributors

Brett Ball is a PhD student at the University of Florida in the College of Journalism and Communications. Her focus is in health communication, particularly on interpersonal communication's impact on health decisions. Brett's research interest include how social network structures along with race and ethnicity influence the health outcomes of student-athletes. In addition, her interest expands to interventions for health disparities in underserved communities. Brett is an emerging scholar who desires to effectively translate her research to her target audience.

Erin D. Basinger (PhD, University of Illinois at Urbana-Champaign) is an assistant professor of health communication at the University of North Carolina, Charlotte. Her research centers on interpersonal processes in health contexts. Specifically, she considers how individuals cope with stressors (e.g., grief and loss, chronic illness) in the context of their interpersonal and family relationships.

Kelly A. Chernin (PhD, Pennsylvania State University) researches Chinese and Hong Kong social movements and the role technology plays in shaping the memory of mass occupations. Her dissertation, "After a Rainy Day in Hong Kong," focused on Hong Kong's political and social conditions following the 2014 Umbrella Movement. She has also written about this topic for various popular press publications. Chernin has worked with the University of Florida's Center for Public Interest Communications and is now an assistant professor at Appalachian State University.

Andrew I. Cohen (PhD, University of North Carolina, Chapel Hill) is director of the Jean Beer Blumenfeld Center for Ethics and associate professor of philosophy at Georgia State University. He is author of *Philosophy, Ethics, and Public Policy* (2015), and has published on themes in contract theory and moral repair. He is completing a book on the ethics of apologies. With co-PI Jennifer A. Samp, he received a grant from the NEH to study moral injury among those who have served in the US armed forces.

Elizabeth A. Craig (PhD, University of Oklahoma) is an associate professor in the Department of Communication and a faculty partner with The Center for Family and Community Engagement at North Carolina State University. Her teaching and research are in the areas of interpersonal and family communication where she examines a number of communication processes and competencies that contribute to managing close relationships. Specifically, she focuses on mental health, family adversity, and the communication of resilience.

Timothy Curran (PhD, University of Georgia) is an assistant professor at Utah State University in the department of Languages, Philosophy, and Communication Studies. His research examines the links between interpersonal communication competency and both mental and physical health factors.

Amy L. Delaney (PhD, University of Illinois at Urbana-Champaign) is an assistant professor of communication at Millikin University. Her research emphasizes interpersonal processes in health contexts, investigating relational dynamics of depression, pregnancy, diabetes, and chronic illness.

Maryam El-Shall (PhD, University of California, Irvine) is an assistant professor of English at Santa Fe College. Her research and writing span a wide spectrum of themes from mental health and subjectivity to Marxism and post-colonial theory.

Elizabeth Flood-Grady (PhD, University of Nebraska-Lincoln) is a post-doctoral associate in the STEM Translational Communication Center in the College of Journalism and Communications at the University of Florida. Her research focuses on translational communication in health and clinical decision-making contexts. She studies strategic message design in the context of clinical research participation and recruitment and how interpersonal and family communication influence health decisions among individuals with stigmatized illnesses. To date, she has published in several interdisciplinary journals, including *Health Communication, Journal of Clinical and*

Translational Science, and *Chronic Illness* and has received grant funding to support her research.

Joy V. Goldsmith (PhD, University of Oklahoma), is a professor of health communication at the University of Memphis. She conducts communication research examining family caregivers, providers, patients, health literacy, health equity, and communication interventions. Her body of work reflects the undertakings of her research partnerships that seek to improve patient, caregiver, and provider communication across chronic, advanced, and terminal illness. She is co-creator of the COMFORT model and curriculum, which provides COMFORT-related communication research and training information and offers provider, patient, and family resources. She is founder of and co-directs the Center for Health Literacy and Health Communication at the University of Memphis and serves as an affiliate faculty member in the School of Public Health.

Dorothy Hagmajer is a science and health communication graduate student at the University of Florida. She is primarily interested in how medical students and trainees develop strategies for success and professional fulfillment. Currently, her work focuses on the application of cognitive restructuring as a means of mitigating burnout in health professionals.

Cynthia A. Hoffner (PhD, University of Wisconsin-Madison) is a professor in the Department of Communication, Georgia State University. Her research focuses on media psychology, specifically psychological aspects of media uses and effects. Her recent work explores issues related to media and mental health; use of new media technologies for emotion regulation; the role of emotion in media selection and response; and parasocial relationships with media figures. Her recent research has appeared in communication and psychology journals, including: *Health Communication*; *Stigma and Health*; *Journal of Health Psychology*; *Cyberpsychology, Behavior and Social Networking*; *Psychology of Popular Media Culture*; *Journal of Broadcasting & Electronic Media*; *and New Media & Society*. She is an associate editor of the *International Encyclopedia of Media Effects* (2017).

Jody Koenig Kellas (PhD, University of Washington) is professor of communication at the University of Nebraska-Lincoln. Her research and teaching focus on interpersonal, family, and health communication. She studies how people communicate to make sense of identity, difficulty, health, and relationships. She is founder of Narrative Nebraska, dedicated to understanding the ways in which communicated sense-making, narratives, storytelling content, process, and functions can be translated to enhance individuals' and families' well-being. She has published over fifty articles and chapters and received national awards for her scholarship.

Gary L. Kreps (PhD, University of Southern California) is a University distinguished professor and founding director, Center for Health and Risk Communication, George Mason University. His research examines the information needs of vulnerable populations, including those facing serious socioeconomic, cultural, and health challenges. He examines access to and use of relevant health and risk information for making informed health decisions and participating actively in health promotion activities. His research findings drive development of evidence-based programs to reduce structural, economic, cultural, and bureaucratic barriers to well-being, as well as to prevent, prepare for, and respond to serious health risks and crises. His many research honors include the Research Laureate Award from the American Academy for Health Behavior and the NCA/ICA Outstanding Health Communication Scholar Award.

Dylan M. McLemore (PhD, University of Alabama) is an assistant professor of public relations at the University of Central Arkansas. His research concerns the dissemination of persuasive information, perceptions of that information, and its effects, particularly in the areas of health and politics.

Andrea L. Meluch (PhD, Kent State University) is an assistant professor of communication studies at The University of Akron. Her research focuses on the intersections of health, organizational, and instructional communication. Specifically, she is interested in issues of organizational culture, mental health, and social support. She has published in *Communication Education*, *Southern Communication Journal*, *Qualitative Research in Medicine & Healthcare*, *Journal of Communication in Healthcare*, and the *Journal of Communication Pedagogy*. She has also authored/co-authored more than a dozen book chapters and encyclopedia entries.

Jessica Moore (PhD, 2007, University of Texas at Austin) is a faculty member at St. Edward's University and a marriage and family therapist. Her research examines the processes through which cognition and communication facilitate individual and relational health and well-being. She teaches courses in interpersonal communication, relational communication, health communication, and research methods, among others, and has received numerous citations and awards for excellence in teaching. Her work appears in many publications including *Communication Reports*, *Women's Studies* *in Communication, Positive Communication in Health and Wellness, Novel Applications for Virtual Communities in Healthcare Settings*, and the *Ohio Communication Journal*.

Sara "Sarie" Norval (MA, Kansas State University) teaches communication at Tidewater Community College in Chesapeake, Virginia, and Palomar College in San Marcos, California. Her research focuses on leveraging communication methods to authentically reflect individual experiences through ethnography, autoethnography, and ethnodrama. Specifically, she explores how theatre, especially the script itself, serves as a communication tool for those with ADHD, anxiety, or who may be on the autism spectrum.

Cameron W. Piercy (PhD, University of Oklahoma) is an assistant professor in the Department of Communication Studies at the University of Kansas. His expertise is in relationships and digital media use in organizations. He is especially interested in socio-technical relationships. His research has been published in *New Media & Society, Communication Research, Qualitative Health Research, Communication Studies*, and *Computers in Human Behavior*.

Sarah E. Riforgiate (PhD, Arizona State University, Tempe) is an associate professor in the Department of Communication at University of Wisconsin, Milwaukee. Her research concentrates on the intersections of organizational and interpersonal communication, particularly regarding public paid work and private life to increase understanding and develop practical solutions to improve interactions. Research projects include communication pertaining to work-life concerns, emotions in organizations, conflict negotiation, organizational leadership, and policy communication. Her work has been published in *Communication Monographs, Journal of Family Communication, Management and Communication Quarterly, Western Journal of Communication*, and the *Electronic Journal of Communication*.

Jennifer A. Samp (PhD, University of Wisconsin-Madison) is professor in the Department of Communication Studies at the University of Georgia (UGA). Using survey, real-time, and laboratory-based observational methods, Dr. Samp's work illuminates how and why individuals do not always respond the same way when managing relational problems and conflicts with close friends, romantic partners and family members. Dr. Samp is a fellow of the UGA Owens Institute for Behavioral Research, a faculty affiliate of the UGA Center for Risk Communication, and a faculty affiliate of the Emory University Center for Injury Control. Her research has been supported by grants from the National Institutes of Health, UGA Research Foundation,

UGA Owens Institute for Behavioral Research, and the Arthur W. Page Center. With co-PI Andrew I. Cohen, she received a grant from the NEH to study moral injury among those who have served in the US armed forces.

Kristina M. Scharp (PhD, University of Iowa) is an assistant professor of communication at the University of Washington and a director of the Family Communication and Relationships Lab. She researches difficult family transitions such as parent-child estrangement and the processes by which family members cope with their distress. Featured in journals such as *Communication Research*, *Human Communication Research*, and the *Journal of Family Communication*, she is particularly interested in ways people navigate entering and exiting the family. Her research has also garnered attention from outlets such as *The New York Times*, *Forbes-India*, *PBS*, *NPR*, and the *Wall Street Journal.*

Sarah Smith-Frigerio (PhD, University of Missouri) is an assistant professor in the Department of Communication at Columbus State University. Her research involving the representation of mental health concerns in both entertainment and news media has been published in *Health Communication*, *The Howard Journal of Communications* and in the anthology *President Donald Trump and His Political Discourse*. She is also interested in how individuals use digital media to build social capital, advocate, and manage stigma around issues of mental health.

Shawn Starcher (PhD, Kent State University) researches interpersonal communication, family communication, and health communication. More specifically, he examines how parents and children discuss topics and manage privacy regarding mental health and how that influences those family members. He is currently a member of the National Communication Association, Eastern Communication Association, Central States Communication Association, and Ohio Communication Association.

Yulia A. Strekalova (PhD, MBA, University of Florida) is assistant research professor in the College of Journalism and Communications and director of Educational Development and Evaluation in the Clinical Transnational Science Institute at the University of Florida. Her research is situated in the general areas of health communication, health education, and social interaction. She is particularly interested in examining the implications of virtual conversations for health engagement, literacy, and decision-making in mental health and cancer. Dr. Strekalova has also worked as an evaluator on a number of projects in the area of health education (consumer-focused) and training (trainee-/provider-focused).

Sachiko Terui (PhD, University of Oklahoma) is an assistant professor in the Department of Communication and Film and co-director of the Center for Health Literacy and Health Communication at the University of Memphis. Her research addresses communicative challenges pertaining to linguistic and cultural aspects of health and health management, communication interventions, health literacy, and health disparities experienced among marginalized and underserved populations. Her recent projects center in interdisciplinary collaborations, including communities and healthcare organizations.

Erin K. Willer (PhD, University of Nebraska-Lincoln) is an associate professor in the Department of Communication Studies at the University of Denver. Her scholarship as an artist/researcher/teacher engages narrative, art, and embodied methodologies in order to harbor sense-making, empathy, compassion, community-building, and health in the face of difficult life experiences, including grief and loss. Dr. Willer's research has focused on social aggression among girls and women, as well as infertility and perinatal loss. She is the founder of The Scraps of the Heart Project (www.scrapsoftheheartproject. com), a community-based research collective dedicated to empowering families and educating communities about baby loss through story and creative arts. Dr. Willer's work is published in journals such as *Communication Monographs*, *Journal of Family Communication*, *Health Communication*, *Communication Studies*, *Journal of Social and Personal Relationships*, *Personal Relationships*, and *Qualitative Communication Research*.

Alaina C. Zanin (PhD, University of Oklahoma) is an assistant professor of organizational and health communication at Arizona State University. Her research interests include structuration, sensemaking, and framing theories as well as organizing issues related to power, control, resistance. Her work is published in journals, such as *Small Group Research*, the *Journal of Applied Communication Research*, *Qualitative Health Research*, *Health Communication*, and *Management Communication Quarterly*.